Upon This Granite

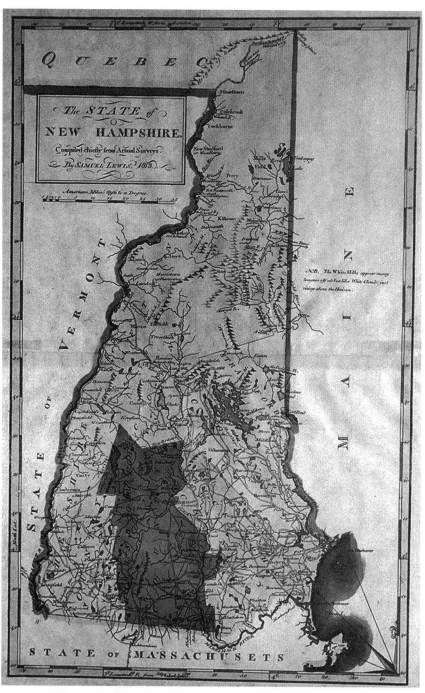

This rare 1813 map of New Hampshire was given to the author by the Reverend Doctor Douglas Horton, a former dean of Harvard School of Divinity. At the time of his death, Reverend Horton lived in Randolph, N.H. (Photo by Cote Photography.)

Upon This Granite

CATHOLICISM IN NEW HAMPSHIRE
1647–1997

Wilfrid H. Paradis

PETER E. RANDALL PUBLISHER
PORTSMOUTH, NEW HAMPSHIRE
1998

Additional copies available from
The Roman Catholic Bishop of Manchester
The NewMarket Agency
Box 3210, Manchester, NH 03105-3210

Peter E. Randall Publisher
Box 4726, Portsmouth, NH 03802-4726

Design: Tom Allen, Pear Graphic Design

Library of Congress Cataloging-in-Publication Data

Paradis, Wilfrid H.
  Upon this granite : Catholicism in New Hampshire, 1647-1997 /
  Wilfrid H. Paradis
      p.   cm
Includes bibliographical references and index.
    ISBN 0-914339-75-3 (cloth: alk. paper). — 0-914339-76-1(pbk. : alk. paper)
    1. Catholic Church—New Hampshire—History. 2. Catholic Church. Diocese
of Manchester—History. 3. New Hampshire—Church history.
I. Title.
BX1415.N45P37 1998
282'.742—dc21
                                                                98-40729
                                                                     CIP

Front cover: Granite sculpture in the outline of New Hampshire is by
Roger Belisle of Hooksett and the photograph of old St. Mary in Claremont is by the Reverend Albert G. Baillargeon of Rochester.
Rear cover: The coat of arms of the Diocese of Manchester. The arms are
composed of a silver (white) field upon which is displayed a red cross of
the Christian faith. In the center is a sheaf of five arrows, an emblem taken
from the seal of the "Colony of New Hampshire," adopted in 1776. The
five arrows denote the then five counties bound together in a strong
union. The staff in the midst of the arrows is the symbol of Saint Joseph,
titular of the Cathedral-Church in the See of Manchester.

This book is dedicated to all those who lived the history of Catholicism in New Hampshire.

Among them are "The People's Bishop," Leo E. O'Neil, who died on November 30, 1997, and the devoted father and mother of the author, Wilfrid Z. Paradis and Alice Dugré Paradis

This history was published with a grant from the Diocese of Manchester. The text, however, is solely the responsibility of the author.

Contents

APPENDICES

List of Photographs

Two professional photographers, Raymond Cote of Cote Photography and Gerald Durette of The Camera Shop, both in Manchester, and one nonprofessional, Reverend Albert G. Baillargeon, have been most helpful in providing the photographs in this book. For their skillful work and for their time, this author is most appreciative. The present editor of *Tidings*, Matthew J. McSorley, and his staff deserve similar credit.

Preface

This history is intended for all those who are interested in the development of the Catholic Church in the state of New Hampshire. While the text is based on considerable research in church and public archives and countless publications, it is presented without footnotes or other academic embellishments to simplify the reading of this history. Readers desiring further information on the subject may consult the notes and photographs of the author in the possession of the museum of the Diocese of Manchester.

As it is noted elsewhere, the historical evaluations and interpretations are solely those of the author and he takes full responsibility (or blame) for all of them.

The author's fascination with the history of Catholicism and that of New Hampshire began in high school and intensified through his doctoral studies and his years of ministry in the priesthood, a great deal of it in this state.

As in virtually all human enterprises, this author was encouraged and assisted by a large number of people. Three deserve special mention. Monsignor Albert W. Olkovikas, who has been the chief financial planner for the diocese since the late 1950s and a strong supporter of this history project, provided invaluable financial and personnel information not available elsewhere. Mr. Joseph W. Fobes, a precise and tireless worker, shared considerable previously unknown data learned from his years of working in diocesan archives, particularly in the areas of church property (land and buildings) and insurance. Mrs. Judith Hall Fosher, the founder and director of the Diocesan Museum, in addition to her personal support, contributed several of the photos and illustrations that would very likely not have survived without her attention. To all of them, this writer is infinitely grateful.

Finally, the qualities of this text are due to the editorial work of Ms. Doris Troy of Amherst, Massachusetts, and Ms. Christine Fosher of Lawrence, Kansas. The shortcomings are, like the content, to be attributed entirely to the author.

PART I

FORMING A CATHOLIC COMMUNITY
1647–1884

ONE

European Voyages of Discovery and Early Settlements

Voyages of Discovery 800 (c)—1614 A.D.

The identity of the first Catholic explorers and the first Catholic settlers in what is now the state of New Hampshire is shrouded in mystery. Some historians believe that the first Catholic visitors, as well as settlers, were Irish who were driven from their home in Iceland by Scandinavians from Norway during the ninth century. If, indeed, the Irish were the first Catholic explorers and settlers, they were either absorbed or exterminated by the native population, or returned to their homeland.

According to two sagas first written down in the early thirteenth century, Leif Ericsson, the Norwegian navigator and a convert to Catholicism, accidentally discovered the so-called Vinland in the year 1000 A.D. located somewhere along the eastern coast of North America. An attempt by the Vikings to establish a colony or colonies there a few years later ended in failure, largely because of the hostility of the indigenous population. One colony was, evidence indicates, at L'Anse aux Meadows at the northern tip of what is now Newfoundland. Whether the Vikings ever settled farther south along the coast is a matter of dispute among archaeologists and historians.

An interval of some five hundred years was to take place before the great voyages of European exploration began. Many of these explorations were made by men from Catholic countries. To speak of a Catholic shipowner, navigator, explorer, or sailor at the time under consideration is a redundancy–a superfluous addition. Until the Protestant Reformation

1

swept Europe, beginning with Martin Luther in the last years of the 1510s, virtually everyone was at least nominally Catholic. One could hardly boast of a Catholic Hernando Cortés, a Francisco Pizarro, or a Hernando De Soto to name but three among the most notorious of this breed of rapacious despoiler. It was the nationality of the navigator's or explorer's flag, rather than his religion, that established the legitimacy of his discoveries.

For whatever religious significance that it may have, in addition to determining the confessional allegiance of the missionaries, the first of the great explorers, as everyone has been taught, was Christopher Columbus, a Genoese who, sailing for Spain, first sighted land, most likely the island of San Salvador in the Bahamas, on the evening of October 11, 1492. During a second Columbus voyage the following year, one of the priests accompanying the large colonization party, on Epiphany, January 6, 1494, celebrated the first Mass in North America for which a record exists, in a temporary church at Isabella on the island of Española, now the island of Santo Domingo–Haiti.

Three of the great powers in Western Europe were to claim possession of much of the eastern coast of North America: England, France, and Spain. England's claim was based on the voyage of Giovanni Caboto (John Cabot), a Genoese Catholic like Christopher Columbus, who, sailing for England in 1497, touched land at what was probably Newfoundland. On the basis of that voyage, England claimed title to all of North America east of the Rockies and north of Florida. France's claim was based on a voyage of exploration by Giovanni da Verrazzano, an Italian, in 1524, commissioned by the Catholic King of France, Francis I. Verrazzano's expedition mapped the coast of the United States from North Carolina to Maine, including the future New Hampshire. Spain's claim rested on a voyage of exploration by a Portuguese navigator, Estevan Gomez, who sailed for that nation, in September 1524. His expedition mapped the coast of North America from roughly the Cape Cod area to Cape Breton Island, Nova Scotia. Copies of his map show the White Mountains and identify the mouth of the Piscataqua River as the Bay of St. John the Baptist, and the Merrimack River as the River of St. Anthony. Cabot, Verrazzano, and Gomez were all seeking a passage to Japan and China, or fabulous wealth as found in Mexico and Peru.

Many other early explorers were to sail along the coast of New Hampshire, not counting the very likely appearance of fishing vessels from such places as Portugal, Brittany, the French and Spanish Basque lands, Spain, France, and England. Among those who certainly saw the coastline of New Hampshire were Bartholomew Gosnold (1602); Martin Pring (1603), who examined the Piscataqua River for some nine to twelve miles upstream; and George Waymouth (1605). All three were English and Protestant.

In a second voyage of exploration made along the coast of the future New England in 1605, Samuel de Champlain sighted the White Mountains from Casco Bay, discovered the Isles of Shoals, and landed at what is now Odiorne Point, where he gave presents to some native people whom he found there. Champlain, therefore, actually set foot on the soil of present New Hampshire. It is impossible to imagine that the explorers who preceded him did not do so as well. Although there is no documented evidence for it, some have speculated that Mass may have been celebrated during the landing on New Hampshire soil, as Champlain was known to have a chaplain on board ship whenever that was possible. This is only conjecture, however.

A final voyage of exploration will be noted: that of John Smith of England in 1614. In that year, he examined the coast from the Penobscot River to Cape Cod and made a map, the best to that date, and published it two years later in a book entitled *Description of New England*. It is John Smith who gave New England its name; prior to that, the area was called North Virginia.

Early Permanent Settlers

Two other significant events of this period with regard to the English deserve mention: the founding of Jamestown by the Virginia Company of Plymouth on the north bank of the James River in May 1607, and the founding of Sagadahoc by the Virginia Company of London on a spur of land on the west bank of the Kennebec River in August 1607. Both colonies were to experience nearly indescribable hardships. Jamestown persevered and became the first permanent English colony in North America; Sagadahoc was abandoned by the colonists before the winter of 1608.

While the English were busy laying claim to and attempting to settle the east coast of North America, the French were equally occupied in the same pursuit. In 1603, King Henry IV of France commissioned Pierre du Guast, Sieur de Monts, to colonize Acadie, a region defined as extending from the 40th to the 46th degree of latitude; that is to say, from roughly what are now the states of New Jersey and Pennsylvania to the south to what are now Nova Scotia and the Ottawa River to the north. This means that what is now New Hampshire was included in territory claimed both by England and by France.

France's first attempt to colonize what is now New England occurred in 1604. In that year, the expedition of the Sieur de Monts landed on an island in the Sainte Croix River (between Maine and New Brunswick), where the first Catholic chapel was built and where the first Mass was celebrated in July 1604 by the Reverend Nicholas Aubry, a priest from Paris. The establishment of French settlements and missionary posts along the Atlantic seaboard progressed very slowly after this initiative and led to many confrontations with the English to the south.

After the Treaty of St. Germain-en-Laye in March 1632, ending a war between England and France, the authorities on both sides informally agreed to set the dividing line between New France and New England at the St. George River on the Atlantic seacoast and the Kennebec River inland, although this was not one of the terms of the treaty. By this agreement, New Hampshire fell entirely within the boundaries of English territory, at least along its Atlantic coast. France's first permanent colony was established by Samuel de Champlain at Quebec on the St. Lawrence River in 1608, one year after the founding of Jamestown in Virginia. New England's first permanent English colony was established early in 1621 by the Pilgrims at Plymouth, now in the state of Massachusetts. Many of these settlers were dissenters from the Anglican Church who migrated to the New World to live according to their own religious beliefs.

The anti-Catholic character that was to mark the future of most of New England was set less than three weeks after the departure of the *Mayflower* from England. On November 3, 1620, the royal government granted a patent for the founding of a colony between 40 and 48 degrees north latitude to the Council of New England. This grant, among other things, stipulated that no Roman Catholic could go to the colony without first taking the Oath of Supremacy, something a Catholic could not do in conscience.

New Hampshire's first permanent colonies were founded barely two years after Plymouth. In the spring of 1623, a small group of settlers, led by David Thomson, established themselves at Odiorne Point. This eventually expanded to become Rye and Portsmouth.

Although there is some dispute about this, it is believed that in the same year as the settling at Odiorne Point, the Hilton brothers, Edward and Thomas, and their associates established another fishing and trading center on a neck of land eight miles up the Piscataqua River that they called Northam, later to be renamed Dover. These settlers, at both locations, entered the wilderness for motives of gain rather than religion, for profit rather than piety, in contrast to the religious motives of the Plymouth colony. They hoped to achieve their goals by fishing, trading, mining, and, undoubtedly, by the sale of lumber and wood products.

In contrast, the next two colonies founded in New Hampshire were of religious inspiration, with their roots in the Massachusetts Bay Colony, which had been established in the Salem-Boston area in 1628–1630.

Exeter was founded in 1638 by the Reverend John Wheelwright and many of his followers, on land purchased from the Native Americans on the Squamscott River (also known as the Exeter River). Reverend Wheelwright had been expelled from the Massachusetts colony by the General Court for his non-Puritan religious convictions.

Also in 1638, the Reverend Stephen Bachiler, a minister with strong Puritan ideals, was the leader of a group that settled the fourth New Hampshire town, Hampton. These four towns grew slowly. New Hampshire's fifth town, Dunstable, was not incorporated until 1673, some thirty-five years after Exeter and Hampton.

It has been estimated that the total nonindigenous population of New Hampshire in 1642 was about one thousand. Recognizing their individual and collective weaknesses, all four towns voluntarily joined the Massachusetts Bay Colony, the last in 1642. One of the effects of this union was that all Massachusetts laws became applicable in the four towns with hardly any exception. New Hampshire remained politically united with Massachusetts until 1679, when it became a royal colony by order of the King of England, Charles II.

By the end of the period of the voyages of discovery and the early settlements (800–1646 A.D.), there were no Catholics known to be residing in New Hampshire. French missionaries had not yet made any effective contacts with the Native Americans, and the French had not ventured in any numbers west of the Kennebec River. Protestant-Catholic hostility would break out in the years to follow.

TWO

Ruinous Nationalistic and Religious Sectarianism 1647–1783

Anti–Catholicism

Responses to Catholicism in New Hampshire for the next 136 years, between 1647 and 1783, can be documented from two perspectives: the overall anti-Catholicism of the European settlers and their descendants, with a few exceptions, and the conversions to the Catholic faith of many of the Native Americans. This section will consider the recurring anti-Catholicism of the white population (with the exceptions), while a subsequent division will discuss the choice made by a good number of the Native Americans to side with the French and, frequently, to adopt their religion. Because of their alliance with the French, the next section will also review, in summary, the seven wars in which the Native population of New Hampshire was forcibly involved between 1675 and 1783.

In noting and describing certain aspects of the anti–Catholicism of the English colonies, it must also be recorded that an equally virulent anti-Protestantism existed in New France, where Protestants were treated in ways similar to Catholics in New England. Animosity was the most evident area of reciprocity between the English and French colonies.

In 1647, some six years after New Hampshire had been joined politically to Massachusetts Bay, the colony passed a law regarding Catholic priests. By its provisions, any Jesuit, seminary priest, or ecclesial person ordained by the authority of the Pope or See of Rome was forbidden to enter or live within the jurisdiction of the colony, roughly what is now Massachusetts, Maine, and New Hampshire. A person convicted of being a priest was to be banished or otherwise punished as the courts saw fit.

Punishment could be as severe as perpetual imprisonment. A priest who escaped after being sentenced to perpetual imprisonment, or one who had been banished, was to be, on due conviction, put to death if he returned to the jurisdiction of Massachusetts Bay. Exceptions were made for Catholic priests who might be shipwrecked or who were present on diplomatic business. There is no evidence that this law was ever applied, although priests in Maine were sometimes harassed and, on at least two occasions, killed.

Therefore, it can be said that the history of Catholicism in New Hampshire was inaugurated by a legal act against Catholic priests.

When King Charles II established New Hampshire as a crown colony in 1679, removing it from the jurisdiction of Massachusetts, the vote was granted by the first legislature to male Protestants who were at least twenty-four years of age and who possessed property valued at twenty pounds. With this royal enactment, the oath of allegiance to the king was administered to every voter. Legally, the colony of New Hampshire merely reenacted the legislation of Massachusetts under which it was sustained for more than thirty-seven years. At that time, there were only 209 qualified voters out of a total population of more than 2,000. No one of European descent in the province was known to be Catholic.

A brief glimmer of hope occurred for Catholics in the British colonies of North America with the ascension of James II, the former Duke of York and a Catholic, to the throne of England on February 16, 1685. His attempts to improve the religious situation of large numbers of his subjects, including instructions to the government of the Massachusetts colony to provide liberty of conscience to all, demonstrated a more tolerant policy toward religion. James II's extension of that policy to universal liberty of conscience in 1687 was translated in New England into a plan to send Catholic priests to the Native Americans of Maine, funded by the assets of the New England Company for Evangelization of the Indians. Unfortunately, this monarch established the Dominion of New England in order to create one centralized government for all New England and to eliminate popularly elected assemblies in favor of a royally appointed governor, a royally appointed council, and royally appointed judges.

King James II's antidemocratic bias and his pro-Catholic stance were repulsive to the vast majority of the settlers in the province of New Hampshire. In reality, his religious policies had little substantial effect on these colonies. He was dethroned and replaced, after a brief reign, by King William III, who restored the former restrictions on religious freedom. One of the results of the deposition of James II was war between England and France. That war spread to America, where it extended and intensified an already existing conflict between the French and English into King William's War, which did not end in the colonies until 1698.

After a period of self-government since 1679, New Hampshire entered a second union with Massachusetts Bay in 1690. This was to last only until 1692, when New Hampshire became a province for the second time, a status that it would retain until the eve of the American Revolution. It was during this second union with Massachusetts, on October 7, 1691, that the province received a new royal charter that extended liberty of conscience in the worship of God to all Christians (except papists) inhabiting, or who would inhabit or be resident in, the province. Using the royal charter as a base, the Massachusetts legislature passed a law forbidding the French to reside in or occupy any of the seaports or frontier towns within the province, including New Hampshire, beginning January 2, 1693, unless they were licensed by the governor and his council. Nothing in the law was said about Irish or English Catholics.

Though New Hampshire became an independent province in 1692, it shared the same governor general with New York and Massachusetts, beginning with Richard Coote, Earl of Bellemont, who arrived in New York on April 2, 1698, and visited New England the following year. Massachusetts, and undoubtedly New Hampshire, was not enthusiastic about him, for he was an outsider, a king's man in politics, and an Anglican. However, he had the redeeming qualities of being anti-Catholic and anti-French.

Blaming the French missionaries residing with the eastern Native populations for alienating them from the English and instigating the murder of English settlers during King William's War, he succeeded in having the Council and the General Court of Massachusetts pass a bill, approved by the House on June 17, 1700, which decreed that no priest could legally be present, as a priest, in Massachusetts territory (which included Maine) after September 10, 1700, under penalty of perpetual imprisonment. If a priest so condemned escaped and was recaptured, he was to be put to death. This law did not apply beyond the St. George River on the coast of Maine and the Kennebec inland. Harboring a Jesuit or priest carried a fine of two hundred pounds (a share going to the informer), the pillory for three days, and surety, or guarantee, for good behavior. This new law, based on that of 1647, elicited nothing but strong approbation in neighboring New Hampshire.

Shortly after the end of the French and Indian War in 1763, it was reported to the Holy See by a knowledgeable source that in the provinces of New England and New York one might find a Catholic "here and there," but with no opportunity to practice his/her religion, for no priest could visit. This same source went on to say that there was not much likelihood that Catholic priests would be permitted to enter those provinces, as the majority of the residents belonged to denominations bitter to Catholicism.

At that time (1763), there were a dozen towns in New Hampshire with a population of more than one thousand inhabitants. Portsmouth was the largest with about 4,500, and Londonderry was the second at approximately 2,500. When the first formal census was taken in the province of New Hampshire in 1767, it was found that there were 53,000 residents, almost evenly divided between men and women. Because of the near impossibility of reaching everyone in the large expanses of wilderness, the actual population may have been significantly higher. Of the roughly 250 townships existing in New Hampshire today, 60 percent were erected between 1715 and 1765.

In asserting that there were, at most, but a few isolated Catholics in New Hampshire in the seventeenth and eighteenth centuries (up to at least the American Revolution), one must consider some accounts that place a number of French in Boston in 1731, perhaps as many as a thousand, involved in illegally building ships for the French and Spanish. Even if this was an inflated figure, one could reasonably wonder if the same illegal shipbuilding went on in Portsmouth or even at some of the minor ports of New Hampshire.

Irish Catholic presence in New Hampshire is somewhat better documented. One form of evidence is the frequency with which Irish names were given to towns in New Hampshire and the surprising number of Celtic names in the provincial records. There is reason to believe that some of the Scotch-Irish who settled in Londonderry beginning in 1719 came from the south of Ireland and were Irish with no admixture of Scotch. To the extent that any were Catholic, this identity was eventually lost, especially because of the lack of a Catholic community and Catholic clergy. These Scotch-Irish, including those from the middle and southern counties of Ireland, settled in other towns in southern New Hampshire. Among these were Peterborough, Dublin, Antrim, Stoddard (once called Limerick), and Gilsum (chartered as Boyle).

Several eighteenth-century New England towns had Irish schoolmasters who had most likely fled the English persecutions in Ireland. Their immigration to the colonies continued until the outbreak of the Revolutionary War. A number of these schoolmasters were from the central and southern counties of Ireland, thus at one time presumably Catholic. Some of these schoolmasters taught at Peterborough, New Boston, Antrim, Concord, Somersworth, Canterbury, Weare, Exeter, Boscowen, Northfield, and Newport. A number of these schoolmasters and many of their students became famous in the history of New Hampshire. There is no evidence that any retained their Catholic identity.

Fear of Catholics in the American colonies, including New Hampshire, intensified again shortly after the Treaty of Paris in 1763. Among the issues causing concern were: the granting of religious freedom by the English government to French Catholics in Canada; the episcopal ordination of a Catholic bishop for Quebec in 1765, with the tacit permission of the British government; and the presence, officially sanctioned, in 1767, of a Catholic priest on the St. John River, Nova Scotia, to whom the Native Americans of Maine made the long journey for his ministrations.

Protestant-Catholic tension was further aggravated by the presence of English troops in the American colonies, particularly in Boston. Many of the latter, judging by the names, were Irish and perhaps Catholic. It is even possible that among the British soldiers who fired on a mob of colonists in Boston in March 1770, killing five and wounding several others—causing what is called the Boston Massacre—were some Catholics.

It is also known that after 1769, anti-Catholic books were circulated, anti-Catholic sentiments were expressed at town meetings, and similar impassioned sermons and public announcements were made by a number of Protestant ministers.

Political decisions by the English government in relation to the American colonies frequently had an effect on the latter and the new British possession of Canada. One was the dismantling of the forts between Canada and the American colonies. Another was the Proclamation Line of

1763, which reserved the region between the Alleghenies and the Mississippi River from Florida to 50 degrees north latitude for the use of the Native American tribes. Colonists already beyond the crest of the Alleghenies were ordered to withdraw.

Between 1765 and 1773, a number of resented British laws, aggravated by skirmishes with the colonists, further complicated the situation. These proved to be steps leading to the American Revolution. One of the final and most critical steps was the passage of the Quebec Act on June 22, 1774, which: legalized the practice and support of the Catholic religion in Canada; exempted Catholics there from the Test Oath, affording them an opportunity to participate in the civil and military life of the country; restored ancient French property and civil laws; and reestablished the boundaries of the province as in the days before the conquest—that is, the area west of the Alleghenies and north of the Ohio River was attached to Canada.

Many interpreted the Quebec Act as another betrayal by the British by which the American colonists were made to sacrifice their own liberties to give dominance to the religion of their enemies. There was even fear that the British and Canadians would join forces to attack and subjugate the politically agitated American colonies.

Political reality, however, pointed to the fact that some accommodation with French Canada by the British was greatly preferable to creating an enemy on the northern border of their American colonies. As for the American colonists themselves, they attempted to attract the French Canadians to their cause, notably with a conciliatory address by the First Continental Congress in September–1774, and a congressionally mandated mission to Canada consisting of Benjamin Franklin, Samuel Chase, and Charles Carroll of Carrollton (a Catholic), and Charles Carroll's cousin, Father John Carroll, a priest of Maryland. The mission was largely unsuccessful.

Once the American Revolution broke out, participation by Catholics from the thirteen colonies was necessarily on a minor scale. At the time of the Declaration of Independence, it is estimated that there were no more than 20,000 to 30,000 Catholics in the entire country; that is, about 1 percent of the 2.5 million colonists. They were cared for spiritually by approximately twenty-six to thirty priests. In New England, not one single priest was left on its soil, even among the Native Americans. There were no openly professed Catholics either, except for some members of the Abenaki tribes, mostly residing in Maine, with a few living on New Hampshire soil.

If there were no openly professed Catholics at the time of the outbreak of the American Revolution, there was probably a certain number who were either hiding their Catholic religious affiliation or who had abandoned it for a variety of reasons. Most of these appear to have been Irish; a smaller number may have been French. It is known, for example, that the number of Revolutionary War soldiers from New England with Irish names was high, if not the figure of three thousand cited by one historian.

Other Catholics, it is known, did participate in the American Revolution. A certain number of French Canadian Catholics volunteered for service on the American side. The names of foreign officers such as Thadeusz Kósciuszko, Count Casimir Pulaski, Marquis de Lafayette, and Captain John Barry are recognized by all students of American history.

Without a doubt, the greatest asset to the Americans in the Revolution was the entrance of France into the conflict on the side of the United States. The French navy and ground troops, as well as French supplies, ensured an American victory. One illustration of France's decisive intervention was the battle of Yorktown, where French soldiers and sailors outnumbered the American Revolutionary forces three to one. In various ways, Catholic Spain also contributed to winning the American Revolution.

The presence of French troops on American soil and of French ships in some harbors had a lasting effect on the future of Protestant-Catholic relations throughout the country, including New England. It was during the visit of the French fleet to Boston for two months in 1778 that Mass, for the first time, began to be said on a regular basis in northern New England, with the exception of the religious services for the Native Americans of Maine. Mass was celebrated both on board the ships of the fleet and in the barracks on Governor's Island, where the sick and wounded of the French expeditionary force were given medical attention and hospitalization.

With the return of French ships to Boston in the summer of 1780, another hospital was opened in the west end. At these hospitals, liturgical services were undoubtedly available to the French civilians living in Boston, such as the French consul and his staff and a good number of French merchants who looked after the needs of the military and of French commercial interest in general. These two hospital chapels probably became the first regular meeting places for the Catholics of Boston.

The departure of the French fleet at the end of December 1782 did not mark the end of Catholicism in Boston and New England. The French consul and his staff remained behind, and some French officers and military personnel chose not to return to France but to stay permanently in the United States. They were joined by some French merchants who expected to profit from an anticipated increase in French-American trade. These French, as well as a nucleus of Irish who were not as visible because they were mostly laborers, became the soil from which sprouted the Catholic Church in New England.

It has been estimated that the entire number of men who enlisted in the Continental Army during the American Revolution was 231,791; of this figure 12,497 were from New Hampshire. Though official statistics list a smaller number, it has been calculated by some that nearly half were killed or disabled. In a report made to Congress in 1790, it was calculated that one in eleven of the male population of New Hampshire had served in the American Revolution. All in all, despite the real hardships imposed on the state by the war for independence, there was little direct physical impact on New Hampshire and no fighting took place within its borders.

The First Catholics: Native Americans 1623–1798

When the English Pilgrims landed at Plymouth in 1620, it is estimated that the Native American population of New England was about 50,000. Of these, perhaps four or five thousand resided in what is now the state of New Hampshire. All of the tribes of southern New England, plus the Abenaki of Maine and Nova Scotia; the Delaware and Powhatan of the Middle Atlantic states and Virginia; the Sauk, Fox, Kickapoo, Pottawatomi, and Blackfoot in the Midwest were of the Algonquian language group. This means that despite language variations, these tribes could communicate verbally with each other.

After the Pequot population was virtually destroyed by Massachusetts in 1637, a conflict that New Hampshire was too distant to experience, the colonists of what is now New England lived in relative peace with the Native Americans for some thirty-eight years, until 1675.

Catholic missionary activity in what is now New Hampshire probably began among the Sokwakis. These Native Americans, with their main fort at Squakheag, a site near the present Northfield, Massachusetts, also occupied the banks of the Ashuelot River. Some scholars believe that they also used the Connecticut Valley, up to the Mascoma River, as their hunting grounds. Father Gabriel Druillettes, a Jesuit and an experienced missionary, is reported to have visited the Sokwakis in their own territory in 1650 and 1651. It has also been speculated that the headwaters of the Merrimack River had been, at some time, the site of a Jesuit mission, or, at least, that the Penacooks, established near the town of the same name, were visited more than once by Jesuits from Maine.

Some have interpreted the *Jesuit Relations,* the contemporary reports made by Jesuit missionaries to their headquarters in France, as indicating that the order's Abenaki missions extended onto what is now New Hampshire soil, more likely in the regions of North Conway, Chocorua, Ossipee, Winnipesaukee, and, perhaps, into the Merrimack Valley. There is other evidence that would seem to indicate that a Catholic mission existed somewhere in New Hampshire, or that Jesuits had extended their missionary journeys into what is now the Granite State.

As previously noted, between 1675 and 1783, the Native Americans of New Hampshire became involved in seven separate wars—with six of these having a European counterpart. Many of the tribes sided with the French, some moving either permanently or temporarily to what is now the province of Quebec; others cast their lot with the English. Even more tragically, some tribes split between the two. Those who tried to remain neutral found it extremely difficult, if not impossible, to do.

During King Philip's War (1675–1676), for example, large numbers of Native Americans moved to reservations in New France, including Sokwakis who lived on the Connecticut River and Penacooks who resided on the Merrimack River. Leading the Penacooks to New France was their chief Wanalancet, son of the great Passaconaway. Many raids were made by the French and their Native American allies on the English settlements of New Hampshire during King Philip's War. Some of the warriors were members of tribes from New Hampshire. During the three years of this war, some six hundred white settlers of New England were killed, thirteen towns were destroyed, and as many as six hundred buildings were gutted by fire. Native American losses of men, women, and children have been estimated at a staggering three thousand.

The active missionary work of the Jesuits among the Native Americans of New Hampshire, and the permanent or temporary residence of many of the Native Americans in New France, obviously influenced their attitudes toward the policies of the French as well as toward the Catholic faith. These converts were the first Catholics of New Hampshire.

King William's War (1689–1697), the second in the series of seven, was the most prolonged. It resulted in the further killing and dispersion of the Native Americans from New England, for countless centuries their home and hunting grounds. Hostilities first broke out between the Abenakis in Maine and the English in 1688 and lasted some ten years, except for an occasional truce. When King James II was dethroned and replaced by William III and Queen Mary II in 1689, the conflict extended to Europe, where France declared war on England on the side of the deposed James II.

This war raged over much of New England, including New Hampshire. Many—and perhaps most—of the raiding parties on the side of the French were made up, at least in part, of members of New Hampshire tribes. During this war, the four New Hampshire towns of Portsmouth, Dover, Hampton, and Exeter, and their environs, and the adjoining Maine settlements of York, Kittery, and Berwick, experienced about four hundred killed, wounded, or taken captive. The Peace of Ryswick, which ended the war between France and England in 1697, simply provided for a return to the territorial status of 1679 in North America.

This war had two results of particular interest to the Catholic history of New Hampshire. One was the conversion to the Catholic faith of a number of Englishwomen taken prisoner during the Native American/French raids who were eventually ransomed by the French of New France from their Native American allies. Three of these women were captured at Cocheco (Dover) in June 1689, and another two were made prisoners at Oyster River (Durham) in July 1694. Such conversions among the women prisoners of war were a cause of great distress to their families in New Hampshire and to the authorities of the province. Even more unusual—even startling—was the decision of one of the Oyster River captives, Mary Ann Davis, to enter the Ursuline convent at Quebec in 1698, where she was given the name of Sister Saint Benedict. She died a professed religious of that community on March 2, 1749, more than fifty years after entering religious life.

These Englishwomen, converted to the faith, were the first individuals from New Hampshire of European ancestry to become Catholics.

A second consequence of King William's War was the first celebration of Masses on the soil of present New Hampshire for which there is an official record. These Masses (there were two) were celebrated on July 16, 1694, after the French and Native American attack on Oyster River. Twenty houses were burned down, five of these being of the fortified garrison type; anywhere from ninety to one hundred people were killed; and some thirty were taken captive. Following the battle, perhaps amid the dead bodies and certainly in sight of the smoldering ruins, the two chaplains, Father Louis P. Thury and Father Vincent Bigot, s.j., each celebrated Mass for their charges—the two hundred to three hundred Catholic "praying Indians" involved in the attack.

Queen Anne's War, called the War of the Spanish Succession (1702–1713) in Europe, again imposed hardships on English and Natives alike. Some New Hampshire Native Americans withdrew, either permanently or temporarily, to New France as others had done during the two previous wars; others fought for the French against the English; and a number remained faithful to the English. Oyster River (Durham) was attacked at least seven times during this war alone. The English retaliated by raiding the Pigwacket country (Fryeburg, Maine–Conway, New Hampshire, area), ambushing Native Americans on the Merrimack River, and launching an armed excursion to Lakes Ossipee and Winnipesaukee in 1711.

During Queen Anne's War, Governor Dudley of Massachusetts reported in 1706 that many of the English captives held by the French had converted to Catholicism, some entering the nunneries and others marrying French Canadians. Other English captives intermarried with the Native Americans and remained with them, preferring, as one historian analyzed it, the "wigwam to the cot where they were born."

With the Treaty of Utrecht, ratified in April 1713, Great Britain secured the Hudson Bay region, Newfoundland, and Acadia. However, no clear determination was made concerning the ownership of Maine, from the Kennebec River eastward, and New Brunswick. This was to cause continued strife between the English and French, not to mention the indignation, anguish, and wrath of those who rightfully claimed the land as their own, the true Natives.

Dummer's War, also know as Lovell's or Father Rasle's War, was a strictly local war pitting the ever-expanding, land-hungry English against the Native Americans who were defending their homes, growing fields, and hunting grounds. Hostilities began in 1718; peace treaties with various groups of Native Americans were not signed until 1725, 1726, and 1727. Again, many towns in New Hampshire were devastated. New Hampshire Native Americans, both those living on their lands in the province and those domiciled on reservations in New France, joined their kin, the Abenakis of Maine, on many, if not most, of the attacks.

During this war, two assaults were made by the English on Norridgewock on the Kennebec River in Maine in order to capture or kill Father Sebastian Rasle, s.j., who was accused of stirring up the Native Americans against the European colonists. The first expedition was under the command of Colonel Thomas Westbrook of New Hampshire. Failing to find Father Rasle, who had fled, his home and the chapel were pillaged and his strongbox was taken, or, more accurately, stolen.

The items in this strongbox were given to various institutions but the box itself was retained by Colonel Westbrook, who gave it to his daughter Elizabeth, who married a Major Waldron of Dover. Their great-grandson, Edmund L.S. Waldron, a convert and a Catholic priest in Maryland, gave the strongbox to the Maine Historical Society in Portland, where it remains today.

A second raid on Norridgewock on August 23, 1724, consisting of about one hundred troops led by two officers from Maine, killed Father Rasle and about eighty Native American defenders and burned the village, including the chapel. It was reported that many of the dead bodies of the Native Americans were found in a defensive circle around Father Rasle.

Roughly between the end of this "local" war around 1727 and the beginning of a more general war in 1745, some major changes were taking place in New Hampshire that would affect both the colonists and the Natives. On March 8, 1740, England enlarged the territory of New Hampshire and gave it greater responsibilities. On that date, the King's Privy Council in London granted New Hampshire 3,500 miles of territory long claimed and settled by Massachusetts. The next year, King George II gave New Hampshire its own governor and forced the province to assume a greater share of the financial and military personnel burdens of any future wars These decisions were made to curb, or at least moderate, the growing independence of the Massachusetts colony that was to lead to the Revolution of 1776.

Another change, primarily distressing to the Native Americans, was the mounting pressure placed on them by the population growth of the English colonists. For example, the colonist population of New Hampshire rose from 10,755 in 1730 to 23,256 in 1740, a growth of 116.2 percent in ten years. It then expanded by another 18.2 percent during the next decade. Native American living space, growing fields, and hunting grounds decreased proportionately.

The fifth war in the sequence of seven was fought between 1745 and 1748 primarily over the succession to the throne of Austria; this one was known as King George's War. It was during this conflict that the great French fortress of Louisbourg (Nova Scotia) was captured by English and colonial troops in June 1745, using plans prepared by Major William Vaughn of Portsmouth and the active participation of a New Hampshire regiment of five hundred men. On the soil of New Hampshire itself, the Native Americans and the French found that they could no longer roam the province at will, as they had done previously, for the colonists had moved the frontier—in effect, their line of defense—to a line drawn from Rochester, to Boscowen, Concord, Hopkinton, Hillsborough, Keene, and Westmoreland. Despite British and colonial strength, in these and adjacent towns about one hundred people were killed, wounded, or captured between July 5, 1745, and June 17, 1749, a period of almost four years. War casualties among the raiding Native Americans were sustained by eastern Abenakis, Sokwakis, Penacooks, and other western Abenakis, the last three being largely from New Hampshire.

One of the distressing lessons learned by the pro-French and frequently Catholic Native Americans of New Hampshire as a result of King George's War was that their territory and mobility in that province had been further greatly reduced. The greater security and dominance of the English colonists had been achieved: (1) by the construction of a string of forts and garrison houses from the Maine border to the town of Rumford (now Concord) and down the west bank of the Merrimack; (2) by organizing regular armed patrols; and (3) by reinstituting a policy of bounty payments to volunteers who killed enemy Native Americans on their own.

King George's War was concluded at the end of 1748 by the Treaty of Aix-la-Chapelle. This was an inconclusive war both in Europe and in North America. As part of the settlement, Cape Breton was returned to the French, nullifying the brilliant capture of Louisbourg.

Except for the Catholic Native Americans of New Hampshire living on the soil of the province and those in exile in New France, to whom may be added the women converts among the English taken as prisoners to New France, there were no others who could have been identified as Catholics in what is now the Granite State. The Reverend Arthur Brown, Anglican rector of Queen's Chapel, Portsmouth, confirmed this fact when he wrote in 1741: "Nor Quaker, nor Baptist, nor Papist, nor Heathen, nor Infidel [is] known among the population."

The absence of Catholics of European stock in New Hampshire did not change with the forced deportation of Acadians, who were both French and Catholic. These Acadians resided on British soil in what is now Nova Scotia and were considered a menace. The fear was that they would act as an infiltrating fifth column should England engage in another war against France. On the other hand, the French found it next to impossible to understand how the Acadians could remain loyal to Protestant Britain.

Despite the fact that England and France were then at peace, some 12,000 Acadians were deported and had their properties confiscated and turned over to new owners. Thus was accomplished a cruel and very likely unnecessary episode in the history of the colonies of British America. By the end of the deportation, some 1,200 Acadians, from 16.7 percent to 20 percent of the whole number that had been captured and expelled, were forcibly relocated in Massachusetts. There is no evidence, however, that any were settled even temporarily in the neighboring colony of New Hampshire. Most of the Acadians in Massachusetts returned to Acadia once they were able to do so, soon after the French and Indian War that ended in 1763.

This French and Indian War, also known as the Seven Year War, began in 1754 in North America, some two years earlier than in Europe. One of the major causes of the conflict on this continent was for control of the Ohio Valley, which was then a buffer zone between the English and the French.

During the years 1754 to 1760, the numerous Native Americans siding with the French, many being Catholic and having among them warriors either currently or formerly from New Hampshire, took part in almost every military action against the English and their allies. Despite Native American forays into New Hampshire, particularly down the Connecticut River Valley, fewer than fifty settlers were killed or taken captive during the nine years from 1754 to 1763. A few of the reasons for this relatively low casualty figure among the colonists were: an increase in European population to 39,093 in 1760; the establishment of new towns and forts, which effectively further crowded the Native Americans off their own lands; and the decrease in the number of Natives, due to war, disease, and a continuing migration to New France.

One of the several causes for the defeat of the Native Americans in the French and Indian War was the aggressiveness of Rogers' Rangers. These fighters, led by Robert Rogers of New Hampshire, were recruited mainly from New Hampshire, principally in the vicinity of Amoskeag Falls (located presently in Manchester).

Certainly the best-known exploit of Rogers' Rangers was the attack on the St. Francis reservation, also known as Odonak, on the St. Francis River in New France. This reservation was the refuge for large numbers of Native Americans who sided with the French, including many with New Hampshire roots.

Ordered by Sir Jeffery Amherst, commander of the British and American forces, to attack this settlement and either destroy or neutralize it, Major Rogers and his Rangers traveled from Crown Point (New York) by boat and then on foot through the wilderness to Odonak. Attacking at night with 142 men, the Rangers burned the village to the ground, including the chapel; killed an undetermined number of men, women, and children; and retreated with a considerable amount of loot, all within three hours. This one action disrupted the St. Francis mission for some eight or nine years. Rogers and his Rangers had virtually eliminated an enemy of the previous one hundred years.

Among the treasures carried away by the Rangers was a statue of the Blessed Virgin made of silver weighing between ten and thirty pounds. Estimates vary on this point. The retreat became a desperate effort as the Rangers were pursued by some three hundred French and Native Americans seeking vengeance. Suffering from hunger, the cold, the primitive ruggedness of the terrain, and the knowledge that they were being tracked like animals, many Rangers never made it back to safety.

Their hunger was such that some, it is said, turned cannibal and ate the bodies of their deceased comrades. It is not surprising, either, that under the circumstances the Rangers discarded or hid the treasures that they had carried away from the St. Francis mission. The two Rangers who stole the silver Virgin are believed to have hidden it somewhere in northern New Hampshire. One theory has the statue concealed in the Cowas meadows above Lancaster. As neither Ranger made it to safety, the hiding place has never been identified, and there is no record that the statue has ever been found. Occasional searches are still made to look for it.

The French and Indian War was concluded by the Treaty of Paris in 1763. It was an overwhelming triumph for the English. Among the treaty's provisions, France lost all of its lands in New France, except for the two small islands of St. Pierre and Miquelon, both south of Newfoundland. England's boundaries were extended at the expense of France to include New France and all its territory east of the Mississippi, except New Orleans. France was forced to cede to Spain the port of New Orleans and the rest of Louisiana west of the Mississippi.

The impact of this war on New Hampshire was massive. Previously, the province had provided only several hundred soldiers for the wars, most of which took place in the disputed territory between New York and New France. In 1759, however, the number from New Hampshire serving in the military, not counting those who remained within the province, had expanded to nearly one thousand.

Besides the Native Americans of Maine—whose religious liberty was recognized by the province of Massachusetts as early as May 1775—there were, at about the same time, other Abenakis located on ancestral lands at Mississquoi (Vermont), Memphremagog (Vermont–New France), Cowas, the upper Androscoggin River, and a reduced band of Pigwackets in the Freyburg, Maine–Conway, New Hampshire, area. These tribes, the last three named being at least partially on New Hampshire soil, split on the issue of the American Revolution, as did those in northern Maine.

Generally, the Native Americans of New Hampshire who migrated to New France at the beginning of the Revolution, or who lived there already, sided with the British crown, at least in the initial phases of the war. New France had been British since 1763, it should be remembered. The Native Americans who remained in New England from Cowas to Passamaquoddy Bay, in great measure fought primarily for the Americans. Also, in 1775, there were an estimated seven hundred western Abenakis scattered from Lake Umbagog (New Hampshire–Maine) to Lake Nemphremagog. Tumkin Hagen, who resided at Umbagog, was regarded as their chief. Also in 1775, it appears that the bulk of the Cowassucks were living in the upper

Cowas area near present Lancaster, New Hampshire. There is no clear account of the movements of Tumkin Hagen's Native Americans during the American Revolution, or of the Cowassucks in the upper Cowas. At the time of the signing of the Treaty of Paris in 1783, which ended the war, there were still an unknown number of Abenakis remaining in New England, including New Hampshire.

By 1798 at the latest, except for isolated individuals or small groups, all the Native Americans had left the state of New Hampshire, apparently most for Quebec. Later reports of Native Americans in northern Vermont or New Hampshire and in western Maine would likely have been hunting and trading parties. An English visitor at Odonak in 1807 or 1808 found Cowassucks, Ossipees, and Pigwackets, formerly from New Hampshire, living there. While the visitor did not mention it, there must have been others from the Androscoggin, Connecticut (in addition to the Cowassucks), and Merrimack Rivers domiciled there as well.

Thus came to an end the presence of the original inhabitants and owners of what is now New Hampshire. Many of these were also Catholics, the first of this faith on this land.

THREE

Troubled New Beginnings
1783–1787

Catholics in the United States

One year after the Peace of Paris of 1783, which officially ended the American Revolution, there were twenty-four priests in all of the thirteen original states. Nineteen of these were in Maryland and the remaining five were stationed in Pennsylvania. Four years later, in 1787, it was estimated by various sources that the entire Catholic population of the thirteen states stood between 24,000 and 30,000.

Except for Maryland and Pennsylvania, no state had as many as one thousand Catholics at that time. New Hampshire, with an estimated population of roughly 100,000 in 1784, is not listed as having any among its residents, although it is likely that there were a small amount of French merchants at Portsmouth, and perhaps a few working-class Irish scattered here and there.

Declining French Influence

It has been well documented that the history of Catholicism in New England between 1780 and 1788, with the exception of the Native American experience, was in large measure French. When the French armed forces left the United States in 1782, a sizable number of French Catholics continued to live in the New England area. For the most part, these French Catholics were the consuls and their staffs, former soldiers, and enterprising businessmen anticipating brisk trade between France and their war ally. They were thought to number between three hundred and six hundred scattered between New Haven, Connecticut, and Machias, Maine. One such Frenchman, Jean Toscan, was French vice-consul in Portsmouth.

French influence in Boston, and possibly in all New England, began to decline around 1787 with a substantial decrease in French residents. Among those remaining in New England, however, some still hoped to obtain the services of a Catholic priest.

A Minor Irish Presence

Almost unnoticed was the increase in the number of individuals with names from southern Ireland living in Boston and the rest of Massachusetts in the years after 1760. A solid base of evidence is available for the conclusion that this particular Irish immigration came mostly by way of Newfoundland. In a good number of instances, Ireland itself was the direct place of origin. These south Irish immigrants generally held humble posts in Boston society as porters, laborers, fishermen, temporary guards, and all too often as inmates of the local almshouse during the winter months.

It has been calculated that out of a Boston population of 15,520 in 1770, 1,368 were Irish—that is, about 12 percent of the population. Being on the migration route separating Newfoundland, Nova Scotia, New Brunswick, and coastal Maine from Massachusetts, it is not unreasonable to conjecture that some Irish, at least a small number, ended their search for a permanent home in New Hampshire, more likely in a seaboard town.

It is unlikely that these "invisible" Irish were aware of the presence of their coreligionists, the French, and even less likely that they would have joined together in any common religious effort.

France Refuses to Supply a Priest for Boston

Endeavors to obtain the services of a priest during this time, primarily by the French Catholics of Boston, were unsuccessful despite at least two major attempts. Much of the difficulty stemmed from the fact that the French government was opposed to French migration to the new American states, and logically to granting aid for a Catholic church in Boston, or elsewhere for that matter. This latter policy was based on the fear that

French influence in the United States would be harmed by any aid to Catholic churches in America, and the belief that the slightest appearance of interest in the Catholic faith would reignite the former anti-Catholicism so prevalent in most of the former English colonies.

France's refusal to subsidize a Catholic church in Boston and the failure of the French in that city to obtain the services of a priest resulted in another delay in Catholic missionary activity in New Hampshire. Later, that activity was to come from Boston—the population, commercial, and cultural center of New England.

FOUR

Anti-Catholic Legislation Affecting New Hampshire 1784–1968

Second Constitution of the State of New Hampshire 1784

One of the consequences of the separation of the American colonies from England was the need to provide for a system of government. Before 1776, New Hampshire had already experienced four different forms of government. On January 5 of that fateful year, some six months before the Declaration of Independence, the Fifth Provincial Council, meeting at Exeter, having voted itself into a special convention, adopted a constitution that would remain in effect until the end of the war. It was never presented to the people for ratification. New Hampshire, nevertheless, became the first American colony to adopt a constitution in defiance of British threats. This pioneer constitution, which ran to only 911 words, proved to be an adequate vehicle to carry the state through the Revolution, but lacked the precision, the detail, and the sophistication to guide New Hampshire in the postwar years.

Preparing and passing a new constitution for the state was no easy matter. A proposed constitution, prepared by a constitutional convention convened in Concord in 1778, was turned down by the voters in 1779. It is believed that this was the first constitution in human history to be rejected by the people in a democratic and peaceful manner. Voters, according to this rejected constitution, were to be all the male inhabitants of the state of lawful age who paid taxes and professed the Protestant religion. Catholics would have been disqualified from voting and holding office.

Another constitutional convention was assembled in 1781 with the instruction that it was to remain in session until a new government was approved by the people. The voters finally approved the fourth proposed constitution, the third prepared by the constitutional convention of 1781, in an election on October 31, 1783. This constitution went into effect on June 2, 1784. Consisting of 6,944 words, it ranks second in age in American history. Only that of Massachusetts is older.

There were several provisions in the document that were prejudicial and unjust to Catholics as well as to other non-Protestant Christians, members of non-Christian religions, and people who belonged to no church, such as agnostics and atheists. These clearly unfair laws against these categories of people are all the more bizarre in that the Bill of Rights of the same constitution guarantees: equality regardless of race, creed, color, sex, or national origin; the rights of conscience; the right to worship God according to the dictates of one's own conscience and reason; and the assurance that no person of any particular religious sect or denomination was ever to be compelled to pay toward the support of the teacher or teachers of another persuasion, sect, or denomination. Illogically, this same constitution went on to specify that only Protestants could serve in the house of representatives, the senate, as members of the governor's council, and as governor. This religious test for state office was to remain in the state constitution for more than ninety years, until 1877.

At variance too with the spirit of the freedoms of conscience and religion and the equality of all faiths before the law was a provision of article 6 of the Bill of Rights that was not amended by the citizens of New Hampshire until 1968. Article 6 began by acknowledging that morality and piety, rightly grounded on evangelical principles, gave the best and greatest security to government and laid in the hearts of individuals the strongest obligations to due subjection. That knowledge, it continued, was most likely to be propagated through society by the institution of public worship of the Deity and by public instruction in morality and religion. In order to promote those important purposes, article 6 decreed that the people of the state had a right to empower—and did by the constitution fully empower—the legislature to authorize, from time to time, the several towns, parishes, bodies corporate, and religious societies within New Hampshire to make adequate provision, at their own expense, for the support and maintenance of public Protestant teachers of piety, religion, and morality. Each town, parish, body corporate, or religious society was recognized as having at all times the exclusive right of electing their own public teachers and contracting with them for their support and maintenance.

Town-Supported Protestant Churches 1640–1819

Passage of the second constitution did not revoke the old Puritan system (dating back to the early 1640s, when Massachusetts assumed temporary control over the province of New Hampshire), which permitted every town and parish to impose taxes upon its inhabitants for the purpose of building and maintaining a meetinghouse and for paying the salary of a minister chosen by the majority of the town or parish. The majority of voters in almost every community being Congregationalists, they regularly imposed taxes to build and maintain Congregational meetinghouses and to pay the salaries of Congregational ministers.

This religious, or ministerial, tax was no small financial matter. In fact, it was the largest single item in the annual budget of the town, much larger than the school or road taxes. Nonpayment of this tax could result, on conviction, in imprisonment or the confiscation of property. Even household furniture and furnishings were not exempt from seizure—not even dishes.

Abolishment of the town-supported Protestant churches was in great measure due to the Reverend Dan Young, a Methodist minister from Lisbon, New Hampshire. Elected to the state senate in 1816, he introduced a bill that eventually became known as the Toleration Act. His bill, had it passed, would have abolished compulsory religious taxation. That year Reverend Young was able to muster only three favorable votes besides his own in the senate.

The following year, the same bill received half the twelve votes of the senate. In the third year, the bill passed the senate by a large majority but was tied up in the house of representatives. In 1819, the year marking the opening of the new state capitol building in Concord, the bill passed the senate for a second time, and under the leadership of Matthew Harvey, Speaker of the House, and Dr. Thomas Whipple Jr. of Wentworth, the bill's sponsor, it was approved by that body by the hardly impressive vote of ninety-six to eighty-eight. It was signed into law on July 1, 1819, by Governor Samuel Bell of Londonderry, who had supported the bill. As this was not a matter regulated by the state constitution, it did not require approval by the voters of the state.

Gradual Elimination of Anti-Catholic Provisions 1784–1968

Attempts to abolish the religious test from the constitution for holding the offices of governor, governor's council, state senator, and member of the house of representatives were not successful until 1877. At the constitutional convention convened in 1791, an amendment broad enough to include Roman Catholics and deists among those eligible for elected state office was defeated thirty to fifty-one. Another proposal, intending to strike from the constitution those clauses that required officeholders to be of the Protestant religion, was approved by the convention but rejected by the people.

Passage of the already mentioned Toleration Act in 1819 had not drawn a clear line of separation between church and state. Among the problems not settled were: the aforementioned constitutional law that provided that only Protestants could be elected to certain state offices; church property left exempt from civil taxes, thus providing an indirect subsidy to religion by the state; and the fact that some towns still held an endowed income from lands set aside in the colonial period for support of the ministry. These towns still turned over that income to support ministers elected by the voters in a town or parish.

Other points to be resolved were: that courts still retained the power to define blasphemy, profanity, and profanation of the Sabbath; and the fact that in 1868 the Supreme Court of the state, in the case of Hale *v.* Everett, had even assumed the power to decide that a religious society of Unitarians in the town of Dover could not vote to hire a certain pastor who was not, in the opinion of the court, a "Christian."

By 1850, New Hampshire was the only state in the union in which Catholics could not hold elected office at the state level. In early November of that year, a constitutional convention of 290 members was called to order at Concord. Franklin Pierce, who had recently returned from the Mexican-American War, was elected president of this body. This convention ultimately approved fifteen amendments for presentation to the people, including the abolishment of religious qualifications for elected state office. Pierce was among those who spoke in favor of that particular amendment. All fifteen amendments were rejected by the voters at the polls on March 8, 1851. The amendment to abolish the religious test received only 9,566 votes.

The constitutional convention then decided to propose for a second time three of the previous fifteen amendments for ratification. One of the three was the abolition of the remaining religious test. Once again it was rejected by the voters at the election of March 9, 1852. For various reasons, no further constitutional conventions were held for the next twenty-four years.

On December 6, 1876, the sixth constitutional convention was convoked in Concord and was in session for eleven days. Thirteen amendments were approved for proposal to the voters. Among these amendments were: the elimination of the word "Protestant" from article 6; the abandonment of the religious test for the offices of governor, governor's council, state senate, and house of representatives; and the addition of a new provision to article 83, stating that "no money raised by taxation shall ever be granted or applied for the use of the schools or institutions of any religious sect or denomination."

Election results on March 12, 1877 were a mixture of victory and defeat for the Catholics of New Hampshire. On the positive side, the voters narrowly abolished the religious test by a vote of 28,477 to 14,231. That was only a mere five votes over the required two-thirds majority. It must be noted, however, that the religious test law had not been strictly enforced by the legislature since the Civil War. On the negative side, the voters of New Hampshire again defeated the constitutional amendment that would have removed the word "Protestant" from article 6 of the Bill of Rights. Further, they approved an insertion in article 83 that prohibited the granting or application of money raised by taxation to schools and institutions of any religious sect or denomination.

The eleven amendments receiving the required two-thirds majority were proclaimed by Governor Person Cheney, a Republican, on April 17, 1877. The removal of the political ban against Catholics holding elected state office went into effect in 1879.

A seventh constitutional convention, held in early 1889, proposed seven amendments to the voters. Once again, one of these was the striking of the word "Protestant" from article 6 of the Bill of Rights. Again it was defeated by a good margin. A somewhat similar amendment proposed by the eighth constitutional convention was voted down in 1903.

Reference to "public Protestant teachers" in article 6 of the Bill of Rights of the Constitution of New Hampshire was finally deleted by a vote of 142,111 to 67,697 in 1968, 184 years after the state constitution went into effect in 1784. After taking into account that a certain number of voters did not read or understand the proposed amendment, it is surprising that at a date as late as the mid-1960s more than 67,000 citizens apparently wished to maintain a religious bias in the state constitution.

FIVE

Early Catholic Missionary Efforts 1788–1808

Turbulent Beginnings 1788–1792

New England was far from fortunate in the first three priests who settled in Boston with the apparent intention of remaining there permanently.

The dubious distinction of being the first resident priest in Boston and the founder of the first Catholic church in New England for Europeans belongs to a man with the impressive name of l'abbé Claude Florent Bouchard de la Poterie. This priest, born in France, arrived in Boston in the summer of 1788 as a chaplain in the French navy. While in Boston, he jumped ship—that is, he deserted the navy—and at the invitation of some French residents he established a Catholic church at 18 School Street, Boston, in an abandoned French Huguenot Protestant church. His first Mass celebrated in the School Street Church on Sunday, November 2, was what may be properly identified as the first public Mass in Boston in an edifice dedicated to Catholic worship.

Father Claude Florent Bouchard de la Poterie proved to be a devious and highly undesirable character. In addition to deserting the French navy, he used a title to the nobility to which he appeared to have had no right (that of de la Poterie). He was flamboyant in expression to the point of bringing ridicule on himself; he ran the Boston church into heavy debt; and he alienated both Father John Carroll, superior of the mission in the United States residing in Baltimore, and the French consul in Boston. An already highly unacceptable situation was further aggravated when it was learned from the archbishop of Paris and from other sources that the abbé de la Poterie was not a clergyman proper for ministry and that in consequence of impropriety of conduct, apparently of a moral nature, his faculties had been withdrawn from him in Paris.

Reacting to this information, as well as to the abbé de la Poterie's conduct in Boston, Father Carroll suspended him in a letter dated May 20, 1789. After unsuccessfully attempting to start a division in the Catholic community, he left Boston on July 8, 1789, and traveled to New York, Rhode Island, Connecticut, New Hampshire (localities unknown), and appears to have made his way to Quebec City to petition to work there as a priest. He was refused.

To replace the abbé de la Poterie, Father Carroll offered the Boston parish to Father Louis de Rousselet, who at that time was residing in Philadelphia. Accepting the invitation, he apparently arrived in Boston in early September 1789. Like his predecessor, Father Rousselet was French, and similarly, it was discovered, he had been suspended from the exercise of his ministry in his native land. (Father Rousselet had a relative by the name of Nicholas Rousselet who married a woman from Portsmouth and lived in that port community for a period of time. It appears likely that Father Rousselet visited him there, possibly around 1789.)

Father Rousselet's ministry could hardly be called overwhelmingly successful in Boston. In December 1789 it was reported that the active participants in the parish consisted of one American, three or four French, and a score of "poor Irish." To add to his woes, the abbé de la Poterie returned to Boston, probably in December 1789, and, despite his suspensions both in France and the United States, insisted on participating actively in the Christmas Eve services against the wishes of Father Rousselet, then the "legitimate" pastor. In the ensuing physical clash between the partisans of the two priests, the greater part of the furniture in the church was destroyed. Christmas Eve services featuring a confrontation of Catholic clergymen and a church wrecking were certainly cause for amusing wonderment in the Yankee community of Boston.

The abbé de la Poterie finally left Boston and the United States for good on January 19, 1790. However, seventeen days before his permanent departure, a third priest arrived in Boston on January 2. He was the Reverend John Thayer, an American born in Boston of Unitarian parents, who became a Congregationalist minister. During a trip to Europe, he converted to Catholicism in Rome in 1783. After studies with the Sulpicians in Paris, he was ordained to the priesthood four years later with grandiose plans to make all of New England Catholic; he was the first Yankee priest.

Father Thayer's presence in Boston—and his undeniable zeal—did in fact, bring an immediate increase in the size and level of activity of the Catholic community. More Irish began to attend church and to have their children baptized, and some Protestants were attracted because of Father Thayer's New England background. He also proved to be a forceful but not always tactful polemicist in his sermons, printed tracts, and frequent newspaper articles in defense of the Catholic Church and its teachings.

Unfortunately, the rivalry between the abbé de la Poterie and Father Rousselet was succeeded by one between Father Rousselet and Father Thayer, the French siding, for the most part, with the former, and the Irish, almost unanimously, with the latter. After hearing from both factions by mail, Father Carroll, on June 1, 1790, appointed Father Rousselet the sole pastor because of prior residence, age, and having been invited to Boston at the request of the congregation. Father Thayer was directed to establish himself in any other place in New England of his own choice. This he refused to do and remained in Boston. Consequently, as Father Thayer celebrated Mass and held his other religious services in the church on School Street, Father Rousselet exercised his ministry from the rectory. In some cases, at least, partisans of one faction would not use the spiritual ministrations of the priest of the other faction.

While this conflict was at its peak, Father Carroll was in Europe receiving episcopal ordination as the first bishop of Baltimore, which included all of New England. On his return, he decided to go personally to Boston to resolve the confused and bitter ecclesiastical situation simmering there. Before his departure for New England, he received on March 9, 1791, letters from France and a copy of one from the bishop of Coutance containing information very prejudicial to the character of Father Rousselet. On the following day, he wrote to Father Rousselet informing him that on receiving the letter, all powers and faculties granted by him were revoked. On the same day, he also informed Father Thayer that he was to replace Father Rousselet as pastor.

Bishop Carroll did come to Boston around May 25, 1791, and remained there for about three weeks. He was surprisingly well received by the population, but was unable to effectively heal the breach between Fathers Thayer and Rousselet and their respective supporters. In fact, the situation deteriorated to a point where a schism was at least implied by the opponents of the strong-willed and authoritarian Father Thayer.

In summary, by the autumn of 1792, the Catholic community of Boston had been organized with a priest at its head for four years. The first two pastors, de la Poterie and Rousselet, were priests who had been previously suspended in France and were eventually suspended again in the United States by Bishop Carroll. Father Thayer, the third pastor, engaged in a disedifying struggle with Father Rousselet for the pastorate of Boston, a contest that divided the French and Irish parishioners. One disastrous consequence of these ecclesiastical skirmishes was that only a handful of literally hundreds of Catholics in Boston participated in the worship of that church. This unhappy and scandalous situation was to be remedied with the arrival in Boston of the fourth pastor, the Reverend Francis Anthony Matignon, on August 20, 1792. He would remain in Boston until his death twenty- six years later. Father Matignon is rightly regarded as the true founder of the Catholic Church in New England.

Founding of the Church in New England on a Sound Base 1792–1810

Father Matignon was born in Paris on November 10, 1753. He received a degree in theology at the Sorbonne and was ordained to the priesthood on September 19, 1778. After his ordination, he returned to the university and received his doctorate in theology in 1785. This erudite priest was soon assigned to teach at the then famous theological college of Navarre in Paris. Among his penitents was Jean Louis Cheverus, who was at that time a student at the College Louis-le-Grand.

Refusing to take an oath to support the civil constitution of the clergy demanded of all clerics by the revolutionary government of France, Father Matignon fled first to England, and, after a brief secret visit back to France, sailed for the United States, arriving in Baltimore on June 24, 1792, with three other French priests, all Sulpicians. Bishop Carroll assigned him as pastor of Boston when he arrived on August 20, 1792. Father François Ciquart, a Sulpician, one of his companions aboard ship, accepted to work among the Native Americans of Maine.

Once in Boston, Father Matignon immediately assumed charge of the parish. Father John Thayer, whom he replaced, departed for the South to try out the mission fields of Norfolk and Portsmouth, Virginia. He did not find satisfaction there. Between 1792 and 1803 he wandered from one part of the United States to another, and even went to Canada to solicit funds for a church in Albany, New York, without ever being able to settle down. On several occasions, up to 1789, he returned to Boston, where he assisted Father Matignon, and then Father Cheverus when he arrived in October 1796. It is not known if he ever traveled to New Hampshire.

Father Thayer left the United States in November 1804, never to return. In Europe he spent some time in London, La Trappe (France), and Dublin. By February 1811, he had moved to Limerick, Ireland, where he led an ascetic life and had a vast number of penitents. At his death in 1815, he left his entire estate to Father Matignon, who, following Father Thayer's directions, used the money to begin an Ursuline establishment in Boston. That convent was to involve several people from New Hampshire. Thus ended the life of the first "Yankee" priest, the third pastor of Boston.

There remained in Boston one more priest in addition to Father Matignon: Father Louis de Rousselet, who had been the second pastor of Boston, after the abbé de la Poterie. Father Rousselet had, after being dismissed by Bishop Carroll in his letter of March 10, 1791, gone to Maine to minister to the Native Americans. He did this despite the fact that Bishop Carroll had stripped him of all ecclesiastical powers and faculties. Father Rousselet is also known to have exercised ministry among the French around Boston, at least on occasion. He returned from his 1791 voyage to Maine in early December of that year, and again went to minister to the Native Americans in the summer of 1792. In early September of the latter year he was back in Boston, where he met the new pastor, Father Matignon, who had arrived in that city on August 20. Father Rousselet was soon employed by the French of royalist convictions, thus against the ideals of the French Revolution, as editor of the second French newspaper in Boston, which began publication on December 10, 1792.

Instead of the confrontation that might have been expected between the present and this former pastor, Father Matignon, by his kindness and tact, was able to bring Father Rousselet to regularize his status with Bishop Carroll. This was done sometime in mid-January 1793, under conditions laid down by the bishop of Baltimore. Shortly thereafter, on January 19, 1793, Father Rousselet publicly announced that he was ceasing the publication of his newspaper and leaving Boston to respond to a call to exercise his priestly ministry on the island of Guadeloupe. There, he was guillotined in the fall of 1794 in a massacre of royalist supporters. A history of Guadeloupe relates that he died bravely, encouraging and ministering to his fellow prisoners. Not long after the news of Father Rousselet's edifying death reached Boston in April 1795, the last member of his French supporters finally joined Father Matignon's congregation.

Father Matignon was to remain alone in Boston until the arrival of Father Jean Louis Cheverus on October 3, 1796. By his exemplary life, his piety, his intelligence, and unfailing courtesy to his people, Father Matignon was able to increase the income of the parish, pay the debts incurred in 1789, make extensive repairs to the church both inside and outside, and purchase new furnishings. Of far greater importance, he attracted the former Catholic nonchurchgoers, and softened the anti-Catholic prejudices of a number of Bostonians. To symbolize his permanent presence among his people, he became an American citizen in the summer of 1796.

During his first four years in Boston (1792–1796), Father Matignon made only two missionary voyages. The first was in the early fall of 1793, during the presence of Father Thayer in Boston. In October, Father Matignon made a missionary trip to Newburyport and then went as far north as Portsmouth, New Hampshire, most likely by ship, both to get acquainted with and to minister to the Catholics of the area. These visits were repeated in February 1794. On both occasions the Catholics served were all French. Father Matignon's visits to Portsmouth in 1793 and 1794 were truly the first of a missionary nature to individuals of European stock in New Hampshire.

Father Matignon's nearly solo ministry of four years was to end, as it has been said, with the arrival in Boston of Jean Louis Cheverus on October 3, 1796. With him the activity of the Catholic Church would be extended to large areas of New England.

Like Father Matignon, Jean Louis Cheverus was born in France at Mayenne on January 28, 1768. Also like Father Matignon, he took refuge in England in mid-September 1792 because of the French Revolution. He remained in England for nearly four years, where he learned English and served first as a teacher and then as a chaplain. He was persuaded to come to New England by the many letters he received from Father Matignon, whom he had known while a student in Paris.

By early 1797, Father Cheverus had begun to visit the missions north and south of Boston, and to search out the Catholics in those areas. After visiting Newburyport in early 1797, Father Cheverus went on to Portsmouth, where he ministered to some French families named Prilay and Louis. In early June he traveled to the southern missions, where he is known to have gone as far as Plymouth, Massachusetts. On his return to Boston, Father Cheverus visited the Native Americans of Maine for the first time. This was a journey that he was to make almost every year until his return to France in 1823, even in times of war or the threat of war. Beginning in 1797, he began to locate other Catholics in Maine, mostly Irish, and ministered to them as well.

Father Cheverus made a second trip to New Hampshire in 1797, this time to Bedford. There, in September, he baptized three children, the offspring of two Catholic families. It was on this occasion that he lodged in the home of Theodore Goffe, a Presbyterian, who was to be received into the Catholic Church with his wife and children some thirty-four years later. In 1798, he was again in Portsmouth, on July 27, but he does not appear to have stopped there in 1799.

By the end of three years of missionary apostolate, Father Cheverus had made Catholic history in New England. He was the first English-speaking Catholic missionary to cover most of the coastal area and minister to the Catholics scattered along this territory. Building on the pioneer efforts of his predecessors, he extended the missions in the matter of the distance traveled and the frequency of visits.

During this period and afterward, there was a slow but real growth in the Catholic population. On May 1, 1798, Father Matignon estimated that there were from six hundred to seven hundred members in the Boston congregation spread over New England. At that time, most of them were in the city of Boston and in Maine. Almost all, excluding the Native Americans, were Irish. It is not known how many of the 183,868 people in New Hampshire, counted in the federal census of 1800, would have professed themselves of the Catholic faith. The number was certainly very small.

Fathers Cheverus and Matignon received another invaluable coworker from France in the person of Father James René Romagné, a friend of Father Cheverus since childhood. He remained with the Maine Native Americans for nineteen years, from 1799 to 1818. In the fall and winter of 1805–1806, he began to minister to the Irish at Newcastle,

Maine, and environs. It appears that he also made at least two visits to Portsmouth to baptize, in 1815 and possibly 1818.

Father Cheverus is known to have visited Portsmouth again in February 1800. Between 1801 and 1810, he may have continued to visit there on three or four additional occasions. Portsmouth was not a regular mission stop, as were Salem and Newburyport in Massachusetts, for example. In February 1807, however, Father Cheverus baptized seventeen people in Portsmouth over a period of eight days. Once again, after the record of this visit, the archives remain silent until 1811, when Cheverus, now the first bishop of Boston, returned to Portsmouth.

This seemingly pointless recitation of visits by Catholic missionaries is simply to indicate that some form of religious activity was taking place within New Hampshire. Unfortunately, the present state of research has not yet revealed a great deal about the precise nature or extent of that activity.

In addition to the growth of Catholicism and the ever-expanding missionary effort in much of New England, a few other events of the period need to be noted: the flare-up of anti-Catholic sentiment (a reminder of the past and a foretaste of the future); and several outbreaks of yellow fever in various parts of the country, notably in 1791, 1793, 1798, and 1800. In 1798, in Boston, for example, more than a hundred people had died by October, about one-fourth being members of the little Catholic congregation. This apparently disproportionate number of Irish among the victims is most likely a somber reflection on the poverty and lack of hygienic and medical facilities available to them.

On a far happier note, the Catholic congregation of Boston on March 31, 1799, voted to build its own Catholic church, the first in New England, not counting Native American chapels in Maine. Construction of the church, built on plans drawn up by the famous architect Charles Bulfinch, moved along very slowly because of difficulty in raising funds. Completion was made possible in good measure by contributions from Protestants. Bishop Carroll came to Boston and dedicated the building, named the Church of the Holy Cross, on September 29, 1803, the feast of St. Michael the Archangel. This historical treasure and architectural masterpiece was eventually torn down and replaced by commonplace office buildings.

SIX

The New Diocese of Boston 1808–1853

The Episcopacy of Bishop Jean Louis Cheverus 1808–1823

As early as 1802, Bishop Carroll requested from the Propaganda Congregation in Rome a division of the huge diocese of Baltimore. In due course, it was decided that new dioceses would be established in Boston, New York City, Philadelphia, and Bardstown, Kentucky.

On April 8, 1808, Pope Pius VII in two briefs made Baltimore a metropolitan see and named four suffragans to the four new dioceses. Father Cheverus was named bishop of Boston. He was Bishop Carroll's second choice for the office. His first had been Father Matignon, who categorically refused and even threatened to return to France if the bishop of Baltimore persisted. Father Matignon seems to have declined for a number of reasons. In addition to thinking that Father Cheverus was better suited for the responsibility, he must have taken into account his age (he was fifty-five), as well as his natural shyness and humility.

Father Cheverus's ordination to the episcopacy did not take place until November 1, 1810, however. The originals of the two briefs of Pope Pius VII were delayed in Italy because of the embargo laid upon American vessels due to a phase of the Napoleonic wars. Father Cheverus was ordained to the episcopacy in Baltimore on the strength of authenticated copies of the briefs that reached Baltimore by way of France.

Bishop Cheverus was officially installed in Boston's only Catholic church, the Cathedral of the Holy Cross, on Sunday, December 22, and presided over the celebration of Christmas three days later. His episcopal authority and responsibilities extended over all New England.

At the time of Bishop Cheverus's episcopal ordination in 1810, there were but three churches and three priests, counting the bishop himself, in all New England. The churches were the Cathedral of the Holy Cross in Boston, the new church (1808) at Damariscotta Mills in Maine, and the log chapel for the Native Americans at Pleasant Point, also in Maine.

The priests, in addition to the bishop, were Father Matignon, who generally remained in Boston, and Father James Romagné, who ministered to the Penobscots and Passamaquoddys and frequently made his winter quarters at Newcastle, Maine. At that time, the Catholic population of Boston was estimated at about 720, and that of all New England at no more than 1,000. The Catholic population of New Hampshire was still so small that it had never been listed in church census figures.

By the spring of 1811, Bishop Cheverus was again making his missionary journeys, including his lengthy visits to Maine. On his return from Maine in 1811, he again visited Portsmouth, where on September 21 he baptized the son of an American officer at Fort Constitution.

Even during the War of 1812, Bishop Cheverus continued his apostolic and missionary journeys. In 1812 he is known to have made an additional visit to Portsmouth on his return from Maine after a stop in Portland. In 1814, despite the fact that the English occupied some territory in New England, including, by October, the whole country east of the Penobscot River, neither Father Romagné nor Bishop Cheverus was disturbed, nor were the Native Americans.

His only concessions to the war were to persuade Father Romagné to go to Boston with him for a while and to travel by land, rather than by sea, to avoid interception by British ships. On their way back to Boston by stagecoach, the usual visits were made to Portland and Portsmouth.

Other recorded pastoral visits made to New Hampshire between 1814 and 1823, the year of the permanent departure of Bishop Cheverus to France, were: Father Romagné to Portsmouth during November 1815 and, possibly, to the same place in December 1818; Bishop Cheverus may have visited the same city during 1822; later that same year the bishop visited Claremont twice, both on his way to Montreal and on his return. Father Charles D. Ffrench o.p., ministered in Claremont during 1818; and Father William Taylor preached a mission in Claremont during June 1822. These four visits to Claremont are described below.

As valuable as Bishop Cheverus was to New England, so was Father

Matignon to Bishop Cheverus. His close friend and colleague, whom he had known and esteemed since his student days, died in Boston on September 19, 1818, at the age of sixty-five. He had spent twenty-six years in Boston as pastor of the Church of the Holy Cross. His death marked the passing of the true founder of the Catholic Church in New England.

It was also during the years of the episcopacy of Bishop Cheverus that two other steps were taken to root more firmly the Catholic Church in the soil of New England: the training of young men for the priesthood and the introduction of the first women religious in New England.

As early as 1813, Bishop Cheverus began the training of young men for the priesthood in his rectory in Boston. By 1823, this cathedral-rectory-seminary was evidently abandoned in favor of sending the candidates elsewhere to established houses of study.

In Boston itself, Bishop Cheverus completed the building of a convent and school around Christmas of 1819. In June 1820 he traveled to Montreal to meet four Ursulines—two professed sisters and two novices–who had been trained at his request at Three Rivers—in order to escort them to Boston. As soon as the Ursulines arrived, they began to teach catechism. In September 1820, they opened a day school with more than one hundred young girls as students, divided between morning and afternoon sessions. Thus New England had its first real parochial school. Its primary purpose was the education of poor Catholic children. A secondary development was an academy that later accepted non-Catholic young women as well.

Bishop Cheverus was not to remain in the United States for very long after the establishment of the Ursulines in Boston. In the spring of 1823, he received letters from France informing him that he had been appointed bishop of Montauban at the request of the king of France, Louis XVIII.

Despite the fact that he personally did not want to leave, and in spite of the formal protests of Catholics and non-Catholics alike, he finally gave in to the pressures put on him from France. He sailed from New York on October 1, 1823. From Montauban, Bishop Cheverus was promoted to Bordeaux in 1826, and was made cardinal-archbishop of that see on February 1, 1836. He died on July 19, 1836, greatly mourned both in New England, where he had spent twenty-seven years, and in France.

In 1817, some six years before the departure of Bishop Cheverus, only Massachusetts and the province of Maine had churches and resident clergy. In Rhode Island, Connecticut, Vermont, and New Hampshire there were neither churches nor resident clergy because, as Bishop Cheverus wrote, "there are almost no Catholics." During the last four to six years of Bishop Cheverus's episcopacy in Boston, the construction of five new churches was either in progress or completed. One in progress was at Claremont, New Hampshire, the first in the state. The Catholic population in New England also rose significantly, from no more than 1,500 in 1817 to an estimated 4,500 around 1823, including the 700 Native Americans in Maine.

Catholic Population Growth of New England Mainly Irish Immigrants 1815–1845

While the increase in the Catholic population in New England between 1815 and 1845 can rightly be accounted for by: (1) the reproduction of the older Catholic stock; (2) a fairly encouraging number of converts; and (3) a certain number of immigrants from other European countries, the major part of the growth must be attributed to the immigrants from Ireland. It is a demographic fact that during this period, in marked contrast to the Mid-Atlantic states or the Midwest, New England received very little immigration other than Irish. The federal census of 1850, for example, showed that while the six states of New England contained little more than one-tenth of the total population of the country, they had one-fifth of the Irish-born population. This Irish immigration was more pronounced in Massachusetts and Connecticut than in New Hampshire.

There were several major and generally tragic causes for the exodus from Ireland. These may be summarized under three categories: an astonishing increase in population in Ireland; a deterioration in economic conditions; and a number of famines caused by the failure of several potato crops, beginning in 1817.

Economic progress, unfortunately, failed to keep pace with the boom in population: In fact, quite the opposite occurred. One must recall that during the period under consideration, 90 percent of the people of Ireland were sustained by agriculture. After a period of prosperity from 1784 to 1815, agricultural prices fell drastically, and wretched weather, bad harvests, unpaid rents, and famished farmers clamoring for assistance turned the owners away from farming to pasturing sheep and cattle. This move by the owners forced 2 million to 3 million people from the land.

During the same period, Irish industry entered a stage of distress and actual decline. Competition from a more financially, industrially, and commercially powerful England, combined with the removal of the last protective duties in 1824, virtually ruined the exportation of woolen, linen, and cotton goods. The same occurred with the manufacture of glass and shipbuilding and in the fisheries. Artisans and industrial workers found themselves sharing the plight of those in agriculture. These conditions reduced half the population, at a minimum, to live virtually on only one article of food—the potato, a delicate as well as fertile root.

From 1817 to 1844, because of blight and excessive dampness, there were more or less extensive and varying degrees of failure of the potato crops in 1817–1818, 1821, 1825, 1829–1830, 1832–1834, 1836, and 1839–1842, some fourteen subnormal harvests in about twenty-seven years. These were, most unfortunately, simply forerunners of the great catastrophes that began in 1845.

Again, regrettably, it is impossible to obtain and tabulate accurate statistics on the number of Irish immigrants who entered New England, and specifically New Hampshire, between 1815 and 1845. Official statistics for that period are grossly unreliable. One imprecise indication, according to existing data, is that 65,095 Irish came to New England during the period 1820–1845. The number of immigrants fluctuated each year, increasing with the severity of the famine in Ireland and decreasing during the years of depression in the United States, such as those that began in 1819 and 1837.

During this early period, the destination of Irish immigrants probably depended more on oceanic routes of commerce to the United States than on an individual's personal preference. Few, up to the end of the period under consideration (1815–1845), came directly to Boston because the ships from England were too small, few had steerage accommodations, and the cabin fares were too high for most immigrants. Consequently, the vast majority had to make the crossing on commercial vessels.

One of the few such possibilities for immigration to New England by commercial ship was provided by the timber trade. These ships picked up timber, frequently in New Brunswick, and delivered it to many seaport towns in Ireland, a country by then drastically denuded of trees. As these ships seldom had much cargo on the westward voyage, their relatively large size provided a great deal of space for emigrants at a low fare.

The majority of the Irish who landed in New Brunswick had no intention of remaining on British soil. The goal of most was the United States. Many proceeded overland, from New Brunswick, and settled along the coast of Maine. Most appeared to have gone on further to New Hampshire, Massachusetts, and beyond.

A more popular way was to set out from Canada by ship for ports in Maine, Portsmouth in New Hampshire, Boston, or wherever else employment could be found, or where relatives or friends made their homes. For example, in 1842 the steamer *Huntress* carried 525 passengers from St. John, New Brunswick, and Eastport, Maine, to Portsmouth.

In summary, for about a quarter of a century, from 1817 to 1842 at least, the Irish emigrants who came to New Brunswick and then continued on to New England, either overland or by sea, would seem without question to represent the chief immigration that this area received. While the New Brunswick route to New England predominated, the Irish arrived by other routes as well. Some came by ship directly to Boston from Ireland, such as from Limerick and Dublin. Liverpool began to draw an ever-increasing number of Irish passengers, a trend that eventually led to a preponderant share of the traffic. By the 1840s the trip from Liverpool to Boston was about as inexpensive as that from Ireland to New Brunswick.

In 1844 another improvement took place: A Boston packet line carrying mail, goods, and passengers was inaugurated from Liverpool that set out to capture the immigrant market. Thus, a new era was born: The Liverpool–Boston route displaced the New Brunswick route as the most frequented way to New England, and the method of transporting immigrants passed more and more from commercial ships to passenger ships.

The Extraordinary Story of the Barber Family and Other Conversions to Catholicism

While Irish immigrants started to flow into New England, another drama began to develop that would have an impact on Catholicism in the state of New Hampshire. This was the conversion of the Barber family and the reception into the Catholic Church of from 100 to 150 people in Claremont and the vicinity. These converts were the third group of residents of New Hampshire to join the Catholic Church, following many Native Americans and some women of the province who were captured by the

French and Native Americans during the frequent wars and were converted to Catholicism by French missionary priests.

These notable events in Claremont, which seem to have no parallel in the history of Catholicism in the United States, began with the Reverend Daniel Barber, rector of the Episcopal church in that community.

One of his abiding concerns as a clergyman was the validity of his priestly ordination. At the age of twenty-seven, he resigned from the Congregational ministry because he doubted the validity of his ordination and joined the Episcopal Church, in which he was ordained to the priesthood in 1787. For the next thirty years he served, as he said, without the least doubt or suspicion concerning the correctness and validity of his Episcopalian priesthood.

After some thirty years, however, the doubts about the validity of his Congregational ordination returned concerning his Episcopalian ordination. By this time, he had been pastor of the Union Episcopal Church in Claremont for some twenty-four years. In one of his attempts to resolve this problem, Barber traveled to Boston to seek the advice of a Catholic priest. There he met and discussed the matter with Father Cheverus, then the bishop-select of Boston.

In addition to explaining the principal differences between the Catholic and Episcopal Churches, Bishop-select Cheverus gave him several books to study at home. These books were widely read by the members of the Barber family, and by a number of the members of the parish.

Not long after the Reverend Daniel Barber's visit to Boston, which was probably in 1810, his youngest son, one of four children, Virgil Horace, brought his family to Claremont for a summer holiday. At the time, Virgil, an Episcopal priest like his father, was principal of the Episcopal Academy at Fairfield, New York (near Utica), and rector of the local parish.

Father and son discussed the troublesome question of the validity of Episcopal orders, using the books given to Daniel by Bishop-select Cheverus. The Reverend Virgil H. Barber had been married to Jerusha Booth since September 1807. Five children were born of the union between 1810 and 1816: Mary, Abigail, Susan, Samuel, and Josephine. All evidence points to a happy marriage based on love and mutual respect,—and a rarer quality—a willingness to sacrifice for one another.

On his return to Fairfield, New York, bearing one of Bishop Cheverus's books given to him by his father, Virgil pursued with interest the question of the validity of ecclesiastical orders and the identity of the true church founded by Jesus Christ. As his father had visited Bishop-select Cheverus in Boston, Virgil sought in 1816 the counsel of the Reverend Benedict J. Fenwick, s.j., then the administrator of the vacant episcopal see of New York.

In addition to an in-depth discussion of the religious subjects that perplexed Reverend Barber as well as the tenets of the Catholic Church, Father Fenwick gave him some books to study and offered, when he returned to New York, to review any matter that might seem unclear to him.

Through all of this difficult period of search, Virgil Barber discussed all matters with Jerusha and used her as a sounding board and critic for his ideas and reasoning.

Within several months, Virgil Barber returned to Father Fenwick in New York and made his profession of faith in the Catholic Church. He then went back to Fairfield, where he resigned as rector of the Episcopal church and as principal of the academy, not without being subject to, it is said, the disbelief of his parishioners and the personnel of the academic community.

The seven Barbers—Virgil, Jerusha, and their five children—then moved to New York City, where Father Fenwick assisted the new convert in opening a private school for boys, which soon was well attended. Not long after the arrival of the Barbers in New York, the rest of the family was received into the Catholic Church, beginning with Jerusha.

On September 23, 1817, five days after the first communion of Virgil and Jerusha, the real drama of the Barbers began. On that day, they asked Father Fenwick, who was visiting their home, under what conditions could they enter religious life, if indeed that was even possible. This desire originated with Virgil, who felt called to the Catholic priesthood as he had previously to the Episcopal ministry. Jerusha, certainly with a love that has known few equals, consented to his proposal, if this arrangement was possible and if suitable provisions could be made for their five children, especially the youngest two, Samuel and Josephine, who were both under four years old.

Father Fenwick, who claimed that he was aware of previous cases of this kind in England, answered in the affirmative but counseled prayer, patience, and careful thought, principally because the parents were the sole means of support of the children.

Despite the almost hopeless nature of this case, a solution was proposed and agreed upon. Father Fenwick, who had been recalled to Georgetown by his superiors shortly after the request of the Barbers, was able to convince, with considerable difficulty, his own Jesuit superior and the archbishop of Baltimore, Leonard Neale, to consent to the extraordinary petition of Virgil and Jerusha. Part of the agreement reached was that the three oldest daughters would be taken by the Visitation Sisters of Georgetown with their mother, Virgil would join the Jesuits, and Samuel and Josephine (the latter being about thirteen months old) would be cared for by Father Fenwick's mother, a widow who lived nearby. It was further agreed that the two youngest would remain with Mrs. Fenwick until Samuel was old enough to be schooled by the Jesuits and until Josephine was of age to join her mother and three older sisters at the Visitation convent.

This proposed arrangement was accepted by all. Virgil entered the Jesuits, Jerusha the Visitation Sisters, and the five children were separated as planned. Despite a number of unexpected problems that affected the Barbers, both Virgil and Jerusha advanced toward their goals: his ordination as a Jesuit, and her religious profession as a Visitation sister. One of the unexpected problems may have been the temporary concern that Mrs. Barber was again with child. When the two youngest children reached the appointed age, Samuel became a student at Georgetown and Josephine, in her turn, joined her mother, by then Sister Mary Austin (or Augustine), at the Visitation Academy.

In the fall of 1818, on what appears to have been a temporary return from his studies in Rome, Virgil Barber, known as Brother Jerome in religion, went to Claremont with Father Charles D. Ffrench, an Irish Dominican convert, then stationed in New York. While in Claremont, Father Ffrench celebrated Mass and preached. His were the first Masses celebrated in western New Hampshire since the possible celebration of the Jesuits among the Native Americans in the seventeenth and eighteenth centuries. During his brief stay there, Father Ffrench baptized seven converts from among the Barber, Tyler, and Chase families, including the wife of the Reverend Daniel Barber.

Not long after the visit of his son Virgil and Father Ffrench to Claremont, the Reverend Daniel Barber resigned from the Episcopal parish in Claremont on November 15, 1818, and on the subsequent Sunday gave his farewell sermon in a spirit of friendship, peace, and harmony. He then went to Georgetown, where he pursued his studies in the Catholic faith. A few months later, he received conditional baptism from Bishop Cheverus.

By early 1822, Daniel Barber had returned to Claremont and resumed the work that he had begun in the name of the Catholic Church. In June of that same year, 1822, Bishop Cheverus sent a Father William Taylor to Claremont to preach a short mission there.

More additions were made to the Catholic community, including Captain Bela Chase, his wife, and their three children from Cornish, New Hampshire, and probably the rest of the Tyler family, consisting of the father, three daughters, and a son, William, who later became the founding bishop of Hartford, Connecticut.

During the summer of 1822, Bishop Cheverus himself paid two visits to Claremont, first on his way to Canada and then on his return. By then it had been determined that Virgil Barber would be sent there after his ordination.

It was perhaps during one of the two visits of Bishop Cheverus in 1822 that Daniel Barber was given minor orders—tonsure, porter, exorcist, and acolyte—and possibly permission to preach. It was probably on one of these same occasions that Daniel Barber made a gift of some land in Claremont on which to build a Catholic church.

Another phase in this amazing story was reached on January 23, 1820, when Virgil Barber and Jerusha, his wife, met in the Georgetown convent chapel to take their religious vows. Mrs. Barber, now Sister Mary Austin, took her vows as a Visitation sister, and Virgil followed by pronouncing his as required by the Society of Jesus. All five of their children were present. Mary, the oldest, was then ten, and Josephine, the youngest, was not quite three and a half.

Virgil Barber was ordained to the priesthood by Bishop Cheverus in Boston on December 3, 1822. Shortly thereafter he left for Claremont, where he arrived probably before Christmas to begin his ministry.

As the Catholics of Claremont were few and for the most part poor, Father Barber traveled to Canada, notably to the Diocese of Three Rivers, to solicit financial assistance. One of the reasons for choosing Three Rivers for soliciting funds was certainly the fact that the first four women religious to minister in the Diocese of Boston—the Ursulines—were trained for ministry there.

Moreover, Quebec was the closest source of Catholic sympathy and help available to Claremont and to all of New England. With these funds, Barber was able to build a small brick church connected with the domicile of his parents. This structure is still standing, the oldest Catholic church in New Hampshire. On occasion, it is still used for worship, particularly during the summer months.

Father Barber made another trip to Canada in the winter of 1823–1824 to collect more funds, which he used to add another building to the home of his parents, chiefly to lodge student boarders. Both the Barber homestead and the second building just mentioned have since been razed. No photographs or archaeological evidence has yet been found concerning these two buildings.

Father Virgil Barber, with the assistance of his own father, Daniel, established a secondary school for boys not long after the Jesuit arrived in Claremont. Known as the Claremont Catholic Seminary, it was the first Catholic high school for boys in New England. By March 17, 1823, there were at least fifty pupils enrolled, both boarders and day students. Tuition, board, and room combined was one dollar per week.

The fortunes of this school varied considerably over the years. While in 1824 Father Barber was obliged to refuse admittance to nearly twenty applicants for lack of space and sufficient teaching personnel, in 1825 he was forced to close the school for nearly two years for financial reasons. After another tour by Father Barber to collect money in the second half of 1826, the academy opened its doors once again in June 1827. After the departure of Father Barber from Claremont in February 1828, Daniel Barber continued the school, but this attempt failed after a short period.

A more personal misfortune struck the Barber family in early 1825. On February 8, Mrs. Daniel Barber died of influenza in the Claremont family home, having received the last sacraments from the hands of her son. Her funeral was the first in St. Mary Church and she was also the first to be buried in the new Catholic cemetery situated behind the church. The exact location of her grave in now unknown, and no monument or plaque commemorates the first burial in the first Catholic cemetery in New Hampshire.

Rather numerous were the absences of Father Barber from Claremont, in addition to his trips to collect money for St. Mary Church and the Claremont Catholic Seminary. In the fall of 1825, for instance, he was in Baltimore for the episcopal ordination of his old friend and mentor, Father Benedict J. Fenwick, s.j., as the second bishop of Boston. From Baltimore, Father Barber and Bishop Fenwick traveled to Georgetown, where with Sister Mary Austin, Virgil's wife, arrangements were made for their daughter Mary's reception at the Ursuline convent in Boston and her sister Abigail's with the Ursulines at Quebec City in the province of Quebec. It was on this occasion, November 14, 1825, that the Barbers, husband, wife, and five children, all met together for the last time.

Eventually all five Barber children entered religious life. It seems that Virgil Barber had taken this for granted. Besides Mary and Abigail, Susan and Josephine left Georgetown, in 1827, the first for Ursulines at Three Rivers and the second to join the same congregation in Boston. Not long after, Samuel entered the Jesuits at White March, Maryland. He was ordained to the priesthood on September 22, 1839. Samuel had a distinguished career as a Jesuit that included the vice presidency of Georgetown College and the presidency of Gonzaga College in Washington in the District of Columbia.

In April 1826, Father Barber made a successful missionary voyage to Hartford, Connecticut, and in the fall of that year he was commissioned by Bishop Fenwick to make a pastoral tour to the East, which brought him to Dover, New Hampshire, to minister to the Irish living there. From Dover he went to Bangor, Eastport, and the two Native American settlements in Maine, homes of the Penobscots and Passamaquoddys.

At that time there were only three priests in all New England in addition to Bishop Fenwick: the Reverend Patrick Byrne stationed in Boston, the Reverend Dennis Ryan in Maine, and Father Barber in New Hampshire. Five of the nine existing places of worship were without pastors.

During the spring and summer of 1827, Father Barber reached the peak of his optimism, concerning both the number of new converts and the success of the academy. This proved to be the calm before the storm. Storms struck simultaneously from two directions. One was financial: by the winter of 1827–1828, the financial situation had become desperate. The second, the more serious and unresolvable problems, were the bitter quarrels, most likely over money and property, that broke out in the Barber family, with Virgil on one side and his father, his brother Trueworth, and his sister Mrs. Laura McKenna on the other.

Recognizing the futility of the situation, the Jesuit superior recalled

Father Barber to Georgetown, for he certainly could not evict the other Barbers from their own home. As a result, Claremont would not become a permanent parish until 1870, many years after Father Barber's departure and death.

Mr. Daniel Barber spent his last years in Maryland visiting the various Jesuit houses and old Catholic families of the area. He died at St. Inigoes in that state on March 24, 1834, and was buried in the cemetery of the Jesuit mission there. Father Virgil Barber, after working among the Maine Indians and later teaching at various Jesuit institutions, including Georgetown College, died on March 25, 1847.

The Barber family story, told here in summary, has been a source of inspiration for some and one of bewilderment, even of disapproval, for others. Those inspired would most likely point first to the faithful and firm response to God's grace of both Virgil and Jerusha, and then to that of their four daughters and one son. Those who either question or disapprove would invoke several reasons. Among their predominant concerns might be the apparent inferior status given to the bond of marriage to that of the priesthood and religious life: One could leave the lower to ascend to the higher. Another, even closer to the human heart, was the virtual abandonment of five children, depriving them of mother and father and placing their entire welfare—physical, psychological, emotional, and material—into the hands of others. A historical judgment in this case has no other appeal than to divine authority.

At this stage of research concerning Virgil and Daniel Barber and their families, as well as the "Claremont converts," it is not clearly known what aroused their doubts concerning the validity of the priestly orders in the Episcopal church. The initial concern of Daniel Barber on the subject of ordination moved him to leave the Congregational Church and become an Episcopal priest in 1787. This was followed by the uncertainty of both Daniel and Virgil Barber relative to the priestly order in the Episcopal Church. Virgil was admitted into the Catholic Church in either late 1816 or early 1817; his father received conditional baptism very likely in early 1819. Both of these conversions antedated the Oxford movement in England, which had similar concerns and objectives. That movement, however, did not flourish until the period 1833–1845, sixteen or more years after the Barbers joined the Catholic Church.

Additional Converts to Catholicism

Other converts to Catholicism during the period 1825–1846 with some link to or roots in New Hampshire were: Fanny Allen of Vermont, the daughter of the famous Revolutionary War hero Ethan Allen, who had previously been baptized in the Episcopal Church by the Reverend Daniel Barber; Orestes Brownson, who was ordained a Universalist Church minister at Jaffrey, New Hampshire, on June 15, 1826, and served for two years as minister of that denomination at Walpole, beginning in the summer of 1832; and Theodore Goffe and his family, from Bedford, New Hampshire, who, as previously mentioned, walked to Boston to be instructed in the faith and were baptized there by Bishop Fenwick on November 15, 1831.

Other converts with some New Hampshire affiliation were Stephen Burroughs, John Holmes, William E. Hoyt, and Edward Putnam. An interesting and often edifying story could be told about each of them.

Defections from the Catholic Church

Despite the increase in the number of Catholics, it is quite evident that because of the small number of Catholic churches in New Hampshire (as late as 1855 there were only three) and an equal number of clergy, the outflow, or rate of defection, of Catholics greatly exceeded the gain by conversion.

Reasons for the Continued Growth of New Hampshire

There were some positive signs of continued increase in the number of Catholics in New Hampshire. One was the steady growth of the state. New Hampshire's population rose from 141,885 in 1790, shortly before the missionary visits of Fathers Matignon and Cheverus, to more than 318,000 in 1853, the year of the founding of the Diocese of Portland, which, as we shall see, included New Hampshire as well as Maine.

In short, the population of the state grew by 184,188 between 1790, the year of the episcopal ordination of John Carroll as the first bishop of Baltimore, and the eve of the outbreak of the Civil War some seventy years later (1860).

In addition to the availability of land, there were many other reasons for the growth of the state. Among these were relative improvements in the speed and comfort of transportation. New Hampshire's first highways were the ocean, rivers, lakes, and other bodies of water. Then came the building of roads, especially turnpikes. By the fall of 1794, a weekly stage-coach ran between Boston and Concord, with several intermediate stops.

Turnpike construction, generally toll roads, chartered by the legislature of the state, began in 1796. As early as 1819, there were already approximately 460 miles of turnpikes within New Hampshire. In time they linked virtually the entire state. The original toll on the first turnpike was one cent for ten sheep or hogs, and three cents for a four-wheeled vehicle.

Canals offered an additional way to travel. In 1803, the Middlesex Canal opened between the Charles River at Boston and the Merrimack River at Chelmsford, Massachusetts. By 1815, one could travel by canal boat from the capital of Massachusetts to that of New Hampshire. As for the Connecticut River, it was made navigable as far north as Walpole, New Hampshire. Short side canals and locks allowed boat travel up various tributary rivers.

While canal travel was highly practical for heavy freight, it was far from ideal for passengers. First, canal boats were quite slow: The trip from Boston to Concord, upstream, took five days; that in the opposite direction consumed four days. Another great disadvantage was that the Merrimack River was generally closed between December and April. A stagecoach or carriage trip over the same distance took less than half of canal time. Moreover, turnpikes crisscrossed the state; canals, on the other hand, were few in number heading to only a few destinations in New Hampshire.

A new and faster means of transportation began to replace the canals and make the turnpikes less attractive: the railroads. In 1830 there were only thirty–two miles of railroad track in the whole United States; by 1900 there were 175,000. New Hampshire participated vigorously in their construction. East Boston, Massachusetts, was connected to Portsmouth, New Hampshire, between 1837 and 1840, and Boston was linked by rail to Manchester and Concord in 1842.

In 1851 an all-rail route was completed between Boston and Montreal, although passengers and freight had to use seven different railroad companies to negotiate the distance. This route, in particular, opened New England to the flood of French Canadians who began migrating here, especially after the Civil War.

By 1900 there were already 1,239 miles of track in New Hampshire; of these 1,179 were controlled by the Boston and Maine. Many of the construction workers on these lines were Irish escaping the famine, and the discrimination and outright persecution by the British. A good number of these workers eventually settled somewhere along the rail lines that they had built in New Hampshire.

Another attraction for immigrants to New Hampshire were the cotton and woolen mills. The first cotton mill in the state began operation at New Ipswich in 1804. By 1870, five years after the Civil War, there were important cotton factories in twenty-seven New Hampshire communities, and fifty-three fairly large woolen mills. Immigrants also worked in other industries and some began to operate their own small neighborhood businesses. Relatively few Catholic immigrants to New England took up farming or commercial fishing, however. Working hours in most industries were long and working conditions almost universally harsh.

The Native American Movement

A shameful but hardly surprising consequence of the rising tide of immigration was the revival of hostility toward the Catholic immigrants, particularly the Irish. Anti-Catholicism had been relatively dormant in the United States since the American Revolution.

An outbreak of anti-Catholicism occurred during the Native American movement of the 1830s and 1840s and flared up at least three more times in the Know-Nothing movement of the 1850s, the American Protective Association (APA) movement of the 1890s, and the Ku Klux Klan (KKK) movement of the early twentieth century. In addition to the hostility generated by the new Catholic immigrants, the Native American movement was fueled by the revival of what can be called a "fundamentalist" movement in a number of the Protestant churches in the United States. Interdenominational societies were formed to convert Catholics, and large segments of a growing Protestant press were blatantly outspoken and highly biased against papists.

Anti-Irish and anti-Catholic clashes in New England were relatively common during this period, notably in Boston. Some occurred in that city in 1823, 1826, 1828, and 1832. Undoubtedly one of the most disgraceful episodes in the religious history of New England happened in

Charlestown, Massachusetts, in 1834: the burning down of the Ursuline convent boarding school for girls, Mount Benedict.

The destruction of this institution by fire has a place in the history of New Hampshire Catholicism as some of the principals involved-on both sides—the arsonists and the convent's personnel,—were from the Granite State. At the time that the convent was vandalized, looted, and set on fire there were forty-four students at Mount Benedict and ten members of the Ursuline community. Among the choir nuns were Sister Mary Benedict Father Virgil Barber's eldest daughter, and Sister Mary Ursula (Sarah Chase of Cornish, New Hampshire), a sister of Captain Bela Chase and one of the Claremont converts.

After a series of confrontations between some officials of Charlestown and the Ursuline sisters, including an unwarranted and shameless inspection of the convent by the former, a hostile crowd gathered in the area of the Catholic institution on the evening of August 11, 1834. Among the more menacing milling about were numerous laborers employed by several brickyards in the neighborhood. A good number of these men had been recruited from New Hampshire.

One of the New Hampshire brickmakers was John R. Buzzell, who was described as a towering young giant and a locally famous "fighting man." He is reported to have been the first to break in the convent door. John Buzzell and many in the mob believed, among other things, that a nun was being held there against her will.

Meeting little resistance, John Buzzell and the mob had no difficulty evicting the nuns and students. They then ransacked, robbed, and set fire to the building. On the pleading of Bishop Fenwick, the Catholics, mainly Irish laborers, were morally restrained from taking revenge.

Of all those brought to trial for this outrageous incident, only one was found guilty and sentenced to hard labor in the state prison for life. This sole convicted person was only sixteen years old. Bishop Fenwick and the superior of the Ursuline convent were among the thousands who petitioned for his pardon, including many other Catholics. After considerable official hesitation, this young man was pardoned by the governor of Massachusetts in October 1835.

The final outcome was that no one was ever punished for this cowardly crime and neither the nuns nor the diocese was ever compensated for the loss. During his trial, John Buzzell was found "not guilty," a decision that caused loud applause in the courtroom and cheering in the streets. He was also showered with compliments and gifts of money from the public.

In the latter part of 1838, an attempt to reopen the Ursuline convent was made in Roxbury, this time with Mother Mary Benedict Barber as superior. This foundation failed in 1840–1841 and the Boston Ursulines disbanded, the members retiring to convents in Quebec, Three Rivers, and New Orleans.

Native American hostility was not restricted to the Charlestown convent, as it has been noted. Other incidents, of varying magnitude, also occurred several more times in Boston and such places as New York, Lowell, Bangor, New Haven, Wareham (Massachusetts), Norridgewock (Maine), and Burlington (Vermont).

In 1831 and 1832, unsuccessful efforts were made to burn down the new church in Dover, New Hampshire. These anti-Catholic depredations were certainly intensified by the publication of mendacious and inflammatory books, and the equally scurrilous attacks by certain preachers and lecturers.

New Hampshire's First Parish: St. Aloysius (Later St. Mary) Dover 1830

It was in this inimical atmosphere that the first Catholic parishes were established in New Hampshire. The earliest among these was St. Aloysius in Dover. By 1830, Dover had a population of 5,449, making it the foremost industrial center in New Hampshire. Around 1819 a group of about twenty Irish immigrants had settled there, most of them employed in the local textile mills. More Irish settled there from that year onward. Among the Catholic pioneers were John Burns and Philip Scanlon.

In response to the frequent and urgent pleas of the Irish Catholics of Dover, Bishop Fenwick sent Father Virgil Barber of Claremont on a voyage eastward in the latter part of 1826, as previously mentioned. He celebrated the first Mass in Dover in the courthouse on Sunday, October 22, 1826, before a large congregation, it is said, of all religious denominations.

As a result of Father Barber's favorable recommendations and his own impressions during a personal visit to those places in 1827, Bishop Fenwick instructed the Reverend Charles Ffrench, an Irish Dominican, to build churches at Eastport and Portland in Maine, and at Dover in New Hampshire. This was accomplished between 1827 and the summer of 1835.

The cornerstone of the church in Dover was blessed by Father Ffrench on May 14, 1827, and the completed structure was dedicated by Bishop Fenwick on September 26, 1830. Two months later St. Aloysius was created as a parish and the Reverend Michael Healy was appointed the first pastor. As mentioned, attempts were made by Nativists, or persons inspired by them, to burn down the church in 1831 and again in 1832.

This first parish in New Hampshire, in continuous existence since 1830, served many surrounding communities for many years, at one time extending from Newburyport, Massachusetts, to South Berwick, Maine.

A Unique Mission Priest: Father John B. Daly, o.f.m.

One of Dover's pastors, the Reverend Patrick Canavan, an energetic worker who arrived there in July 1834, began receiving some part-time assistance in the vast missionary field of New Hampshire in 1837 from the Reverend John B. Daly, an Irish Franciscan. Originally assigned to Vermont, he extended his missionary work to include the northwestern part of Massachusetts and, over the years, to much of New Hampshire.

For example, his mission list for the years 1837–1840 included twenty-seven stations spread over three states—Vermont, Massachusetts, and New Hampshire. His six stations in New Hampshire in those years were Claremont, Cornish, Charlestown, Lebanon, Hanover, and Keene.

To fully appreciate the magnitude of his efforts, one need only recall that this travel was done mostly before the building of the railroads and generally over hardly passable roads. It is known that Father Daly also visited Manchester, Lakeport, Laconia, and Lancaster (this latter town way up in the northern part of New Hampshire), from 1844.

This priest, described by his contemporaries as being of a generous but irascible character, is said to have boasted that in his some nineteen years as a missionary in Vermont, Massachusetts, and New Hampshire, he never slept under the same roof for two consecutive nights.

In fact, Father Daly was so possessive of his missionary field that he had to be directed several times to leave by the Ordinary of Portland, Bishop Bacon, before he reluctantly agreed to do so. He left New England in the spring of 1856 and eventually settled in New York City, where he died on December 11, 1872, at the age of seventy-seven.

More Native American Outbreaks and the Slow Growth of Catholicism 1843–1848

By 1843 it was estimated that the Catholic population of all New England was 68,133. Massachusetts was listed as having 47,941 of that number. New Hampshire was deemed as having 1,064 Catholics, by far the lowest on the list of New England states.

At the time, there were only two priests who ministered in New Hampshire: Father Canavan at Dover, and Father Daly, the circuit rider. The lack of enthusiasm for migration to New Hampshire by Catholics can be explained, at least in part, by two factors: the Anti-Catholic provisions of the state constitution, and continued flaring-up of the Native American movement.

This movement, which had experienced a remission for a few years, began to heat up again in the early 1840s. With the economic depression that began in 1837, the Nativists shifted their emphasis from anti-Catholicism to the disastrous effects of cheap foreign workers on labor wages, the standard of living, and, ultimately, the security of the jobs of the American working class.

Native American outbreaks, most of them violent, took place in Philadelphia; Boston; Providence; and Bangor, Maine. Through the American Republican Party, the Nativists were able to hold successful meetings in various parts of New England and to elect their candidates to public office.

This second outbreak of Nativism, although more violent than in the 1830s, was also short-lived. Broader issues, such as the fates of Texas and Oregon, the future of slavery, and the prelude to the war with Mexico, attracted the attention of the American public.

Famine in Ireland and the Exodus to America

By coincidence, the temporary ebb of Nativism was accompanied by a deluge of emigration from Ireland. Between 1841 and 1871, some 2.1 million Irish made their way to the United States; roughly two-thirds of these were

Catholic. Their immigration to New Hampshire is reflected in the fact that in twenty years—1846 to 1866—the number of Catholic parishes in New Hampshire grew from one to ten. This same phenomenon took place throughout New England, and in other parts of the United States as well.

This exodus from Ireland, one of the major human tragedies of the nineteenth century, was caused primarily by the repeated failure of the potato crop due to the blight. Adding to that calamity was the simultaneous failure of other crops, such as those of wheat, oats, turnips, beans, and onions, because of disease. Pigs became victims of starvation, and cattle herds were decimated by an epidemic that began in 1838.

Tens of thousands of people died of starvation and an even greater number perished from cholera, dysentery, and other diseases that followed in the wake of the famine. In time, this famine and its dreadful consequences reached into almost every stratum of Irish society. A number of English laws aggravated the economic situation of Ireland and intensified the misery of the people.

Departure from Ireland did not necessarily end the intense sufferings of large numbers of the emigrants. Sailing vessels became infected with typhus, which spread through steerage. Great numbers died at sea and countless more drew their last breath after reaching their destination. This was more common in or near the port cities along the St. Lawrence River than in those along the east coast of the United States.

Inevitably, the arrival of the Irish placed considerable strain on the charitable institutions of many American communities. In addition, massive efforts were made by Catholics and the general public to send money and food for those who remained in Ireland. Fortunately, the physical condition of the passengers arriving from Ireland in Boston began to improve in 1849, and further progress was made in subsequent years.

Founding of the Second and Third Parishes in Manchester and Portsmouth

It was in the circumstances just described that the second and third Catholic parishes in the state of New Hampshire were established: St. Anne in Manchester in 1848 and St. Mary (later Immaculate Conception) in Portsmouth in 1851.

By this time, the Diocese of Boston had its third bishop, John Bernard

Fitzpatrick. He was ordained coadjutor to Bishop Benedict Fenwick in 1844 at the age of thirty-two, and succeeded the latter at his death on August 11, 1846.

Father John B. Daly, o.f.m., seems to have been visiting Manchester for a number of years before 1844. It was in that year that he advised Bishop Fenwick that a Catholic church would soon be needed in that community because of the number of Catholics settling there. A plan to build a church in 1847 was canceled when Bishop Fitzpatrick became aware of the fact that the deed to the land, donated by the Amoskeag Manufacturing Company, provided for lay trustees, a provision totally unacceptable to him.

It is doubtful that any deviousness was intended by the company. Trustees were undoubtedly standard in the Protestant churches previously endowed with free land by the Amoskeag. The Catholic Church is one of the few Christian denominations that still distances its lay members from ownership of church property. Trusteeism, which places the management of the property and the funds of the parish in the hands of elected lay trustees, was never to become a reality in the Catholic Church of New Hampshire, and, therefore, never a cause of contention or division.

This Catholic building project lay dormant until Father William McDonald was sent to Manchester in the latter part of 1848 as the first resident priest and pastor. Born in Ireland, Father McDonald was ordained for the Diocese of St. John, New Brunswick, in 1842. On June 17, 1848, he transferred to the Diocese of Boston, from which, after a brief period of probation, he was sent to Manchester, where he remained until his death on August 26, 1885.

Father McDonald proved to be a providential choice for the mission assigned to him. A brief assessment of his qualities reveals that he was serious, industrious, faithful, resourceful, a good manager, and a devoted priest in every respect. His piety and moral standards reflected one of the stronger trends among the churchmen of his time: He was strict, even severe.

Having been born in a rigorously Catholic environment in Ireland, William McDonald was prepared for the priesthood in an equally rigid French Canadian seminary, that of the Grand Séminaire in Montreal. These influences of home and education—Ireland and Quebec—gave him a puritanical perspective, or, in Catholic terms, a near Jansenistic view of life.

Two out of many possible examples will underscore this tendency. One was that he would refuse to enter a restaurant located in a hotel—a public house—even to attend a parish function. If a similar party was held on parish property, he would be present. A second indication of this mind-set was that he would not allow laywomen to enter the church sanctuary, even to dust and clean; rather, he would do this himself. A contemporary account has him covering his hair with a cloth before beginning this cleaning chore. This prohibition of women in the sanctuary did not extend to those consecrated to the religious life. Once the Sisters of Mercy arrived at St. Anne's in July 1858, he turned this function over to them.

Father McDonald was far more than the one-dimensional person who emerges from the information that can be gathered from church archives. Other facets of his personality and thinking can be learned, for example, from testimony that he gave before a committee of the Senate of the United States inquiring into the relations between labor and capital (employer and employee). Father McDonald's testimony was taken in Manchester on October 15, 1883, by the chairman of the committee, Henry W. Blair, one of the two senators from the state of New Hampshire. At the time of the interrogation, Father McDonald had lived in Manchester for some thirty-five years and had been a priest for more than forty. The Diocese of Manchester was founded just six months after his appearance and one year and ten months before his death.

In addition to the many things that he had to say about the relations between labor and capital in New Hampshire, Father McDonald's testimony is noteworthy for its blunt challenge to federal authority and for his interjection of several extraneous subjects that he judged important to the city at large and to the Catholic community in particular. His understanding of the city in regard to the working class, Senator Blair stated, was greater than "almost any other citizen of Manchester . . . particularly that of the Catholic segment of the population."

At one point in his testimony, Father McDonald went beyond the purpose of the interrogation and affirmed that he personally "had indirectly contributed more wealth to the Amoskeag company, and all the other companies in Manchester, than any other individual." This he had done, he explained, by protecting their property and keeping the Irish honest so that they would not steal or cheat the Amoskeag. He made it very clear that the company had never acknowledged or rewarded him for this, even when he appealed to the Amoskeag board for financial assistance when he built St. Anne Church (in either 1848 or 1849).

During his testimony, one is surprised to find several challenges to the authority of the federal government to interject itself into the affairs, as he saw it, of the legislature of the state of New Hampshire. His reasoning was that the mills and corporations had been brought into existence and incorporated by the state legislature and that the "United States" had no right "to come here and interfere with these things." Moreover, Father McDonald questioned the small size of the Senate committee (ten in all) and its legal right to divide itself, as only two members came to Manchester. Strangely, perhaps even facetiously, he even noted that a committee should not be in even numbers: "There's luck in odd numbers." Despite some rather heated exchanges with Senator Blair on these subjects, neither was able to sway the mind of the other.

The transcript of this discussion indicates that Senator Blair remained the more composed of the two and used less strident language than the pastor of St. Anne. At one point, Father McDonald affirmed his pro-state position by informing the senator: "My old friend, the State of New Hampshire, has legislated well for the rising generation, and wishes all the children to be educated."

On the subjects directly related to the Senate committee's inquiry, Father McDonald expressed some points of view that are of interest. For example, while he noted some lack of harmony between employer and employee in the mills, he attributed this to a general condition where the worker always complained about the employer. He also told Senator Blair that the condition of the working people, supposedly the men, women, and children, was improving and that the "operatives," as he called them, were well clad. Moreover, he even considered that the hours of the work week, then eleven hours a day, would do, as they were down from thirteen or fourteen hours sometime before 1852 or 1853. As one can see, the perception of the work week, as well as that of social justice and humane treatment, has changed considerably since the 1880s. As a sort of summary on this aspect of the interrogation, Father McDonald stated, "No person in Manchester need want of anything if they are sober, frugal, and proper in the use of their money. I speak of it in church and everywhere."

On the subject of the housing provided by the Amoskeag, the tenements occupied by the operatives, he conceded that the sanitation needed no improvement but that the houses themselves should be equipped with steam heat and have flat roofs. The purpose of the steam, he explained, was to heat the whole house or apartment evenly and in all its rooms, and the flat roof was to eliminate the angled room walls and to prevent the sun from striking directly on the slate roofs, which produced unbearable heat in the summer. Father McDonald added that he knew of this condition personally, as he had visited the sick in these attics.

Father McDonald concluded his testimony on a rather triumphal tone by remarking that the Know–Nothings of the 1850s had not driven the Catholics out of Manchester and added, "I am not driven out . . . but I am almost in a condition to see that we are driving somebody else out." This enigmatic and somewhat vindictive statement did not identify the person or group to be expelled. Senator Blair, apparently sensing some unpleasantness to follow in the testimony, politely but abruptly dismissed Father McDonald at this point.

At the time of Father McDonald's arrival in Manchester in 1848, there were from three hundred to six hundred Catholics in the city, a minuscule number in a total population of somewhat less than 13,000. After purchasing land on the corner of Merrimack and Union Streets, construction of a church was begun in May 1849. The dedication of this church to St. Anne took place on April 4, 1850. Up to that time, the favored location for Sunday Mass had been the old Granite Hall, at the northwest corner of Elm and Merrimack Streets.

This first Catholic church had neither lighting nor heating facilities. Parishioners brought their own fish-oil lamps to church for both these purposes. A far worse deficiency was the shoddy construction of the building. It had to be torn down within two years of its completion because of the danger that it would collapse. A new church was erected on the same corner; that is St. Anne's as it is today. No sketch or photograph of the first church building has ever been found.

Just three years after establishing St. Anne's, Bishop Fitzpatrick of Boston made his second and final foundation in New Hampshire: That was St. Mary Parish in Portsmouth, later to be renamed Immaculate Conception. Portsmouth has the distinction of having one of the oldest Catholic presence's in the Granite State. Father Gabriel Druillettes, a Jesuit, stopped there in 1651 while on a diplomatic mission to Massachusetts on behalf of New France.

A local tradition has Father John Thayer, the first New Englander to be ordained to the Catholic priesthood, conducting the first services there in the early 1790s. A French priest, Father Louis de Rousselet, at the time pastor of Boston, may have preceded him. It is well documented that Father Matignon, and then Father Cheverus, made numerous pastoral visits there between 1793 and 1823.

An occasional visitor was Father James René Romagné, who spent nineteen years with the Abenaki Indians of Maine. Bishop Fenwick made a stop at Portsmouth in 1833. After St. Aloysius Church in Dover was erected and dedicated (1830), the Catholics of Portsmouth journeyed there for their spiritual ministrations.

Later, the Dover priest traveled to Portsmouth to care for the Catholics. Mass in Portsmouth was celebrated successively in many places, beginning with the home of Dominic Peduzzi, an Italian and a candy-maker, who was among the first in that city to openly declare his Catholic faith.

When the Catholic population of Portsmouth reached about three hundred in 1851, Bishop Fitzpatrick sent Father Charles McCallion there as the first pastor on November 21, 1851. With the assistance of two lay-men, a choice lot was obtained at the corner of Summer and Chatham Streets for $1,500.

A wood-frame church was built, in large measure by lay volunteers, and dedicated by Bishop Fitzpatrick on October 8, 1852, despite the displeasure and interference of the Know–Nothings.

The American Party (Know-Nothings) 1852 ff.

After a brief lull, anti-Catholicism began to build again in the United States around 1847. In 1852, various anti-Catholic forces organized into the American Party, popularly known as the Know–Nothing Movement. It spread very quickly through many parts of the United States, including Massachusetts, Maine, and New Hampshire. The causes for its intolerance, bigotry, and violence have been pointed out in previous discussions of the anti-Catholic movements.

Anti-Catholic disturbances began in New England in 1847 and increased in intensity up to the mid-1850s, when they reached their highest pitch. Again, Boston was the scene of some of the earliest disturbances,

disturbances that extended to the neighboring communities of Roxbury, Cambridge, and Watertown. All of those altercations occurred between 1847 and 1852.

Adding fuel to an already roaring anti-Catholic fire was the visit to the United States of Archbishop Gaetano Bedini as envoy of Pope Pius IX, ostensibly to settle, as best he could, some trustee disputes, and to report to Rome on the state of Church affairs in this country. An additional task was to try to convince the government to accept a papal envoy to the United States. Archbishop Bedini arrived in New York on June 30, 1853.

While he was at least civilly received in many places, the major effect of his visit was to provoke anti-Catholic outbreaks in many parts of the country, including New England, notably in Massachusetts and Maine. Catholic churches were stoned or blown up; the houses of Catholics were damaged; priests were threatened, and, in a least one case, physically attacked; Irish servant girls were under suspicion of planning to poison their employers; church basements were believed to be arsenals of weapons, and so on.

At Ellsworth, Maine, in October 1854, Father John Bapst, s.j., was tarred, feathered, and ridden otherwise naked on a rail in retaliation for his opposition to the reading of the Protestant Bible in the local public schools. Protestants and Catholics did not accept each other's translation of the Bible. This humiliating and savagely traumatic treatment deeply affected Father Bapst's health as well as his emotional and psychological well-being. While he did have some subsequently productive years, he finished his life in an insane asylum, where he would wake screaming that his Ellsworth tormentors were attacking him again.

On this troubled and violent scene appeared a certainly bizarre and possibly deranged figure by the name of John S. Orr, who called himself the Angel Gabriel. To play his chosen part he customarily wore an ample white garment and carried a trumpet. In his mind he apparently came to believe that he had been given the exalted mission of bringing about the destruction of the Catholic Church. While he was obviously an outlandish figure, his appeals to violence attracted some of the more vicious anti-Catholic elements wherever he traveled with his peculiar and provoking message.

John S. Orr made appearances in many towns in Massachusetts and is known to have visited New York, New Hampshire, and Maine. In Nashua he persuaded his sympathizers to attack the homes of the Irish in the neighborhood called "the Acre," but the rioters were dispersed by the local mayor and the police.

In early July 1854, Orr's inflammatory words resulted in the destruction by fire of the Catholic church at Bath, Maine. After being arrested, fined, and ordered to give bond for good behavior in Massachusetts, he was not allowed to speak publicly again anywhere in the United States.

Anti-Catholic prejudice in New Hampshire, in addition to what has already been mentioned, was expressed in many ways. There were recorded anti-Catholic incidents in Peterborough, Newmarket, Manchester, Dover, Portsmouth, and Greenville.

Tradition has it that Father Charles McCallion, the pastor of the Catholic church in Portsmouth, while on a pastoral visit to Newmarket, was attacked in the house in which he was lodging. He was successfully defended, it is said, by the Catholic women of the neighborhood, who poured scalding water on the aggressors. In 1855, Father Edward Turpin, a priest of the Diocese of Boston, was attacked in the home of Anthony Halloran in Greenville while he was hearing confessions.

Manchester, undoubtedly because of its growing Catholic population, appears to have been the scene of the most violence in New Hampshire during the Know-Nothing period.

One confrontation broke out on the night before the Fourth of July in 1854. In addition to the religious question, a number of other issues, national and local, split the Irish Catholics from the majority of the rest of the community. The tension between the groups broke into open conflict when some Irish youths built a bonfire in downtown Manchester to celebrate the eve of Independence Day. The police were obliged to extinguish the fire several times. A crowd, as could be expected, gathered at the scene. The Irish youths responded by throwing rocks and injured several of the onlookers.

In retaliation, at daybreak on July 4, a large number of men assaulted the Irish quarter of Manchester. Ten to fifteen houses were almost completely destroyed, and hundreds of Irish sought safety in the woods nearby or in the homes of neighbors.

The mob then closed in on St. Anne Church, the only Catholic church in town, and shattered the stained-glass windows. The police, it was reported by possibly prejudiced Catholic sources, were either unwilling or incapable of stopping the highly aroused attackers. Further damage to

both property and people was prevented by a Mr. John Maynard, a coura-
geous Protestant who lived across the street from the church. Mounting
the steps of St. Anne's, he succeed in getting the attention of the mob and
shaming it for its conduct. His words had their desired effect: The mob
broke up without further violence. When Mr. Maynard died nearly forty
years later, in early May 1894, a special resolution was drawn up in his
honor by representatives of the Catholic community in Manchester, and
the bells of St. Anne were tolled at the hour of his funeral.

St. Anne parish was to be the target of at least two more Know-Nothing assaults, one in 1858 and the other in 1859. In 1858, at least one
attempt was made to burn down the convent, then under construction,
destined for the soon-to-arrive Sisters of Mercy. Fortunately, the fire was
discovered and the alarm sounded before any great damage was done.
From then on until the arrival of the sisters, the convent was occupied,
and guarded, by a Catholic family by the name of Holland, parishioners
of Father McDonald.

The final attack on St. Anne parish had a certain lugubrious humor
about it: Firemen attempted to burn down the church building! The occasion was an all New England Firemen's Muster, generally known for their
rowdiness, which took place in Manchester, September 13–14, 1859. This
event attracted fifty-five firefighting companies, consisting of 2,500
firemen, with their engines and paraphernalia. It also drew a large crowd
of spectators including, according to a contemporary Manchester newspaper, an avalanche of gamblers, pitchmen, and prostitutes.

On the evening of September 13, a fight broke out in a saloon on
lower Elm Street when an out-of-town fireman, it is said, discovered that
a gambler had paid him off in counterfeit money. This fight spread to
nearly every saloon in the city, and there were many of them. To climax
the evening, the rampaging firemen decided to burn down St. Anne's, just
a few blocks from Elm Street and hardly farther away from Merrimack
common, the site of the muster.

By then, the outnumbered police had been able to organize and to
place themselves between the church and the firemen. The presence of the
sheriff with a double-barreled shotgun certainly contributed to a change
of heart and plans by the would-be arsonist-firemen!

Know-Nothing power, through the American Party, won impressive
political victories in many states. In Massachusetts, for example, it elected

the governor, every member of the state senate, and 376 of the 379 members of the house in the November 1854 elections. With this near-absolute control of the government, many anti-Catholic laws were passed. American Party victories were also achieved in Rhode Island, Maryland, and Kentucky. Its impact was nearly as strong in other states, such as Tennessee, New York, and Pennsylvania.

Despite the fact that Franklin Pierce, a Democrat from New Hampshire, was president of the United States, the American Party also won political control of the Granite State. By the end of 1854, it is recorded that there were 249 Know-Nothing lodges throughout the state. In the spring elections of 1855, the American Party saw elected its candidate for governor, Ralph Metcalf of Newport, all three U.S. congressmen (the number allotted to New Hampshire at that time), and gained control of both the state senate and the house of representatives.

Governor Metcalf's first inaugural address can be read today as an almost textbook enumeration of the American Party's antipathies toward Catholics and immigrants. Governor Metcalf was elected to a second term by the state legislature, as required by law, because he did not win a majority of the popular vote. By the end of his second term in 1858, the American Party was in its death throes around the United States. In New Hampshire, despite its one-time dominant position, it accomplished very little in implementing its anti-Catholic and anti-immigrant programs.

One of the major reasons for the demise of the American Party was that the country was more seriously divided by the slavery issue than by ethnic or religious differences. Many, moreover, had been alienated by the violence of the Know-Nothings as well as by their secrecy.

The passage of the Kansas–Nebraska Act in 1854 estranged the anti-slavery Know-Nothings and further divided the North and the South. From this very muddled political situation the Republican Party was born, and by 1856 the American Party was no longer a serious factor, at least in most elections.

SEVEN

The Diocese of Portland (Maine) and New Hampshire 1853–1884

Establishing the Diocese of Portland 1853

Aware of the increasing Catholic population of the United States, including New England, the Holy See, usually at the request of the American bishops, continued to create new dioceses in this country. In New England, the Diocese of Hartford was established in 1844 with the Reverend William Tyler, Father Virgil Barber's nephew and a one-time student at his Claremont Catholic Seminary, as the first bishop.

In 1853, Rome founded two more dioceses in New England: one for Vermont, with Burlington as the See city; the other for both Maine and New Hampshire, with Portland as the headquarters of the bishop. Counting Boston, this raised the number of dioceses in New England to four.

A bishop of Portland was not ordained and installed until 1855 because Rome's first choice refused the appointment. The second choice was the Reverend David W. Bacon, a native of Brooklyn, New York, then forty-one years old.

After being ordained bishop at St. Patrick Cathedral in New York City, he was installed in Portland on May 31, 1855. This ceremony was deliberately kept low key in order to attract as little Know-Nothing attention as possible. For example, in addition to Bishop Fitzpatrick of Boston, there were only six priests present, two being Jesuits. Moreover, as late as 1870, Bishop Bacon's street attire was that of a layman rather than the church-mandated distinctive garb of the Catholic clergy. This, too, is most likely attributable to his concern about the anti-Catholicism that continued to lie smoldering in some quarters.

Further Growth 1855–1874

There are no reliable statistics concerning the number of Catholics in Maine and New Hampshire at the time of the arrival of the first bishop of Portland. In 1855, Bishop Bacon estimated that there were 40,000 spread over both states. There are sound reasons to believe that this was an underestimate, very probably of a deliberate nature: Bishop Bacon did not wish to alarm the anti-Catholics, nor did he desire to add to that alarm in subsequent years by charting the growth of the Catholic population. Consequently, the number of Catholics in the Diocese of Portland was still listed officially at the same 40,000 in 1865, some ten years later.

On Bishop Bacon's arrival, he could count twenty churches and nine priests, five diocesan and four Jesuits, spread over the two states. New Hampshire's share was three parishes, at Dover, Manchester, and Portsmouth, and the old mission of St. Mary at Claremont. At that time, there were only three priests residing in New Hampshire: Father Patrick Canavan in Dover, Father William McDonald in Manchester, and the itinerant missionary, Father John B. Daly, loosely based at Claremont. The Portsmouth parish did not have a pastor when Bishop Bacon arrived. Fortunately, a small number of New Hampshire towns were served, at least on occasion, by priests, from Maine and Massachusetts.

Bishop Bacon was to remain bishop of Portland until his death on November 5, 1874. During these more than nineteen years, thirteen parishes were founded in New Hampshire. The first was at Nashua. It is very likely that the first Catholics in that community, except, perhaps, for isolated individuals, came to work on the construction of the railroads.

According to existing records, the first Mass was celebrated in Nashua during 1850 in the home of Daniel Dempsey by the Reverend Timothy O'Brien from Lowell, Massachusetts. At least six other priests visited there between 1850 and 1855. For Nashua's first pastor, Bishop Bacon chose the Reverend John O'Donnell, who was assigned there effective November 7, 1855. This Ireland-born priest remained in Nashua until his death twenty-six years later, in 1882.

The first church, consecrated to the Immaculate Conception, was dedicated by Bishop Bacon in December 1857. By then, the Catholic population had grown to six hundred. Nineteen years later in 1875, the chiefly Irish–born population of the parish and those of Irish descent had reached 2,300. This growing parish, in its initial stages, also served Concord, Penacook, Milford, Hollis, Jaffrey, and Merrimack.

As for Father O'Donnell, he became one of the very prominent members of the community. He was elected to the public school board and had a public school named after him, the latter a unique honor in the history of Catholicism in New Hampshire. After a new parish church was built between 1905 and 1909 and dedicated this time to St. Patrick (in 1910), the old church was eventually turned over to the Lithuanian community and became St. Casimir Church.

In 1856, Father Isidore H. Noiseux was assigned by Bishop Bacon of Portland to all the territory in the Connecticut Valley. Over the years, he extended his mission territory not only in the Connecticut Valley from the Ashuelot River to the Canadian boarder, but also to the White Mountains and beyond. It is known that he ministered in towns such as Groveton, Berlin, Gorham, Franklin, Laconia, Lakeport, Lebanon and North Conway.

Having been authorized by the bishop to personally select a community in his area for a parish, in 1857 he chose the town of Lancaster. The first Catholics in this remote area of New Hampshire, excluding the Native Americans in previous centuries, appear to have come from Ireland as early as 1833. Mass was celebrated there, according to one historian, in the dwelling of Patrick Connary, on May 4, 1850. The ubiquitous Father John B. Daly also ministered there in the town hall during either 1854 or 1855. Father Noiseux and his people soon purchased the lot on which the present church stands and used the buildings already on the property, with some improvements, for both the chapel and a residence.

This priest, a French Canadian, spent nearly twenty years as pastor of Lancaster; he was assigned to Brunswick, Maine, in 1876. The sheer extent of his mission labors, under great trials and hardships, places him in the first rank of the pioneer priests of the western and northern parts of the Granite State. Equal to the Franciscan, Father Daly, and the Dominican Father Ffrench, in zeal he was without their eccentricities and occasional irascibility. After some six years outside New Hampshire, he returned in 1882 as the founding pastor of St. Rose of Lima in Littleton. He is buried in Littleton, where his tomb can be visited today.

Two more parishes were established between 1856 and 1859: Great Falls (now Somersworth, 1856), and Exeter (1859). The claim of Salmon Falls (now Rollinsford) to be the sixth oldest Catholic parish in New

Hampshire is tainted by the fact that it was actually a mission of Great Falls from 1856 until 1870. However, its brick church, dedicated in 1859, although much renovated, is still the house of worship of the Rollinsford Catholics and one of the historic monuments of the diocese.

Between 1862 and 1873, Bishop Bacon established eight more parishes in New Hampshire. These were spread throughout the state. A first Catholic parish was erected in the communities of Keene (1862), Concord (1865), Claremont (1870), Laconia (1871), and Suncook (1873). Two additional parishes were founded in Manchester—St. Joseph (1869) and St. Augustine (1871)—raising the total to three in that city. Nashua was given a second, St. Aloysius (St. Louis de Gonzague) in 1871. Two of these parishes, St. Augustine in Manchester and St. Aloysius in Nashua, have the distinction of being, in the order mentioned, the first two national parishes in New Hampshire: Both were for French Canadians.

The Founding of Catholic Education in New Hampshire

It was also during the episcopacy of Bishop Bacon that: (1) the first religious community arrived in New Hampshire; (2) the first religious education program was established in a parish; and (3) the first Catholic school was founded, not counting the Claremont Catholic Seminary (1823–1828) instituted by the Reverend Virgil Barber, s.j., with the assistance of his father, Daniel Barber.

There is no documentary evidence of any formal religious instruction for children or youth in any of the parishes of New Hampshire, whether for girls or for boys, before Sunday school was begun at St. Anne in Manchester during 1856. This program, which enrolled nearly four hundred pupils, was taught exclusively by the pastor, Father William McDonald. Before that time, it appears that the responsibility for the religious instruction of the young was left to the home and to whatever they could glean from church services and sermons.

Recognizing the feebleness of such a situation, a defect that was further aggravated by the fact that the only schools—the public schools— were in reality, in the minds of many, Protestant schools, Father McDonald built a convent at the corner of Union and Laurel Streets in Manchester, beginning in 1857, with the purpose of inviting a community of religious women to Manchester.

With the support of Bishop Bacon, he was able to obtain the services of five Sisters of Mercy from Providence, Rhode Island. They arrived in Manchester by train on July 16, 1858, wearing lay clothing because of the fear of possible Know-Nothing mischief and hostility.

This community was to have a profound influence on the Church and far beyond the boundaries of New Hampshire. The superior of the founding sisters, Mother Frances Xavier Warde, a strong-minded and extraordinarily energetic woman, for example, founded some seventy religious institutions in the United States, having establishing beforehand some twelve in her native Ireland. There have been many other Sisters of Mercy of similar caliber.

Shortly after their arrival in Manchester, the community opened evening classes for adults at the convent. That September, extensive free schools were inaugurated for girls. During the same autumn (1858), Mount St. Mary, a boarding school, was begun in the northern half of the convent at 435 Union Street. This became one of the first schools for girls in New England—and by many estimates, one of the best. This school subsequently moved to Hooksett (1909) and then to Nashua (1948). In 1992 it was merged with Bishop Guertin High School due to financial and other pressures.

In January 1859 a school was opened for boys in the basement of St. Anne Church, under the direction of Mr. Thomas Corcoran. He remained principal of that school until his retirement in 1893. Unarguably, Mr. Corcoran, who served as a teacher in Manchester for some thirty-four years, did more than any other person to prepare nearly two generations of young Catholic men for respect and service to the community and country, and for an interested and devoted role in their church. In this sense, he was most valuable Catholic in Manchester of that period.

In 1861, a Manchester school district voted to give the Catholics the use, free of charge, of the Park Street School, a former public school, not then in use (Park Street is now Lake Avenue). Mr. Corcoran remained there as principal, with the assistance of several Sisters of Mercy, until his retirement.

In March 1863, the city school board voted to take financial responsibility for the Park Street School. This included salaries for all the teachers as well as maintenance. Financial support by the city for Catholic schools extended until, in 1868, it involved one grammar school, three middle schools, and eight primary schools, with a total enrollment of 1,029 pupils.

In addition to Mr. Corcoran's salary, the city also paid the wages of up to twelve Sisters of Mercy. Their salaries were comparable to those of the regular public school teachers, and the nuns were allowed to wear their habits. This arrangement was discontinued between 1868 and 1869, primarily, it can be assumed, on the principle of separation of church and state.

This "Manchester Plan," involving the financial subsidizing of parochial schools by the public school board, was not unique. Similar arrangements were attempted in several other communities. The better known were in Poughkeepsie, New York, in 1873, and in Faribault and Stillwater in Minnesota in the early 1890s. All were eventually abandoned, as it was in Manchester.

From 1858 onward, the Sisters of Mercy expanded into an impressive number of apostolates in Manchester, including visiting and caring for the sick and elderly at home, founding orphanages, homes for the elderly, a hospital, a residence for working young women, and an infant asylum. They also established schools at Portsmouth, St. Joseph parish, Manchester, Laconia, and Dover, all by 1884. Only the Portsmouth school failed after three years, for financial reasons.

French Canadian Migration to New Hampshire

It was also during the years that New Hampshire was a part of the Diocese of Portland that a second major migration group, an overwhelming majority of them Catholic, joined the Irish in settling in New Hampshire: These were the French Canadians of the province of Quebec. Some 40,000 are said to have migrated to the United States between 1831 and 1844. Many sought temporary asylum after an unsuccessful uprising for independence by some French Canadians against the British in 1837–1838. Most who remained in the United States during this period lost their Catholic identity.

The tempo of immigration from French Canada to New England accelerated as the decades went by. Between 1850 and 1900, the net French Canadian increase in New England was about 340,000. At least another 660,000 are believed to have spent some time in this country before returning to Canada.

Sometime around 1860, the French Canadians began migrating to

New England specifically to work in the textile industry, particularly that of cotton, although they could be found in large numbers in other jobs as well. By 1900 the French Canadians constituted more than 18 percent of the total population of New England. After 1900, emigration from Quebec began to slacken because of industrial development in Canada and the opening of the lands to the west in that country for colonization.

In New Hampshire, the number of French Canadian residents rose from 1,780 in 1860 to 76,000 in 1900. By that last year, Manchester had a French Canadian population of 23,000—that is, 40 percent of the total population of the city. Other centers, in decreasing numbers of French Canadian population, were: Nashua (8,200), Berlin, Somersworth, Suncook, Claremont, Laconia, and Concord (2,000).

Multiple were the reasons for this mass exodus from the province of Quebec. Among these were an astonishing growth in population, despite emigration; subdivisions of land among heirs that made farms too small to adequately sustain a family; poor, nonproductive soil, particularly north of the St. Lawrence River; a dry climate and a short growing season; a shortage of cash in the province that hobbled business; poor roads, which impeded the shipment of produce and hampered communications; after 1820, the appearance of the wheat midge, an insect that cut into the region's leading crop; and the overall lack of skill of the French Canadians in both agronomy and husbandry.

New Hampshire's first French Canadian parish was established on May 14, 1871, in Manchester by the Reverend Joseph Augustin Chevalier. For approximately one year before his arrival, the spiritual needs of the French Canadians in Manchester were taken care of by a Father Cléophas Demers, who was assigned as an assistant to Father McDonald at St. Anne. At the time of the founding of this first French Canadian parish, to be called St. Augustine, there were from 2,000 to 2,500 individuals of this ethnic group in Manchester out of a population of 6,000 Catholics. After worshiping in several places in Manchester, Father Chevalier and his people completed a church building that was dedicated by Bishop Bacon on November 27, 1873. This building is still the parish church.

Over the years, this became a flourishing parish with schools for girls and boys, an orphanage, a large parish hall (St. Cecilia), and a home for aged women. The school for girls opened in 1881, the first bilingual school in the state of New Hampshire. It was confided to the Congregation of

Jesus and Mary. These sisters thus became the second Catholic religious order in New Hampshire following the Sisters of Mercy. To say that the school of the Sisters of Jesus and Mary at St. Augustine was bilingual from its establishment is inaccurate. In reality, the school day was largely, and often nearly exclusively, conducted in French. This language was mandatory even during recess and its use was monitored by the sisters. This pattern of school life was not only the desire of some of the parents who wished to live here as they had in the province of Quebec; it was also based on the reality that the teaching nuns, who were almost exclusively French Canadians, could not speak or understand the language, or, if they spoke it at all, did so badly and with an accent. If there were exceptions, they were rare.

The situation improved gradually over the years with the admission of native New Englanders into the various French Canadian religious communities. After World War II, French began to disappear from the schools. Currently, if taught at all, it is presented as a foreign language. One of the legacies of the past is that there are still a number of older people educated in these schools who at the close of the twentieth century speak neither English nor French correctly. Most of these live in communities with a large concentration of French Canadians where French is frequently the common language of communication at home, among relatives and friends, on the street, and, more rarely, in commerce.

After the founding of St. Augustine in 1871, eighteen additional French national parishes were officially erected in New Hampshire, the last being St. Joseph in Berlin, established in 1941. In addition, from approximately 1910 to 1940, forty other parishes were considered "mixed." These were parishes where both English and French were used, frequently with a homily in both languages at the same liturgical service; in many instances, it was the same sermon. English is now the dominant language in all the parishes of the diocese, including the "national" parishes. (Newer Spanish, Vietnamese, and Portuguese Catholic immigrants are discussed later.)

Catholics and the Issue of Slavery

Other issues that agitated the community while New Hampshire was still a part of the Diocese of Portland were those of the indissolubility of the

Union and the bitter division over slavery. These were finally resolved legally but not sociologically by the Civil War (1861–1865).

Slavery had existed in New Hampshire. The census of 1765 listed more than six hundred slaves and a number of free blacks. While a third resided in Portsmouth, there were slaves in more than fifty other towns. Most slaves in New Hampshire were house servants and not field hands. Without the passage of any law, slavery simply died out gradually in the state beginning in the 1780s, in some measure because it was not economically profitable.

When the confrontation on the issue of slavery reached near war proportions, the opponents of slavery could find but slight support for their position in the official teaching of the Catholic Church. While it was true that Pope Gregory XVI condemned the slave trade in 1838, he did not repudiate slavery itself. In fact, no pope throughout history ever condemned domestic slavery as it existed in the United States.

American bishops, for the most part, kept silent on the issue. No Catholic bishop is known to have spoken publicly in favor of emancipation during the pre–Civil War years.

Few Catholic laypeople would have argued in favor of abolition; traditional moral theology gave them no grounds on which to do so. In fact, even the Constitution of the United States acknowledged slavery, in a very embarrassing way. Slavery was only abolished by the thirteenth amendment, passed in 1865.

Economic status, particularly that of the Irish immigrants, became an important factor in this situation. The Irish realized that if the black slaves were freed, particularly all at once, they would compete with them for jobs at the bottom of the economic ladder, where most of them found themselves. Consequently, a strong majority of the Catholics of the Northeast were against freeing the slaves. Catholic theology and economic necessity combined to validate their position.

When the Civil War erupted, however, the Catholics of New England rallied for the most part to the cause of the North in order to save the Union, but initially not to abolish slavery. One can safely conjecture that this was the attitude of most of the clergy and the Catholic laity in New Hampshire: They were anti–abolitionist and anti-emancipation, but anti–secessionist and pro–union.

Irish enlistment in the Union Army during the Civil War was to have a significant influence in improving native-born American attitudes toward this immigrant group and Catholics in general, although it did not eradicate anti-Catholicism either completely or permanently.

It has been estimated that some 144,000 Irish served in the Union Army. How many of the approximately 31,500 to 39,000 men from New Hampshire who participated in the war were Irish Catholics is not known. From various sources it can be determined that the number was relatively high. For example, several military companies from the state were commanded by Irish captains.

One of the outstanding figures from New Hampshire in the war was Captain Michael T. Donohoe, who by his patriotism, bravery, and leadership ability rose to the rank of a brevetted brigadier general. In 1862, while still a captain, Michael T. Donohoe helped to raise a virtually all-Irish regiment in New Hampshire, the Tenth Volunteers. The city of Manchester furnished the greater part of six companies for the Tenth. This regiment conducted itself gallantly in battle. Other states, including Massachusetts and New York, raised one or more Irish regiments.

At least one incident in New Hampshire marred the almost united front supporting the Civil War. These were riots triggered by the passage of the Conscription Act of March 3, 1863, by the Congress of the United States. By this act, the federal government claimed the authority to draft individuals into military service. This law was patently unjust in that an individual could be excused from service either by paying the government $300 or by providing a replacement. It certainly placed the safety of the rich ahead of that of the poor. Violent riots broke out in many cities, including Boston and New York. In New York, several hundred people were killed or wounded. Large numbers of the rioters in those cities were Irish, many subject to the draft.

In New Hampshire, an unruly crowd at Portsmouth prevented the draft from taking place as scheduled on July 14 and 15, 1863. During confrontations on July 16, one Irishman was arrested and another was shot in the thigh. The fact that both victims were Irish added considerable irony to the incident. It must be remembered that an Irishman on his way to comply with the draft in Portsmouth could possibly pass a HELP WANTED sign in a store window that added "NO IRISH NEED APPLY," or carry a newspaper under his arm containing ads with the same warning.

Troops from the office of the Provost Marshal, some Marines, the entire garrison at nearby Fort Constitution, and a number of citizens brought the Portsmouth draft riot to an end by the following morning, July 17.

The First Vatican Council 1869–1870

The First Vatican Council, which was held in St. Peter's Basilica in Rome, was the first ecumenical council ever to involve the participation of Americans, as the previous council, that of Trent, was held between 1545 and 1563.

Bishop Bacon, the spiritual leader of Maine and New Hampshire, could be said to have been one of its silent members in that he did not make any oral or written interventions. He was one of the 136 participants, however, who signed a petition requesting the council not to define the primacy and infallibility of the pope as a dogma of faith. This position was most likely taken because he recognized that there was already sufficient hostility in Maine and New Hampshire against the Catholic Church and the pope without creating another issue certain to produce more conflict.

Bishop Bacon was not in Rome for the votes on primacy and infallibility taken on April 24 and July 18, 1870. He had obtained permission from Pope Pius IX to leave the Eternal City because of illness and departed on January 31, 1870. He was one of a large number of bishops who left rather than remain and vote against papal primacy and infallibility, either because they did not agree, or, like Bishop Bacon, because they found the timing of the definition inopportune. Once the definition was promulgated, he adhered to it, and preached approvingly on that subject in his diocese.

Bishop Bacon died in a hospital in New York City on November 5, 1874, just a few hours after returning from Europe by ship a very ill man. During the nineteen years of his episcopacy, Catholicism made great progress in Maine and New Hampshire, largely because of strong Irish immigration and the initial phase of French Canadian migration across the border from Quebec.

New Hampshire's Black Bishop: James A. Healy 1875–1884

Portland's second bishop was the Reverend James Augustine Healy, a priest of the Diocese of Boston. Among his distinctions were those of being the first bishop in the United States with a black racial background and having been legally born a slave.

His father, Michael Morris Healy, was born in Ireland. Michael Healy migrated to Georgia by way of Nova Scotia and began by degrees to build up various cotton plantations and to acquire slaves. At the time of his death, on August 29, 1850, he was the proprietor of fifty-seven slaves.

The records, as scant as they are, show that Michael Healy, in 1829, took for his wife a Georgia-born mulatto slave girl who went by the name of Eliza Clark, or Eliza Smith. At the time, she was a few months over sixteen years old; he was about twice that age. There is no official record of a marriage ceremony, nor of any subsequent validation by a priest, despite Michael Healy's assertion that the union had been regularized by the Church.

Eliza Healy legally remained a slave all her life. According to the law of Georgia, all children of a union followed the condition of the mother. Thus, all ten children of Michael Healy and the slave Eliza were not only partially black but also fully slave. James Augustine, the eldest, was born on the plantation on April 6, 1830.

Deeply concerned about the future of the children, Michael Healy brought them out of the South once they were judged to be old enough. James was the first to be taken north before he reached the age of eight. It is virtually certain that James never saw his mother again, and that he never returned to his birthplace.

Michael Healy first entrusted the education of James, once he was in the North, to the Quakers. After a chance meeting with the recently ordained coadjutor bishop of Boston, John B. Fitzpatrick, Mr. Healy educated his sons and daughters in Catholic institutions. Four of Mr. Healy's sons—James, Hugh, Patrick, and Sherwood—were in turn enrolled at Holy Cross, Worcester, the first two in the college and the younger two in the grammar school. It was arranged for the eldest daughter, Martha Ann, to live with the family of Bishop Fitzpatrick's sister in Boston and to go to school there.

Eventually all the surviving Healy children were secretly brought out of the South, the last three, Josephine, Eliza, and Eugene, after the death of their mother and father (both died in 1850; the first expired in May and the other in August).

James Healy graduated ranking first in the first college graduation class at Holy Cross in 1849. This young man's desire to become a Jesuit was frustrated by the fact that the novitiate of the society was in Maryland, a slave state. His black ancestry, his partially African features, and his legal status of slave ruled that out. Instead, he applied and was accepted by the Diocese of Boston.

Realizing that it was extremely dangerous to send him to a seminary in the South, where, in any case, he would not have been accepted, Bishop Fitzpatrick enrolled James first in the Grand Seminary in Montreal, a Sulpician institution (1849–1852), and then at St. Sulpice in Paris. He was ordained in this latter city on June 10, 1854, at the age of twenty-four.

This young priest's plans for further study in Europe were canceled when his brother Hugh died. Hugh had managed the family and its financial affairs since the death of the parents in 1850. It now became James's responsibility to replace Hugh in this task.

Father James Healy was the first of several in his family whose vocations turned to the religious life. His brother Patrick, who was fair skinned, was able to attend the novitiate in Maryland and become a Jesuit. During a distinguished career, he served as president of Georgetown University for a number of years. Alexander Sherwood, like his brother James, was ordained for Boston.

One sister, Josephine, became a nun at l' Hôtel Dieu in Montreal, where she died on July 23, 1879, after a brief five years in community. Eliza also went to Montreal in 1874 and joined the Congregation of Notre Dame. During her religious life, Eliza served as superior in houses in Montreal, Vermont, and on Staten Island, New York.

Another sister, Martha, had joined the same Congregation of Notre Dame ten years before Eliza. Another brother, Michael, chose a career at sea and attained national renown as a full captain in the Revenue-Marine (now the Coast Guard) for his numerous heroic rescues in the waters around Alaska.

Ample historical evidence forces one to conclude that Father James Healy wanted to conceal his racial ancestry, at least through most of his

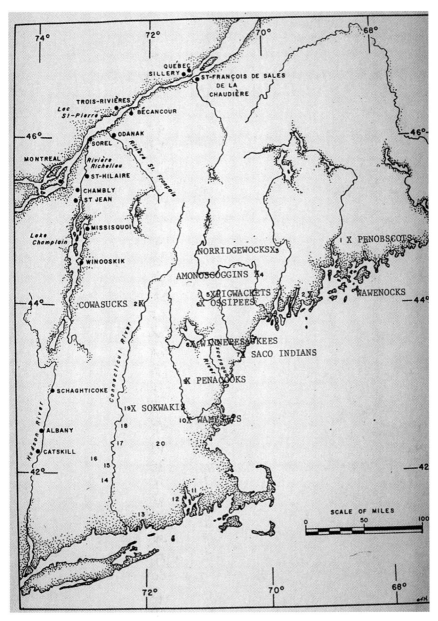

1. Location of some of the native American tribes in what is now New Hampshire and other proximate parts of New England in the seventeenth century.

2. Samuel de Champlain, a French explorer, discovered the White Mountains (from his ship at sea), the Isles of Shoals, and the Merrimack River. He also landed and visited the Native Americans at what is now Odiorne Point. In 1608, he founded Quebec City.

3. This contemporary painting (based on old records) shows the Oyster River (Durham) Meeting House where the first Mass on what is now the soil of New Hampshire may have been celebrated July 18, 1694. (Photograph by the Reverend Albert G. Baillargeon. Painting in the collection of the Durham Historical Society.)

4. *Church of the Holy Cross in Boston, the first Catholic church built in New England (except for Native American chapels in Maine) was dedicated on September 29, 1803. Charles Bulfinch was the architect. The church was torn down to make way for office buildings.*

5. *Catholic converts Theodore and Anna Goffe and their children of Bedford, New Hampshire, walked to Boston to receive religious instruction. They were baptized there on November 15, 1831. (Photographs in the collection of the Bedford Historical Society.)*

6. *(right) Bishop Jean Lefeb-vre de Cheverus, born in France, was the first bishop of Boston which then included all of New England. He arrived in Boston on October 3, 1796 and served as bishop between 1810 and 1823 when he returned to France.*

7. *(below) This is the re-enactment of the departure of a French Canadian fami-ly from Quebec for New England probably in the 1840s before the railways. Such a trip could take from two to three weeks. (Com-pare this photograph with that of the Vietnamese fam-ily shown later.)*

8. The home of the Barber family adjacent to old St. Mary's church in Claremont. The family home was torn down around 1912.

9. Saint Mary Church, Claremont, was the first Catholic Church erected in New Hampshire and is still used occasionally for worship. It was built by Reverend Virgil Barber s.j., in 1823-1824. Behind the church is the first Catholic cemetery in the state. The building across the street is the Episcopal church where the Reverend Daniel Barber, Virgil's father, was rector until his resignation on November 15, 1818. (Photo by the Reverend Albert G. Baillargeon.)

10. Father William McDonald was the founder in 1848 of Saint Anne Parish, the first Catholic church in Manchester. He died as pastor of that parish on August 26, 1885.

11. Father Isidore Noiseux was appointed pastor to all missions in the North Country in 1856. His territory extended from the Ashuelot River to the Canadian border to the north, and east across the White Mountains to the area of Gorham and Berlin, and occasionally beyond.

12. Interior of Saint Joseph Church completed in 1869, now the cathedral, prior to extensive renovations and enlargement before 1894.

13. Present appearance of Saint Joseph Cathedral in Manchester. Dedicated in 1869. (Photo by the Reverend Albert G. Baillargeon.)

14. Bishop James A. Healy, the spiritual leader of both Maine and New Hampshire (1875-1884), was the first African-American Catholic bishop in the United States.

15. Bishop Denis Mary Bradley, a native of Ireland, was the first bishop of the Diocese of Manchester, 1884-1903.

16. *In 1858, Mother Frances Xavier Warde became the founding superior of the Sisters of Mercy in New Hampshire. In her lifetime, she established 12 religious institutions in her native Ireland and some 70 in the United States.*

17. *Thomas Corcoran, often called the ideal Catholic teacher of his day, was the principal of the school for boys at St. Anne's in Manchester from 1859 to 1893.*

18. *The old Park Street (now Lake Avenue) School, a former public school, served as the first Catholic school for boys in Manchester under Mr. Thomas Corcoran beginning in 1861.*

19. These eight Sisters of Mercy were photographed in 1949 before the changes in religious habit brought about by the Second Vatican Council.

20. This elegant bridal dress was worn by Sister Mary Geraldine McCarthy on the day of her profession of vows as a Sister of Mercy to symbolize her espousal to Christ. She later changed into her religious habit which she wore until her death at the age of 90 in 1978. This gown is on display at the Diocesan Museum. (Photo by Gerald Durette.)

21. *The Sheridan Guards was organized in Saint Anne Parish, Manchester, on August 30, 1865 by veterans of the Civil War. In 1898 all 68 members volunteered for service in the Spanish American War and was designated as Company B, First New Hampshire Volunteer Infantry. One enlisted man, Corporal William H. Dervin, died of typhoid fever in Georgia. The Sheridan Guards is shown here at a national drill in Washington, D.C. in 1887. (Photo from the collection of Richard Walsh a grandson of William Sullivan, fifth in the back row of this picture.)*

22. *This photo taken in 1892 is a group of Sisters of Jesus and Mary and their students at Saint Augustine Parish in Manchester. The Sisters had arrived in the parish in 1881, the first French Canadian order of women to settle in New Hampshire. (Photo by Langley. From the private collection of Robert B. Perreault.)*

23. Saint Anselm College is the oldest of six Catholic colleges in New Hampshire. Classes began there in 1889. Pictured is the administration building, the first structure on the campus. (Photo from the collection of the Manchester Historic Association.)

24. This photograph was taken October 11, 1893 on the occasion of the dedication of Saint Anselm college. In the center is Bishop Bradley who invited the order of Saint Benedict to the diocese. (Photo from the college archives.)

25. To commemorate the beginning of the twentieth century, Bishop Denis M. Bradley asked the parishioners of Saint Joseph Cathedral parish to contribute gold trinkets, coins, medals, rings, etc. to make a chalice. Enough gold was collected for a chalice, a ciborium and the upper part of a monstrance. The chalice and paten are pictured here. (Photo by Cote Photography.)

life. To that end, he discouraged research into his life and background. On some occasions he even fabricated a genealogy for his mother. In at least one biography, she is described as the descendant of an aristocratic southern family. In answer to inquiries, Father James Healy is reported to have said himself that she was from Santo Domingo; another response was that his mother was from an old Virginia family. It was only after he felt settled and secure in Portland that he would admit that she was an octoroon; that is, she was one-eighth black.

There is no evidence that Father James Healy, as either seminarian, priest, or bishop, had anything to do with black Catholics outside of the diocese he was serving, Boston first, then Portland. Had he made a powerful denunciation of slavery before the Civil War, or had he vigorously condemned the evils of segregation after the conflict, he would have, in time, undoubtedly ranked as one of the great bishops of his era.

One final and painful duty is to report the collective decision of the Healy brothers and sisters to sell the slaves whom they had inherited from their father. Since his death, the slaves had been leased for labor on other Georgia plantations, thus providing income for the Healys living safely and comfortably up north.

On orders from Father James Healy, with the unanimous approval of his brothers and sisters, fifty-one slaves were disposed of by the estate on January 1, 1855, for almost $30,000. During the following year, the remaining six slaves were sold on long-term credit to Georgia farmers. Payment was completed in 1861, the year of the beginning of the Civil War. There were, however, some defaults among the new owners.

Father Healy was to spend more than twenty years as a priest of the Diocese of Boston. After a brief assignment as chaplain to a home for orphan boys and assistant at a church, Bishop Fitzpatrick transferred him to the cathedral staff, made him his personal secretary, and assigned him to organize a diocesan chancery office.

One of his first tasks was to assist Bishop Fitzpatrick in combating the Know-Nothings, who were swept into virtually total political power in Massachusetts by their victories in the 1854 elections. It was during these years that he acquired a reputation as an outstanding preacher, one that he would retain for the rest of his life, and as a champion of social justice, particularly for his vigorous public defense of the rights of immigrants.

He also served as rector of the cathedral and, at least on one occasion, was given full powers of attorney for the diocese. In mid-July 1863, he was involved in calming the Catholics, particularly the Irish of Boston, who rose against the unfair Conscription Act.

When Bishop Fitzpatrick died on February 13, 1866, and was succeeded by Father John J. Williams, the latter, shortly after his episcopal consecration, sent Father Healy to replace himself as pastor of St. James parish, Boston. At that time, St. James was considered to rank just below the cathedral in importance in the diocese.

Father Healy remained at St. James until he was appointed the second bishop of Portland on February 12, 1875. At the time of his episcopal ordination in the cathedral at Portland, on June 2, he was forty-five years of age. Bishop Healy lived long enough to celebrate his silver jubilee as ordinary of Portland, dying August 5, 1900.

During his episcopacy, he became one of the most influential bishops in New England, partly because of his personal friendship with Bishop (later Archbishop) Williams of Boston. On practically every issue, he sided with the conservative members of the hierarchy. As a pulpit orator, it is recorded, he had few equals and was in frequent demand around the country. His letters are pithy, sometimes humorous, and often contain a barb against people or events that did not please him.

Despite the goodwill toward Catholics generated by the Civil War, Bishop Healy's episcopacy, like that of Bishop Bacon, was marred by anti-Catholicism. This time it was stirred up by the Evangelical Alliance, founded in the United States in 1867, an association of ex-nuns and ex-priests, real or pretended; and by some secret societies. This anti-Catholicism was more feeble than before the Civil War: It crested in 1875 and 1876, and slowly subsided between 1877 and 1887.

One of Bishop Healy's first decisions as ordinary of Portland was to make a pastoral visitation of the entire diocese. This he undertook the year of his arrival (1875), accompanied by the Reverend Denis M. Bradley, the chancellor of Portland and his private secretary. The two covered an astonishing amount of territory during which Bishop Healy confirmed more than four thousand children and preached over one hundred sermons. By then, many communities could be reached by train. Away from the railroads, however, especially in the far northern portion of Maine and the westernmost parts of New Hampshire, the two traveled by stagecoach and buggy. This diocesan-wide visitation was repeated in 1878.

With his newly acquired knowledge of Maine and New Hampshire, Bishop Healy began an expansion of parishes and, to a lesser extent, of Catholic schools. In the Granite State eleven parishes were created between 1875 and 1883. Eight were established in communities previously without a Catholic parish: Lebanon (1875), Gorham (1876), Rochester (St. Mary, 1876), Newmarket (1878), North Walpole (1878), Fisherville (now Penacook, 1880), Littleton (1882), and Wilton (1882).

The three others were all French Canadian national parishes; St. Mary, Manchester (1880); St. Martin, Great Falls (now Somersworth, 1882); and Holy Rosary of Rochester (1883). These eleven parishes brought the total number in New Hampshire to thirty. Five of these parishes were French Canadian national parishes, and a good number of the others used both English and French in their religious services.

Bishop Healy attempted to meet the needs of French Canadians by requiring that all priests learn both English and French, and that they preach in each language at every Mass, if the congregation was linguistically mixed.

School openings, as might be expected, lagged behind the creation of new parishes. In 1882 the Sisters of Mercy made their first viable school foundation in New Hampshire outside of Manchester, at St. Joseph parish, Laconia, with four sisters and 134 students. The next year they opened Sacred Heart School at St. Mary parish, Dover, with an enrollment of 450 boys and girls and a teaching staff of seven Sisters of Mercy.

In 1883, the third religious community of women religious was admitted to New Hampshire as schoolteachers, after the Sister of Mercy (1858) and the Congregation of Jesus and Mary (1881). These were the Sisters of Holy Cross, who began the second bilingual school of the state in the basement of St. Aloysius Church, Nashua, in November, with an initial enrollment of 550 boys and girls in the care of five sisters.

In summary, by the time of the foundation of the Diocese of Manchester, on April 15, 1884, six parishes had parochial schools; three of these possessed separate buildings for boys and girls. Their total enrollment was 1,323 boys and 1,610 girls. In these schools, the instructional staffs were composed of forty-four Sisters of Mercy, eight Sisters of Jesus and Mary, an equal number of Sisters of Holy Cross, and one layman, Mr. Thomas Corcoran.

At St. Patrick Orphanage, Manchester, six Sisters of Mercy gave instruction to seventy girls. Thus, the total number of children receiving Catholic school education in New Hampshire in 1884 was 3,003.

PART II

THE CATHOLIC COMMUNITY
OF THE
DIOCESE OF MANCHESTER
1884–1997

EIGHT

The "Golden Years" 1884–1903

The Founding of the Diocese of Manchester

By 1884, the number of Catholics and of Catholic institutions in New Hampshire were sufficiently elevated to create a diocese. The Granite State was the last in New England to receive this distinction because, it has been said, of its persistent anti–Catholicism. At that time, the exact Catholic population was not known. One source, in 1884, estimated it at 45,000.

The following year, perhaps after a more thorough census, the *Catholic Directory* set the figure at about 60,000, in a total state population exceeding 347,000—about 17 percent of the census figure.

At the foundation, there were thirty-one parishes, ten chapels, thirty-seven priests, and five convents. The women religious teachers and those in other ministries numbered eighty-nine: sixty-five Sisters of Mercy, twelve Sisters of Jesus and Mary, and an equivalent number of Sisters of Holy Cross. The Catholic school population and the number of teaching personnel have already been mentioned.

Bishop James A. Healy, bishop of the Diocese of Portland, nominated the Reverend Denis Mary Bradley as the first bishop of Manchester, a choice that was approved by the Holy See.

Denis M. Bradley was born in Knockeen, near Castle Island, County Kerry, Ireland, on February 25, 1846, the first child of Michael Bradley, a farmer, and Mary Kerins. Five other children were born of this union.

Not long after the unexpected death of her young husband in the spring of 1854, and that of the youngest son, John, then only a few months old, Mrs. Bradley and her children emigrated from Ireland and joined one of her sisters in Manchester, New Hampshire.

After working in the mills for a time, Mrs. Bradley's principal occupation in Manchester became that of operating a boardinghouse in a rented home on Laurel Street. Denis was placed in a private school and, afterward, in the school for boys at St. Anne taught by Mr. Thomas Corcoran. Beginning in his tenth year—that is, at the age of nine—Denis began to work in the mills during the summertime. After finishing his course at the Park Street School, he found permanent employment there.

Once his mother learned of his desire to become a priest, she gave him her savings of $300 in gold, a princely sum at the time, to help pay for his education. Denis, then slightly over eighteen years old, first attended Holy Cross College, Worcester, from 1864 to 1867, where he successfully passed two classes each year by means of concentrated studies.

From Holy Cross, he went to Saint Joseph Seminary in Troy, New York, where he completed his philosophical and theological studies. On June 3, 1871, now twenty-five years of age, he was ordained to the priesthood in the seminary chapel by the bishop of Rochester, New York.

On June 14, 1871, Father Bradley was appointed an assistant at the cathedral in Portland. In 1873, he was named rector of the parish, and when Bishop Bacon went to Europe the following year, he was commissioned chancellor and rector of the only two parishes in Portland, the cathedral and St. Dominic.

When Bishop Healy arrived in Portland in June 1875, as the second ordinary, Father Bradley was immediately reappointed as chancellor and rector of the cathedral. In 1875 and 1878, as has been noted, he accompanied Bishop Healy on his pastoral visitations, that of 1875 covering an astonishing three thousand miles.

In 1879, after five years of arduous work and travel, Father Bradley's health, never robust, failed him. When a curative trip to Europe did not restore his health sufficiently to pursue his dual tasks, he asked Bishop Healy to be replaced. The latter sent him to Manchester, the city where he had spent his youth, to assume, on June 17, 1880, the pastorate of St. Joseph parish. There is good reason to believe that, even at this early date, Bishop Healy had already selected Father Bradley as his first choice for the projected new diocese in New Hampshire, and wanted him in that state to learn firsthand about conditions there.

There were at the time five hundred families in St. Joseph parish, consisting of 2,550 individuals, plus 93 single men and women. A perception of the level of religious practice there can be gained by noting Father Bradley's calculation that 2,030 attended Sunday Mass; only 520 did not.

Father Bradley's pastorate proved to be very successful at every level. On the spiritual plane, for example, the Redemptorists preached a much appreciated combined parish mission and renewal programs in April and October 1882, and he, Father Bradley, strengthened his personal bonds with the Sisters of Mercy, bonds that had been more than somewhat frayed by Bishop Healy's domineering, and occasionally caustic, dealings with that community.

On the construction plane, he completed a school for boys that was being built on his arrival, provided new furniture for it and the girls' school, and, in 1883, built a new school for the girls as well. On the financial plane, by various fund-raising activities, he reduced the rather substantial parish debt by two-thirds.

As planned by Bishop Healy, the Holy See established the Diocese of Manchester, covering the whole state of New Hampshire, in a decree dated April 15, 1884. Father Bradley was chosen the founding bishop and was ordained to that office by the archbishop of Boston, John J. Williams, on June 11, in the Cathedral of St. Joseph in Manchester. Bishop Healy gave the homily. At the time, Bishop Bradley was thirty-eight years old.

Third Plenary Council of Baltimore 1884

One of the first duties of the new bishop of Manchester was to attend the Third Plenary Council of Baltimore, which was held from November 9 to December 7, 1884. That council has been evaluated as having been the most important ever held on the soil of this country.

Present were sixty bishops, fourteen archbishops, seven abbots, thirty-one superiors of religious orders, eleven superiors of major seminaries, eighty-eight theologians, and a host of minor officials. So thorough were the decrees passed by this council that they remained the law of the church in this country for many decades.

Despite Bishop Bradley's obvious lack of episcopal seniority, he was appointed to the committee that prepared the decrees on the Catholic faith and the office of bishop.

Bishop Bradley was accompanied to Baltimore by two priests from New Hampshire: the Very Reverend John E. Barry, the vicar general and pastor of St. John the Evangelist, Concord, and the Reverend William McDonald, pastor of St. Anne parish, Manchester. Father Barry served as theologian to the committee on the sacrament of marriage; Father McDonald, very likely out of deference for his age, was not assigned to any committee. His presence at Baltimore seems to have been a reward for his selfless and caring services for the previous thirty-six years.

First Synod of the Diocese 1886

In order to implement needed legislation in New Hampshire, Bishop Bradley convoked the First Synod of the Diocese of Manchester in the cathedral on November 4, 1886. In essence, the synod promulgated the decrees of the Second and Third Plenary Councils of Baltimore during the morning, and in the afternoon session diocesan consultors were appointed as well as members of other curial offices.

A roll call established that forty-two of the forty-five priests of the diocese were present at the synod. An attempt to hold a second synod was not begun until November 3, 1964, almost exactly seventy-eight years later. As we shall see, this second synod was never completed.

The Growth of Catholicism

Bishop Bradley remained active in the administrations of St. Joseph parish and in other affairs concerning the city of Manchester even after his episcopal ordination and the appointment of a rector for the cathedral.

For example, he became personally involved in enlarging the girls' school; the building of an episcopal residence; moving and remodeling the old rectory into a home for the Christian Brothers, who arrived to teach in St. Joseph parish in 1885; completing the five-story St. Joseph orphanage for boys (1887); excavating a basement under the cathedral where Mass could be celebrated for the children; expanding the home for elderly ladies; opening Sacred Heart Hospital (1892), the first Catholic institution of this kind in the state; greatly enlarging the cathedral and installing new stained-glass windows (1892); and dedicating the bigger and renovated cathedral church on April 15, 1894, the twenty-fifth anniversary of the building and the tenth of the Diocese of Manchester.

Highest priority during Bishop Bradley's episcopacy was given to the establishment of parishes, missions, and stations, particularly in the distant and scattered parts of New Hampshire. In order to help subsidize these foundations, Bishop Bradley, not long after he became bishop, established the Poor Mission Collection, which has been taken up yearly ever since.

Between 1884 and 1902—that is, in about eighteen years—thirty-six new parishes were canonically erected. Twenty-five of these were in communities that had never had a Catholic parish. By the time of his death in 1903, there were sixty-seven parishes in New Hampshire, and approximately an additional sixty-seven missions were regularly visited by priests.

Seven of the parishes established by Bishop Bradley were French Canadian, raising the total to ten. St. Raphael, while not legally a national parish, was founded in 1888 for the German-speaking Catholics of Manchester and vicinity. St. Hedwig, also in Manchester, established in 1902, became the first of three Polish national parishes in the diocese.

Another method used to reach the unchurched and to attract converts was the employment of missionaries to preach around the state in 1900, 1901, and 1902. These efforts appear to have been very successful. Unfortunately, with the death of Bishop Delany in 1906 (Bishop Bradley's successor), all sustained evangelization efforts came virtually to a halt until the diocesan centennial in 1984. In substance, no aggressive effort to evangelize was mounted for some three-quarters of a century.

Another heartening sign during the period 1884–1903 was the increase in the number of religious communities of both men and women in New Hampshire. Religious communities of women grew from three to eight during these years. The new communities were the Sisters of Charity of Sherbrooke (1885), the Benedictine Sisters (1889), the Sisters of the Presentation of the Blessed Virgin Mary (1889), the Sisters of Charity of Providence (1892), and the Sisters of the Precious Blood (1898), the last a contemplative order.

Among the first four orders of men to settle in the diocese, three were composed entirely of brothers, and the other mainly of priests. These were the Christian Brothers (1885), the order of St. Benedict (1888), the Brothers of the Sacred Heart (1889), and the Marist Brothers (1890). By 1903, these twelve communities of men and women numbered more than five hundred. Of these four communities of men, only the Benedictines remain in New Hampshire.

Other functioning institutions at the time of the death of Bishop Bradley were five orphan asylums with over four hundred children, four homes for the aged, five homes for working girls, one night refuge for girls, four hospitals, and one infant asylum.

Catholic schools also flourished during these years, largely in response to the mandates of the Third Plenary Council of Baltimore of 1884 and the diocesan synod of 1886. Between 1884 and 1903, twenty-nine Catholic elementary schools were founded in New Hampshire.

Fifteen of these schools were originally staffed entirely by laypeople until they were replaced by members of religious communities, or until they were forced to close, generally for financial reasons. Lay staffing was not to become common again until after the Second Vatican Council. Total Catholic elementary school attendance by 1903 had reached 12,581 students, not counting 855 boys and girls receiving instruction in orphanages.

In the same year (1903), secondary education for boys was provided in five parishes: three in Manchester and one each in Dover and Nashua. There were five secondary schools for girls, four in Manchester and one in Dover. In attendance were 1,050 boys and 300 girls.

In 1903, there was only one Catholic college in New Hampshire, St. Anselm, with a faculty of seventeen Benedictine priests and an enrollment of one hundred students, both at the secondary and college levels. Classes had been inaugurated there in 1889. During its early years, St. Anselm was essentially more of a secondary school than a college.

Bishop Bradley had invited the Order of Saint Benedict to New Hampshire from a monastery in New Jersey for two reasons. One was to look after the spiritual welfare of the immigrant German Catholics in the diocese. These Benedictines, several originally from Germany, founded St. Raphael parish in Manchester in 1888 and are still ably ministering there in 1997. A second goal was to establish an institution of higher learning, a Catholic college. Bishop Bradley, in his correspondence, urged haste in achieving this second objective. One of his fears, he confided to the Benedictines, was that they would be preceded by a religious order of men from French Canada, a situation that he did not favor or want. As mentioned, St. Anselm began classes in 1889; no French Canadian order of men ever established a college in the state. This was not to be true for women religious, however. River College (1933) in Nashua and Notre

Dame College (1950) in Manchester were founded by the Sisters of Presentation and the Sisters of Holy Cross, respectively.

The Spanish-American War 1898

One of the sources of division in the American Catholic Church, as it was, in fact, a matter of dissension among citizens at large, was the declaration of war on Spain by the United States in 1898. Once war was declared, however, Catholics responded patriotically by joining the armed forces and, once more, the sisterhoods furnished selfless service to the sick and wounded in military hospitals, as their predecessors had done during the Civil War.

In New Hampshire, the Sheridan Guards, a Catholic military organization, established in Manchester by Father William McDonald after the Civil War, is said to have volunteered to a man to serve in the Spanish-American War as a company of the New Hampshire Third Regiment. It has been estimated that there were about four hundred Catholics in that regiment, including those in the Sheridan Guards. This regiment did not see combat because the United States quickly crushed the Spanish military forces.

One unusual result of the war was the imprisonment of 1,600 Spaniards, mostly navy personnel, at Camp Long, Seavey's Island, in Portsmouth Harbor, from July to September 1898. These Spanish prisoners, most probably all of the Catholic faith, received much attention and assistance from the bishops of Portland and Manchester and from the priests of St. Mary parish (now Immaculate Conception) of Portsmouth.

Continued Immigration

Two of the linchpins to an understanding of New Hampshire Catholicism between 1884 and 1903 are the unceasing flow of immigrants into the state and a new wave of anti-Catholicism.

While by 1900 Irish immigration to the United States had been reduced to modest proportions, French Canadian migration to New England continued to be very heavy. It is estimated that at the turn of the century, French Canadians represented 16 percent of the population of the state of New Hampshire, and one-fourth of the residents of Manchester.

By 1865, the German influx equaled that of the Irish, and from that year to 1900 around 700,000 came to the United States. Over 35 percent of these immigrants were Catholics; relatively few settled in New Hampshire. Only one parish was founded for them in the diocese, as it has been noted, St. Raphael in Manchester.

Polish immigration to New Hampshire left a more lasting mark than did the German. A minor immigration between 1854 and 1870 was followed by the great immigration of 1870–1910, during which more than 1.6 million came to this country. In 1902, with about 850 Polish people in Manchester, St. Hedwig was founded as a national parish.

Five years later, in 1907, the Felician Sisters of Buffalo, New York, opened the first Catholic school for Polish children in New Hampshire. It is still in operation today under the guidance of the same community of religious.

A Polish national parish, St. Stanislaus, was founded in Nashua in 1908 and staffed originally by diocesan priests. In 1927 it was entrusted to the Missionaries of Our Lady of La Salette. A third was opened by diocesan priests in Claremont in 1920. Dedicated to St. Joseph, it is still staffed by a diocesan priest. Significant Polish colonies also established themselves at Franklin and Winchester.

Lithuanians began arriving in the United States in about 1868. While a number settled in Manchester, Lincoln, and elsewhere in New Hampshire, only those in Nashua were able to establish their own parish: St. Casimir was opened in 1906 by the LaSalette Fathers.

In the last quarter of the nineteenth century, migrants began arriving from Syria, among them both Melkites and Maronites, churches of the Oriental Catholic rite. They came for reasons similar to those of migrants from other nations: overpopulation at home; primitive methods of agriculture; the lack of industry, commerce, and business opportunities; and religious or ethnic persecution.

After being served by itinerant missionaries for many years, the Melkite church of Our Lady of the Cedars was canonically erected in 1963, and a Maronite church, dedicated to St. George, was canonically established at Dover in the same year.

There was a sufficient number of Ukrainian Catholics in Manchester to open St. Mary Church in 1906. These three are the only Oriental Catholic parishes in New Hampshire: one Ukrainian, one Melkite, and one Maronite.

While close to 5 million Italians came to the United States between 1820 and 1930, relatively few chose to seek their future in New Hampshire. Larger and more prosperous states, particularly the cities, held greater attraction. This was unfortunate for this state, as it deprived both the civic community and the Catholic Church of the cultural, economic, and religious contributions that they could have made here. It should be noted, however, that among the emigrants from the Papal States, which were forcibly merged into Italy in 1869, there was some strong anti-Catholicism, particularly among those who worked in granite quarries. This anti-Catholicism was the consequence of their poor treatment in the Papal States. One New England town that received a number of these laborers with this mentality was Barre, Vermont.

One frenzied and disgraceful incident in Rome in the 1880s confirms the anti-Catholicism among some of the residents of the former Papal States. On the night of July 13–14, 1881, an unruly and jostling mob, "shouting taunts, blasphemies and insults," attempted unsuccessfully to cast the dead body of Pius IX into the Tiber River from the Ponte Sant'Angelo. Pius IX's remains were being carried, supposedly secretly, from the Vatican Palace to the place he had chosen for his entombment, the church of San Lorenzo fuori le Mura just a few miles away.

The Portuguese, who came to this country in far smaller numbers than the Italians, rarely ventured farther north than the border of Massachusetts. Again, New Hampshire was deprived of their economic and cultural potential.

Further migrations to New Hampshire with any significant Catholic import are dealt with in proper chronological sequence.

The Knights of Columbus and Other Church Societies

From their first years in New Hampshire, these immigrant groups, as well as the earlier arrivals, founded a wide variety of societies to take care of their religious, social, and some aspects of their economic needs. Each ethnic group brought with it some of the parish organizations its members had known in their country of origin. While few written records of these societies remain, it can be conjectured that from the very beginning virtually all the parishes, missions, and stations had societies for married women, married men, single women and men, and even organizations for youths and children. A few of the better known were: the Altar and Rosary Society, the Ladies of St. Anne, the Children of Mary, the Holy Name Society, the League of the Sacred Heart, the Apostleship of Prayer, the Catholic Daughters of America, the Daughters of Isabella, among a great many more. These Catholic organization—parochial, diocesan, national, and occasionally international—have proliferated to the point that the 1996–1997 *New Hampshire Directory,* published by the Office of Communications of the diocese, lists twenty-five such groups. In addition, it recognizes one lay missionary group, three secular institutes, and ten full secular orders. It is easy to note, however, that the names, styles, and objectives have changed a great deal over the years to meet the needs of a shifting church and society. All of these organizations, past and present, have been or are largely composed of and managed by laypeople. They deserve a full study of their own.

Certainly the most successful Catholic organization in the United States is the Knights of Columbus. This organization was founded in New Haven, Connecticut, in 1882 as a result of the inspiration and work of a local priest, Father Michael J. McGivney. Its highly laudable purpose was to offer fraternal assistance to Catholic men to better enable them to preserve their faith and to care for their families. Its goals were charity, unity, fraternity, and patriotism. One of its best-known and appreciated features is its insurance program, which currently (1997) provides over $32 billion of coverage to its members worldwide.

New Hampshire's first council, Council #92, was established in Manchester in 1895. The following year, three more were founded in Concord, Nashua, and Portsmouth. By 1899, after only seven years of existence in the state, there were a sufficient number of councils to create a State Council Jurisdiction. This organization has experienced consistent growth so that by early 1997 it had sixty-eight active councils in every part of New Hampshire, with a total membership of over 7,179. Worldwide there are more than 11,000 councils.

This organization's contribution to the Church and to society, as they have been to the members and their families, has been considerable. On the national level, it has invested millions of dollars in the campaign against abortion and in another in support of some form of federal assistance for the parents of students in Catholic schools who are being penalized for exercising their freedom to make an educational choice.

In New Hampshire, the Knights of Columbus have given notable assistance to those with kidney disease as well as to those who are mentally challenged in some way. The diocesan summer camps for boys and girls (Fatima and Bernadette), the Oblate Retreat in Hudson, a scholarship program, and financial assistance to support religious vocations are among the worthy causes that have been aided or subsidized by the Knights.

Renewed Anti-Catholicism

Protestant attitudes toward Catholics during the period 1884–1903, while much improved, were still far from ideal. As late as 1875, a New Hampshire historian referred to the French Canadians as bigoted, priest-ridden, and averse to changes in laws, customs, and the processes of labor. This was undoubtedly attributed by this gentleman to the corrupting influences of their Catholic faith and their benighted clergy. There is no evidence, however, that New Hampshire was affected by the level of virulence of anti-Catholicism that plagued certain parts of Massachusetts.

Contributing strongly to the anti-Catholicism of this period was the founding in 1887 of the American Protective Association, also known by its initials, the APA. For some years the association grew slowly, but in 1892–1893 it began to spread rapidly, like a malignancy. Among the causes for its expansion were: the seemingly endless arrival of Catholic immigrants; the rise in the number of parochial schools; the exercise of political power by Catholics in the Democratic Party; the overall progress made by Catholics in the business and economic fields; the financial panic of 1893; and some gross lies. One of the lies was that the Catholic Church was preparing to take over the United States by insurrection and massacre. APA propaganda was so successful that, at its zenith, it claimed 2.5 million members in twenty-two states.

Some ripples of the APA movement lapped over into New Hampshire. In 1894, Bishop Bradley noted in his biographical information on the clergy, that a Manchester American Protective Association newspaper accused a local priest of a serious breach of morality. Unfortunately, subsequent information indicates that the charge was not without foundation.

In the same year, the celebration of Bishop Bradley's tenth anniversary as ordinary was marred by unspecified activities of the APA. Finally, in September 1895, an evangelist by the name of Rush of Boston gave two anti-Catholic lectures at the Opera House in Peterborough on behalf of the APA. To the credit of the residents of Peterborough, only sixty-eight people, including children, attended the first lecture, and a mere twenty-eight were present for the second.

To the Turn of Century

During Bishop Bradley's episcopacy, all the ecclesiastical celebrations mandated by the Holy See were duly observed in the diocese, including the beginning of the last year of the century at midnight on December 31, 1899, and the beginning of the twentieth century at midnight on December 31, 1900.

On this latter occasion, Bishop Bradley invited the donation of objects of gold by the faithful, such as jewelry and coins, to make a souvenir chalice. Enough gold was collected from 1,800 donors to make a new-century offering of a chalice, ciborium, and part of a monstrance. (The rest of the monstrance is of a baser metal.) All three of these precious objects are still used in the cathedral for worship on special occasions.

On examining these three sacred articles, one can easily be emotionally moved not only by their value and purpose, but even more so by the faith and sacrificial generosity of the donors. For the greater part, they were poor, earned unjustly low wages, and worked inhumanely long hours under generally wretched conditions. This is a gospel story in modern dress, that of the widow's mite (Mt 12:42f; Lk 21:2f).

While the Diocese of Manchester responded alertly and faithfully to the spiritual appeals from the Holy See, it does not seem to have been affected to any degree by the philosophical and theological controversies that disturbed the Catholic Church in Europe and in the United States, especially in the late nineteenth and early twentieth centuries. Two of the major controversies of the time were Americanism and Modernism.

A search of the archives of the diocese failed to uncover any significant information on or reaction to Pope Leo XIII's January 1889 Condemnation of Americanism in *Testem Benevolentiae,* the first questioning of American orthodoxy by Rome. Even Pius X's condemnation of Modernism, which has been defined as a synthesis of all the heresies of the time, in sixty-five propositions in 1907, in the decree *Lamentabili,* and in a subsequent encyclical, *Pascendi,* failed to elicit local response of any kind.

Among the reasons for this lack of involvement in key Church issues were certainly the small size of the diocese, the primitive means of communication available in the world and country, the mediocre quality of seminary training that produced a pious and loyal but non-scholarly clergy, and the comparative remoteness of New Hampshire from the centers of controversy. Bishop Bradley's lack of a contentious character certainly contributed to the theological tranquillity of the diocese.

Another document of seminal importance to the Church issued during the episcopacy of Bishop Bradley was the encyclical of Pope Leo XIII entitled *Rerum Novarum*, promulgated in 1891. It has since been called "the Magna Charta on which all Christian activities in social matters are ultimately based."

In a church whose primary focus and efforts had always been on charity, this encyclical had little immediate effect in New Hampshire. Even when local wages were far below what was needed to support a family, thus forcing a wife and children to work; when working hours were inhumanely long; when the workplace was dangerous and unhealthy; when there were no benefits for sickness, unemployment, and retirement; and a host of other valid complaints, a call to justice was not understood. An appeal to charity was made instead. Most did not seem to recognize that charity usually becomes necessary when justice does not prevail. Direct calls for justice did not begin until the episcopacy of Bishop Brady (1945–1959), and reached maturity under his successor, Bishop Primeau (1960–1974).

This new emphasis on justice forced many changes in the Catholic Church's organization and its way of dealing with any social and economic problems. Charity, while absolutely essential in many circumstances, frequently keeps the recipient dependent on the continued generosity of the donor. Justice, on the other hand, can mean the permanent transfer of autonomy, with its dignity, to the beneficiary.

Obviously, the concept of justice is not new in the Church: It is listed as one of the four cardinal virtues—prudence, justice, fortitude, and temperance.

Corporation Sole

Another matter of constant concern to the Church was settled in New Hampshire during the episcopacy of Bishop Bradley, that of the ownership of church funds and property. It has already been noted that the Bishop of Boston, at a time when the entire state was a part of that diocese, refused free land from the Amoskeag Manufacturing Company for the first Catholic church in Manchester (St. Anne) because it hinged on the acceptance of lay trustees. The ownership of assets and property was obviously subject to civil law; their management was, in the greater part, a matter of church law.

This reluctance—and in most cases the outright refusal—to accept laypeople as partners in the ownership of church funds and property most likely arose from two sources: the hierarchical structure of the church, and the recurring disastrous and scandalous consequences of lay participation in the ownership and management of the church's financial resources.

It cannot be ignored that the Catholic Church's structure and governance were molded during the emperor phase of the Roman Empire in the West (27 B.C.–476 A.D.), and to a lesser degree that of the East to the fall of Constantinople in 1453 A.D. Perforce, the Church was influenced in many ways by its contact with imperialism for a number of centuries. These forms of government did not allow for much democratic participation, if at all.

Of more immediate importance, however, were the experiments in lay participation, notably by the election or appointment of trustees, that caused major divisions—some bordering on schism—in places such as Baltimore, Buffalo, Charleston, New Orleans, New York City, Norfolk, and Philadelphia.

In other places, such as the Diocese of Manchester, where at least some of the property was held in the name of the local pastor, this system proved to be no more successful. As early as 1886, Bishop Bradley was complaining to his attorney, John M. Mitchell, that the heirs of the pastor were occasionally claiming ownership of the church funds and property held in his name and that a more reliable and secure method had to be found to protect the church.

One means was the corporation sole. This was a legal entity whereby the property was to be held in the name of the bishop, not as an individual, but as a moral person who would exist perpetually through his successors. A corporation sole was first created by the legislature of Maryland in favor of the archbishop of Baltimore on March 23, 1833. This system was subsequently widely adopted. Bishop Bradley was able to have similar legislation passed in his favor and that of his successors on March 7, 1901. Since then, all diocesan church funds and property, with few exceptions, are legally in the name of "The Roman Catholic Bishop of Manchester and His Successors."

Even the guarantee of a corporation sole has not kept the Catholic bishops of Manchester totally immune from some aggravations. In the case of Bishop Guertin, it happened after his death. Because of the vagueness of his will, some of his heirs, taking advantage of this, demanded a share of his estate. In order to prevent a wider publicity to this challenge, the diocese settled generously with them out of court, despite the fact that his executor was convinced of the invalidity of their claims.

An incident related to Bishop Brady had a humorous aspect to it. While attending the funeral of a pastor at Guardian Angel parish in Berlin in 1959, the relatives of the deceased emptied the pockets of Bishop Brady's suitcoat while he was in church thinking that it belonged to their deceased relative! When Bishop Brady became aware of this during the drive back to Manchester, he had his chancellor-chauffeur turn around to reclaim his property, successfully.

Death of the First Bishop

Bishop Bradley died at 2:29 A.M. on Sunday, December 14, 1903, at the age of fifty-seven years, nine months, and eighteen days. The cause of death was later attributed to cancer of the stomach. His funeral, attended by state and municipal officers, including the governor, and by Protestant ministers, brought the city to a standstill. Public schools were closed, and even every electric car in Manchester came to a stop in place out of respect for two minutes at precisely noon. He was interred in the new crypt in the basement of the cathedral under the main altar. Perhaps the best evaluation of the first bishop of Manchester has been expressed in the four words on a tablet under the first station of the cross in the cathedral dedicated to him: "Pious—Learned—Gentle—Zealous."

Fundamental Changes

For a few decades before the death of Bishop Bradley, a number of fundamental changes had been taking place in the Catholic Church, including that of the United States. Only two, of considerable importance, will be mentioned here.

One was the constant influx of immigrants from many corners of the world, a phenomenon frequently mentioned in this study. While the American Catholic Church was changing in this way, the episcopal leadership became even more concentrated in the hands of one group, the Irish. By 1900, for example, two out of three bishops in the United States were of Irish origin; in New England, three out of four (75 percent) were of this same racial stock. This led, as it shall be seen, to severe ethnic turmoil, and one schism in New Hampshire.

Another fundamental change, of perhaps greater importance, was an evolution in the basic understanding and role of the episcopacy and, consequently, in the very kind of man selected for this responsibility. This basic change was due, in large measure, to the decrees of the First Vatican Council, particularly that defining the infallibility of the pope, and to the many more that mandated the greater centralization of the Church under the leadership of Rome. This perception filtered down to greater centralization of authority and management under the bishops in the decrees of the Third Plenary Council of Baltimore of 1884.

As a result, a number of competent American historians have traced the demise of the active role of the laity in the Church to the end of the nineteenth century, and the debilitating weakening of the independence of the clergy, particularly pastors, to the early years of the twentieth.

Challenges to Episcopal Authority

One of the countless incidents that illustrate the relatively greater independence of parish priests prior to roughly 1900 is that concerning the pastor of St. Bernard, Keene, who exercised his ministry there between 1883 and 1895. Shortly after the Third Plenary Council of Baltimore (1884), Bishop Bradley directed that pastor, as he did many others, to build a Catholic grammar school, as mandated by the council. Initially the pastor refused to do so. After a ping-pong volley of letters between Keene and Manchester, he reluctantly agreed to build a school in 1886. At the conclusion of this project, the pastor simply mailed all the construction bills to the bishop with a letter telling him, in effect: You ordered it, you pay for it.

To further aggravate the situation, the Keene pastor was repeatedly petitioning Bishop Bradley for a transfer to St. Joseph parish in Laconia. His lame basis for the request was that the climate in Laconia was more healthful than that in Keene! Despite the previous numerous discourtesies of this clergyman, Bishop Bradley granted him his wish in 1895. It is not known if his health was any better in Laconia than it had been in Keene; he died in his coveted parish three years later, in 1898.

Other instances where the Bishop's compassion and sense of justice were brought into play, as well as a challenge to his authority were: the habitual use of opium (laudanum) by a pastor to the north, a charge that the pastor denied; the introduction of a new congregation of women religious into the diocese to teach school by the same pastor, without the knowledge, much less the consent, of the ordinary; the boycotting of the Sunday High Mass in a parish to the west by all of the parishioners because the pastor was believed to be cohabiting with his housekeeper, a tactic that did not end the affair; the addiction of a mother superior to alcohol, again to the west, who tried to bribe the silence of another nun with a personal key to the liquor cabinet; and a pastor in a parish neighboring the cathedral in Manchester whose moral conduct, it has been noted, came to the attention of the American Protective Association, thus moving the bishop to send the individual back home to the province of Quebec, where he continued to scandalize the faithful.

With little effort, it can be detected that from the earliest years of the diocese the far north and the remote west of New Hampshire were often used to isolate clergy whose conduct was considered less than exemplary by the bishop and his entourage. The lame principle "Out of sight, out of mind" was frequently in effect. These clumsy and ill-advised attempts to cast problems to the north and west frequently boomeranged back through the portals of episcopal headquarters with irreparable spiritual damage.

As for Bishop Bradley and his jousts with the clergy, this kind and gentlemanly person was frequently the one to be figuratively picked up from the dust. Had he owned a personal coat of arms, as most American bishops did, it could have featured a *chevalier gisant*, a fallen knight.

This ambience in the diocese would change with the new century with the appointment of a bishop fully in harmony with the theological and sociological developments just described.

Episcopal Interference from Quebec

Bishop Bradley was to suffer further and unexpected indignities from a few of the bishops of the province of Quebec. Even a cursory examination of the correspondence between the bishop of Manchester and some of his counterparts in Quebec, who had priests or women religious exercising ministry in New Hampshire, frequently reveals a patronizing tone toward him accompanied by many recommendations (one could easily say directives) on how to deal with their subjects. A reader senses that a favor had been bestowed on the bishop of Manchester, one that could be recalled.

Certainly the most humiliating exercise of this spurious authority over a priest formerly of his diocese, but now incardinated the Diocese of Manchester, was by the Most Reverend Louis-Zepherin Moreau, bishop of Ste.-Hyacinthe from 1875 to 1901.

In either late 1890 or early 1891, Bishop Moreau had the effrontery to have the Congregation of the Propagation of the Faith in Rome appoint Father Pierre Hevey, pastor of Ste. Marie parish in Manchester, to the highest rank of monsignor, that of Protonotary Apostolic. This was done without the knowledge, and much less the consent, of Bishop Bradley or even that of Bishop James A. Healy, who had had jurisdiction over New Hampshire from 1875 to 1884.

Father Hevey had been ordained for the diocese of Ste.-Hyacinthe in 1857 and had served there until 1871, when he transferred to the Diocese of Portland. There is no doubt that Father Hevey was one of the outstanding priests of the Diocese of Manchester. He was in many respects an exemplary clergyman and a great builder at Ste.-Marie in Manchester, as he had been previously at Sts.-Peter and Paul in Lewiston, Maine, where he was pastor from the fall of 1871 to either late 1881 or early 1882, at which time he was sent to Ste.-Marie on March 8 by Bishop Healy.

As neither Bishop Bradley nor Bishop Healy knew the source of the request to Rome on behalf of Father Hevey, the latter bishop wrote to the Propaganda congregation twice to obtain some information. In its response to Bishop Healy, the Propaganda denied all knowledge or participation in the monsignorial appointment but promised to investigate. A second letter informed the bishop of Portland that the appointment of Father Hevey had been made at the solicitation of the bishop of Ste.-Hyacinthe, Bishop Moreau. Rome added that it would be more careful about such matters in the future. In a letter of explanation to Bishop Bradley, Bishop Healy, a person who could be blunt with the truth, added that he hoped that Rome would also be more careful about "what lies they tell." Thus Pierre Hevey became the first Monsignor in New Hampshire and remained the only one with that distinction for several years.

On a larger scale, it must be added that for a few decades toward the end of the nineteenth century, there were a certain number of people in the province of Quebec, including bishops, who believed that because of the heavy migration of French Canadians to New England, particularly to the northern tier of Maine, New Hampshire, and Vermont, these three states would eventually be annexed to the province of Quebec by popular referendum. It is very possible that Bishop Moreau was one of these believers. This was, in effect, a sort of modest French Canadian "Manifest Destiny."

Another galling aspect related to this unprincipled elevation of Monsignor Hevey was his leadership in trying to obtain a bishop of French Canadian ancestry to replace Bishop Bradley upon the bishop's death. In 1894, for example, which was the tenth anniversary of both the founding of the diocese and the episcopal ordination of Bishop Bradley, Monsignor Hevey sent a confidential letter to the French Canadian priests of New Hampshire. In it he expressed some reservation about accepting the invitation that he had received to toast Bishop Bradley in their name at a reception to be given in the bishop's honor. His hesitation, he explained, was based on the plans they had for the future, to obtain a French Canadian successor. A copy of this confidential letter fell into the hands of Bishop Bradley, who wrote across its back, the "insidious" letter of Monsignor Hevey.

It is believed by many, although no written documentation has been found to this effect, that Monsignor Hevey had built the grandiose new church of Ste.-Marie between 1891 and 1898 in part to serve as the cathedral for the first French Canadian bishop of the Diocese of Manchester.

Monsignor Hevey's "insidious" maneuvering with his colleagues in favor of a bishop of French Canadian ancestry succeeded in 1907 with the appointment, as we shall see, of Father George A. Guertin as the third bishop of Manchester. Monsignor Hevey was able to enjoy this victory for three years and two days; he died in retirement on March 21, 1910. St. Joseph's remained the cathedral.

NINE

Shattered Expectations
1904–1906

A New Bishop for Manchester

On January 7, 1904, the bishops of New England, with Archbishop Williams of Boston presiding, prepared a terna—a list of three recommended successors for Bishop Bradley—which was sent to the Holy See. Their first choice, the Reverend John B. Delany, was appointed the second bishop of Manchester. Public announcement of his selection was made on August 9, 1904, exactly the fortieth anniversary of his birth. His episcopal ordination took place in the cathedral before a throng of ecclesiastical and civic dignitaries on September 8. It is interesting to note that the principal consecrator was the apostolic delegate to the United States, the Most Reverend Diomede Falconio, and that one of the assistants was the Most Reverend William O'Connell, then bishop of Portland, and future cardinal-archbishop of Boston.

Little did anyone suspect on this occasion that this healthy, energetic, robust, and ecclesiastically well-connected prelate, from whom so much was expected, would lie in his casket before the same cathedral altar a little more than twenty-one months later.

John B. Delany: Years of Preparation 1864–1904

John B. Delany was born in Lowell, Massachusetts, on August 9, 1864, the eldest of ten children, of whom six survived to adulthood. Both his father, Thomas Delany, and his mother, Catherine (Fox) Delany, were born in Ireland—he in County Galway and she in County Monaghan—and married in that country before coming to the United States in 1857. Settling in Lowell, Mr. Delany earned his living as a custom tailor.

John Delany obtained his early education in a public elementary school in Lowell and then at the local public high school. From there he went to Holy Cross College, Worcester, for two years. He then transferred to Boston College, where he graduated with the class of '87. His preferences, his contemporaries attested, were for English literature and poetry.

During his college years, he published a number of articles and poems in college newspapers, and eventually became the editor in chief of the Boston College *Stylus*. He played the piano well and studied the guitar while a seminarian in Paris. In addition to his love for music, he was also fond of art in all its forms and, it is said, of nature as well.

His temperament was described as gregarious and he made many friends during his relatively short life. While he was known to be refined, it was also observed that he was very determined, some say even obstinate—this latter attribute being evident in the cut of his jaw as seen in his photographs, and observed in his words and actions. Here character and physiognomy appear to have been in harmony. Preferring, it appears, a more missionary diocese than that of Boston, and very likely attracted by the rugged beauty of the state of New Hampshire, he applied to study for the Diocese of Manchester rather than his home diocese, Boston, and was accepted by Bishop Bradley.

In order to provide John Delany and his classmate and lifelong friend, Edward A. Quirk, who applied for the Diocese of Manchester with him, with the needed fluency in the French language, Bishop Bradley assigned them both to Sulpician seminaries, first at Issy and then in Paris, France. They spent the school year of 1887–1888 studying philosophy at Issy and the years 1888–1891 studying theology in Paris itself. There is no doubt that John Delany's four years in Europe were very full and happy ones. Throughout this period he kept a diary, which he used as the base for his letters home. While the diary itself has not been found, much of its content is known from articles he published later, when he became the founding editor of the first diocesan publication, *The Guidon*, in 1898. These articles, copied and most likely revised from his letters home, include perceptive, and frequently humorous, accounts of life in the seminary in Paris, and of the numerous historic places in France, Italy, Germany, Austria, and Switzerland he visited during vacations.

John Delany was ordained to the priesthood on May 23, 1891, by Cardinal Richard, archbishop of Paris. On his way home, he made pilgrimages to various shrines in France, and visited England and Ireland as well. After passing a few days in Lowell with his family and friends, he reported for duty to Bishop Bradley.

His first assignment was as second assistant at St. Anne parish, Manchester, where he remained for two and a half years. From there he was transferred to Immaculate Conception parish, Portsmouth. The extent of his lack of enthusiasm for this assignment can be measured by at least four requests he made to Bishop Bradley in 1893, 1894, 1896, and 1897 to be moved from Portsmouth to the cathedral parish. From his written personal observations on his clergy, it is apparent that Bishop Bradley was hesitant concerning Father Delany's request. His uncertainty seems to have centered on Father Delany's perceived ambition rather than on his abilities, which everyone seemed to recognize.

Another dimension of Bishop Delany's character can be discerned from the remarks he made in his address to the clergy at the traditional banquet following his episcopal ordination. In the presence of the apostolic delegate and a large number of priests, he observed that he had never sought the episcopacy and had never expected to be a bishop, but in consideration of his new position, he stated: "I am the bishop, the whole bishop, and nothing but the bishop." This, to many, must have sounded like a warning or, at least, a caution. This warning was also in keeping with the more authoritarian stance of the post–First Vatican Council and the Third Plenary Council of Baltimore decrees; a study of Bishop Bradley's character and life reveals no similar frame of mind or statement.

It was not until 1898 that Father Delany was temporarily assigned to Hinsdale to substitute for the pastor who was on a trip to Europe. Finally, later in the same year, Father Delany was granted his often-requested wish: He was appointed to the cathedral as chancellor of the diocese and secretary to the bishop. Once in Manchester, at least seven additional assignments were given to him, ranging from chaplain to the cloistered Sisters of the Precious Blood, who founded a monastery in Manchester in 1898, to diocesan director of the Priests' Temperance League.

Without a doubt, Father Delany achieved his greatest renown as the founding editor of *The Guidon,* the first official publication of the Diocese of Manchester, which began to appear in magazine format in October

1898. This publication survived for nine years, suspending operation in October 1907, just sixteen months after the untimely death of Bishop Delany. In addition to carrying articles and features on a wide variety of topics, its editorials, written by Father Delany on both religious and secular subjects, were quite frequently reprinted or commented on in major secular and Catholic newspapers. Father Delany was considered by many in the media to have remarkable insights into the problems of the times. *The Guidon* ceased publication for financial reasons. It was succeeded by *The Magnificat,* a publication of the Sisters of Mercy, which ran almost without interruption from November 1907 to June 1968. Also appearing monthly, it became more of a literary magazine with national appeal rather than a local publication covering matters of particular interest to the people of New Hampshire. It, too, achieved a high reputation for its excellence during much of its existence.

John B. Delany, Bishop 1904–1906

After his episcopal ordination, Bishop Delany's pace continued to be that of a young and vigorous man. In the twenty-one months of episcopal life allotted to him, for example, he established five new parishes. Four of these were in towns previously without a Catholic parish: Ashland (1904), Charlestown (1904), Lakeport (1905), and Harrisville (1906). The fifth was the first and only Lithuanian parish in New Hampshire, St. Casmir in Nashua, founded in 1906.

During the same brief twenty-one months, two more religious orders made their foundations in New Hampshire. The Sisters of the Assumption replaced the lay teachers at Sacred Heart School, Greenville, in 1905 and, in the same year, the Xaverian Brothers relieved the Sisters of Mercy from teaching boys at St. Agnes School in St. Anne parish, Manchester.

Overall, the Catholic school system in New Hampshire appeared to be so rapidly thriving to Bishop Delany that he wrote, on October 2, 1905, that it had more children, according to the proportion of Catholic population, than any other diocese in the country.

Bishop Delany will very likely be best remembered, in addition to *The Guidon,* for something that he planned but was never able to implement. He proposed to spend his summers, aided by a French-speaking priest, doing missionary work in the remote areas of New Hampshire, preaching to fallen-away Catholics and to the unchurched alike. His death, as it has been noted, paralyzed evangelization in the diocese for several generations. In fact, the most sanguine and uncritical observer of the history of the Catholic Church in New Hampshire would be hard-pressed to detect a high priority given to evangelization at any time in its past.

A study of Bishop Delany's brief episcopacy reveals that he was, overall, a forward-looking person and an adept planner. On a minor level, for example, in addition to making several improvements in the cathedral, he had electric lighting installed in that church and in the rectory at his personal expense as a gift to the parish. On the planning level, Bishop Delany purchased two adjoining estates on Pine Street in Manchester, facing Tremont common (now Pulaski Park), where he had hoped to erect a Bradley memorial school, a high school for boys, and one for girls. Funds pledged for this project never materialized and these schools did not come into existence until the opening of Bishop Bradley High School for boys in 1950 and Immaculata High School for girls in the early 1960s, but not on the land planned for them.

In 1905, he also purchased seven acres of land on Bridge Street in Manchester, near Derryfield Park, which was part of the discontinued city farm. For this property, Bishop Delany planned five buildings: an orphanage for boys, an orphanage for girls, an infant asylum, a gymnasium, and a chapel. This project was also abandoned at his death.

Bishop Delany was stricken with appendicitis early in June 1906, a condition that was not immediately recognized by his two local physicians despite a number of warning symptoms. Unusually enough, he had one doctor of clearly Irish extraction and the second of obvious French Canadian background. Why this duplication was believed expedient is not known. One could suspect, and probably correctly, that it was to prevent any accusations of favoritism in either ethnic group. Whatever the reason for the precaution, neither the Irish nor the French Canadian doctor diagnosed appendicitis. When they finally did, it was too late. Peritonitis had set in—a nearly always fatal development in those times.

A specialist, called from Boston to assist in the case, arrived in Manchester by train Thursday morning, June 7. He confirmed the diagnosis: The problem was indeed appendicitis. Bishop Delany was immediately moved from the cathedral rectory to Sacred Heart Hospital a short distance away, and underwent surgery at about noon, in the presence of many priests, local doctors, and nurses. Bishop Delany lingered on after the operation in considerable pain, but remained lucid most of the time.

As news of his approaching death spread throughout Manchester, large crowds gathered near the hospital to wait and pray, even blocking street traffic. He died at 3:45 A.M. on Monday, June 11, 1906. His funeral, on June 14, like that of Bishop Bradley, brought the city to a standstill.

With Bishop Delany were buried the shattered expectations of many who believed that he would have, had he lived, eventually assumed a position of far greater leadership in the Catholic Church in the United States.

TEN

Years of War, Stress, and Depression 1907–1931

Selection of George A. Guertin, Third Ordinary

Manchester's third bishop was to be a priest of French Canadian descent, the first in New England to have both a French Canadian father and mother. For many French Canadians crusading for a bishop from their ethnic background, having one parent from another background, invalidated their requirement.

George Guertin was also the first person born in New Hampshire to be ordained to the episcopal office in the Catholic Church. His selection by the Holy See was due, in large part, to the intervention of the French Canadian clergy of New Hampshire with the apostolic delegation in Washington.

Three French Canadian pastors designated by their confreres made a census of the French Canadians in the parishes of the state. This ethnic group was by then the most numerous in the Diocese of Manchester. Their census was begun, as one contemporary French Canadian publication noted, "hardly after the casket of Bishop Delany had been closed." The census figures were then hand-delivered to the apostolic delegate in Washington by two French Canadian clergymen with the petition that the choice of the French Canadian priests of New Hampshire, Father George A. Guertin, be named to succeed Bishop Delany.

Father Guertin received notice of his appointment in December 1906. He was to preside as bishop for twenty-four years, four months, and eighteen days, the longest to date of any bishop of Manchester. These years would be marked by a number of catastrophic events, in both the religious and secular spheres.

George Albert Guertin was born in Nashua on February 17, 1869, the son of George Guertin, a harnessmaker, and Louise (Lefebvre) Guertin, a homemaker. His elementary education was received first in a public school of Nashua, and then in the newly founded parochial school of his parish, St. Aloysius (St. Louis de Gonzague).

For a number of years he then studied at St. Charles Seminary, Sherbrooke, and subsequently at the seminary of Ste.-Hyacinthe, both in the province of Quebec. For his theological studies, Bishop Bradley enrolled him at St. John Seminary, Brighton, Massachusetts. When ordained to the episcopacy, he became the first alumnus of that institution to be named a bishop. Bishop Bradley elevated him to the priesthood in his home parish of St. Aloysius on December 17, 1892.

Father Guertin, Diocesan Priest, 1892–1907

All of Father Guertin's assignments as a priest were in parish ministry. His first was at St. Augustine, Manchester, where he remained for four years and three months. From there he was transferred to Sacred Heart, Lebanon, a parish in which both English and French were spoken; it also covered a large territory. On October 7, 1900, he was given his first and only pastorate: St. Anthony Church in east Manchester, a so-called "mixed parish," which was developing quickly because of new industries in that part of the city.

During his six-year tenure at St. Anthony's, Father Guertin made many improvements and won the admiration and affection of his people. He was remembered with devotion for several decades after his departure. One of the many signs of progress was the employment of the Sisters of Holy Cross in 1904 to open a school in the church basement.

He is also known to have taken a lively interest in the civic life of Manchester, as he had previously in Lebanon. When he was informed that he had been selected as the third bishop of Manchester, he was thirty-seven years and ten months old, and had been a priest for fourteen of those years.

Episcopal Ordination of Bishop Guertin 1907

A few days after receiving the official notification of his nomination to the See of Manchester, Bishop-select Guertin made the very unusual decision to move into the cathedral rectory, which is no more than two miles from that of St. Anthony. His motive was explained in a sermon that he delivered at all Masses in the cathedral on Sunday, February 17, 1907. In that sermon, he assured the people that St. Joseph would remain the cathedral, that there would be no changes, and that the parish would remain a strictly English congregation. There had been, it is known, many rumors and fears that this bishop select of French Canadian descent would move the cathedral seat to Ste.-Marie in Manchester west, and otherwise alter the status quo.

Father Guertin was ordained to the episcopacy in the cathedral on March 19, the feast day of St. Joseph, the patron saint of the diocese, by the apostolic delegate, the Most Reverend Diomede Falconio, the same prelate who had ordained Delany, in the presence of a huge throng that included high church and civic leaders.

Changes in Emigration Patterns

Like his predecessors, Bishop Guertin had to deal with, for many years, the flood of immigration. Catholic population in the United States grew from 6,259,000 in 1880, to 16,363,000 in 1910, to over 20,000,000 in 1930. Until 1896, most immigrants came from Northern and Western Europe. By 1907, the year of Bishop Guertin's episcopal ordination, 80.7 percent came from the south and east, from countries such as Italy, Poland, Hungary, and the Slavic lands. Responding negatively, immigration to the United States was progressively restricted by Congress by laws passed in 1921 and 1924. As no quotas were imposed on hemisphere migration, French Canadians continued to enter the United States in considerable numbers until the Great Depression in late 1929.

In New Hampshire, the change in Catholic population can be traced by censuses. In a special federal census in 1907, it was determined that there were 127,613 Catholics in the state. By 1923, the number of Catholics had risen to 141,439, and by 1929 to 153,846.

By 1933, the Catholic population had declined to 146,967, because of the return of many French Canadians to Canada as a result of high unemployment in New Hampshire and the migration of other Catholics to states considered to be less affected by the Depression. The total Catholic population of the state did not exceed that of 1929 until 1935.

Continued Expansion of Catholicism

One effect of the growth in population was the need for additional parishes. Between 1907 and 1926, sixteen new parishes were created. Seven of these were in communities previously without a Catholic parish. Seven more of the sixteen were national parishes: Five French Canadian and two Polish. The two Polish parishes were St. Stanislaus, Nashua (1908); and St. Joseph, Claremont (1920).

During the period 1907–1932, the Catholic school population in New Hampshire rose steadily from 13,178 to 22,487. By 1932, there were fifteen high schools with 1,060 students conducted by five religious communities, and sixty-three grammar schools, taught by eleven religious orders.

Three communities of women religious entered the diocese during this period: the Sisters of Joan of Arc (1919), the Sisters of St. Joseph (1926), and the Sisters of St. Martha (1928). The Sisters of both Joan of Arc and St. Martha were introduced as domestic nuns, primarily to care for priests in their rectories. Two communities of men were added as well: The Oblates of Mary Immaculate (1921) and the Missionary Fathers of La Salette (1928).

World War I, 1914–1918

While two events of the early twentieth century—one religious and one partly secular—the crisis over Modernism and the Mexican Revolution— had little or no effect on the Catholic Church in New Hampshire, World War I profoundly affected that Christian community.

Until the actual entrance of the United States into the war, many within the two largest ethnic groups in the Catholic Church in the United States, the Irish and the German, tended to lean toward the Central Powers, and against the Allies, the first because of the persecution of the Irish by the English and the desire for the independence of Ireland, the second because of their attachment to their mother country.

Once war was declared by Congress against Germany, on April 6, 1917, and against Austria-Hungary, on December 7, 1917, American Catholics overwhelmingly rallied to the cause of the Allies.

New Hampshire contributed more than 20,000 people to the armed services; 697 gave their lives to the cause. It has been estimated that nationwide approximately one million Catholics were among the 4,781,172 who served in the armed forces. Only 4 of the 3,989 identified conscientious objectors in the nation were Catholics, and no pacifist priest or bishop was discovered during that war.

While there are no precise statistics available, there are indications that the proportion of Catholics who served in the armed forces surpassed their ratio in the total population of American young men. Many young Catholics felt they had to prove they were faithful Americans.

Bishop Guertin's attitude toward war in general, which certainly included World War I when it broke out, was expressed in an address to the Sheridan Guards on May 6, 1908: "You can have all the Hague conferences for peace that you like, but as there has always been war, there always will be war, but we must limit war as much as we can, and we must at all times be prepared for war." He went on to admonish them. ". . . I want to see you walk straight, aim straight, and when you have to shoot in defense of your country, shoot straight." Bishop Guertin's rather awkward English in this instance simply veiled a truly committed patriotic heart.

The needs of the men and women in the armed services were met by a variety of organizations such as the Red Cross, the YMCA, the Salvation Army, the Jewish Welfare Board, and the Knights of Columbus. This last organization maintained "huts" where all were welcome, and provided recreational facilities, offices, and chapels at 250 centers overseas and 360 stateside. These were staffed by 2,000 "secretaries" and 27,000 volunteers. The Knights of Columbus in Manchester raised $23,700 for the effort.

Catholics participated generously in the purchase of bonds to finance the war. Five huge bond issues were floated. The first four were known as "liberty loans," and the last after the war was over was called the "Victory loan." Bishop Guertin was among the bigger investors; the cathedral parish, for example, invested $15,000 in the fourth loan, and the bishop himself purchased a $5 War Savings stamp for each boy and girl in the cathedral parish schools from the fifth grade up.

The Spanish Influenza 1918

In the fall of 1918, even before the end of the fighting in World War I, a pandemic catastrophe of Spanish influenza overspread a good part of the world, including the United States. About one-fourth of the American population was stricken, and almost 500,000 died of the disease.

In New Hampshire, there were from 2,000 to 2,500 deaths; 434 of these were recorded in Manchester. This ordeal brought forth heroic manifestations of public and private charity. Among the Catholic organizations that gave more than generous assistance were the Notre Dame Emergency Hospital, the Knights of Columbus, and the Circle National Club, a French Canadian private club.

The closing of the schools gave the women religious liberty to assist in the care of the sick in the pesthouses, hospitals, and private households. Seven priests died as a direct result of the epidemic: two in Nashua and one each in Manchester, Dover, Plymouth, Hillsborough, and Newmarket. Four were associate pastors and the other three were pastors without associates; no pastor with an associate died during the epidemic.

It is some interest to note that the Spanish flu was not Spanish in origin but, most likely, American. Virologists believe they have traced its origin to hogs in South Carolina. An American soldier from that state carrying the virus spread it nearly around the world; he did not survive, along with some 21 to 26 million others.

Americanization 1918

One of the effects of World War I was a strong and sustained program to Americanize immigrants that involved adults as well as children. Principles on Americanization were adopted at a meeting of the governors of states and chairmen of Committees on Public Safety, which was convened in Washington in April 1918 by the Secretary of the Interior.

In New Hampshire, the principles concerning schools were interpreted by a Committee on Americanization composed of fourteen members. Three, possibly four, of the committee members were Catholic; one was the superintendent of Catholic schools, the Reverend Patrick J. Scott, and another was a Manchester lawyer, Wilfrid J. Lessard.

Bishop Guertin accepted the interpretation proposed by the New Hampshire committee: (1) all schools were to use English exclusively in the teaching of reading, writing, spelling, grammar, arithmetic, geography, physiology, history, political economy, music, and drawing. English was also to be the administrative language of schools. (2) The exclusive use of English for purposes of instruction and administration was not intended to prohibit the use of a foreign language for the teaching of religion or for conducting religious exercises. (3) A foreign language could be taught in primary schools, if the program outlined by the Department of Public Instruction, or its equivalent, was put into practice.

Bishop Guertin also endorsed a program of evening classes for adults who did not know English or were deficient in it. While the bishop's decisions were accepted in some French Canadian quarters, others expressed reservations or rejected them outright as a capitulation to the "anglicizers."

These bitter and sharp divisions of conviction on the teaching language to be used in the parochial schools of national parishes added another explosive issue to the continuing confrontation between the bishop and his partisans on one side and the unyielding French Canadians on the other.

In recognition for his work as a member of the Committee on Americanization, and for his other services to the Church, Bishop Guertin, on November 19, 1919, appointed attorney Wilfrid J. Lessard as diocesan superintendent of schools, to replace Father Scott, who had resigned for reasons of health. Attorney Lessard became the first layman to serve in that capacity in the history of Catholic education in the United States; he occupied that position until 1932, that is, until shortly after Bishop Guertin's death. Because of his identification with Bishop Guertin and his policies, he became one of the major targets in the Irish–French Canadian controversies.

Prohibition, Woman Suffrage, and Child Labor

Catholics were also involved in at least three other issues that were debated nationally in the early twentieth century: Prohibition, woman suffrage, and child labor.

On the first issue, Catholics leaned more toward moral suasion, that is, to temperance rather than Prohibition, although there were exceptions. That drinking was a problem among some New Hampshire Catholics cannot be doubted, however. The periodic admonitions of the bishop and the diocesan magazine, *The Guidon*, against excessive drinking amply corroborate this judgment. Father Delany, in a sermon before he was appointed bishop, even called saloon keepers "the devil's henchmen." Yet the editorial policy of *The Guidon* was against Prohibition.

After the 18th amendment, the Volstead Act, went into effect nationally on January 16, 1920, some churchmen, including William Cardinal O'Connell of Boston, worked for its repeal. Eventually, recognizing its unworkability, the 21st amendment, repealing Prohibition, was ratified in 1933.

Woman suffrage was also an issue in New Hampshire. When the proposal to amend the constitution of the state to allow woman suffrage was placed on the ballot in the election of March 10, 1903, *The Guidon* firmly opposed it. In a rather lengthy comment on the topic, marshaling reasons for not giving women the right to vote, *The Guidon* concluded that voting was not an absolute right of women, nor was it an essential part of citizenship. Nowhere does the constitution guarantee this right, and universal suffrage, it observed, never prevailed in this or in any other country. On the subject of the oratorical powers of women, a skill needed by politicians, it conceded that some were capable of making good speeches but that like Samuel Johnson it believed: "A woman making a speech is like a dog walking on its hind legs. The wonder is not that it does it well, but that it can do it at all." Naturally, *The Guidon* rejoiced in the defeat of the proposed state amendment.

New Hampshire finally passed the 19th Amendment to the Constitution of the United States, granting woman suffrage, on September 19, 1919. It was finally ratified by the nation on August 26, 1920, and for the first time women voted in a national election.

Many other Catholics opposed the amendment until the end, including James Cardinal Gibbons, archbishop of Baltimore, who feared a confusion of sex roles and the diversion of women from their proper sphere in the home.

A French Canadian priest-author and poet living in Manchester, Father Henri Beaudé, whose pen name was Henri d'Arles, in addition to sharing Cardinal Gibbons's evaluation, saw woman suffrage as a pernicious introduction of Anglo–Saxon ideas into the French Canadian character, a deviation much deplored, he said, by certain eminent members of the clergy in the province of Quebec.

Catholics were also divided on a third issue, child labor. National statistics show that in 1900, one of every five children between the ages of ten and fifteen was gainfully employed. A New Hampshire child labor law passed in 1905 raised the full-time working age to fourteen, but many youths falsified their age in order to find work, and government officials did very little to enforce it.

Bills proposed in the federal legislature to curb child labor in the early 1900s were either defeated by Congress or declared unconstitutional by the Supreme Court.

In 1924, Congress finally succeeded in passing a constitutional amendment giving it "the power to limit, regulate and prohibit the labor of persons under eighteen years of age." While New Hampshire approved the amendment, on May 17, 1933, it never won enough states for ratification. Catholics were divided pro and con on the amendment. One of the leaders against the amendment was Cardinal O'Connell of Boston, who called the proposal "nefarious and bolshevik."

Catholic opposition, such as that of Cardinal O'Connell, was based on the power that it gave the federal government over youths and education; the encroachment upon the proper spheres of state governments; and, more fundamentally, the infringements on individual and parental rights.

The main factors in bringing child labor slowly under some control of the law were compulsory school attendance, increasing the age at which children could leave school, raising the degree of academic proficiency required, and lengthening the school year.

The Labor Strikes of 1922

Another issue involving labor reached the explosion point in February 1922. This was a strike of some 17,000 workers against the Amoskeag Manufacturing Company and the Stark Mills in Manchester. Similar strikes, for essentially the same reasons, were called at mills in Nashua, Dover, Somersworth, Exeter, Newmarket, Allenstown, and Pembroke.

For reasons that are too numerous and complex to discuss here, the New England textile industry had been losing ground to the South since as early as 1910. Many northern manufacturers, including the Amoskeag Manufacturing Company, responded to worsening market conditions after World War I by continuing to vote substantial dividends for the stockholders, subsidized by reducing wages for the workers.

On December 6, 1920, for example, the Amoskeag management announced that it was reducing wages by 22.5 percent, shortening the work week to three days until further notice, and completely closing the mills for two previously unscheduled and unpaid weeks.

Another drastic announcement was posted in all workrooms of the

Amoskeag on February 2, 1922. It read that beginning Monday, February 13, 1922, a reduction in wages of 20 percent would go into effect in all hour and price rates in all departments and that, at the same time, the work week would be increased from forty-eight to fifty-four hours. The new schedule made no exceptions for women and youths. At the time, New Hampshire was one of thirteen states that allowed the fifty-four-hour work week. Only three limited it to forty-eight, and eight, mostly in the South, permitted sixty hours.

The decision either to accept the Amoskeag terms or to go out on strike was placed before the workers in a vote supervised by the United Textile Workers of America (UTW), on February 10, 1922. According to the tabulations of the UTW, 12,150 of the 17,000 eligible workers participated in the vote: 12,032 to reject the company decision, and fewer than 200 to accept it.

Thus began the first prolonged strike in the history of Manchester. This strike did not begin to break up until June 5, when one mill was opened on the conditions set by the Amoskeag. It was finally brought to a conclusion by the capitulation, on company terms, of the UTW and by those still out on strike in a vote taken Sunday, November 26, 1922.

In addition to similar strikes in the New Hampshire communities already mentioned, other strikes against textile mills were called in Rhode Island and in Lowell and Lawrence, Massachusetts.

This strike inflicted much hardship on a high proportion of the people of the New Hampshire cities and towns where they took place and induced many to leave, some temporarily and others permanently. Some individuals and many groups were either mandated or voluntarily attempted to mediate the strike in order to bring it to an end, including the Manchester Ministerial Association, an organization composed of Protestant clergy.

All conciliation efforts failed primarily because the employers, on the one hand, would not negotiate on either hours or wages and the strikers, on the other hand, refused to arbitrate the question of hours: That is, they held to the forty-eight-hour week.

There were a few attempts by representatives of the Catholic Church to negotiate the strike but they were no more successful than the Protestant ministers or secular agencies. The first attempt took place on February 9, just one week after the Amoskeag posted the notices concerning the reduction in wages and the increase in hours, and four days before these new regulations were to go into effect.

On that day, Bishop Guertin met with some Catholic clergy at the cathedral rectory to discuss what action should be taken by the church in this matter. After discussion, it was decided that Bishop Guertin would write a letter to be published in the three Manchester daily newspapers the following evening, Friday, February 10, urging a meeting or conference of the employers and employees with a view to a mutual understanding and agreement before Monday morning, February 13, the day when the salary and hour changes were to go into effect.

They also decided that nothing was to be said about this subject from the church pulpits on Sunday, except to communicate what the bishop might send to the priests. This decision was taken to prevent the clergy from advising the people differently on this issue. While the reason for silencing the parish priests was sound, one of its effects was to give the impression that they did not care enough to become involved. Nothing, however, came of the bishop's initiative. The day after this secret meeting convoked by the bishop, the Amoskeag workers voted overwhelmingly in favor of a strike.

Despite pleas repeated time after time by various parties for him to become involved, Bishop Guertin kept a relatively low profile during the strike until virtually the end. One exception was an appeal read in the Catholic churches of Manchester on March 19, the feast of St. Joseph, patron of the worker and the diocese, and published in the press, in which he again pleaded with both the employers and employees to meet soon for a frank and amicable discussion of the causes of the situation in order to reach an early settlement. Like all other initiatives, this one had no apparent effect.

A second exception to Bishop Guertin's policy of non-intervention was to receive in August a delegation representing the strikers to discuss the situation. As this meeting was off the record, nothing is known about what was said by either side.

In late June, a citizens' strike-mediating committee of ten was appointed jointly by the mayor, the president of the chamber of commerce, and two other prominent Manchester residents. This committee included at least four Catholics; among these four was the Reverend John J. Lyons, pastor of St. Anne parish.

When this committee failed to gain its objective, it was disbanded on

October 4, and replaced by another appointed by Mayor George E. Trudel in accordance with the vote of the Board of Mayor and Aldermen. There were several Catholics on this committee as well. It, too, failed.

An ever-widening breach in the united front of the strikers was opened when the Amoskeag Manufacturing Company decided to resume operations in its Coolidge mill on June 5, under the conditions posted February 2, 1922. Similar decisions were made at the Nashua mills and the Jackson mills in Nashua, and the Pacific mills in Dover. This decision was taken mainly because the governor promised to provide protection by the National Guard to the workers who entered the mills.

Opening the Coolidge mill added violence and an intensification of demonstrations in the mill area, and many protesting strikers were arrested. Nevertheless, the number of strikers returning to work slowly began to rise throughout the summer. Women, who most likely experienced the worst of the effects of the strike through the misery of their children, were the first to enter the gates of the Amoskeag.

Another blow to the union was struck on September 10 when the Amoskeag announced that wages were being raised to those prevalent prior to February 13, 1922; that is, they were being increased by 20 percent for both day and piece work. By October the number of Amoskeag working employees had increased to 7,500, despite the continuing strike.

For his part, Bishop Guertin did not take an active public role in the mediation of the strike until Saturday, October 21. On that day he was able to convene a meeting of representatives of both the employers and the employees at the cathedral residence, their first acknowledged face-to-face encounter since the beginning of the strike the previous February. This parley did not change the position of either side.

After considering the positions taken by both sides, Bishop Guertin then presented a proposal for the settlement of the strike. In essence, he submitted that: the working hours be reduced from fifty-four to fifty-one per week, subject to review no later than February 1, 1923; no discrimination would be exercised against the Amoskeag employees still on strike; and none as well by the strikers against those who had gone back to work since June 5. An answer was requested on the proposal by each party on or before November 1, 1922. At about the same time, the bishop sent a pastoral letter to all parishes in Manchester asking Catholics to pray for the settlement of the strike.

Bishop Guertin's proposal was accepted by ballot by the rank and file but was rejected by management. Despite another meeting of union officials with Bishop Guertin the week following the vote, he made no further public efforts to end the strike.

With the Amoskeag holding the upper hand with seventeen of the corporation's twenty main mills operating, at least in part, with 8,300 functioning looms as of November 1, 1922, the strike was coming to an end. The capitulation of the strikers against the Suncook mills on November 15, and those against the Somersworth and Dover mills not long afterward, on the basis of the fifty-four-hour week, added to the discouragement of those in Manchester still on strike.

Keenly aware of the sacrifices and suffering endured by the strikers and their families, the United Textile Workers union recommended, on November 25, that the strike be brought to an end. On Sunday, November 26, the strikers voted in favor of calling off the strike by a margin of three to one.

Efforts to enact a forty-eight-hour work week in the state legislature proved unsuccessful. The New Hampshire House passed such a bill, but the Senate killed it. A well-organized farm lobby contributed to this defeat because farmers believed that such a law would make it impossible for them to successfully operate their farms.

La Sentinelle, French-Irish Strife

Certainly the most unfortunate and corrosive event that took place during the episcopacy of Bishop Guertin were the clashes between the French Canadians and the Irish, and among the French Canadians themselves. These bitter quarrels that reached their crest in the late 1920s and early 1930s are generally referred to as *La Sentinelle* movement.

Despite sharing the same Catholic faith, the Irish and the French Canadians soon entered into confrontation after the latter began arriving in New England in large numbers after the Civil War. There were a good number of reasons for this, not the least being major cultural differences, competition on the economic plane, and rivalry for control of the Catholic Church, including the episcopacy, the latter being paramount in the minds of many.

That the Irish clergy was divided on the subject of Bishop Guertin cannot be seriously questioned. Moreover, the Diocese of Manchester was further sundered when the French Canadian clergy eventually split into two camps, the partisans of Bishop Guertin and that of his foes. This animosity among the French Canadian priests descended to name-calling: The partisans of the bishop were derisively labeled *"pur laines"* (pure wool), and those opposed to him were scornfully called *"les fessiers"* (the buttocks). The French Canadian laity reflected the cleavage in the clergy with a number taking leadership roles against Bishop Guertin. Tensions and conflicts between French Canadians and the Irish had not been uncommon during the latter part of the nineteenth and the early part of the twentieth century. These confrontations were virtually suspended during World War I, only to be revived during the mid-1920s.

At least three of the complaints of the French Canadians had their genesis in Rhode Island: a campaign to raise funds in favor of the diocesan Catholic high schools of the Diocese of Providence, in which each parish had a quota to meet, which was perceived as forced support of schools that would anglicize French Canadian youths; a controversy over the management of a hospital operated by French Canadians; and the mandate to all parishes to pay for a specified number of subscriptions to the diocesan newspaper, which was regarded as foreign to the language and concerns of the French Canadians.

There were many other grievances as well, such as the small number of French Canadians in diocesan administration, the conviction that the Irish bishops of New England were limiting the number of French Canadian seminarians and priests, and the annual assessment on the parishes in favor of the bishops' national organization, the National Catholic Welfare Conference, which was judged to be in favor of the assimilation of the various ethnic groups. To this basic list of grievances were added several more stemming from local conditions within each New England diocese.

A newspaper founded in Rhode Island in 1924, called *La Sentinelle*, assumed the role of paladin of the French Canadian cause. This newspaper's vindication of French Canadian grievances was carried out, impartial observers would agree, with insults, outrageous language, attacks on the character and private lives of individuals, and outright inaccuracies.

La Sentinelle spread more intensely and widely into the Dioceses of Manchester, Fall River, and Springfield, largely because of the support of a good number of priests of strong character and like mind. Manchester had another link to the Rhode Island newspaper: One of the strongest supporters of *La Sentinelle* and its policies was Mr. Elphège Daignault, a lawyer, and president of l'Association Canado-Américaine (ACA), based in Manchester.

The situation came to a head in Rhode Island when Mr. Daignault, in consort with about sixty others from ten parishes, sued Bishop William A. Hickey of Providence before the Superior Court of the state. The basic purpose of the suit was to prevent parish corporations from following the orders of the bishop to withdraw money from parish funds for diocesan high schools, the Providence Catholic newspaper, and the support of the national conference of Catholic bishops in Washington.

A Rhode Island Superior Court, and subsequently the state Supreme Court, ruled against Mr. Daignault and his associates. On May 4, 1928, the official publication of the Holy See, the *Acta Apostolicae Sedis*, informed the public that Mr. Daignault and all those who had gone to civil court against Bishop Hickey had been excommunicated, and that *La Sentinelle* had been placed on the *Index*.

L'Association Canado-Américaine in Manchester had become deeply involved in these controversies. In mid-December 1924, while attending a convention of a federation of twenty-five French Canadian organizations in Connecticut, the ACA refused to support a resolution to disassociate the federation from a campaign conducted by *La Sentinelle* that was basely insulting and injurious to Bishop Hickey of Providence.

When the officers of the ACA refused to make a retraction of their position at the request of Bishop Guertin, claiming that he was misinformed, the bishop withdrew the chaplains at all levels of that organization in the state of New Hampshire.

Surprisingly, no other bishop in New England, including the archbishop of the Metropolitan See, Cardinal O'Connell, supported his Manchester colleague by taking similar actions. Bishop Guertin stood alone.

The ACA did not make its peace with the Diocese of Manchester until 1936—that is, only after Mr. Daignault and the other excommunicated members made their peace with the church (1929), Bishop Guertin had died (1931), and Mr. Daignault was no longer president of the organization.

In addition to some sixty people excommunicated in Rhode Island, two priests of the Diocese of Manchester, both associate pastors, were suspended by the Holy See for their activities during the *Sentinelle* crisis. Before being reinstated, they were obliged to make an act of submission to the Sacred Congregation of the Council in Rome and to Bishop Guertin, and to apologize in writing to the parishioners of St. Martin, Somersworth, where they had been stationed. Their letter, which was read at every Mass on a Sunday, asked pardon for the abuse of their preaching ministry, their conduct toward the pastor, and the use of their influence to incite division and hatred among the Catholics of that city.

One of the suspended priests had served in Somersworth from 1922 to 1927, and the other far more briefly, from February 28, 1926, to an unspecified date the following year. Understandably perhaps, neither one ever gave a public reason or account of his role in *La Sentinelle*. After their reconciliation to the Holy See and with Bishop Guertin, they led long productive ministries in the diocese.

In historical impartiality, one should examine the accusation made by *La Sentinelle* and others that the Irish held a near monopoly on all the major diocesan positions in the dioceses of New England. A review of the personnel assignments in the Diocese of Manchester for the past 113 years, that is, since its creation in 1884, discloses that the complaint was not without foundation. Without going into specifics, a more diverse administration began in the 1960s, with a few prior exceptions. Since the sixties, the diocesan leadership has been free of ethnic preference. It is hoped that the lessons of the past will smooth the path for the new Catholic immigrants, such as those from numerous Latin American countries, Vietnam, and elsewhere.

Division in the Polish Community

An even more distressing division in the Diocese of Manchester occurred in 1915: the sundering of the Polish Catholic community. In that year, the Reverend Stephen Plaza, an assistant at St. Hedwig's, Manchester, from November 10, 1914, to February 1, 1915, led a sizable number of the members of that parish in founding an independent community.

The grievances of the Polish people were in many respects similar to those of the French Canadians. Among them were disputes over the ownership of church property, the right to appoint or select their own pastors, and the appointment of Polish bishops by the Holy See.

In 1930, the Polish community that separated from St. Hedwig parish, now called Holy Trinity parish, united with the Polish National Catholic

Church. In 1950, that parish became the seat of the Eastern diocese of the Polish National Catholic Church.

That division, caused in large measure by a lack of understanding by the then Catholic leadership of the diocese of the culture, character, and aspirations of many of the Polish people, still lingers today. However, since the end of the Second Vatican Council (1965), relations between the two churches have improved considerably.

The Missionary Rosebushes of Ste. Thérèse

Just a few days before the official end of the Amoskeag strike, on November 22, 1922, a young woman founded in Manchester an apostolic work that was to be of no little consequence to the missionary effort of the church.

On that day, Irene Farley, who had been healed of tuberculosis through the intercession of the yet to be canonized Thérèse of Lisieux, established an organization to which she gave the rather charming but somewhat ambiguous title of Missionary Rosebushes of Ste. Thérèse .

From its inception, the dominant purpose of the society has been the nurturing and expansion of native clergy throughout the mission lands of the church. At the time of her death on February 17, 1961, she had raised $850,000 for the missions. This money contributed to the education of close to eight hundred native priests, and to the financial support of approximately four hundred seminarians then preparing for priestly ordination.

In order to support her apostolate in behalf of seminarians in mission lands and to ensure its future, Miss Farley spent a great deal of time trying to establish a religious order of women. Despite her efforts, she never succeeded. Several women joined her over the years but none appeared to measure up to her standards and expectations. Miss Farley led a very austere life, spending much of her time in prayer and in her ministry, but little money on food, dress, and housing. Not one of her candidates was able to persevere. After her death, mainly because of her exhausting dedication to the missionary work of the church and singular self-mortification, many recommended that her cause be presented for canonization. In anticipation of a possible future effort of this kind, oral histories by her associates, family, and friends have been collected, as have the available archives pertaining to her work. (The oral histories were gathered by Miss Eileen Bruton, who is now a Sister Adorer of the Precious Blood in Brooklyn, New York. All the materials mentioned are in the archives of the Sister Adorers of the Precious Blood in Manchester.)

Following Miss Farley's sudden death in 1961, the Missionary Rosebush Society was confided to dedicated laywomen until 1972. Principal among these was Mrs. Charlotte Farley, a sister-in-law of Irene Farley. On March 1, 1972, the Sisters of the Precious Blood of Manchester, a cloistered order, accepted responsibility for continuing this apostolate.

From its foundation in November 1922 to December 1996, slightly less than $5 million has been sent to the missions, 2,268 scholarships for native seminarians have been established, and at least 2,091 priests have been ordained with some financial assistance from the society. Five of this number are now bishops, and two more are archbishops. This society is still active today.

Anti-Catholicism Renewed

Bishop Guertin's episcopacy, like that of all his predecessors, was not free of anti-Catholicism. One small flare-up began around 1907. By 1914 there were said to be some sixty anti-Catholic journals published in the United States, and several anti-Catholic organizations, such as the Guardians of Liberty, founded in 1911, and the American Minute Men. These anti-Catholic campaigns were brought to a halt by World War I, as the Know-Nothing movement had been by the Civil War.

Anti-Catholicism became more blatant again in the 1920s. The spearhead this time was the Ku Klux Klan. By 1925, this organization claimed from 4 million to 5 million members. The Klansmen had a long list of enemies, including African Americans and Jews as well as Catholics.

The Klan is credited as one of the forces that defeated Alfred E. Smith, a Catholic candidate for the presidency at the Democratic National Convention in 1924, and with having a not inconsequential role in defeating him for the presidency in 1928.

New Hampshire, Vermont, and Rhode Island were never strongholds of the KKK. Little is known about its activities in New Hampshire, as the subject has yet to be studied in detail by competent researchers. It is known, however, that a house on South Main Street in Rochester served as the headquarters of the KKK for New Hampshire, Maine, and Vermont, from February to October 1924.

While New Hampshire had but few African Americans in the 1920s and a small number of Jews, their favorite targets, the KKK did find a plenitude of Catholics, some 30 percent of the population, on which to vent their bigotry and animosity.

It is known that, at least on occasion, the Ku Klux Klan would attend the Sunday services in a selected Rochester Protestant church in full regalia, and contributed, it is said, sizably to the collection. They were advised, however, to hold their cross-burning ritual out of town so as not to upset the sensibilities of some of the residents of Rochester. Subsequently, they moved this activity north to Farmington. By the 1920s there were two Catholic churches in Rochester, St. Mary (founded in 1872) and Holy Rosary (founded in 1883). Farmington, on the other hand, did not become a parish until 1920, and the first church, St. Peter, was not dedicated until December 2, 1924. Thus, the raising of a cross to the sky on the Catholic church in Farmington just preceded the burning of another on the ground by the KKK.

The Presidential Election of 1928

Loosely connected with the anti-Catholicism of the 1920s was the defeat of Alfred E. Smith for the presidency of the United States. Mr. Smith was a Catholic and a prominent Democrat in the state of New York and on the national level. His loss nationwide to the Republican Herbert E. Hoover in November 1928 was by a landslide. In the popular vote it was 21,392,190 to 15,016,443; in the electoral college the margin was 444 to 87. New Hampshire was one of the then forty-eight states won by Mr. Hoover.

While many issues were involved in Alfred E. Smith's defeat, two, in particular, attracted considerable attention. One was precisely his Catholic faith, which he professed publicly, and the other was his opposition to Prohibition. The national prohibition of alcohol had been in effect since the passage of the 18th amendment to the Constitution on January 16, 1919. This amendment had been ultimately approved by every state in the union, with the exception of Connecticut and Rhode Island. (Rhode Island, it should be remembered, has the highest percentage of Catholics of all the states in the Union; that of Connecticut is considerable as well.)

Alfred E. Smith's candidacy aroused a great deal of interest, and even more emotion, in some quarters. Some of the interest and emotions were highly in his favor, and some were strongly against him. For large numbers of Catholics, his election would have been interpreted as a public acceptance of their patriotism and loyalty to the nation. These commitments, it was clear to them, had been challenged and repudiated successively by the Nativists, the Know-Nothings, the American Protective Association, the Ku Klux Klan, and many other groups and individuals. A resolution of this hypersensitive issue would not come until John F. Kennedy was elected president in 1960.

In order to ensure maximum Catholic support for Smith in 1928, the bishops and clergy urged (a word that meant "ordered" in those days) the religious—men and women—to register and to vote. Prior to this time, it would have been considered a highly unacceptable secular activity for women religious to participate in the political process by voting. Entering into their reluctance, would certainly have been the fact that women had only been given the franchise in national elections by the 19th amendment ratified on August 26, 1920, that is just eight years and a few days prior to the Hoover-Smith presidential contest. Moreover, many in the Catholic leadership in this country, as well as in New Hampshire, were adamantly against giving women the right to vote, some of them even seeing this as unnatural to their feminine gender. Bishop Delany's thoughts on the subject have been recorded earlier.

To facilitate their voting, Catholic laymen, and the small number of women who had driving licenses at the time, were enlisted to shuttle the nuns between the convent and the polling station. This writer's father was among those volunteers. While no contemporary narrative of this election day has been found, it can reasonably be said that the sight of these women in a group, dressed in yards of black, blue, brown, gray, and other mournful colors, their faces in great part hidden by wimples and veils, startled more than a few in many of the small towns across the nation. On a whimsical note, one can wonder if any of the nuns rebelled against the regimentation and voted for Hoover!

Whether Herbert E. Hoover or Alfred E. Smith was best suited for the presidency at that time will, of course, never be resolved. Alfred E. Smith was never given the chance; Herbert E. Hoover was in office on Black Thursday, October 29, 1929, the day of the crash of the stock market, and presided over the Great Depression until he was replaced by Franklin D. Roosevelt at noon on March 4, 1933.

The Stock Market Crash of 1929

Bishop Guertin's final years of episcopacy coincided with yet another calamity—the stock market crash of October 29, 1929, which marked the beginning of the most severe economic depression in American history. By the end of 1931, almost 10 million wage earners were unemployed; two years later there were 13 million—that is, one worker out of four.

This depression did not truly come to an end until the beginning of World War II in Europe, in 1939. It had serious consequences for the Catholic Church, as it did for every other sector of American life.

The Death of the Third Bishop

It was during these difficult times that the troubled life of Bishop Guertin came to an end. Signs of physical deterioration seem to have shown themselves as early as 1925. This physical deterioration, as in the case of some illnesses, appears to have been accompanied by gradually advancing psychiatric difficulties.

In 1931, Bishop Guertin's condition worsened to the point that his physician sent him to a psychiatric clinic in Morristown, New Jersey, where he died at 3:35 A.M. on Thursday, August 6, 1931, away from home and with only one New Hampshire person with him, the vicar general, Monsignor Jeremiah S. Buckley. Bishop Guertin was sixty-two.

His death certificate cites as causes of death pulmonary tuberculosis, diabetes, and arteriosclerosis. His funeral took place in the cathedral in Manchester with solemn ceremonies on August 11, and he was buried in the crypt with his two predecessors.

Misfortune followed Bishop Guertin to the end. He was sealed into his crypt below the main altar of St. Joseph Cathedral wearing his valuable ceremonial episcopal ring rather than a simple one, as had been intended by the then vicar general.

At some period between the final illness of Bishop Guertin and the installation of Bishop Peterson, or perhaps before or shortly thereafter, the archives of the former were sanitized. That is, much of the information concerning Bishop Guertin's years as ordinary was destroyed. For one major example, all the correspondence between the diocese on the one hand and the apostolic delegate or the Holy See on the other before 1933 has been removed from the archives. The same is true for other crucial files. The information they contained remains unknown.

A 'Run' on the Amoskeag Savings Bank

An incident during the interregnum—between the death of Bishop Guertin and the arrival of his successor, Bishop Peterson, in New Hampshire (see next chapter)—requires special mention. This was a brief financial panic that involved a 'run' on the funds of one of the most trusted institutions in the state, the Amoskeag Savings Bank. This bank was then located in the heart of downtown Manchester at the corner of Hanover and Elm Streets diagonally across from City Hall.

This run has its place in a diocesan history for several reasons. Among these were that a large number of Catholics, most from the working class, banked at the Amoskeag, and that several prominent Catholics, including the clergy, made determined efforts to protect it from financial harm or even bankruptcy. This incident was also an indication of the growing financial impact that the Catholics of Manchester (and of many other New Hampshire communities as well) had on the economy of the region, an impact readily recognized by the banks.

The difficulties of the Amoskeag Savings Bank began against the background of the economic depression that had been gradually crushing the nation. One aspect of this crisis was the failure of a large number of banks across the United States and the world. One such failure, in fact, occurred directly across the street from the Amoskeag Banks (savings and national) on June 9, 1930. On that day, the state bank commissioner closed the Merrimack River Savings Bank, which resulted in the loss of approximately 50 percent of the savings of the depositors, a great misfortune not lost on or forgotten by the citizens of Manchester and its neighboring towns.

It was in this climate of uneasiness and fiscal suspicion that the Manchester newspapers carried reports concerning the acute financial problems of the Amoskeag Manufacturing Company, by far the largest employer in Manchester. This company, as we shall see, was to fail in 1935.

Because of the shared name, Amoskeag, many believed that there was a close financial connection between the ailing Amoskeag Manufacturing Company and the Amoskeag Savings Bank. In truth, there was none, except the common name.

Consequently, on reading or hearing the information concerning the plight of the manufacturing company, depositors, believing that it was the bank or something affecting the bank, began withdrawing their money from this institution. Customers began closing their accounts in considerable numbers on Thursday, Friday, and Saturday, October 8, 9, and 10. When the bank opened again on the following Tuesday, having been closed on Sunday and Monday, Columbus Day, mobs of people descended on the bank, with Wednesday the 14th and Thursday the 15th being the busiest. With hundreds of people insisting on their money, Amoskeag Savings had to borrow cash from many sources to pay its depositors. Among the cooperating banks were several from Boston, which shipped money to Manchester by train and by truck. By the end of the panic at the close of the day on Friday, October 16, the Amoskeag had lost some $1,181,000 in deposits, an impressive amount in those days.

During the height of the panic, several means were used to reassure the public that the Amoskeag Savings Bank was completely solvent and that it had no link with the Amoskeag Manufacturing Company. Sensibly, for example, the bank had a notice from a leading officer of the manufacturing company printed in the local newspapers stating that these institutions were entirely separate and independent and had no financial connections whatsoever. Letters from the state bank commissioner, the governor, John G. Winant, and the superintendent of the public schools of the city were also made public, expressing belief in the financial soundness of the Elm Street bank. Mr. Willard D. Rank, the state bank commissioner, even attested that the bank had an excess of $1.25 for each $1.00 of deposits.

An even more convincing proof of its confidence in the Amoskeag Savings Bank was given by six other banks in Manchester, which jointly published an ad in the local newspapers in which each offered to lend any person the full amount shown on any Amoskeag Savings Bank passbook and to accept the passbook as security.

On Thursday, October 15, at the peak of the run on the bank, with hundreds inside and outside the building determined to withdraw their savings, the Amoskeag officers called on laity and clergy to address the crowd on the solvency of the institution. Among the laypeople were the state bank commissioner, a former governor, a former bank commissioner, and Mr. Adolphe Robert of the Association Franco-Américaine, a French Canadian insurance company. Mr. Albert J. Precourt and Mr. Joseph H. Geisel, both well-known Catholics and businessmen, were also very helpful in reassuring the crowd. In fact, among all those mentioned above, only the bank commissioner and the former governor were not members of the Catholic community.

To bolster their credibility, bank officials also called upon the clergy to speak to those assembled inside and outside the building waiting to withdraw their money. The Catholic priests who did so were Fathers Alphée Leclerc, pastor of Ste.-Marie parish, Aimé P. Boire, pastor of St. Augustine's, and John E. Finen, pastor of St. Anne's, all in Manchester. Fathers Leclerc and Boire, as undoubtedly requested, spoke in French; Father Finen spoke in English.

An officer of the bank who wrote a contemporary account of this incident apparently could not restrain himself from expressing some bias against the listeners by remarking: "[They] stood still but with no more animation or expression on their faces to indicate that they comprehended than a flock of sheep."

An ultimate vote of confidence in the bank by the Catholic Church in New Hampshire was expressed in a letter from Monsignor Jeremiah S. Buckley, administrator of the diocese, to the Reverend Edward A. Clark, rector of the cathedral and chancellor, dated October 15, 1931. In this letter meant for publication in the local newspapers, Monsignor Buckley, after enumerating his reasons for full confidence in the bank, stated that after examining all the facts, "I do not intend to withdraw one cent of these [the church's] funds from the Amoskeag Savings bank (sic)."

All of these efforts by the bank to explain its financial strength began to take effect (as it has been noted), on Friday, October 16, and by the next day, Saturday, the Amoskeag Savings could report more money received than paid out.

It was in this bleak atmosphere that the Catholics of New Hampshire waited for the appointment and arrival of their next bishop.

ELEVEN

From the Great Depression to World War II 1932–1944

A Fourth Bishop: John Bertram Peterson

Certainly acutely aware of the ethnic divisions and animosities existing in the Diocese of Manchester, the Holy See selected as the next bishop a person who was not identified with either of the two national groups contesting for ecclesiastical dominance—the Irish and the French Canadians. Its choice was the Most Reverend John B. Peterson, then an auxiliary bishop of Boston and pastor of St. Catherine of Genoa parish, Somerville, Massachusetts. It is not beyond possibility that Bishop Peterson's firm ruling hand, developed during twenty-five years as a seminary professor and then as a rector, was taken into account in sending him to Manchester, a diocese deeply divided along ethnic lines, where some priests and laity had either covertly or, in some cases, even openly defied Bishop Guertin. Notice of the nomination of Bishop Peterson to Manchester was received by the apostolic delegate in Washington on May 13, 1932, a full eight months after the death of Bishop Guertin. Bishop Peterson was installed at St. Joseph Cathedral in Manchester on July 14, one day before his sixty-first birthday.

John Bertram Peterson was born in Salem, Massachusetts, on July 15, 1871, the son of a Scandinavian sea captain and an Irish mother. His father is said to have been one of the last to captain sail-powered ships to ports in the Orient. John Peterson's early education was in the public elementary and high schools of the place of his birth. Upon graduation, he continued his studies in a commercial school in Boston, and then accepted employment for a few years in the offices of the Pope Manufacturing Company, also in Boston. His interest gained in business remained with him for life. For a time, he also served as a newspaper reporter.

Deciding to study for the priesthood, he attended Marist College in Van Buren, Maine, and from 1893 to 1895 he was enrolled at St. Anselm College, Manchester, New Hampshire. He then entered St. John Seminary, Brighton, Massachusetts, from which he was ordained to the priesthood on September 15, 1899, at the age of twenty-eight.

On the recommendation of the Sulpician seminary faculty, Father Peterson was sent to Europe for graduate studies, where he spent one year in Paris and another in Rome specializing in church history and related disciplines. His next twenty-five years were spent at St. John Seminary, first as a professor of church history and several other subjects, then of theology (1901–1911), and finally as rector (1911–1926). As rector, he became the first diocesan priest to hold that office. Prior to 1911, the Brighton seminary had been conducted by the Priests of St. Sulpice. Because of his personal dislike for the Sulpicians and his desire to have the seminary directed by priests from his own archdiocese, Cardinal O'Connell, with little dialogue and even less mutual agreement, forced this highly qualified group to leave.

On November 16, 1926, Father Peterson was appointed pastor of St. Catherine of Genoa parish, in Somerville, Massachusetts. In less than a year, on November 10, 1927, he was ordained auxiliary bishop of Boston by William Cardinal O'Connell, the archbishop. Bishop Guertin, an alumnus of St. John Seminary, was one of the co-consecrators. During his years at Somerville, he acquired the reputation of being a skilled administrator, educator, and canonist, and was appointed to a number of diocesan offices. In addition, some of his contemporaries have said that he was a favorite of the children of his parish in Somerville, an aspect of his demeanor that was not always evident later to the clergy of New Hampshire.

Bishop Peterson's appointment to Manchester, according to still-existing correspondence, seems to have been the result of an agreement between Bishop Peterson and Monsignor Francis J. Spellman, then working for the papal secretariat of state at the Vatican. It was obviously an agreement that fell in with the plans of the Holy See. The agreement, suggested by Bishop Peterson, was that he would be willing to accept the vacant See of Manchester in order to free the position of auxiliary in Boston for Monsignor Spellman.

Bishop Peterson's reasoning was that Monsignor Spellman, who was still a young man, should be settled where he would be near the center of ecclesiastical power and more apt to receive a promotion. This plan, in effect, was adopted by the Pope, Pius XI. From Boston, Auxiliary Bishop Spellman was promoted to archbishop of New York seven years later in 1939.

At the time of the arrival of Bishop Peterson in 1932, the Catholic population of New Hampshire stood at about 154,000. These Catholics were served by 163 diocesan priests, and 46 priests from religious orders. Eighty-five churches had resident pastors. In addition, there were forty missions, forty-four stations, and thirty-two chapels. (A station is a place where Sunday Mass is regularly celebrated that is other than a Catholic church or chapel.)

In that same year, there were 32,817 young people in Catholic institutions, including six high schools for boys and thirteen for girls, six academies for girls, sixty parish grammar schools, seven orphanages, and one college (St. Anselm). An understanding of the size of the Catholic Church in New Hampshire can be gained by noting that the second largest denomination in the state in 1936 was the Congregational Church (United Church of Christ), with 22,363 worshipers on its rolls.

The Great Depression

The Great Depression was certainly the most acute and pressing problem faced by the Catholic Church of New Hampshire upon the arrival of Bishop Peterson. His experience as a professor of economics at St. John Seminary served him in good stead in dealing with this crisis; he handled it in a firm and efficient way. Some six months after his arrival, in January 1933, he reduced all customary diocesan assessments by one-third; mandated that all but urgent expenses in the parishes be eliminated; warned that all requests for permission to build or renovate were not even to be made; and that none but essential repairs would be approved during the year. He also cautioned priests not to be beguiled into needless purchases by persuasive itinerant salesmen. In April 1934, he repeated that the era of building had unhappily come to an end, and that the mere maintenance of what was already owned would severely burden diocesan resources.

Concern in the community at large over the effects of the Depression on the financial solidity of the banks moved Bishop Peterson to personally announce from the cathedral pulpit, at the 8 A.M. Mass on Sunday, March 5, 1933, that the banks of Manchester were sound and that there was no cause for alarm or panic. His message was read to the congregation at all the other Masses. During the same year, Bishop Peterson urged the clergy in a letter to make every effort to encourage fidelity to Sunday Mass. His fear was, he explained, that some people were absenting themselves because of embarrassment at their poor appearance or their inability to contribute as generously as of old.

Seat Money and Collections

Bishop Peterson's admonition to the clergy may have been prompted by the fact that, in at least one parish in the diocese, a person entering the church on Sunday was obliged to pass through a turnstile, such as those used in subways and ball parks, where the seat money was collected; in many other churches one had to walk a gauntlet of ushers serving the same purpose at the door.

Seat money was collected in most—and perhaps all—of the Catholic parishes in New Hampshire. Frequently this was done by ushers at the entrance (as noted); in others it was done by ushers who went from pew to pew, from person to person, at the beginning of Mass. This was, of course, separate from the collection, or, in many cases, the two or more collections. Seat money was thought correctly by some to be the equivalent of the poll tax. The latter required payment to exercise a right guaranteed by the Constitution of the United States, the right to vote. Seat money violated the right of the People of God, guaranteed by the constitution of the Church, to free access to the gifts of God, among these a nonmonetary approach to the sacraments. What God gave freely appeared to be subject to an admission fee by the clergy at the door of the church.

Another noisome practice was the auctioning or sale of pews, generally for use at the parish High Mass. By paying the highest price at auction, or by paying a fixed rental price, an individual or family obtained the sole right to a specific pew at a specific church function, usually, as it has been said, at the principal Sunday Mass, the High Mass. This trick-mirrored the basic, fundamental, radical equality of all before God into a distorted image where wealth established a hierarchy of importance even in the parish church. In at least one parish, and probably in many more, a person paying seat rent was given a small ticket, or coupon, which was then returned in the collection basket at the offertory. The major purpose of the ticket transaction was for the clergy to match the number sold against the number deposited in the collection basket or plate to determine the honesty of the ushers.

Church collections also led to some bizarre practices. In most places, at the time of Bishop Peterson and long afterward, the collection (or collections—there were often two and occasionally three) was taken up by the parish priests dressed in cassock and surplice. While the ecclesiastical vesture was undoubtedly meant to show the vital link between the offering of the faithful in the pews and the sacrifice at the altar, its practical result was to shame a good number into increasing their donation because the parish priest was handling the basket and, presumably, watching. When two or more collections were made, it was often a race against time. The priest-collector(s) would kneel briefly in the church aisle during the elevations of the Body and Blood of Christ and then continue to disturb the worshipers for money to the near end of Mass. In-house ecclesiastical humor would have likely considered a "curate" who was unable to finish the mandated collections before the dismissal of the congregation as probably unfit for parish ministry.

In parishes with one priest, it was not unusual for him after the sermon to remove his chasuble and solicit with basket every person present for the offering. At summer resorts with overflow crowds this meant that the celebrant went outside with the basket so as not to exclude anyone. After the collection, Mass was resumed.

During the height of the Depression, in at least one parish (in south Manchester), the pastor would personally go from home to home on Saturday to collect the Sunday offering. A journal kept by the Sisters of the Holy Cross of that parish noted that the collection was made by the pastor in his brand-new automobile. One's sense of indignation can easily be aroused by the mental image of a new automobile parked in front of a very modest home so that the clergyman can collect the Sunday offering from a family on the dole.

It is with relief that one notes the almost total disappearance of the shameful methods used to collect seat rent and the offering. A great deal of the improvement can be attributed to the gradual return to prosperity and a growing sensitivity to the feelings of the faithful, particularly the poor. Of even greater importance were the insights gained concerning the liturgy during and after the Second Vatican Council. Even the second collection, for it has not been abandoned everywhere, is now usually gathered during the post-communion reflection rather than at the apex of the canon of the Mass.

Another practice that has been discarded is the one-hour interval between each of the Sunday Masses. Some parishes operated on this principle, often verbalized as "Get them in, get them out." This haste in the celebration was masked by the fact that the service was in Latin and the priest faced the wall. The same precipitation today in English would leave the celebrant open to the charge of impiety, at the least.

Church collections have not ceased to attract attention; the amount donated the previous week is almost invariably the first item checked in the parish bulletin, and it is also the one that generates the most comments. It is used as the primary index—the Dow Jones—to evaluate the spiritual vigor as well as the financial success of a parish. Pastors are evaluated and ranked by this index as well.

Fund-raising: Legal and Illegal

In the many parishes, and perhaps the majority during the Great Depression, the income from seat money and the collections was not sufficient to meet the minimum needs of the parish. Consequently, the raising of additional funds became a matter of grave concern, even of survival. Parish functions could no longer be held simply to create community. Rare, or perhaps even nonexistent, is the Catholic who has escaped from these fund-raising enterprises. Among them are raffles, card games, plays, movies, penny sales, bingo, dinners, dances, picnics, Monte Carlo nights, carnivals, outright gambling, and countless other schemes. Even boxing, where some skill may be exerted to physically subdue and perhaps injure another person, and professional wrestling, which has almost universally deteriorated into a spectacle of simulated brutality and the verbal insulting of another human being, have been deemed, in certain quarters, to be Christian—if not civilized—means of raising money. For children, boxing or wrestling must seem as just an extension of the mayhem they see on the cartoons that they watch on Saturday morning.

Of these fund-raisers, bingo has been the most enduring and financially successful. Its revenue has contributed greatly to the building and support of parishes, particularly along the border with Massachusetts. These games attracted busloads of people from the Bay State, where, for a long time, bingo was prohibited by law. Because of their sponsorship of this pastime, a few pastors in southern New Hampshire gained the dubious title of "Bingo King."

In some instances, the raising of additional funds by the methods previously listed skirted or even violated civil law. One good, that of the financial solidity of the church, was deemed to have priority over the other. These transgressions included the illegal mailing of raffle tickets and the use of a number of gambling machines and devices prohibited by state or local ordinance. Unfortunately, the clergy spent a disproportionate amount of time involved in these secular activities. In a few parishes, it is known that the priest-organizer, usually the curate, was paid a small percentage of the net receipts, in addition to his salary, to ensure his maximum effort and to reward him for his diligence. It is not recorded if the large number of laymen and laywomen workers were similarly compensated.

The Heart of the Matter

A rarely told story here, which can be called "The Heart of the Matter," is the remarkable generosity of the majority of the faithful in the three honored means of giving—time, talent, and treasure. In countless instances, particularly during the Depression, the giving of the laity came from the hardship of their own lives. From 1930 to roughly 1940, unemployment in the United States reached 25 percent. Many individuals and families were on charity rolls and great numbers were fully dependent on government programs such as the Work Progress Administration (the WPA, the famous initials of the 1930s). Catholic men and women gave from their need and not from their abundance.

Financial Improvement

With the sustained support of the laity, Bishop Peterson was able to report, as early as December 31, 1936, that the financial condition of the parishes and diocese had improved. He then permitted construction and extensive repair only when two-thirds of the cost was already at hand. One year later, on December 31, 1937, he reported that the new debt on all parochial property had finally passed below the $1 million mark.

By the end of December 1941 (World War II having been declared earlier in the month), Bishop Peterson was advising the clergy to take advantage of the then present prosperity to pay their debts or, where there was no debt, to improve the parish property before materials became scarce and costly. A national scramble for generally nonemergency purposes took precedence over the certain critical needs of a country already at war across two oceans, the Atlantic and the Pacific.

On March 1, 1943, he gave a report contrasting the financial condition of the diocese in 1933 with that at the end of 1942. On December 31 of the latter year, he reported that the net parish indebtedness had been reduced to $336,000. This debt was more than $1 million less than in 1933. During the same period, an even larger sum had been spent on construction and property improvements. This remarkable financial achievement is all the more praiseworthy when one takes into account the considerable damage done to church property by the flood of March 1936 and the hurricane of September 1938.

Slower Growth of the Church

One of the major effects of the Depression was the general slowing of Catholic Church growth in New Hampshire. An important factor was that immigration fell to almost nothing—from 241,700 nationwide in 1930 to 23,068 in 1933. In fact, from 1931 to 1936, more people left the United States than gained admission to it.

In the depressed industrial areas of New Hampshire, the workers either moved to more promising communities or, as in the case of many French Canadians, returned to the province of Quebec. From 1932 to 1944, the Catholic population of the state grew by only 15,350 to 169,196. During the same period, only three parishes were founded. Two of these were French Canadian national parishes: St. Theresa, Manchester (1934), and St. Joseph, Berlin (1941). However, the total number of diocesan clergy did rise from 209 (1932) to 254 (1944). In fact, during this period, a significant number of applicants for the seminary were refused. Economic hardship, in this case, was a stimulant to vocations. Among the numerous signs of stagnation and atrophy was the decrease in parish elementary school enrollment from 21,958 to 17,760 between 1932 and 1944.

Decline of the Textile Industry

Undoubtedly the weakest link in the economy of New Hampshire in the 1920s and 1930s was the textile industry, particularly the infirmities of its giant, the Amoskeag Manufacturing Company of Manchester. Bishop Peterson became personally involved on several occasions in attempts to solve the problems of that industry.

On his own initiative, Bishop Peterson successfully mediated a strike that began at the Amoskeag during the week of May 15, 1933. The major grievances of the strikers in this instance were a cut in wages ranging from 20 to 40 percent put into effect in February of that year, and the threat by management to shut down the mills without pay from May 26 to July 31. By this time, the Amoskeag workforce had fallen from a peak of over 25,500 in 1919, to about 17,000 in 1922, to just 7,500 in 1933.

After a thorough investigation into all aspects of the situation, Bishop Peterson proposed three conditions for settling the strike: (1) the reopening of the mills immediately to all who were employed at the time of the closing, (2) an immediate 15 percent pro rata increase in wages, and (3) no discrimination against anyone who had participated in the strike. This plan, which became known as "the Peterson Plan," was accepted by both the trustees of the Amoskeag and the members of the striking United Textile Workers of America by a margin of three to one.

In March and April 1935, Bishop Peterson was in Washington with a committee, apparently delegated by the state of New Hampshire, to lobby Congress in an attempt to find a solution to the plight of the ailing textile industry in New England. Governor Styles Bridges, who had been unable to attend because of illness, subsequently wrote to Bishop Peterson to highly commend him for his April presentation to the congressional textile committee. Impressed by Bishop Peterson's knowledge of and concern for the cotton industry, the governor and council, on August 9, 1935, appointed him chairman of a committee of five members, the State Textile Committee, to investigate the textile situation and to recommend solutions to the problems. One knowledgeable person, certainly reflecting the opinion of many others, evaluated the report presented by this committee as most comprehensive, enlightening, and eminently fair, showing wide study and careful thought.

This report, as penetrating as it was, did not solve the problems of the textile industry in New Hampshire, particularly those of the Amoskeag Manufacturing Company. The Amoskeag shut down operations in September 1935, with the proclaimed intention of reopening in the future. It was never able to do so. The Amoskeag finally applied for reorganization in the New Hampshire bankruptcy court in December 1935. This reorganization never came about, either.

The flood of March 1936, which destroyed or damaged a large percentage of the Amoskeag's property and machinery on the Merrimack River, made a rebirth impossible; it was the coup de grâce. Finally, in July 1936, the master of the court ordered liquidation of the Amoskeag's assets. A remnant of cotton manufacturing struggled on in Manchester until the shutdown of the Chicopee Mill on February 27, 1975.

Bishop Peterson was also a member of the Citizens Committee that took responsibility for the property and equipment of the bankrupt Amoskeag and eventually attracted to Manchester hundreds of small firms that again brought prosperity to the city.

Irish–French Canadian Tensions

Another major task facing Bishop Peterson on his arrival in New Hampshire was the reduction, if not the resolution, of the Irish–French Canadian tensions and rivalries. The French Canadian newspapers, in both New England and the province of Quebec, expressed disappointment on the choice of Bishop Peterson rather than a bishop of their own national origin, either for Manchester or for Portland, which had been vacant at about the same time. They observed with satisfaction, however, that both Bishop Peterson, named to Manchester, and Monsignor Joseph E. McCarthy, assigned to Portland, spoke French, were sympathetic to their ethnic group, were not assimilators, and were eminently qualified for episcopal office. More than a tinge of displeasure was voiced on the reappointment of Monsignor Jeremiah S. Buckley as vicar general, and of a few other Irish ecclesiastical personages. This was compensated for in part, the press continued, by the appointment of some French Canadian pastors that they approved.

Bishop Peterson made his position on the ethnic quarrels unequivocal when he stated at a civic reception in his honor in Manchester on December 13, 1932, that he would do all in his power to discourage hatreds, including ancestral hatred, racial hatred, and religious hatred, and that no cause that sought to help itself by hatred could ever expect any help from him. This sense of fairness and justice, strengthened considerably by the awe (and in some cases, fear) in which Bishop Peterson was held by virtually all the clergy, began a healing process that would last for several decades.

This sense of awe was certainly spurred by his official communications and personal letters to the clergy. On a consistent basis he dealt with them in the same manner that seminary professors and rectors did with seminarians at that time. In his letters he was curt, formal, professional, and on occasion clearly demeaning. On its side, the clergy seemed to accept this type of relationship as normal between bishop and priests.

One of Bishop Peterson's tactics in helping solve the ethnic problem seems to have been the establishment of a ratio of French, Polish, English, and what he called "neutral" priests in the diocese. Who the latter were was never described or identified. In his own hand, he calculated that he needed to ordain three French Canadians to every four English (apparently Irish) in order to maintain the then current ethnic balance. He also determined that the diocese needed—at any time—five priests of Polish ancestry, apparently no more and no less. In order to achieve the proper Polish ratio, he calculated that he needed one-half of a Polish priest every year, that is, one ordination every two years. There seems to have been no understanding, and certainly no provision made, that a priest of Polish or French Canadian descent could serve properly in an entirely English-speaking parish.

Also found in Bishop Peterson's personal papers are brief, often one-word evaluations of some twenty-seven French Canadian priests, mostly not very flattering; the designation "two-faced" is used at least once. This same paper lists all the parishes in the diocese. Each parish is given in its order of importance, from the least desirable to the most. This was the ladder that the priests had to ascend, usually by a small promotion at a time. Overall, this scale was followed very closely by Bishop Peterson.

The Fiftieth Anniversary of the Diocese

Among some other events worthy of note in the 1930s were the celebration of the fiftieth anniversary of the Diocese of Manchester and the sixty-fifth of the dedication of St. Joseph Church in April 1934. These celebrations were kept at a very low key because of the poverty and human suffering caused by the Depression. An unusual feature of the celebrations was the promotion of Bishop Peterson by Pope Pius XI to an attendant of the Papal Throne, a religious honor, and his elevation to the rank of Count of the state of Vatican City, a civic honor. He was one of a very small number of American bishops to achieve the rank of nobleman.

The Spanish Civil War

The Spanish Civil War, 1936–1939, which pitted Loyalists, backed by international communism as well as liberals in many countries, against Nationalists, led by General Francisco Franco, who espoused both fascism and a dominant role for the Catholic Church, caused serious divisions in the United States, even among Catholics. Many ecclesiastical leaders sided with the Nationalists, and the children and youths in Catholic elementary and secondary schools were often led in prayer to petition for the victory of Franco. The news of the end of this embarrassing war was received with genuine relief in the United States.

First Catholic Governor of New Hampshire

On a happier note, Francis P. Murphy, a Republican industrialist from Nashua, was elected the first Catholic governor of New Hampshire in the fall of 1936, and served for two terms until 1941. Before 1878, he would have been prohibited from holding that office by the state constitution solely because of his religion.

National Involvement of Bishop Peterson

Bishop Peterson was the first bishop of Manchester to achieve prominence at the national level. He was a frequent speaker at conventions of the National Catholic Educational Association, and served as president general of that influential organization from 1936 until his death early in 1944. His addresses to the members of that association display considerable erudition. As early as 1930, he was appointed by President Herbert Hoover to serve on a committee entrusted with the task of conducting a survey of the educational situation in the United States. He was one of seven bishops in this country selected by the Holy See in 1938 to conduct an apostolic visitation of all the seminaries and other institutions in this country engaged in preparing youths and young men for the priesthood.

In the early 1940s he was elected vice chairman of the administrative committee of the National Catholic Welfare Conference, and episcopal chairman of the department of education of that conference, both high honors in the episcopacy. He was also elected to or selected to serve in a number of less prestigious national offices.

World War II

Just as Bishop Peterson's early years as bishop of Manchester were overshadowed by the Great Depression, his final years were clouded by the threat and eventual outbreak of World War II. This war was not unexpected by him. In his expressed view, it represented a life-or-death struggle with militant materialism. From the beginning of this war, he urged clergy and laity alike to abide by all the regulations laid down by the government, and issued a number of practical directives, such as the purchase of sufficient parish insurance to cover any damage that might be caused by the enemy.

Approximately 60,000 people from New Hampshire served in the armed forces during World War II. Assuming that 32 percent of these were Catholic, the proportion of Catholics in the general population of the state at that time, some 19,200, participated as either male or female members of the Army, Navy, Marines, or Coast Guard. Another source sets the number at 21,032. Using the above 32 percent, it can be estimated that close to 500 of the 1,595 from New Hampshire who died while in military service were of the Catholic faith. Roughly forty conscientious objectors from this state have been identified—more than half were Jehovah's Witnesses.

One of the primary preoccupations of Bishop Peterson during these war years was to shelter from the draft the seminarians who were eighteen or older. He judged it "of supreme importance" to place promising aspirants in that age group in recognized preparatory seminaries, before or during the scholastic year 1942–1943. In this endeavor he was successful: By 1944, despite the war, there were forty-two diocesan seminarians compared to thirty in 1932. Both the Great Depression and the war strengthened rather than weakened the call to vocations and ordinations to the priesthood in New Hampshire.

Another important contribution to the war effort by the Catholic Church in New Hampshire was the encouragement of adults to buy bonds and children to buy defense stamps. There were seven great bond drives throughout the war period. Bishop Peterson urged pastors to invest parish money and parishioners to subscribe from their earnings to defense bonds. Appeals were made to Catholic elementary and secondary school students, and to those in the Confraternity of Christian Doctrine programs, to purchase defense stamps. These appeals were successful. Catholic school students also collected scrap metal for the war effort. St. Patrick School, Portsmouth, held the record in that category, collecting 119,350 pounds in the latter part of 1942 alone.

The Diocese of Manchester also opened a United Service Organization (USO) center in the Queen City on one of its properties, the former Batch Hospital on Maple Street, now the site of the Mount Carmel Nursing Home. Thousands of service personnel were entertained there. Priests and laity were encouraged by Bishop Peterson to take an active interest in the campaigns to raise money for the USO; to cooperate in the house-to-house drives for that purpose; to contribute what they could to the cause; and, in the case of the clergy, to join local committees.

The Death of Bishop Peterson

World War II still had more than a year to run its course when Bishop Peterson died in Manchester on March 15, 1944, at the age of seventy-two years, eight months; he had served Manchester for almost twelve years, and two months. Archbishop Francis J. Spellman of New York, a longstanding friend, officiated at the solemn pontifical funeral Mass in St. Joseph Cathedral on March 21. Bishop Peterson, like his predecessors, was buried in the crypt there. Monsignor Jeremiah S. Buckley was elected administrator by the diocesan consultors, as he had been at the death of Bishop Guertin.

TWELVE

Horizons Unlimited
1945–1959

The United States c. 1945

Rome's choice as fifth bishop of Manchester nearly coincided with a new era in the history of the United States and that of the Catholic Church in this country. Less than seven months after the installation of the Most Reverend Matthew F. Brady in Manchester, on January 17, 1945, both the war in Europe (June 6) and that in the Far East (August 14) came to an end. This marked the beginning of a period of prosperity and expansion in both the nation and the Catholic Church.

Much of the new prosperity and expansion was attributable to the economic stagnation caused by the Great Depression [1929–1940(c)], and then by shortages that resulted from World War II, both before and especially during the participation of the United States [1939(c)–1945]. In all, these two events created some sixteen years of abnormal economic disorder.

These sixteen years built up a backlog of needs by the American public, which included housing, automobiles, food, and all kinds of consumer goods. For the Catholic Church, it meant a pressing need for new buildings, as well as renovations and repairs of the old. The needs of both the country and the Church could now be met because of the increase in the standard of living of the American people resulting from some fifty years of progress in mass production techniques in industry and the mechanization of agriculture. In summary, there were many needs and ways to produce goods, and there was money to pay for what was desired.

In addition to the massive profits made by most industries and businesses during the war, other sources of accumulated capital were: the savings from higher wages paid to workers, who had few outlets to spend because of the shortages; the savings of many of the veterans; and a new source of capital, the earnings of the large numbers of women in the workplace during the war.

Other factors that contributed to the growth and healthy condition of the Catholic Church after World War II were: a dramatic upsurge in the birth rate; a return to religion by large segments of the American public; and the passage of the GI Bill of Rights in June 1944, which provided some form of education or vocational training to millions of men and women veterans.

It is now well established that by the immediate postwar years, Catholics had achieved upward mobility in education and financial standing, had far better occupations, and were mobile geographically. On the negative side, there was a worsening of Protestant-Catholic relations, after the united efforts of World War II. This discord in ecumenical harmony, as it will be seen, had its repercussions in New Hampshire.

Events on the international level, such as the Korean War and the tensions in Europe between Russia and its satellites and the United States and its allies, while they were costly in lives lost and the huge financial expenses involved, did not greatly disturb the rhythm of life in this country.

Bishop Matthew F. Brady: Background

It was in this historical context that Bishop Matthew F. Brady was called to exercise his episcopal ministry in New Hampshire. Matthew Francis Brady was born in Waterbury, Connecticut, on January 15, 1893, the son of John and Catherine (Caffrey) Brady. His early education was in the public elementary and high schools of his native city, and then at St. Thomas Seminary, Bloomfield, Connecticut.

After completing the preparatory seminary course, he was sent to the American College in Louvain, Belgium. When World War I broke out, he was recalled to the United States and completed his studies for the priesthood at St. Bernard Seminary in Rochester, New York. He was ordained in Hartford, Connecticut, on June 10, 1916.

Father Brady's first assignment was as an associate at Sacred Heart parish, New Haven. From August 28, 1918, to March 1, 1919, he served as a chaplain in the Army Transport Service with the rank of first lieutenant, exercising his ministry mainly on troop ships returning from Europe. After his discharge, he returned to Sacred Heart, New Haven, where he remained until November 1922, when he was assigned to the faculty of St. Thomas Seminary, his alma mater. There he taught English, French (learned in Belgium), and Sacred Scripture for the next ten years.

In 1932, Father Brady was appointed pastor of St. Rita parish, Hamden, Connecticut, where he remained for six years. In 1934 he was given the additional tasks of serving as defender of the bond and promoter of justice for the diocesan tribunal. Appointed diocesan director of the Confraternity of Christian Doctrine, he planned and managed the Fourth National Catechetical Congress, which was held in Hartford in October 1938.

Just prior to that congress, on July 30, 1938, Pope Pius XII named him the fourth bishop of Burlington, Vermont. He was ordained to the episcopacy in that city and installed on October 26.

Bishop Brady served in Vermont from October 26, 1938, to early January 1945, when he became the fifth bishop of Manchester. He is remembered in the history of Catholicism in Vermont for a number of major accomplishments. As his numerous innovations there were, for the greater part, later duplicated in New Hampshire, they will not be described here.

At the death of Bishop Peterson, Bishop Brady was appointed to replace him by Pius XII on November 11, 1944. He was installed at St. Joseph Cathedral in Manchester on January 17, 1945, a day that was marked by a twenty-two-inch snowfall. Bishop Brady's transfer to Manchester can be looked upon as a promotion, but of fairly modest proportions.

Two considerations in sending him to New Hampshire were most likely his ability to speak French quite adequately and the fact that he did not come from a state that had been disturbed by the *Sentinelle* movement, such as Rhode Island or New Hampshire, or to a lesser extent, Maine or Massachusetts.

Bishop Brady: Builder, Administrator

Bishop Brady will be best remembered as a builder and administrator. In that respect, he was much like many of his peers throughout the American hierarchy at that time. Their skills proved to be of great value to a church then faced with a growing population and, as it has been noted, with a heavy backlog of needs created by poverty during the Great

Depression and the acute shortage of materials for civilian use during World War II.

Between 1945 and 1956, twenty-seven new parishes were founded in New Hampshire by Bishop Brady, seventeen being in communities previously without a Catholic parish. These new establishments raised the number of parishes from 88 to 115. He is second only to Bishop Bradley in the number of parishes erected: Bishop Bradley founded thirty-six in eighteen years, and Bishop Brady twenty-seven in eleven years.

In addition, during his episcopacy Bishop Brady authorized the building of forty-seven churches; eleven elementary schools; fourteen convents; five high schools; twenty-nine rectories; eighteen parish halls; three homes for the aged; and the purchase and opening of two summer camps, one for boys at Gilmanton Iron Works and the other for girls at Wolfeboro, named Fatima and Bernadette, respectively.

This nearly incessant pace of building activity was not masterminded in an ornate episcopal residence or even in the seclusion of a private office. Bishop Brady's principal base of operation was a simple secretary-size desk in the chancery office, which was then located on the ground floor of the cathedral rectory. This desk was back-to-back with that of a chancery official, frequently the chancellor, who was barely more than five or six feet away. If the bishop wished to consult with his chancery official, or vice versa, all either one had to do was to raise his voice a few decibels or just lean back a bit and speak in a normal tone. All ordinary business, either with the bishop or with the chancery, was conducted in the open in this office. If any private exchange was thought to be necessary, it was generally held in a rectory parlor at the far northeast end of the rectory hall with both the bishop and the visitor standing.

There is no doubt that, as a modern business practice will attest, a staff or board meeting held standing up will tend to end more quickly than one conducted sitting down. It is not known to be recommended, however, by Emily Post, Gloria Vanderbilt, or Miss Manners.

No time was wasted, either, searching file cabinets for documentation. Virtually all the needed current archives were heaped on the ordinary's desk, where, almost without fail, he was able to quickly locate the papers relative to the business at hand, whether it dealt with blueprints, contracts, correspondence, or some other matter.

Some Personal Characteristics

As it has been noted, Bishop Brady's style of episcopal management and leadership was in many ways typical of the members of the American hierarchy from the latter part of the nineteenth century to the Second Vatican Council (1962–1965). Since the end of that council, the newly appointed bishops have been considerably more pastoral and, some would say, less colorful personalities.

Among Bishop Brady's many advantages was his appearance. All agreed that he had an episcopal bearing: He was tall, had a full head of silvery white hair, a pleasing voice, and an imposing physical presence. Most photographers, in short, would have selected him to portray the ideal American bishop. For others, these very same physical characteristics made him appear intimidating.

In his dealings with people—clergy and laity alike—he presented two contradictory aspects. With his friends and close associates, including his letters to them, he displayed warmth, humor, and even a love for poetry, which he quoted regularly. With the diocesan clergy, he wrote, spoke, and acted quite differently. It was his policy, for example, not to meet his seminarians before their ordination. Most candidates for the priesthood did not see him face to face until the ordination ceremony itself. A priest's first assignment was either given to him orally, after the ordination and a customary breakfast with the ordination class (this assignment, while conveyed in privacy, was given while standing with the bishop), or it came by letter, was brief and in business form and language.

It was not entirely unknown for Bishop Brady not to recognize one of his own clergy or, if he did recognize him, not to remember where he had been assigned. On one occasion, typical of many, he greeted a priest by asking him, "How are things up north?" That individual, who had never been assigned up north, was, in fact, an associate in a parish adjacent to the cathedral. On a few occasions, while visiting a rectory for confirmation or some other function, he would remind a too-talkative priest that it was not necessary to try to entertain him. A priest not wearing a hat was given an episcopal reminder of his neglect of diocesan custom. For an adult of any age to be told to wear his winter black felt or his summer straw panama may have done wonders for his humility but little for his self-esteem.

There is sufficient evidence from participants that during a meeting exclusively with the pastors of the diocese, Bishop Brady said about the associates ("curates," in the language of the times), "You keep them busy, I'll keep them poor." This remark, possibly made in jest, most likely amused the pastors, but was painful for the curates, who detected more truth than guffaws in the statement. In counterbalance, Bishop Brady often said with some emotion, before the entire body of the clergy, that he had the best priests in the United States.

All of the previous bishops of Manchester, with the exception of Bishop Bradley, shared in varying ways and degrees the characteristics of this direct, forceful, occasionally blunt, and generally unapproachable leadership. Bishops Delany and Peterson were the most similar to Bishop Brady in this regard; Bishop Guertin tried resolutely to model himself on this pattern, but was temperamentally unable to do so with much conviction or success.

It should be understood that each one of these bishops was orthodox, sincere, pious, and capable in varying degrees. Like all human beings, they had their moods and peccadilloes, but each was honest and dedicated to the church and its members. Their behavior was simply a reflection of the style that developed and was then expected of, American bishops after the First Vatican Council (1869–1870) and the Third Plenary Council of Baltimore (1884).

This princely attitude of the episcopacy was to be in glaringly sharp contrast with that described by the Second Vatican Council. Three of the sixteen documents promulgated by the council deal specifically with the offices of bishops, priests, and seminarians. Most of the other decrees allude to these ecclesiastical offices as well. All are in the spirit of this admonition taken from the "Decree on the Ministry and Life of Priests," article 7: "The bishop should regard priests as his brothers and friends" and "He should gladly listen to them, indeed, consult them."

As Bishop Brady's direct dealings with the laity were rather limited, consisting primarily of attending meetings, banquets, religious ceremonies, and the like, one can only assume that his episcopal reserve was maintained with them as well on the private and personal level.

Catholic Education

Among Bishop Brady's most notable accomplishments was the expansion of Catholic education, both of Catholic schools and of the Confraternity of Christian Doctrine (CCD).

Enrollment in Catholic elementary schools rose from 17,760 in

1944 to more than 23,000 in 1959; that in Catholic high schools from 1,903 to 4,370 during the same period; and that in Catholic colleges from 429 to 1,513.

Just as remarkable was the growth of the Confraternity of Christian Doctrine. Bishop Brady was one of the pioneers in this country in giving due attention to the religious education of those not attending Catholic schools. He initiated or perfected such programs first in his archdiocese of Hartford, then in Burlington and Manchester. In doing so, he was simply perpetuating a pious work founded in Rome in 1560, approved by Pope St. Pius V in 1571, and mandated by the Code of Canon Law for the United States in 1917.

By 1959, the Confraternity of Christian Doctrine in the diocese had expanded to include 5,960 high school students and 14,021 grammar school boys and girls. In all, a few less than 50,000 New Hampshire children and youths were receiving some formal religious instruction from the Catholic Church in 1959. The CCD programs also included elements of adult religious education, a new endeavor at this time.

Catholic Charities 1945

Another foundation that would have a major effect on the diocese was the establishment of Catholic Charities of New Hampshire in 1945, with the Reverend James R. McGreal (later Monsignor) as the first director, with an initial staff of three. Since its creation, it has expended millions of dollars to alleviate suffering and to enhance the lives of tens of thousands of individuals throughout the state. Over the years it has expanded its outreach, which now includes among its services adoption, maternity care, family counseling, youth programs, assistance to the infirm and homebound elderly, and food for the needy.

Funding is provided by an annual appeal to all parishes, and a special-gifts solicitation directed toward business, industry, and the professions. The success of this annual drive depends on the hundreds of laypeople who volunteer each year to work for the campaign.

Catholic Charities is a prime example of the role played by the laity in the ministry of the Church. Laymen and laywomen are not only the major financial contributors but they are also the preponderant providers of the services offered by the organization.

During the episcopacy of Bishop Brady, Catholic Charities dedicated the first three diocesan nursing homes for the aged in the state. All prior homes of this kind had been parish–sponsored. Two diocesan homes were dedicated in September 1949, at Manchester and Laconia, and one in Dover in November 1958. Two more were opened during the episcopacy of Bishop Primeau, one in Berlin in June 1963 and one in Manchester, the second in that city in September 1969.

Good Shepherd Nursing Home in Jaffrey, the most recent, was acquired and began functioning on January 1, 1990. Catholic Charities also maintains two buildings of apartments for the elderly in Laconia and Manchester. A nursing home for priests in need of such care, dedicated to the memory of Bishop Peterson, opened in Manchester, across the street from Mount Carmel, during the summer of 1995.

The year 1995 marked the fiftieth anniversary of Catholic Charities. One element of the celebration was historical expositions of the organization in a few cities, including the Manchester Historic Association. Another element was to increase the goal of the annual charities appeal to $3 million as part of a major campaign, called "The Future of Our Faith," to raise $18 million for the needs of the 131 parishes and the diocese. Over the years, Catholic Charities has grown into the largest private charitable organization in the state of New Hampshire.

During its fifty years of existence, Catholic Charities has had only three directors; all of them have been members of the clergy. Following Monsignor McGreal, the founder (1945–1963), were Monsignor John E. Molan (1963–1976) and Monsignor John P. Quinn, who was assistant director from 1973 to 1976, and now director since that time.

Role of the Laity

Bishop Brady's views on a number of subjects are of interest and generally reflect those of the vast majority in church leadership at the time. As a national leader of the Confraternity of Christian Doctrine, for example, he recognized the role of the laity in teaching the faith and welcomed the fact that this task was no longer left solely to the clergy and religious. He stopped short, however, of viewing their participation as a right flowing from baptism and confirmation, a right confirmed by the Second Vatican Council. He analyzed it as an apostolate to help the clergy, to make up for a shortage of teachers in the ranks of religious orders, and to substitute for the inability of priests and religious to carry the burden because of the mounting population of the world.

Segregation, Women, and Labor

Bishop Brady's support for the end of segregation was unequivocal: He strongly approved of the federal Supreme Court decision of 1954 and the passage of state legislation prohibiting discrimination because of race, creed, color, ancestry, or national origin.

His position on women was less in harmony with contemporary thinking, however. When World War II came to an end, he rejoiced publicly because women could now return to their rightful place, that is, the home. Bishop Brady would hardly recognize, and much less approve of, our contemporary society, where since the early 1990s more than 53.7 million women over the age of sixteen are in the workplace. By early 1997, some 50 million workers were also mothers. He could have not approved of the new pattern of child-rearing that has developed as a result of their employment. The home is no longer the sole habitat of the child; it is now shared with a nursery school or some such facility.

From his earliest years in the episcopacy, Bishop Brady was recognized as a friend of labor. He has been credited, while bishop of Burlington, for bringing the Bell Aircraft Company to Vermont during World War II, a move that was opposed by many interest groups because they recognized that it would raise wages in other local industries. On the occasion of his death, a state senator observed that "Bishop Brady was one of the best friends labor ever had in Vermont." In New Hampshire, he continued to manifest his interest by establishing a diocesan labor institute and by hosting the Catholic Conference on Industrial Problems in 1947.

Other Developments

Other developments during the Brady years were: The creation of a diocesan federation of the Holy Name Societies and the Leagues of the Sacred Heart; the establishment of the Diocesan Council of Catholic Women, which proposed to gather into one federation all existing societies of Catholic women; expansion of the Catholic Youth Organization (CYO);

and the encouragement of the Catholic War Veterans (CWV), notably in their sponsorship of athletic programs for youth.

Dogma of the Assumption of the Blessed Virgin

In 1950, the Universal Church celebrated the proclamation of the dogma of the Assumption of the Blessed Virgin Mary, the first infallible pronouncement of the pope since the definition of the Immaculate Conception in 1854, and the only one since the founding of the Diocese of Manchester in 1884.

This was celebrated with éclat in the cathedral on November 1, and by mandated homilies in all the churches of the diocese on the following Sunday, November 5. In his report to the apostolic delegation in Washington, Bishop Brady also noted that the secular press had carried the news item adequately and correctly and that there had been no adverse comment on the proclamation of the dogma, either by individuals or by newspapers in New Hampshire.

The Manchester Union Leader

Bishop Brady's relationship to three other groups or organizations during his episcopacy in New Hampshire deserves special attention. These groups were The *Manchester Union Leader,* the French Canadians, and the other Christian churches.

Bishop Brady's relationship with Mr. William Loeb, president and publisher of the *Union Leader,* was unusually warm and cordial and dated back to the days when Mr. Loeb was president and publisher of the *Burlington Daily News* and Bishop Brady the head of the Catholic Church in Vermont. Bishop Brady's endorsement of Mr. Loeb was so positive that he assured the bishop of Providence in 1954 that because of the *Union Leader,* there was no need for a Catholic newspaper in New Hampshire. In fact, he felt that he already had one in that Manchester publication. Mr. Loeb's philosophy was sound, and his relationship with the Catholic Church was regarded, Bishop Brady wrote, as "splendid." When Bishop Brady died, Mr. Loeb entitled his editorial in the *Burlington Daily News* "Heaven Is Richer Today," not a minor compliment.

French Canadians

French Canadian reactions to Bishop Brady were not as unequivocally favorable as those of Mr. Loeb and his newspaper. The archives do show, however, that some French Canadians believed that he had to be given high marks for his impartiality and sense of justice, and for his efforts to encourage the foreign-speaking members of the diocese to retain their language, customs, and culture, not to mention their religion.

In summarizing Bishop Brady's relationship to the French Canadians at the time of his death, in 1959, one newspaper, *L'Action,* editorialized that the people bowed with regret over his grave, shedding tears over the loss of "a great apostle" whose works would never perish in New Hampshire. His ability to speak French, "nearly without an accent," the editor continued, gave great pleasure to his bilingual listeners.

On the other hand, another French Canadian newspaper *Le Travailleur,* published in Worcester, Massachusetts, printed a sarcastic, even vicious, article accusing Bishop Brady of many injustices against specific French Canadians individuals and institutions. Typical of the nine charges was that he had deliberately inflicted on St. George Church of Manchester, a French Canadian parish, the most pitiful administrator–pastor of the diocese. The implication seems to be that this appointment apparently was made to ruin the parish, which is only a few blocks from the cathedral. Despite certain negative evaluations of Bishop Brady, such as those by *Le Travailleur,* the record shows a marked improvement in the relations between the Irish and the French Canadians of the Diocese of Manchester during his administration. The simple passage of time had a great deal to do with this as well.

Reverses in Ecumenism

While the relationship among the Catholic ethnic groups improved during the episcopacy of Bishop Brady, nearly the opposite occurred in the ecumenical movement—that is, between the Catholic and the Protestant Churches.

A growing rift developed after World War II when the Catholic Church either initiated or intensified campaigns to retain an American ambassador to the Holy See; to revoke laws that prohibited the granting of public funds to church-related schools; and to press for free textbooks and bus transportation for pupils of Catholic schools; and a number of other divisive initiatives.

One reaction was the foundation of an organization called Protestants and Other Americans United for the Separation of Church and State (POAW) which issued a manifesto on January 12, 1948, considered strongly anti-Catholic in tone, that placed the POAW and the Catholic Church on a collision course.

Such a collision occurred in New Hampshire on February 3, 1948, when Archbishop Richard J. Cushing of Boston addressed the state council of the Knights of Columbus in Manchester. In his presentation he linked prominent American Protestant leaders with communism, and described the POAW manifesto of January 12 as maliciously anti-Catholic and a force of bigotry.

He also defied the POAW to name the Catholics whom, he said, they had charged were trying to effect a union of church and state, thus striking a blow at the American Constitution. That speech, which was recorded, was broadcast later that evening over local radio station WMUR. This provocative "shot from the cincture" by this often outspoken archbishop did not go unchallenged.

At a meeting held on February 6, the Manchester Ministers Association voted to invite Bishop G. Bromley Oxnam, bishop of the Methodist Church of the New York City area and a prominent officer of the POAW, to Manchester to respond to Archbishop Cushing's address. These clergymen also requested equal time from station WMUR, so that all sides of the controversial matter could be heard, as required by the regulations of the Federal Communications Commission. Bishop Oxnam made his forty-five-minute reply over WMUR beginning at 10:30 P.M. on Sunday, February 15, two weeks after Archbishop Cushing's address was broadcast.

Hindsight certainly demonstrated that Protestant Church leaders were clearly not communists as charged by Archbishop Cushing, and that Catholic leaders were not consciously attempting to effect a union of church and state, as imputed by Bishop Oxnam. In retrospect, the Cushing–Oxnam exchange added nothing positive to the Catholic–Protestant dialogue. Its primary effect was to further chill ecclesial relations in New Hampshire, a condition that would not thaw to any degree until Pope John XXIII and the Second Vatican Council.

National Involvement

Like his predecessor Bishop Peterson, Bishop Brady held many prominent positions at the national level. Among these was the chairmanship of the Episcopal Committee of the Confraternity of Christian Doctrine from 1956 until his death. From 1950 to 1956, he was episcopal chairman of the education department of the National Catholic Welfare Conference, and in 1957–1958, he served as president general of the National Catholic Educational Association.

These last two positions, by coincidence, were also held by his predecessor Bishop Peterson and by his successor, Bishop Primeau. In 1953 he was selected as the chairman of the committee that prepared a bishops' statement on "The Dignity of Man and Its Degradation." From his positions at the national level and from his many public addresses, it can be determined that he was regarded as an expert principally in three fields: religious education, education in general, and the lay apostolate.

End of an Era

Bishop Brady suffered his first heart attack on Sunday, March 3, 1957, while celebrating Mass for patients and staff at the New Hampshire State Hospital, on the occasion of the dedication of a meditation room. He recovered and gradually resumed his normal activities.

The recovery was not to be for very long, however. He collapsed coming down a flight of stairs at the Hotel Vermonter in Burlington shortly before midnight on Sunday, September 20, 1959, while attending the 13th New England Congress of the Confraternity of Christian Doctrine. He did not respond to artificial respiration and died in the stairway before a doctor could arrive.

Bishop Brady is entombed in the cathedral crypt with his four predecessors. In his final testament he bequeathed all his earthly possessions to the Diocese of Manchester, except for a set of golf clubs, which was requested as a memento by one of his close relatives.

This death occurred just a few years before the end of an era in the history of Catholicism in the United States, including the Church in New Hampshire. The Second Vatican Council would begin barely three years after the death of Bishop Brady, on October 11, 1962, and was followed by a period of extensive change, in some cases of a radical nature.

The period 1945–1959, in contrast, was one in which everything seemed possible. The gigantic building projects, the growth of Catholic school education and CCD programs, and the founding of a number of important diocesan organizations, such as Catholic Charities, have already been mentioned.

During the same period the total Catholic population of New Hampshire rose from 168,210 to 220,050; the number of diocesan and religious priests from 189 and 66 respectively, to 271 and 110; parishes from 88 to 115; women religious from 1,087 to 1,618; brothers from 36 to 65; and seminarians preparing for the priesthood of the diocese from 39 to 77. This was a time, indeed, when the horizon seemed unlimited.

THIRTEEN

Second Vatican Council: Renewal and Reaction 1960–1974

A New Time, New Bishop: Ernest J. Primeau

Few, if any, particularly in the United States, could have predicted the major upheavals that were to take place in the Catholic Church shortly after the death of Bishop Brady. This new and frequently disturbing era began inauspiciously enough with the election of John XXIII, the seventy-six-year-old patriarch of Venice, to the papacy in October 1958.

Some three months later, on January 25, 1959, during vespers at the Basilica of St. Paul Outside the Walls, concluding the octave of prayer for Christian unity, he stunned the Catholic world by announcing his intention of calling an ecumenical council, with the promotion of Christian unity as one of its primary aims.

Bishop Brady died almost nine months after Pope John XXIII's public announcement. He did not live long enough to participate in even the principal preparatory phases of that historic event.

That responsibility, including attending the Second Vatican Council itself, became that of the sixth bishop of Manchester, the Most Reverend Ernest J. Primeau. The announcement of his appointment to Manchester was made public by the apostolic delegate in Washington on the morning of Wednesday, December 2, 1959.

Ernest J. Primeau was born in Chicago, Illinois, on September 17, 1909, the son of a French Canadian father born in Montreal and a mother of French Canadian descent, Angelina (La Vigne) Primeau, born in the United States. His elementary education was acquired at Presentation Academy in Chicago and Our Lady Academy in Mantino, Illinois. He attended St.

Ignatius High School and after graduation, spent two years at Loyola University of Chicago. It was during his two years at the university that he discerned that he had a vocation to the priesthood. Accepted by the Archdiocese of Chicago, he was assigned to St. Mary of the Lake Seminary in Mundelein, Illinois, where, after further studies, he was ordained on April 7, 1934.

For the next two years he did graduate work at Mundelein and obtained a doctorate in theology (S.T.D.). From 1937 to 1946, he taught at Quigley Preparatory Seminary in Chicago, principally the fields of mathematics and physics, coached basketball, and served as assistant athletic director. At one point in his involvement with basketball at Quigley, he came into contact with one George Mikan, a seminarian. This George Mikan, after leaving the seminary, eventually became a professional basketball star and was named the best player of the first half of this century. In lighter moments among friends, Bishop Primeau would humorously attribute all of George Mikan's skills and success to his coaching in the seminary: "I taught him everything he knew," he would say.

For the next twelve years, Father Primeau was assigned to Rome. His primary duty there was to serve as rector of St. Mary of the Lake, the Chicago house of studies. This house was maintained principally as a residence for priests doing graduate work in Rome.

During his rectorship, he found time to obtain a licentiate in canon law (J.C.L.) from the Lateran University in 1948, and between 1956 and 1958, he served as an official with the Sacred Congregation of the Holy Office, since renamed the Sacred Congregation for the Doctrine of the Faith. In 1958, after some twenty-four years in the priesthood, he was named pastor of Our Lady of Mount Carmel, one of the large parishes in the city of Chicago.

It was there at Our Lady of Mount Carmel, on November 27, 1959, that he was informed of his appointment to Manchester. He was ordained to the episcopacy by Albert Cardinal Myer in Chicago's Holy Name Cathedral on Thursday, February 13, 1960, and installed in Manchester's St. Joseph Cathedral by Richard Cardinal Cushing on Tuesday, March 15.

As the years of the episcopacy of Bishop Primeau (1960–1974) were dominated and indelibly marked by the Second Vatican Council and its aftermath, as was the Church Universal, a cursory review of that pivotal event and its consequences needs to precede a discussion of this period of Catholicism in New Hampshire.

Preparation for the Second Vatican Council

Less than two months after Bishop Primeau's installation in Manchester, the bishops of the world and other selected experts were asked to submit recommendations for consideration to the pontifical commission for the preparation of the Second Vatican Council. Manchester's response on May 10, 1960, divided into seven parts, clearly demonstrates that the bishop and his advisers did not anticipate either the subject matter or the pastoral tone of the upcoming ecumenical council.

This lack of insight was shared, it must be said, by virtually all the bishops of the United States, and by the vast majority of those in the world as well. Most of the recommendations from Manchester were legalistic in tone, generally lacked a spirit of ecumenism, and reflected a siege rather than a liberating mentality. Many focused on a cosmetic revision of canon law. This attitude would be reversed over the next few years.

Manchester's close involvement with the forthcoming ecumenical council began with the appointment of Bishop Primeau by Pope John XXIII as a member of the pontifical commission for the discipline of the clergy and the faithful on August 8, 1960. He was one of only forty-three people from this country selected to be members of, or consultants to, all the commissions established to prepare for the council.

During the preparatory months (1960–1962), Bishop Primeau's membership on that commission required seventeen separate trips to the Vatican, beginning on November 14, 1960. To assist him in the preparation of the pertinent documentation for these meetings, Bishop Primeau enlisted the services of the Reverend Wilfrid H. Paradis (later Monsignor), a historian, canonist, and educator. He later accompanied Bishop Primeau to the council as his personal secretary and adviser. At the council, Monsignor Paradis was appointed a "peritus," that is, an expert or adviser, to the entire council as well. Two other priests from the Diocese of Manchester were to play a role in the council: Fathers Robert G. Boisvert and Robert E. Mulvee (later Bishop). Each, then doing graduate studies in Rome, was briefly appointed an "assignatore," a task that required taking care of the needs of the Council Fathers, including the distribution and collection of the voting ballots.

When the Second Vatican Council was opened by Pope John XXIII on October 11, 1962, with high medieval splendor, the preponderance of opinion among the bishops of the United States, and very likely among those in many other parts of the world, was that it would last but one session, some even predicting that it would end before Christmas 1962. This conviction was dispelled within the first week when a number of bishops, mainly from Western Europe, were able to wrest the control of the council from the Roman Curia and place it in the hands of the council members themselves.

The council was to last not for one session, but for four. Each of the sessions between 1962 and 1965 lasted approximately three months. The time between sessions was devoted largely to commission meetings, and to the preparation of texts for the consideration and approval of the council members, and eventual ratification by the pope.

Over the four years, the Second Vatican Council promulgated sixteen documents: two in 1963; three in 1964; and eleven during the final session in 1965. This summary will limit itself to dealing with the interventions by Bishop Primeau on three of those documents.

Among the startling innovations at the council was the presence of delegate-observers representing other Christian churches. One of these delegate–observers was the Reverend Douglas Horton of Randolph, New Hampshire, an eminent member of the clergy of the United Church of Christ (the Congregational Church) and former president of the Harvard Divinity School. Doctor Horton, now deceased, holds the distinction, most likely unique among participants in the council, of having never missed a single session and having heard all of the 2,205 spoken interventions. He later published a four-volume diary on the council, one volume for each session. Reverend Horton was so greatly admired and respected by all parties at the council that it was said by many that—if it were possible ecumenically—he should be named the first Protestant Cardinal of the Catholic Church!

Manchester's bishop, the first ever to attend an ecumenical council, was to play an active role in its evolution. Early in the first session (on October 21, 1962), Bishop Primeau was designated executive assistant to the president of a number of committees of American bishops formed to assist the hierarchy in their study of the subjects to come before the Second Vatican Council.

It was also during the first session, in 1962, that he and Bishop Christopher Weldon (now deceased) of Springfield, Massachusetts, were appointed to serve as U.S. representatives on the International Committee of Bishops. This was an informal organization, composed of conciliar members from many parts of the world, that served as an information-sharing organism and as a vehicle for coordinated action among the hierarchies of the world.

Another honor bestowed on Bishop Primeau by the entire council membership was his election by that body, on November 28, 1963, to the Secretariat for Promoting Christian Unity. He thus became one of only twenty-six American bishops to serve on a commission of the council. He was reappointed to a five-year term to that secretariat in June 1975.

Bishop Primeau made five presentations during the council—three oral and two in writing. The oral interventions were: on the Church as a community and as a society, on October 2, 1963; on the relationship of the hierarchy (bishops and priests) to the laity, on October 23, 1963; and on religious freedom, on September 24, 1964. His two written interventions were on religious freedom (September 1964) and on the sometimes feudal relationship between pastors and associates (October 1965).

His oral address on the Church and on the laity received worldwide attention. In his close to ten-minute presentation on the relationship of the hierarchy to the laity, he pronounced the internationally quoted phrase: "Let this talk of their [the laity's] duty of subjection and reverence cease—as if their only duty be stated in these terms: believe, pray, pay, and obey."

As a member of the subcommittee on Religious Freedom of the Secretariat for Promoting Christian Unity, Bishop Primeau played a key role in producing a text on religious liberty that was acceptable to the American hierarchy and public, and in joining those who guided it to an affirmative vote by the entire membership of the council.

Even before the solemn closing of the Second Vatican Council in St. Peter Square on December 8, 1965, its spirit and decisions began to be implemented in the Diocese of Manchester. Renewal was facilitated in a physical way by the centralization of virtually all diocesan departments and offices in a new administration building, at 153 Ash Street, Manchester, which was dedicated on the afternoon of Sunday, August 9, 1964. Since then, diocesan administration has expanded to the point that two additions (modules) have been constructed onto the building, and a separate annex has opened on Concord Street.

Renewal mandated by the Second Vatican Council began, most appropriately, with the liturgy. Not only was it the first subject to be examined, but it was also the first, in a sense, Pope Paul VI remarked later, "in intrinsic worth and importance for the life of the Church." It is through the liturgy, especially the divine Eucharistic Sacrifice, that "the work of our redemption is exercised."

The "Constitution on the Sacred Liturgy" *(Sancrosanctum Consilium)* was the first document completed by the council. It was promulgated by Pope Paul VI in St. Peter's Basilica on December 4, 1963 before a vast majority of all the bishops of the world, who had previously given the text an astoundingly favorable vote of 2,147 in favor to an anemic and statistically insignificant 4 against.

Among the areas of liturgical life to be renewed, according to the decree, were the Eucharist (the Mass), the sacraments and sacramentals, the divine office (the breviary), the liturgical year, sacred music and art, and church furnishing. Over a period of several years after the council ended on December 8, 1965, a large number of documents were issued by the Holy See that elaborated on and explained the liturgical renewal mandated by the bishops and the Sovereign Pontiff.

These various phases of renewal, particularly the Mass and the sacraments, were fully and faithfully implemented in the Diocese of Manchester with few major complaints and but minimal opposition. For instance, there was little or no demand for the Tridentine Mass, that is, the Eucharist in Latin in the form used before the council. Liturgical renewal, overall, was widely welcomed and accepted by the faithful.

A major innovation was the introduction of the vernacular—the language of the people—in the liturgy, including the Eucharist. The vernacular was introduced into the Mass in the United States by a decision of the bishops of this country that became effective on the First Sunday of Advent, November 29, 1964, slightly less than a year after the promulgation of the "Constitution on the Sacred Liturgy." Now, for the first time since Latin became an obsolete language about one thousand years ago, the average person in a Catholic church could actually understand the celebrant at the altar!

While Latin was an obsolete language for virtually everyone, the vernacular used in some of the Catholic churches of New Hampshire, such as French, Polish, and Lithuanian, had become, or was becoming, unknown to a significant number of the members of the national parishes. Those not knowing the language, or who could not deal with its subtleties and nuances, were a great many of the children and youth, plus, in many cases, the non-foreign-speaking spouse of one of the parents.

Recognizing this, Bishop Primeau gently recommended, in a letter dated September 12, 1964, that some of the Masses in these national parishes be celebrated in English for the spiritual welfare as well as the understanding of those who could not handle the foreign language. In this category were twenty-two parishes: One Lithuanian, three Polish, and eighteen French Canadian. While other factors probably contributed in part to the decision, two pastors, that of St. Mary and St. George, both in Manchester, accepted retirement rather than introduce English into the liturgy of the parish.

Introducing English in the Polish parishes presented other problems. The predominant difficulty was the fact that no Polish text of the Mass was then available. Poland, still behind the Iron Curtain, was too besieged to implement this aspect of the Second Vatican Council, as well as many others. Second, in the minds of some, introducing Polish in the liturgy would have appeared as mimicking the Polish National Catholic Church, a separated church, which had been using the vernacular since not long after its founding during the last decade of the nineteenth century.

An Unfinished Diocesan Synod

Among the first major efforts to implement the Second Vatican Council in the diocese was the convocation of a synod, meant to be the second in its history. The first had been held under Bishop Bradley on November 4, 1886. The precise purpose of the second synod was to renew the laws and regulations of the diocese in the pastoral language and spirit of the Second Vatican Council as well as in conformity with present legislation of the Catholic Church, for the pastoral good of the People of God and their salvation.

This synod was solemnly convoked by Bishop Primeau at a Pontifical High Mass in the cathedral on Pentecost Sunday, June 6, 1965, and the one and only session to promulgate documents was held in the same church on Sunday, June 30, 1968, three years later.

Many innovations were incorporated in the preparation of this synod. First, it was decided that the synod's basic structure would be patterned on that of the Second Vatican Council. Accordingly, the preliminary work was divided among twelve preparatory commissions. The membership of these commissions was an even more radical departure from custom at that time. Among the 316 official members were 177 diocesan priests, fifty-four men and women religious, and eighty-five members of the laity.

From the onset, a basic objective was to involve by direct participation, as many people as possible. One means to achieve this goal was consultation with the Catholic community of New Hampshire on several occasions. First, the people of the diocese were asked to submit recommendations to the preparatory commissions at the beginning of the process; later, they were invited to make a critical evaluation of the documents as they emerged from the coordinating commission and had been made suitable for publication by the writing committee (see below).

The first general session of the members of the twelve commissions preparing the synod was held at Immaculata High School in Manchester on November 3, 1965, with more than three hundred clergy, religious, and laity in attendance. The twelve preparatory commissions then met separately, over several months, at their own pace and as often as they deemed necessary, until they estimated that they had completed their tasks.

The recommendations of the preparatory commissions were then passed on to a coordinating commission of thirty-six laypeople, religious, and diocesan priests, to whom Bishop Primeau had confided the functions of coordinating the work and recommendations of the preparatory commissions. Its primary function was to eliminate the numerous duplications and to supply the many essential ecclesial subjects not treated by the synod up to that point.

This hardworking coordinating commission of dedicated members met twenty times between the organizational meeting of February 9, 1966, and December 6 of the same year.

It became glaringly evident during the meetings of the preparatory commissions, and then of the coordinating commission, that the vast majority of the people of the diocese, including much of the clergy leadership, were not ready for a synod patterned on the renewal and reforms promulgated at the Second Vatican Council.

Essentially, as one could expect, the thinking of the newly named "People of God," including those in New Hampshire, was that of a church basically unchanged in doctrine, morals, discipline, and liturgy for roughly the previous four centuries. The status of the faithful in the diocese was analogous to that of the vast majority of American bishops at the Second Vatican Council who expected to be home by Christmas of 1962 after some cosmetic changes and adjustments to the Church. In retrospect, the underlying need for a fruitful Second Synod would have been a long and intensive period of education and prayer.

However, in order to salvage as much as possible of the sound work done in the preparation of the synod, Bishop Primeau appointed a writing committee to put into pastoral language the decisions of the coordinating commission, and to supply any essential information not covered by the previous preparatory bodies. Between May 1967 and May 1968, the writing committee of three Monsignors—William J. Collins, Philip J. Kenney, and Wilfrid H. Paradis, and Father Robert G. Boisvert, with "ad hoc" assistance from a few others—lay, religious, and clergy with specialized expertise—produced six documents for diocesan-wide circulation and study. These were, in order: "The Church Witnessing" (on the missions), "The Church Teaching," "The Church of New Hampshire in Dialogue" (with Christians and all people of goodwill), "The Church Worshiping," "The Church of New Hampshire in the Modern World," and "The Eastern Catholic Churches."

Each of the six proposed synodal documents was submitted to the entire diocese for study and critical comment. This was done in conjunction with the "Year of Faith" (June 30, 1967–June 30, 1968) decreed by the Holy See and presented as "Operation FIRE," the acronym for Faith Intensified by Renewal and Education.

During this most intensive program of consultation ever attempted by the Diocese of Manchester, 10,000 copies of the full text and more than 800,000 copies of the "Operation FIRE" bulletins were distributed. These bulletins were attractive four-page summaries of each of the six proposed synodal documents that were intended for distribution to the people in the diocese at weekend Masses.

Each document was formally introduced at a diocesan-wide meeting by a nationally recognized expert on the subject under consideration, and followed by group discussions and reports to the full assembly. Recommendations from these diocesan-wide assemblies, and the numerous meetings held in parishes and by other Catholic organizations, were examined by the writing committee and used to revise the text.

Five of the six documents, excluding "The Church of New Hampshire in the Modern World," which was judged to need some improvements because of its socially radical nature, were officially promulgated by Bishop Primeau before an overflow congregation of laity, religious, and priests in the cathedral on Sunday, June 3, 1968, following a concelebrated Mass of the Holy Spirit.

While four more documents were completed and circulated, and three more produced by the writing committee, either in full or in part, the second synod was simply allowed to die out. In other words, nothing further was officially decreed or done about it.

Unofficially, Bishop Primeau, who was well acquainted with the Roman Curia, gradually became convinced that it would not approve a synod document in the form and content of that of the Diocese of Manchester. Among the most evident problems that he could detect was that it was not sufficiently juridical in that it attempted to attract and persuade rather than to mandate and legislate. This same dissension or division was duplicated in the diocese between those who favored the Roman and those who preferred the diocesan position. This rift, it will be seen, extended over a broad range of issues. On this discordant note, the synod was allowed to die, bringing to a conclusion the most extensive consultation ever undertaken in the diocese, and many would say, the broadest program of adult education as well.

Consultative Structures

This synod was but one of a large number of projects designed to renew the Catholic Church in New Hampshire during the episcopacy of Bishop Primeau. A number of these innovations were consultative bodies, something new in the structures of the diocese.

Among these were: A Diocesan Pastoral Council initiated in 1965; parish councils (now pastoral councils) made mandatory in 1969; lay school boards in every parish with a school, also begun in 1969; a Diocesan Council of the Laity, initiated on an interim basis in 1970; and deanery pastoral councils, requested by the bishop in the fall of 1973.

Initially, the parish councils (pastoral councils) were designed to have more than consultative authority. In certain defined and limited circumstances, a council could override the veto of a pastor by a two-thirds vote.

The pastor could then appeal to the Diocesan Board of Conciliation for a final judgment. Some clergy felt uncomfortable—even betrayed—by the possibility that the parish lay council could reverse one of their decisions. According to this way of thinking, priestly authority was the final norm rather than an objective analysis of the merits of the problem at hand. This dilemma for some was definitely resolved by the new Code of Canon Law promulgated in 1983. It decreed that the pastoral councils were indeed merely consultative. In fact, while they were recommended, they were not even made mandatory. Parish finance councils, on the other hand, were made obligatory, but with no greater power to decide than the pastoral council.

Some of these consultative bodies, composed either fully or largely of laity, are no longer active. Those still in existence are parish (pastoral) councils, lay school boards, the Diocesan Council of the Laity, and a Diocesan Pastoral Council of twenty-nine members.

A Diocesan Sisters' Council, which was founded in September 1969, essentially to provide a forum to exchange views among the numerous communities of women religious, to allow them to act jointly when opportune, and to advise the bishop and diocesan offices on matters of concern to the Catholic community, became dormant in the fall of 1979. Women religious, given their community loyalty, apparently found it difficult in many instances to adapt to cooperative ministry with others. Subsequently, however, the sisters organized into the New Hampshire Leadership Conference of Religious.

New Hampshire's Catholic clergy were more successful in their organizational efforts. A free Association of Priests was organized on November 22, 1966, and a Senate of Priests, elected by the clergy, held its first meeting on May 24, 1967. Its first president was Monsignor Colin A. MacDonald.

The function of the senate, established by church law, was to assist the bishop in the governance of the diocese. Both the Association of Priests and the senate underwent numerous changes during the following years.

The association was perceived by many as divisive largely because membership was on a voluntary basis and was viewed by some as being controlled by the "liberal element" in the clergy. It was replaced, on the recommendation of the senate and the approbation of the bishop, by a Presbyterium, an organization of all priests in 1970. The Senate of Priests was transformed into a Council of Priests in late 1983 and early 1984, to conform with the norms of the new Code of Canon Law, which went into effect on Sunday, November 27, 1983.

Christian Life Centers

As adult religious education was recognized as one of the foundation stones and a major source of energy for renewal, the second diocesan synod, in the document "The Church Teaching," mandated the creation of what came to be known as Christian Life Centers.

The purposes of these centers were: adult religious education; the formation of catechists at all levels; the preparation of ministers for worship roles; education in social justice; and the reaching out to the community to fulfill its spiritual, intellectual, social, psychological, and recreational needs. The first diocesan Christian Life Center was established in the Dover deanery at the request of the deanery clergy in the fall of 1969.

In the same year, the Franconia deanery inaugurated, on its own initiative, a mobile catechetical center, and the Berlin area employed a full-time religious education coordinator to serve the four parishes in the city. By the fall of 1971, there were ten Christian Life Centers in the diocese serving eleven deaneries, Manchester east and west having decided to share the same facility.

These centers have had a checkered and uneven existence. Several have gone out of existence and others are functioning at a minimal level. On a few occasions, during the early years, a scattering of center personnel were accused of near heresy, or at least of teaching rather doubtful doctrine and morality. This stage appears to be a thing of the past. Essentially, Christian Life Centers were intended to generate cooperation among the parishes of a deanery in the use of personnel and resources, particularly the financial burden. Inter-deanery cooperation was also expected and encouraged. It was theorized that in countless instances, what could not be afforded or done by one parish alone could be managed by several operating jointly. Certainly the single most important reason for the languishing of the Christian Life Center movement is the fact that a large number of parishes have always acted alone and independently and now find it difficult to breach the parish border and cooperate with others. The Church's catholicity—that is, its universality—can easily be overshadowed by provincialism or parochialism.

Lay Ministries

It was also during the late 1960s and the early 1970s that new lay ministries began to take root in the parishes. The first layperson to be appointed as a full-time religious education coordinator was Ms. Sheila McQuillen, at St. Joseph parish, Dover, in the fall of 1969. The first woman religious to assume the same task was Sister Angeline Whidden, r.s.m., who was employed by St. Catherine parish, Manchester. The following July 1, sister Claire Leboeuf, c.s.c., became the first non-ordained person in the diocese to officially join a parish pastoral staff, that of St. Anthony in Manchester.

Episcopal Vicars

Further evidence of the determination to renew the diocese had come on June 25, 1967, with the appointment of Monsignor Wilfrid H. Paradis as episcopal vicar for renewal, one of the first in the United States to hold that title.

Episcopal vicars are relatively recent in the structure of the Church; it is an ecclesiastical office created after the Second Vatican Council. An episcopal vicars appointment and functions are now governed by the new Code of Canon Law, canons 476 to 481. In effect, an episcopal vicar has the same authority (the Code uses "power," c. 479 §2) as the bishop himself over a specific territory or over a defined area of church life, such as renewal, education, administration and social welfare. As vicar, it was Monsignor Paradis's task to propose, facilitate, and implement plans for the updating of the diocese. Most of the innovations mentioned above as well as those discussed below were formulated and carried out by that office.

Another element in the plan for renewal was a broad delegation of authority. This consisted partly in the appointment of three episcopal vicars, with authority respectively over Christian Formation, Community Affairs, and Administration; the selection of twenty diocesan consultors (all clergy); and the appointment of a dean in each of the then existing nine deaneries (again, all clergy).

With some adjustments and fine-tuning, these new structures that went into effect on January 12, 1969, are still the foundation for diocesan administration as it now exists.

Bishop Odore Gendron later modified the existing diocesan structure from that of vicars to one of secretaries. The main effect of that change was to allow laypeople to serve as chief administrators of diocesan offices. Sister Pauline Lebel, c.s.c., was appointed the first non-ordained diocesan secretary, that of Education, in January 1986. At the turn of the century and millennium she remains the only non-ordained person to ever have held this rank.

Renewal Team and Priorities

As it was the conviction of Bishop Primeau and the episcopal vicars that priorities had to be established in order to give a sense of direction to the diocese, a Renewal Team was established. This Renewal Team, consisting of the bishop and the three episcopal vicars, usually accompanied by the vicar general, visited the priests of all the deaneries around the state in the spring of 1970, in order to elicit recommendations on the priorities of the Catholic Church in New Hampshire.

Their recommendations were then presented to the deans, who selected those that appeared to be of the greatest concern and established five priorities. These focused on religious education, the continuing education of the clergy, the resolution of the Catholic school problem (mostly financial), the practice of the social gospels, and the implementation of the diocesan synod.

Recognizing the need to develop these basic commitments into more practical terms, the Renewal Team again visited the deaneries in the spring of 1971. This time it met with the clergy in the afternoon and with the members of the parish councils in the deanery during the evening. Separate assemblies were held for the women religious, also in the afternoon. The reflections and recommendations made at these thirty meetings (ten clergy, ten laity, ten sisters) were analyzed by the deans and the Renewal Team, and nineteen statements on the practical implementation of the five priorities were identified and selected. These statements were transmitted to all the organizations of the diocese at every level with the directive to keep them in mind in preparing local goals or programs. No further diocesan-wide consultations on the goals, priorities, and programs of the Catholic Church in New Hampshire have been attempted since that time.

Other Innovations

Three additional innovations during this period are worthy of mention: the creation of a Board of Conciliation and Arbitration, which was approved by the Senate of Priests on January 22, 1970, and used at least once with success; the invitation extended to the clergy at large on June 8, 1967, to submit the names of priests suitable for the office of bishop, an invitation that was later extended to key laity and religious; and the introduction of "cooperative planning," which was an agreement between the Diocese of Manchester and separately with the Sisters of Mercy, Holy Cross, and Presentation of Mary to participate as partners in discussing, planning, and assigning women religious personnel to the new emerging ministries. This latter initiative was quickly and quietly abandoned in favor of other, less formal means of cooperation.

Like several other post–Vatican II innovations, the Board of Conciliation and Arbitration was allowed to lie dormant. However, it was later revived as two boards, one for Conciliation and a second for Arbitration, and are listed in the 1996–1997 *New Hampshire Catholic Directory.*

Progress in Ecumenism

One of the more satisfying results of renewal was the birth and growth of ecumenism in the Catholic Church in the state of New Hampshire. While isolated ecumenical gestures had been made in the past, almost always initiated by the Protestant churches, modern ecumenism for Catholics began on Saturday, January 19, 1963, when Bishop Primeau invited eighty Protestant, Orthodox, and Catholic clergymen to meet at St. Anselm College, Manchester, to observe the week of universal prayer for Christian unity.

With the passage of the tradition-shattering "Decree on Ecumenism" by the Second Vatican Council, approved by Pope Paul VI on November 21, 1964, ecumenical activity by the Catholic Church in New Hampshire was greatly accelerated. A step of major importance was the appointment of a Commission on Ecumenism for the diocese by Bishop Primeau in early 1965.

This commission, in addition to its Catholic members, included representatives from virtually all the major Protestant denominations in the state. The meetings of this commission provided the first forum in New Hampshire for dialogue between Catholic and Protestant leaders. The commission's first president was the capable Very Reverend Placidus Riley, o.s.b., then president of St. Anselm College.

One of the major challenges of these early years after the Second Vatican Council was to establish the relationship of the Diocese of Manchester to the New Hampshire Council of Churches. That council, founded in 1944, composed of most of the major Protestant denominations in the state, had been created to further Christian life and action in New Hampshire.

In response to the always courteous and sensitive invitations of the members of that council, the diocese named observer-delegates to most of the committees of that organization, beginning in 1967. It finally became an associate member in 1975, several years after the Council of Churches amended its charter to make Catholic membership possible. As it shall be seen, the diocese did not become a full partner until January 17, 1984.

Multicultural Ministries

New Hampshire's Catholic diocese began its systematic and sustained involvement in the missions of Latin America in the early 1960s. This involvement with Latin America was prompted by an appeal from Pope John XXIII to the churches in the United States and Canada to come to the aid of that part of the Catholic world. In 1961, Bishop Primeau announced the establishment of Manchester Mission to coordinate the diocese's efforts in Latin America, and appointed Monsignor Philip J. Kenney as director of that apostolate.

In October 1963, four volunteers from the Diocese of Manchester— two priests, Monsignor Thomas F. Duffy (pastor) and Father Edwin W. Milne, and two Sisters of Mercy, Sisters Pauline Chabot and Sebastian Callahan—after four months of specialized training in Mexico—inaugurated a mission at Our Lady of Perpetual Help Parish in Cartago, Colombia.

Over the years this parish, originally consisting of 15,000 individuals and an extensive territory, has been greatly developed on the spiritual, human services, and material planes.

Sister Sebastian died at the mission on January 31, 1965, and was buried in Cartago, a fitting place for a woman dedicated to the evangelizing and charitable apostolates of the Church. The medical and health programs established by Sister Sebastian have been directed since 1966 by Miss Claire Aucoin of Henniker, New Hampshire, who was joined later by Janice Gagné of Plymouth. Their work is directed toward people of all ages in need of food, shelter, and safety as well as developmental and educational opportunities.

Since the inception of Our Lady of Perpetual Help in 1963, four diocesan priests, five Sisters of Mercy, and at least ten laypeople from New Hampshire have served there, as well as a few Peace Corps volunteers.

Moreover, many other laity from New Hampshire have served as Papal Volunteers for Latin America (PAVLA), in Chile, Peru, British Honduras, and the Caribbean islands. Within the United States, other laywomen and laymen have served as volunteers with the Extension Society and other home mission groups serving in the South and Midwest. On the diocesan level, priests, women religious, and laity have served the large numbers of Spanish–speaking people who migrated here from many different countries of South and Central America as well as the Caribbean islands, including Cuba.

Annual collections have been held in the churches of the diocese for the Manchester Mission in Cartago and for the Church in Latin America since 1964. Moreover, a second collection for the missions is assigned yearly to each parish in New Hampshire by the director of Mission Affairs. Many parishes voluntarily take up at least another collection a year in favor of some specific mission of their own choice.

In addition to its multifaceted ministry to the Hispanic, the diocese began focusing on the Catholics of Southeastern Asia, notably the Vietnamese, who fled from their homes and countries during or after the ill-conceived, brutish, and disastrously unsuccessful war in Vietnam. In more recent years, particular attention has been paid to the newly arrived Portuguese Catholics, primarily in the Nashua area.

In cooperation with the Migration and Refugee Services of the United States Catholic Conference and the Catholic Legal Immigration Network, Inc., a diocesan office facilitates refugee sponsorship, family reunification, orientation and case management for new refugees, counseling, the clarification of immigrant status, the application for visas or citizenship, and similar services.

National and International Involvement

Along with his responsibilities in the Diocese of Manchester, Bishop Primeau served on a number of national committees and on two Roman commissions. In the conference of U.S. Catholic bishops, he was appointed to committees, frequently as chairman, dealing with Latin America, Catholic college students, canon law, seminaries and priestly training, education, pastoral research and practices, the selection of bishops, and the establishment of boundaries for dioceses and provinces. Like his predecessors, Bishops Peterson and Brady, he was elected president general of the prestigious National Catholic Educational Association, in 1965, 1966, and 1967.

In August 1966, he was invited, and accepted, to serve on the executive committee of the Extension Society, a home mission organization. His involvements on the international level have been mentioned, except for his appointment as a consultor to the Vatican Congregation of Bishops, on November 12, 1976, after his resignation and retirement as bishop of Manchester. The major task of this Vatican Congregation is to recommend candidates for the episcopacy in the dioceses and archdioceses of the Church around the world.

Effects of Church Renewal: Negative and Positive

While the renewal of the Catholic Church in New Hampshire has had many positive effects, there were also a good number of changes with a negative impact that were experienced in New Hampshire, as well as nationwide. These changes affected the areas of belief, attitudes, and religious practice. For example, weekend (Saturday evening and Sunday) attendance at Mass fell from about 71 percent in the late 1950s to below 50 percent in the early 1970s.

Acceptance of birth control by lay Catholics reached nearly 90 percent by the early 1970s, and nearly two-thirds of the Catholic clergy were in agreement. As it will be seen, there was an alarming increase in the resignation of priests and in the permanent departure of women religious from their communities.

Catholic high school and elementary school enrollments were also adversely affected. The high school population in New Hampshire dropped from 4,370 in 1959 to 2,981 in 1973; and elementary registration, which rose from more than 23,000 in 1959 to 24,405 in 1965, then plummeted to 11,942 in the fall of 1973. The number of women religious in the state went from 1,679 in 1959 down to 1,370 in 1973, with only 438 remaining in Catholic school education. This exodus bordered on the near desertion of a key ministry in the church. By 1973, there were 218 laypeople teaching the Catholic (elementary and secondary) schools of the diocese.

An equally troubling factor was that registration in Confraternity of Christian Doctrine programs did not increase as fast as the Catholic schools were losing students. That indicated that greater numbers of Catholic elementary and secondary age students were not receiving any kind of formal religious education. Nationwide, by 1976, there were 6.6 million in these categories, a disturbingly high number.

In New Hampshire, overall, the number of Catholic elementary and secondary school students receiving formal religious instruction, that is, either in Catholic schools or in CCD programs, rose from 49,531 in 1959 to only 55,141 in 1973, an increase of just 5,610. During the same period, Catholic schools, elementary and secondary, lost 13,852 pupils. That equates to a loss of 8,242 students.

On the positive side, during the period 1959–1973, the Catholic population of New Hampshire increased by more than 43,000 and eleven new parishes were established, mostly in the southern tier of the state. The number of active diocesan priests remained relatively steady, despite resignations, retirements, and deaths, the number slipping from 254 (1959) to 249 (1973). In 1973, there were forty-three priests who were either retired, on sick leave, or absent, all new phenomena in the diocese.

Resignation of the Diocesan Bishop

On January 30, 1974, Bishop Primeau became the first bishop of Manchester to resign from office. This became effective at 9 A.M., local time. In his written statement on that occasion, he explained that he could no longer fulfill the role that had been entrusted to him. He observed that his sixty-four years of life, thirty-nine years of priesthood, and fourteen years as bishop had been intensive, particularly during the last two decades. They had, he concluded, taken their toll "physically and emotionally." On the same day as his resignation, he took the oath of office as apostolic administrator, at the request of the Holy See. He held this position until his definite departure from the diocese on June 4, 1974.

On that day, Monsignor Thomas S. Hansberry, the vicar general, was elected administrator by the diocesan consultors. Shortly after his departure from Manchester, Bishop Primeau became director of Villa Stritch in Rome, a residence provided by the U.S. hierarchy for American priests who work for the Holy See, and for those Americans who visit Rome on official Church business.

After several years in Rome, Bishop Primeau returned to the United States, where he lived in retirement first in Arizona and then in New Hampshire. He died in Manchester on June 6, 1989. The inscription on his grave in St. Joseph Cemetery rather concisely summarizes his life, as the epitaph for Bishop Bradley did his: "Father of the Second Vatican Council. Learned and Perceptive Churchman. Kind and Gentle Pastor. A Man of Good Humor. He Enjoyed Life in the Lord."

Preliminary Character Profile

An elaboration of Bishop Primeau's just quoted epitaph will give a better understanding of the Catholic Church in the United States between 1909 and 1986, the years of the life of this prelate.

For the first fifty-three years of his life, Bishop Primeau lived in a church that had remained basically unchanged since the Council of Trent (1545–1563)—that is, since the Counter-Reformation began in the mid–sixteenth century. During this phase of Church history, Ernest J. Primeau was educated, ordained, received a doctorate, taught in a preparatory seminary, served in Rome for twelve years, and was appointed the bishop of Manchester. Unquestionably, he was deeply marked by these experiences. They are certainly the reasons why he and his advisers were able to propose only a small number of essentially cosmetic changes in the Church, most of them canonical in nature, when asked by the Holy See to submit subjects for discussion at the Second Vatican Council. There is no evidence of any change of mind or heart in Bishop Primeau during the near two years that he served on the Vatican Commission for the Discipline of the Clergy and the Faithful.

Shortly after the formal opening of the council on October 11, 1962, a gradual and deepening change began to take place in Bishop Primeau's way of thinking about the Church and its role in the modern world, a change that affected a good number of the bishops at the council. This change in him was reflected in his leadership in renewal between roughly 1964 and 1973.

A third and final phase began to insinuate itself in Bishop Primeau's evaluation of the Church and its efforts at renewal. This occurred, as already indicated, in 1973 and perhaps slightly before. By this time, he was publicly stating that the era of renewal was over (it had lasted less than ten years). Part of the problem, he indicated, was that too much time and effort had been spent on bringing about changes in structure and not enough on prayer. Much of his dismay stemmed from the polarization—the often acerbic division—that had accompanied renewal, among and within the laity, the religious, and the clergy. Some of this phenomenon is described in this book.

An observer would have believed during the immediate post–Vatican Council period (1965–1973) that Bishop Primeau's intellect was primarily attracted to the renewalists but that his heart, sentiment, and instincts remained with the pre-Vatican traditionalists. In this internal battle between mind and heart, there is usually no clear victor. Pragmatically, the winning side, if it may be called that, is generally the one that emerges in control, in this case clearly the conservative element in the Catholic Church.

These changes in Bishop Primeau's thinking were obviously brought about by the events of the time. Another element, however, needs to be taken into account: his character and personality. Above all, he was a very adaptable person. After living in Chicago and Rome, he became a contented and adjusted resident of New Hampshire without any apparent stressful period of transition.

In addition, Bishop Primeau never showed the slightest trace of envy in a number of very trying personal circumstances. He was also quite sensitive and sentimental; it was not uncommon for him to show tears in his eyes at the news of the illness of a friend or associate.

Strangely enough, given his French Canadian background, with a father born in Montreal, and his experiences in Rome, where French was often used as a diplomatic language, Bishop Primeau had little command of the language. While he could speak it in a rudimentary and generally incorrect fashion, he had never studied the language at any level of his formal educa-

tion. All of his homilies and conferences in that language were "ghost" written. Even his reading of the prepared text was enough to make the "ghost,"
if present, cringe in his seat or pew. He was fluent, however, in Italian, a far
more useful language for someone dealing with the Holy See. In fact, his
reading of French sounded more like an oration in Italian than it did one in
French. Despite the inelegance of his French, his French Canadian hearers
were pleased that he made the effort and overlooked the quality.

Above all, Bishop Primeau enjoyed the company of people and inter-
acting with them, particularly priests with whom he was the most familiar and at ease. Given a choice between a lively conversation and a visit to
a museum, a historical sight, or attendance at a movie or concert of any
kind, he would without hesitation select the conversation. Such exchanges
of views could go on for hours well into the night. One ploy, frequently
made use of, was for him to begin a discussion on a controversial subject
and then slip quietly out of the room as the others heatedly expressed
their views without even noticing his departure.

One of Bishop Primeau's major difficulties was in the exercise of his
authority. His preference and style, demonstrated over fourteen years,
were to lead by example and persuasion. This style was reinforced by his
strong desire not to offend—even to please—everyone. Some took advantage of this, perhaps thinking his attitude was a weakness. One example,
among many, will be cited. A pastor in Auburn, a town neighboring Manchester, refused to install a new altar facing the people as mandated by
liturgical law and required by the bishop. Despite several mild admonitions on this subject, the pastor, knowing that no punishment would follow, resolved the problem by placing an ordinary table along a wall of the
sanctuary and pulling it out to the center when he knew the bishop was
coming to the church.

A more serious example of Bishop Primeau's fear of offending took
place on the occasion of a New England Religious Education Congress
hosted by the diocese on the campus of the University of New Hampshire,
in Durham, during the latter part of August 1973. Among the speakers
approved beforehand by the bishop for this congress was Father Daniel
Berrigan, s.j., a poet, but also a nationally known peace activist, anti–Vietnam War protester, draft card burner, and invader of draft board offices.
When Father Berrigan's acceptance of the invitation became public, a
number of archconservative organizations and individuals protested

vehemently that he should not be allowed to speak at the congress, especially on government property, namely the University of New of Hampshire, a state college.

Among the most outspoken and powerful objectors was the then governor of New Hampshire, Meldrim Thomson Jr., a true ultraconservative Republican largely educated in the pre–World War II South. So outraged was the governor that at one point he threatened to call out the National Guard to keep this pacifist priest off state property. The *Manchester Union Leader,* always a strong supporter of this governor, joined him, by articles and editorials, in opposing the appearance of Father Berrigan at the university. Gone were the days when the bishop of Manchester could think of the *Union Leader* as his diocesan newspaper, as Bishop Brady had in the 1950s.

Confronted this way about a decision he had already made, Bishop Primeau tried several avenues to have Father Berrigan withdraw his acceptance to attend and speak at the conference, which, by the way, attracted more than 10,000 participants. Finding no one willing to approach the Jesuit for him, and being unwilling to retract the invitation on his own, Father Berrigan himself spoke at the congress, much to the delight of the several thousands who heard him. Governor Thomson, probably analyzing his political options in a state that was about 30 percent Catholic, did not call out the National Guard and eventually kept silent.

Bishop Primeau was the first ordinary of New Hampshire to emphasize and insist upon the continuing education of the clergy and the religious education of the adult Catholic community, along with that of the children and youth. Prior to the council, a seminary education was considered good for life, and the religious education of the laity received in grammar and high school was thought to be sufficient for an entire life as well. Bishop Primeau was the first, and is still the only one of the eight bishops of Manchester to date, to earn a doctoral degree in addition to the honorary degrees bestowed abundantly on the members of the American hierarchy, particularly by Catholic colleges. During his fourteen-year tenure, he sent more priests away for graduate studies than did all of his predecessors combined. Moreover, all members of the clergy were encouraged to take courses and degrees. A special fund was established to pay, at least in part, for this continuing education. To ensure that all priests had an opportunity for education, courses were offered for them around the diocese on a variety of subjects relevant to the priest as a person and helpful for his ministry. These programs have since been expanded and are thriving today.

At the same time, effective steps were taken to provide opportunities for the religious education of the laity. Soon after the Second Vatican Council, nationally prominent speakers were invited to address the Catholics of New Hampshire; preparations for the second synod and "Operation FIRE" provided hundreds of meetings around the state and during its course distributed roughly 1 million pieces of educational materials (cf. above); ten Christian Life Centers were founded covering the entire state; and numerous other opportunities for religious education and formation were devised and presented as well.

From the days of the Second Vatican Council, Bishop Primeau professed himself the friend and advocate of the rights and active role of the laity in the church. As was mentioned previously, he announced his promotion of the laity in an internationally acclaimed oral presentation to some two thousand bishops from around the world assembled at the Second Vatican Council. In his address of October 23, 1963, he stressed that the place of the laity was not one of subjection to the ecclesiastical order, and that its duties were not defined solely by to "believe, pray, pay, and obey." Even before the end of the council, Bishop Primeau began to build numerous structures to give voice, role, and responsibility to laymen and laywomen. In particular, it should be noted that in the early years after the council, Bishop Primeau, as it has been related, proposed to give more than consultative voice to the laity in the parish councils of the diocese. His plan to give them power to override a veto by the pastor under certain circumstances was nullified by the new Code of Canon Law published in 1983. A powerful indication of the importance of the laity in his mind is the fact that he chose to be buried at St. Joseph Cemetery among the laity rather than in the cathedral crypt reserved for bishops. By the end of Bishop Primeau's episcopacy in New Hampshire, the Diocese of Manchester had given as much recognition to the laity as the most advanced in this regard in the nation. A second reading of chapter 12 will reassure the reader of this fact.

Strangely enough, despite his strong and persistent advocacy of the laity, Bishop Primeau was ill at ease, even uncomfortable, with women, both on an individual basis and in small numbers; large groups presented no particular difficulty. This was not an unusual phenomenon among priests of his generation. For many, this could be accounted for by their general isolation from women since their freshman year in a minor high school seminary when they were about fourteen years of age. A good number never really learned how to socialize on an adult-to-adult basis with women. In Bishop Primeau's case, however, he entered the seminary in philosophy, that is in the third year of college, when he was about twenty years old. Consequently, a reason other than the one just given must likely apply. One of Bishop Primeau's contemporaries in the seminary confided that he had a similar problem, which he attributed to his seminary training. There is no doubt that some of the writings of the Fathers of the Church, and later those of the theologians of the Middle Ages, held strong antifeminine views that affected the seminary staff and, through it, the seminarians themselves. In defining the role of women, one could begin with the story of the seduction of Adam by Eve and go on from there. A practical result of this formation was that Bishop Primeau, while vaunting the rights of the laity, declined to appoint fully qualified women to positions of authority on the diocesan level on the grounds that the clergy would either resent or resist their authority. Theory and practice were in conflict here.

Renewal for Bishop Primeau presented him with at least three intellectual and emotional challenges. The first and most obvious was the conflict created by the contrast between the first fifty-three years of his life, which had been in a peaceful and rock-solid stable church absolutely sure of itself on every point, and his final twenty-six years or so. After 1962 major transformations occurred: there was questioning, excitement, chance, and, finally, division and confrontation.

A second dilemma was a matter of loyalty. During his twelve years at the Chicago House in Rome (1946–1958) and later in his ministry, this affable priest made countless friends, many of them prominent conservatives, such as Alfredo Cardinal Ottaviani, head of the Holy Office; Amleto Cardinal Cicognani, at one time Apostolic Delegate to the United States and later Secretary of State for the Holy See; and Giovanni Battista Montini, who was elected pope in 1963 and took the name Paul VI; among many more. Father and later Bishop Primeau was very conscious of their ecclesiastical orientation and their power to reward or to withhold favors and promotions. To them and their peers he owed his appointment to Manchester and shortly thereafter to the Commission on the Discipline of the Clergy and the Faithful preparing the Second Vatican Council.

Generally coinciding with the beginning of the council, he made equally good friends with a large number of the most influential theologians and other intellectuals in the Catholic world. Among these were: Fathers John Courtney Murray, s.j., Yves Congar, o.p., Gregory Baum, Hans Kung, Andrew Greeley (he had been a former student of his at Quigley), and Monsignor William Onclin. From the friendship point of view, Bishop Primeau was placed between the two opposite camps of the Church and the council.

A third concern related to renewal, which proved to be the most crucial and emotionally exhausting, was the division produced in the American Church by the implementation of the council, including the Diocese of Manchester. This more than any other factor brought about the "physical and emotional" toll that he mentioned in his statement of resignation.

FOURTEEN

A Time for Evaluation 1975–1990

From History to Chronicle

From roughly the end of Bishop Primeau's episcopacy, it becomes nearly impossible to present history in the true sense of the discipline. Individuals and events appear too close to the observer to ascertain the importance and the ultimate long-range influence that only future years will reveal. Consequently, most of what follows is simply a chronicle—a relation—rather than an interpretation or analysis of the events of the time under consideration. It is with this in mind that one should examine the Church in New Hampshire since approximately 1975. Everything is said, however, with the understanding that the judgment of history is rarely ever final and is subject to refinement and even revision.

The Seventh Bishop of Manchester: Odore J. Gendron 1975–1990

Bishop Primeau's resignation as bishop of Manchester coincided roughly with the end of the period of intense renewal in the Catholic Church in the United States and the often severe confrontations that took place between the extremists at both ends of the spectrum—left and right. While the tensions between these extremists continue nearly forty years after the end of the Second Vatican Council (1962–1965), they are not as widespread and, as a rule, are less acrimonious.

The period of relative calm achieved in the mid-1970s was too frequently attained by outright defections from the Catholic Church, generally by those who were disenchanted with the changes, overwhelmed by sheer emotional and physical exhaustion, or, in many cases, by the con-

viction that the decisions of the Second Vatican Council and postconciliar documents had not been fully and faithfully implemented in this
country and the dioceses.

It was most likely with this new situation in mind, one that required
stabilization, that the Holy See selected Monsignor Odore J. Gendron, a
priest with a great deal of pastoral experience, as the seventh ordinary of
the Diocese of Manchester.

Bishop Gendron was only the second bishop of Manchester to come
from an essentially pastoral background—that is, the greater part of his
ministry was in a parish—first as associate and then as pastor. Until that
time, the only other bishop with similar experience was George Albert
Guertin. Both Bishops Bradley and Delany had been chancellors, perhaps
the most frequent stepping-stone to the episcopacy; Bishop Peterson had
been a seminary professor and rector; Bishop Brady spent several years on
the faculty of a minor seminary; and Bishop Primeau passed twelve years
in Rome as the head of a house of graduate studies for priests. Of the two
auxiliary bishops, Robert E. Mulvee has also been a chancellor, and Joseph
Gerry, o.s.b., the former abbot of St. Anselm College.

Odore Joseph Gendron was born in Manchester on September 13,
1921, the son of a shoemaker, François Gendron, and a homemaker, Val-
ida (Rouleau) Gendron. Odore was one of three children. His brother,
Mancy, also became a priest, the first ordained member and then superior
general of the Pius X Lay Institute in Pointe au Pic Quebec, Canada. His
sister, Rolande, worked thirty-eight years for the *Manchester Union Leader*
in the circulation department and assisted her mother in taking care of
the family. In order to afford the education of their children, Mrs. Gendron supplemented the family income by taking in boarders, a not
uncommon occurrence at the time. As early as the late 1860s and early
1870s, Mary Bradley had done the same to pay for her son Denis's education to the priesthood.

Odore, for his part, worked summers at manual labor when he was
old enough. On the occasion of his fiftieth anniversary of ordination to
the priesthood in 1997, Bishop Gendron, reminiscing on his youth, spoke
of his father and his sister as "very" people–oriented (as he was also judged
to be), and his mother as the most reserved and retiring member of the
family. During the same interview, he remembered a very unified home
atmosphere in which there were no disagreements, a near unique phe-

nomenon in any generation. There was, the bishop added, never a time when he did not want to become a priest.

Young Odore received his elementary education at Sacred Heart School on the west side of the city of Manchester. After grammar school he was sent to Canada, where he spent four years of high school and two years of college at St. Charles Barromeo Seminary at Sherbrooke in the province of Quebec. From 1942 to 1947, mostly war years, he studied philosophy and then theology at St. Paul Seminary, Ottawa, Ontario. During his seminary years, he related later, he saw Bishop Peterson, his ordinary until his death on March 15, 1944, only once. During this interview, in which Bishop Peterson examined his school record, he seemed very happy with the marks in this seminarian's folder. It is unlikely that he ever spoke to Bishop Peterson's successor until the day of his ordination, as the latter, Bishop Brady, had no policy or plan to meet his future priests before ordination day.

After eleven years of seminary training—six at Sherbrooke and five at Ottawa—Odore J. Gendron was ordained to the priesthood by Bishop Matthew F. Brady at St. Joseph Cathedral in Manchester on May 31, 1947. Successively, his assignments as associate pastor were at Guardian Angel parish, Berlin; Sacred Heart parish, Lebanon; and St. Aloysius of Gonzaga in Nashua. In 1965, he was given his first pastorate at Our Lady of Lourdes parish in Pittsfield. Just two years later he was transferred to St. Augustine parish, the oldest French Canadian national parish in the state of New Hampshire, then a prestige assignment.

In 1966, while serving as pastor in Pittsfield, he began a ministry that was to have high priority in his life for a number of years. In January of that year, he was appointed vicar for French-speaking women religious of the diocese. In that capacity, he looked after the spiritual needs of these nuns.

In February 1971, Bishop Primeau asked Monsignor Gendron to resign the pastorate of St. Augustine in order to serve, on a full-time basis, the English speaking as well as the French-speaking women religious of the diocese. On April 1, 1972, he was appointed the first episcopal vicar for women religious in the history of the Diocese of Manchester.

In addition to his ministry with women religious, Monsignor Gendron, who had been appointed a prelate of honor to His Holiness by Pope Paul VI on December 22, 1970, with the title of Reverend Monsignor, was given responsibilities regarding the clergy. Elected to the Senate of Priests by the clergy, he was chosen the second president of that body in 1970, and reelected the following year.

In January 1974, Bishop Primeau, recognizing Monsignor Gendron's effective work with priests, appointed him the first episcopal vicar for the clergy. In that capacity, he also acted as chairman of the diocesan clergy personnel board, a major responsibility. At the time of his episcopal appointment, he was serving as episcopal vicar for both clergy and religious. At various periods, he also served as notary for the diocesan marriage tribunal (1960), as a founding member of the diocesan pastoral commission elected by the clergy (1965), and as diocesan consultor from January 1969 until his appointment as bishop.

Bishop Gendron was ordained to the episcopacy in the Manchester Cathedral at 3 P.M. on Monday, February 3, 1975, by Bishop Primeau, assisted by the co-consecrators Bishop Edward C. O'Leary, ordinary of Portland (Maine), and Bishop Timothy J. Harrington, then auxiliary bishop of Worcester. Bishop Gendron was only the second of the seven ordinaries of Manchester to be born in New Hampshire. The other, Bishop Guertin (1907–1931), was born in Nashua in 1869.

A Time to Evaluate

While it may not have been intended or even perceived, a kind of moratorium was put into effect on a number of organizations and activities in the diocese beginning in approximately 1975. This will become apparent in this text in reviewing the first years of the episcopacy of Bishop Gendron. In some ways, this was beneficial and even necessary, for at least two reasons. First, it allowed for an appraisal, an evaluation, of all that had been done, in some cases rather precipitously, in the name of renewal between roughly 1965 and 1975. Second, it gave the new bishop an opportunity to develop his own leadership style and to establish his own priorities for the Catholic Church in New Hampshire.

One minor but certainly visible sign of the shift from the previous ten to eleven years was the return to the use of the pectoral chain and cross with street dress (abandoned by Bishop Primeau), and the more frequent use of cassock, purple sash, and purple ferrailo (ample cape) on social occasions where either street dress or ecclesiastical vesture would have been appropriate.

Two Early Priorities

Two of Bishop Gendron's early decisions were to indicate the direction of his episcopal style. One was the motto on his coat of arms, "Unity in Charity," and the other was the pledge, frequently given, to be both a visible and a pastoral leader. "Unity in Charity" was now a realizable goal precisely because the passions created by the postconciliar period had to some extent burnt out. His pledge to be both a visible and a pastoral leader was achieved by his efforts to acquire an intimate and extensive knowledge of every facet of the life of the Church in New Hampshire. His major project to achieve this goal was a pastoral visitation of each parish in the diocese begun in the fall of 1980.

Pastoral Visitations

These pastoral visitations were the most extensive and intensive ever undertaken by a Catholic bishop in New Hampshire. It has been noted that Bishop James A. Healy, then spiritually responsible for both Maine and New Hampshire, undertook a pastoral visitation of the parishes (that of 1875, it is said, covered some 3,000 miles) of both these states in 1875 and again in 1878; travel for these visitations was by train, stagecoach, and one presumes, by boat (at least) to cross rivers, and horseback. The only other systematic and detailed formal visitation of the parishes of New Hampshire had been conducted by Bishop Ernest J. Primeau in the late 1960s. The other bishops, one from Portland (Bishop David W. Bacon) and the six episcopal leaders of the Diocese of Manchester prior to Bishop Gendron, kept in personal touch with the parishes at the time of confirmation, and, less frequently, at church dedications and other religious or social functions. Seldom were "spur-of-the-moment" visits made by any of these bishops.

Bishop Gendron's visitations were unique in many ways. Each visit, for example, was preceded by an in-depth inventory of the parish made by the pastor and the parish council (now known as the pastoral council) following a very detailed questionnaire prepared by the bishop and his staff with considerable prior consultation.

This questionnaire directed the parish council to evaluate the life of the parish in the areas of liturgy, worship, Christian education, finances, youth activities, community affairs, and anything else that pertained to its ministry and spiritual and material well-being. These evaluations in each area were to be supplemented by a consideration of what remained to be done, how these goals could best be achieved, and what assistance was deemed needed from the diocese and the deaneries.

These evaluations, which were eventually to encompass some 130 parishes, began in late September 1980, and would extend over a period of some two and a half years. Bishop Gendron's objective was to complete this crucial phase of his ministry before the celebration of the centennial of the creation of the diocese, which was to occur in 1984. The first two parishes to experience this new approach to episcopal concern were St. Theresa in Henniker and St. Peter in Concord.

In essence, each visitation extended over a period of some thirty hours. As a rule, two parishes were visited each weekend, when the bishop's schedule allowed. One visit began on Friday noon and ended Saturday evening; the second commenced on Sunday morning and came to a close on Monday at about noon.

Each visit incorporated at least the following activities: the celebration of the Eucharist by the bishop followed by a reception for the parish at large; an all-embracing meeting with the parish council; a similar meeting with the parish youth group; a visit, where one existed, with the students and staff of the Catholic school; a time for individual parishioners to speak with the bishop privately, for those who wished to do so; and dialogue with the pastor, the pastoral associate(s), and the parish staff.

Each visitation was followed up by a lengthy report prepared by the bishop's secretary (Monsignor Francis J. Christian) on all that had been discussed with the various groups and individuals. This report was then sent to the parish so that it could be shared by all concerned. Based on the visitation and the report, each parish was requested to identify two goals to achieve during the subsequent year and to report on the status of the implementation of these goals at the end of the year.

Following his unprecedented and highly successful visitations to the parishes, Bishop Gendron then undertook and especially designed visitation of the monasteries and convents of women religious and the similar institutions of religious priests and religious brothers in New Hampshire.

Fortified with this mass of information, in addition to the actual experience of living in the parishes with the clergy, staff, and laity, Bishop

Gendron was superbly equipped to deal with the life of the Catholic Church in New Hampshire. And it is obvious that it greatly influenced him in shaping his own priorities and programs. In effect, this visitation, one not repeated since then, became the foundation and centerpiece of his administration.

It is regrettable, however, that this vast amount of then current and pertinent information about the parishes and religious communities in the diocese has not been either kept up-to-date or used more extensively in preparing for the future of the Catholic Church in New Hampshire. This lack of continuity, or follow-up, had been experienced in previous diocesan programs, such as "Operation FIRE" described under the administration of Bishop Primeau.

Bishop Gendron and the Clergy

In his persistent efforts to be a visible and involved presence, Bishop Gendron paid particular attention to both the needs of the priests and their experience and insights with regard to the present and future of the Church in New Hampshire.

This closeness and exchange of views between bishop and priests did not exist in this diocese, nor hardly anywhere else for that matter, prior to the Second Vatican Council. It is clear from archival evidence and the oral tradition of the priests themselves that Bishops Guertin, Peterson, and Brady had no meaningful informal contacts with the clergy. Few priests ever saw the bishop's residence, for example, any closer than driving or walking by his home. This was not unique to New Hampshire; this was the style and custom around the nation. A theological wall had been built separating the bishop from his closest collaborators.

Nothing certain can be said about either of the first two bishops of Manchester, Bradley and Delany. There is neither enough archival material nor reliable diocesan tradition to make a sure judgment. Based on what little evidence that remains, one would likely conclude that Bishop Bradley had a pre–Vatican I (1869–1870) mentality and thus was close to his clergy. His correspondence points that way. On the other hand, Bishop Delany (whose episcopacy lasted a mere twenty-one months) was the first of the more lordly bishops more distant from the clergy, not to mention the laity.

Bishop Gendron was to improve more widely on the bond of visible union between himself and the clergy initiated by Bishop Primeau. This was achieved in a variety of ways, including informal breakfast meetings with moderate-size groups of clergy at the bishop's residence. For the majority of those present, this was the first time ever in the home of their spiritual leader. These breakfasts were followed in 1986 by informal meetings of groups of about twelve, in the same age category, again in the bishop's domicile. These gatherings began at 10:30 A.M. and consisted of prayer together, discussion, and lunch, in that order. Subject matter for the discussion was determined by the groups of participants themselves for the purpose of identifying current trends in the diocese and to assist the bishop in meetings those needs.

The Diocese's First Auxiliary Bishop

From the onset of his episcopacy, Bishop Gendron recognized the need for an auxiliary. This need was based on both the growth of the Catholic population of New Hampshire and the many new structures and programs that were required to properly minister to the spiritual needs of the faithful. Most likely his future absences because of the parish visitations were also taken into consideration. His petition to the Holy See for an auxiliary was honored by Pope Paul VI on February 15, 1977. On that day it was publicly announced that Monsignor Robert E. Mulvee had been appointed to that office. Monsignor Mulvee was the virtually unanimous choice of the clergy, as he was of everyone who knew or worked with him.

Bishop Mulvee received episcopal ordination on April 14, 1977, just one day short of the ninety-third anniversary of the founding of the Diocese of Manchester. With his episcopal ordination, he became the first auxiliary bishop in the history of the Catholic Church in New Hampshire.

Robert E. Mulvee was born in Boston in 1930, the son of the late John F. and Jennie T. Mulvee. After his primary and high school education in the Boston area, he spent two years at St. Thomas Seminary in Bloomfield, Connecticut; two years at St. Paul Seminary in Ottawa, Ontario; and four years at the American College in Louvain, Belgium, from where he was ordained to the priesthood on June 30, 1957.

On his return to New Hampshire, he first served as chaplain at St. Charles Orphanage in Rochester and volunteered for parish work at St. Leo parish in Gonic. Later he ministered at St. Peter parish in Farmington and at St. Catherine parish in Portsmouth. In 1960 Father Mulvee was named associate pastor of St. Joseph Cathedral in Manchester by Bishop Primeau.

Recognizing his talent and pastoral skills, in 1961 Bishop Primeau assigned him to graduate work at the North American College in Rome. He completed his doctorate in canon law at the Pontifical Lateran University in 1964, and that same year he was granted *post-factum* a master's degree in religious education from the University of Louvain. As mentioned, he served as an "assignatore" at the Second Vatican Council.

In July 1964, upon his return to the diocese, Bishop Primeau appointed Father Mulvee assistant chancellor. Subsequently, he was named to a number of additional diocesan posts, including notary and judge of the diocesan tribunal, diocesan consultor, the bishop's master of ceremonies, and secretary to the second diocesan synod. Father Mulvee also served as a member of the diocesan vocations commission, the diocesan liturgical commission, the diocesan pastoral commission, and the building and real estate board.

In October 1966, Father Mulvee was made a papal chamberlain by Pope Paul VI and, in 1970, the same sovereign pontiff raised him to the rank of Prelate of Honor to His Holiness. Monsignor Mulvee was appointed chancellor of the Diocese of Manchester in April 1972 by Bishop Primeau, the post he held at the time of his selection as auxiliary bishop in February 1977. After his ordination to the episcopacy, Bishop Mulvee was named vicar general of the diocese.

On June 15, 1977, two months after his episcopal ordination, Bishop Mulvee was appointed to succeed Bishop Gendron in the offices of clergy personnel director and chairman of the clergy diocesan personnel board, two positions of key importance in the assignments and pastoral care of priests.

On the national level, Bishop Mulvee was elected as a member of the bishops' national advisory council in 1978. He also served for three years on the board of bishops for the North American College (where he had studied), and on the committee for the nomination of officers for the national conference of Catholic bishops. He was also elected vice chairman of the New England Council of Church Leaders, a group consisting of the ecclesiastical directors of most of the major religious bodies in the six New England states.

On February 19, 1985, the papal Pro-Nuncio for the United States, Archbishop Pio Laghi, announced that Bishop Mulvee had been appointed by Pope John Paul II the seventh bishop of the Diocese of Wilmington (Delaware). He was installed in that diocese on April 11, 1985. From Wilmington, he was transferred to Providence (Rhode Island) as coadjutor bishop with right to succession in early 1995. Some two years later, in 1997, with the resignation or Bishop Louis E. Gelineau, Bishop Mulvee assumed the title and responsibilities of Bishop of Providence. This diocese, which includes the entire state of Rhode Island, has a Catholic population of more than 644,00, nearly twice that of New Hampshire.

New Programs 1976–1980

Simultaneous with his efforts to establish a sound rapport with the clergy and the faithful, Bishop Gendron began to establish what would become a large number of programs that were new to the diocese. In this regard, he appears to have exceeded all of his predecessors. As early as 1976, the year following his episcopal ordination, he inaugurated a national program sponsored by Catholic Relief Services called "Operation Rice Bowl," whose goals are to satisfy the immediate food needs of the hungry around the world and, in addition, to fight the root causes of that hunger by initiating and supporting long-range programs for that purpose. As 25 percent of the monies collected remain in the diocese, they greatly help local poverty programs.

That same year (1976), there began the annual New Hampshire Catholic Charismatic Services Pentecost Celebration, which is still held at St. Mary Church, Manchester, and attracts large numbers of devoted and enthusiastic faithful from the entire New England area. St. Mary parish remains the epicenter of the charismatic movement in New Hampshire.

Respect Life programs, sponsored by the National Conference of Catholic Bishops, were initiated in the diocese in a formal way in 1978. Their objective is to instill a commitment to the value and dignity of all human life, from conception to grave. The programs include concern about hunger; poverty; care of the elderly; the disabled; pregnant women; disadvantaged children; and all situations where the value and dignity of human life are threatened. Obviously, abortion, an assault on the right to life itself, is primary among these concerns.

Parish councils, now called parish pastoral councils, founded in virtually all parishes in the late 1960s by express mandate of Bishop Primeau, were given additional support in 1978 by the establishment of an annual Parish Council Assembly. These assemblies, which provided information, resources, and support to council members, unfortunately were never more than a marginal success. Records indicate that these assemblies never attracted more than three hundred participants nor more than sixty parishes, that in 1985. They have been discontinued for lack of interest.

In contrast, the founding of Emmaus House, also in 1978, has been a lasting and successful enterprise. Administered by the Office of Youth Ministry of the diocese, it is located at 286 Concord Street in Manchester in a building that is three stories high and contains several meeting areas, a lounge, and more than fifty additional rooms. This structure, originally an infant asylum conducted by the Sisters of Mercy, was refurbished (painted, washed, varnished, and so on) by young people from all over the state between January and March 1978 under the direction of Rick Rouse, then the diocesan youth director. Most of the furniture was donated by interested supporters of the house.

This facility was inaugurated in the spring of 1978 with a retreat for the youth of Holy Angels parish, Plaistow. That fall, Rick Rouse was forced to withdraw because of a brain tumor. This dedicated young man was replaced by Sister Bernadette Turgeon, a sister of Notre Dame de Namur, who, in 1997, was still co-director of Emmaus House as well as the head of the entire department of Faith Development.

Emmaus House now provides Christian experience programs of great variety for youth from the age of junior high school through young adults. In addition to being available to prepare teenagers for confirmation throughout the state, the ministries of Emmaus House extend to consultations and training for religious educators, youth ministers, and parents of teenagers. Staff members are also ready to provide programs either at Emmaus House or in the local parish setting.

Another program involving young people has also had considerable success. A project called More House (named after the English saint Thomas More), initiated by the Reverend Frederick J. Pennett, chaplain, is planned and coordinated by the Catholic Student Center at the University of New Hampshire in Durham. Its purpose is to address some aspect of poverty or social injustice in a specific civic community in New Hampshire. This endeavor is funded by New Hampshire Catholic Charities and administered jointly with the Department of Campus Ministries.

This unique program, lasting some eight weeks each summer, usually involves six to eight college students who live in a community experiencing some form of social problem. These students, who have various majors in college, study the situation from all aspects and angles with the assistance of the community, the local church, and the expertise provided by the university. A report is then prepared on their findings, and possible remedies are recommended. The first two projects, in successive summers, in Pittsfield and Franklin were so well received that they have been continued each year in towns and cities around New Hampshire.

An evangelization program of historic proportions was also launched in 1980: the "Rite of the Christian Initiation of Adults" (RCIA). This creative and exciting new program is actually a return to the practice of the early church in initiating, preparing, and receiving prospective candidates into the Christian community. The rite was introduced by the Sacred Congregation for Divine Worship, a commission of the Holy See, in January 1972, in the spirit of the directives of the Second Vatican Council on the renewal of the liturgy.

This period of initiation, or catechumenate, can extend over a period of six months to three years, depending on many factors, the most important, obviously, being the disposition of the candidate. The process consists of the following catechetical stages: The pre-catechumenate, the catechumenate, and purification (enlightenment). A basic component is the involvement of the whole community to which these catechurnens will be bonded by their baptism. This initiation, ideally, culminates in the reception of baptism, confirmation, and the Eucharist at the Easter Vigil service. In 1996, for example, there were 167 adult baptisms and a far larger number of previously baptized people who were, for the most part, received into the Catholic Church in New Hampshire by means of the Rite of the Christian Initiation of Adults.

In response to the Pastoral Statement on Handicapped Persons, published by the United States Conference in 1978, Bishop Gendron established the Office of Ministry with the Handicapped in 1980 with the Reverend Richard P. Tetu, then chaplain at the Laconia State School, as the first director. This office's primary functions, directed to both the physically and mentally challenged, were to provide properly tailored religious education, housing suitable to a person's physical or mental condition, and accessibility to church buildings and other facilities. While these are goals that remain in progress, handicapped accessibility to most churches and many other diocesan buildings is now possible.

In addition to the concerns for the handicapped, the diocese, through its own Secretariat for Community Affairs, continued its involvement in seeking and providing better housing for the disadvantaged. Attempts to achieve this end have been entrusted to the now entitled Diocesan Bureau of Housing and Housing Services. One example of its work was the opening in 1980 of a home for the developmentally disabled in Peterborough, a facility for eight adults and two houseparents. At the time (1980), the Bureau of Housing had plans for three additional group homes. Projects of this nature are generally devised in cooperation with the other churches and civic organizations in the community and funding is sought from local, state, and federal agencies as well as from private foundations

The Permanent Deaconate

One of the major innovations undertaken in the diocese by Bishop Gendron was the establishment of the permanent deaconate. This project was not begun until 1980, well over ten years after it was introduced in the Catholic Church of the United States. On several previous occasions it had been considered but rejected by the leadership of the diocese.

Bishop Gendron selected the Reverend Leonard R. Foisy as the first director of the diocesan permanent deaconate program effective September 1, 1980. Father Foisy was well qualified for the position, having exercised many teaching and administrative tasks while a member of the Sulpicians in both the province of Quebec and the United States. His final assignment with the Sulpicians, before returning to the Diocese of Manchester in the summer of 1980, was that of rector of St. Mary Seminary and University in Baltimore, Maryland, the oldest and most prestigious institution of that kind in the country.

An extensive and in-depth search for candidates for the permanent deaconate, begun before the appointment of Father Foisy, resulted in the selection of twelve men, all married. This early process had been carried out under the attentive leadership of Monsignor John F. Burke. These future deacons held their first weekend meeting, an orientation session, on September 5–7, 1980. It launched an intensive training program that was to last more than three years, a preparation period designed to frequently involve the spouses of the candidates. In fact, wives of the candidates who had been negative to their husbands' applications for the deaconate were not considered for the program.

Many outside experts were employed to assist in the process of formation with the diocesan director. On July 27, 1982, Father Foisy received the aid of an assistant, Sister Eileen Tierney of the Congregation of Notre Dame (c.n.d.), who came to New Hampshire from Connecticut. A clear indication of the care with which the candidates had been screened, selected, and trained is the fact that all twelve original candidates were ordained to the permanent deaconate by Bishop Gendron in a ceremony at St. Anselm Abbey church on December 10, 1983.

New Hampshire received a number of other permanent deacons when they moved to the state from other jurisdictions. In early 1997, there were twenty-one active in the diocese. On September 12, 1984, at his request, Father Foisy, previously named to the pastorate of St. Mary parish, Manchester, resigned as director of the permanent deaconate office and was replaced by co-directors, Sister Eileen Tierney and Father Francis L. Demers, a member of the Missionary Oblates of Mary Immaculate (o.m.i.). Eventually the responsibility for the permanent deaconate was transferred to the Reverend Marc F. Guillemette, the current holder of that position.

A considerable impetus was given to pastoral ministry in the diocese with the decision of Bishop O'Neil to begin the preparation of a second group of men for ordination to the permanent deaconate to join the twenty-one already active in New Hampshire.

The application phase for this program began in February 1997. One hundred-nine names were submitted as possible candidates, and made application for this formation program. All of these applications were carefully studied by Bishop O'Neil, the director of the permanent deaconate in the diocese, and a specially appointed recommendation committee.

Once the applications had been evaluated, Father Marc F. Guillemette, the director of the permanent deaconate office, personally interviewed each of the 109 applicants. In June, Bishop O'Neil, the director, and the committee accepted forty-seven of the candidates for the next step of the process. During that phase, Father Guillemette visited each candidate in his home. This involved, he related, some 2,900 miles of travel in virtually every corner of the state. In addition to the personal visit and interview at home, both the applicants and their wives, (if they were married), underwent psychological testing, as do all the candidates for the diocesan priesthood. Wives were included in the screening process because they inevitably play a vital part in the life and ministry of their husbands.

From this remaining group of forty-seven, a class of twenty-eight was selected by the bishop, director, and committee. Of the twenty-eight, twenty-five of these men are married and three are single. The youngest, thirty-five, is from Nashua; and oldest, from Plymouth, is fifty-seven. Their geographical distribution over the eleven deaneries in New Hampshire is: six in Nashua (the most numerous); five each in Dover and Salem; four in Manchester East; three in Laconia; two in Lebanon; one each in Concord, Keene, and Manchester West, and none in the northern deaneries of Berlin and Franconia.

The preparation of this class of candidates for ordination to the permanent deaconate will extend over a period of four years—in contrast to the three years of the first class—and will involve three components: Theological, pastoral, and spiritual formation.

Their theological training will be provided by Notre Dame College in Manchester, where they will study such subjects as Scripture, systematic theology, ethics, ecclesiology, church history, and the sacraments. These classes, which will begin in January 1998, will be offered either in the college classroom or via Tele-learning on computer. Candidates with a bachelor's degree may earn a master's degree in theology, and those without a bachelor's will be awarded an appropriate certificate of study. Detailed and extensive plans have also been made for the spiritual and pastoral formation of the candidates, and for the wives when deemed important to their future life and ministry.

This second class of candidates for the permanent deaconate—beginning more than seventeen years after the first—is scheduled to be ready for ordination and ministry by late 2001 or early 2002.

The Process 'Renew'

Added to the flurry of activities newly inaugurated or already existing in the diocese was that of a process called "Renew." This process—as it was named, rather than a program that has a definite terminal point—had been developed and successfully used in the Archdiocese of Newark, and subsequently spread rather extensively across the United States. In New Hampshire, it came to the attention of both the Diocesan Council of the Laity and the Office of Pastoral Planning, directed by Father Paul F. McHugh. In order to learn more about the process, seven people from the diocese attended a four-day training session in Newark especially designed for core diocesan teams.

On their return, a team visited around the diocese to explain "Renew" to the clergy, parish councils, and other interested parties. As a result, twenty-five parishes opted to implement this Newark renewal experience. This process, as it could be reasonably be expected, was adapted in part to fulfill the particular needs of this diocese. It was not made mandatory by Bishop Gendron; it was, in effect, an entirely volunteer effort.

Core groups from the twenty-five volunteer parishes held a leadership training session in Concord on January 16–17, 1981. During that spring and summer, the diocesan core group continued the preparation of the parish core groups, a training that involved planning as well as prayer, the latter being called the "cement" of the entire project. This process was designed to extend over five separate sessions of six weeks duration each over a period of roughly two and a half years. Obviously, this was a serious and burdensome commitment for all those involved.

These twenty-five parishes began the first six-week session in the fall of 1981. This first phase of the five was on the theme "The Lord's Call." This was followed by the subjects "Our Response to the Lord's Call," "Discipleship," "Empowerment by the Spirit," and finally "Evangelization," the latter being a fundamental goal of the parish, as it is that of the Church. Members of the parish became involved in the process primarily through the Sunday liturgy (the Mass), abundant take-home materials, and numerous structured small-and-large group activities.

Prayer support was solicited by the distribution of special prayer cards, which the participants were urged to use every day. Moreover, these cards were distributed in hospitals, nursing homes, and wherever they might be used. By the fall of 1982, more than 47,000 of these prayer cards had been given out around the diocese.

Despite the fully volunteer aspect of the process and its two-and-half-year commitment, the record indicates that at least 47 of the roughly 130 parishes (61 percent) in the state participated in "Renew" and that many thousands shared, in some fashion, in the experience.

New Programs 1981–1984

While the process "Renew" was being adapted and implemented, a number of additional programs continued to be introduced in the diocese at frequent but irregular intervals. Among these was the holding of the first annual Respect Life Conference in 1981, at St. Mary parish, Manchester, the focal point of many of the innovations of a spiritual dimension in the diocese. This Respect Life conference has been held there yearly ever since with ardent participation.

During the same year, on September 5, Sister Bernadette Turgeon, director of Emmaus House, sponsored the first Diocesan Youth Day at Trinity High School in Manchester. This event, a twelve-hour program consisting of some thirty workshops, entertainment, and the celebration of the Divine Liturgy, attracted nearly six hundred teenage boys and girls from around the state, including about one hundred from the north. This popular event has been held annually drawing close to one thousand young people jointly to pray, discuss, and rejoice.

Attention to the youth of the diocese, as can be expected, has always been a primarily concern. In fact, organized activities for young people began in 1947. At that time, much attention, in addition to Catholic schools and the Confraternity of Christian Doctrine, was devoted to athletics. In many parishes, membership on an athletic team depended on fidelity of attendance at the religious instruction program.

In 1982, an additional two programs were introduced in the state, and both are still operational at the writing of this history. One that has left a deep imprint on the life of the faithful was the establishment of the Department of Spiritual Renewal Services under the leadership of the Reverend Marc R. Montmigny, who also headed the Diocesan Office of Worship. This highly committed and charismatic priest headed this department until he was replaced, on July 1, 1993, by the Reverend John M. Grace. Father Montmigny, who correctly observed that "the Parish is at the center of the Church," innovated or improved a large number of spiritually centered activities to stimulate the inner growth of all in the diocese.

Four years after the founding of the Department of Spiritual Renewal

Services, in 1986, all primarily spiritually oriented undertakings were placed under one umbrella department. By 1997, this reorganized department consisted of: the Office of Evangelization, New Hampshire Charismatic Renewal, Joseph House (a retreat center located in St. Mary parish), the Center for Spiritual Direction, the Cursillo Movement, Young Adult Ministry, La Rencontre (a French Canadian renewal movement), the Office of the Marian Apostolate, and the Men of St. Joseph (a movement aimed at intensifying the Christian life of men). As indicated, Father Montmigny was succeeded by Father Grace, an equally intense and dedicated priest, who is the only Catholic clergyman in the diocese to have been formally university-trained in spiritual formation.

Mindful of those who are in grief or pain, Bishop Gendron oversaw the creation of a Diocesan Conference for Separated/Divorced under the sponsorship of the Office of Family Services, a branch of New Hampshire Catholic Services. Inaugurated in 1982, this conference involves not only the separated and divorced, but also all those who are touched by these often tragic occurrences, such as members of the family, friends, the parish clergy, and interested religious. The first conference consisted of eight lectures, a brown-bag lunch (rather than a served dinner to mark the seriousness of the assembly), and a closing liturgy.

Diocesan Newspapers

Amid the many successful new enterprises in the diocese, there was at least one highly disappointing, and expensive, failure: the termination of the diocesan newspaper *Concern*.

Since the founding of the diocese in 1884, the only widely circulated publication to achieve notable success, until past the mid-1990s, was *The Guidon*, which appeared from 1898 to 1907 (cf. chapter 8). From 1907 until May 1971—that is, for some sixty-four years—there was, in effect, no diocesan-wide publication intended for the Catholic public at large.

In May 1971, during the episcopacy of Bishop Primeau, a second newspaper was launched, with the title *The Messenger of the Manchester Diocese*. Seven months later, in January 1972, this newspaper was renamed *Concern*, and was published under the direction of several successive editors until December 19, 1982. At no time did either the short-lived *Messenger of the Manchester Diocese* or *Concern* achieve the quality or popularity of *The Guidon*.

In fact, to supplement in part for the paucity of information in *Concern,* Bishop Gendron, through the Office of Communications, established a newsletter called *Inter Nos* ("Among Us"), designed to communicate with pastors and their associates and coworkers. This ill-named newsletter, suggesting to many a privileged inner circle, ceased publication in September 1988 to coincide with the launching of a newly created newspaper, the fourth, called *Tidings.* With this new beginning, Bishop Gendron proposed to improve the quality of the diocesan newspaper, and through it to provide more information—particularly on subjects of more interest to people in New Hampshire—in a more appealing format.

Tidings made its debut, in tabloid format, in December 1988. Since then it has expanded considerably in size, frequency of appearance, range and quality of articles, and use of color. By 1997, it had grown from eleven issues a year to a twenty-issue-per-year newspaper, and to more than twice the original number of pages. It is making visible progress toward its triple goals of providing information, instruction, and, as the editor termed it, "uplift" to its readers.

Because of its greater scope and better quality, a newsletter called *Notations from the Office of Communications,* which began appearing in December 1988 to replace *Inter Nos,* was discontinued in December 1992. Most of the credit for this performance is due to the current editor, Matthew J. McSorley; the administrative assistant, Mary Balon; and the assistant editor, John B. Haywood.

Anyone with a mildly critical eye can note at least two major shortcomings in most of the Catholic newspapers in the United States, including New Hampshire. One is the near total absence of varying or controversial points of view. This lack of debate includes topics that have not been definitely decided by the Church. In summary, in most ecclesiastical jurisdictions, the diocesan newspaper is considered solely a "house organ" limited to one point of view. Consequently, other valid, if controversial, points of view remain unspoken, or, in this case, unwritten. This is at least one reason that many find these newspapers bland and uninteresting and will not either buy or read them.

Another weak point is the apparent unwillingness of the publishers to address themselves to the moral principles that underlie many of the social ills within the boundaries of the state. Dread of being accused of practicing "politics in the pulpit" by secular agencies has, it appears, kept the posi-

26. Bishop John B. Delany, the second bishop of Manchester (1904-1906), right, is shown with Mayor John F. Fitzgerald of Boston, center, greeting Archbishop William H. O'Connell at the pier in Boston on the latter's return from Rome on March 13, 1906.

27. The funeral of Edward N. Fugère, M.D. took place at Saint Marie church in Manchester in 1912. Note the rear wheel of the horse drawn hearse and the dress of the mourners. (Photo by Edward A. Belisle. From the private archives of Robert B. Perreault.)

28. Bishop George A. Guertin, third Bishop of Manchester (1907-1931), left, on horseback at Cap of Dunloe, Ireland, around 1920. With him is the Reverend Dennis C. Ling, a priest from the New Hampshire diocese. The identity of the attractive colleen on the pony is unknown.

29. Wilfrid J. Lessard, a lawyer, served as superintendent of schools for the Diocese of Manchester from 1919 to 1932. He was the first lay person to hold this position in the United States.

30. This editorial cartoon, which appeared in the December 1, 1919 edition of the Concord (New Hampshire) Evening Monitor, shows an enraged Uncle Sam hurling an immigrant into the ocean. This anti-immigrant stance may be in danger of being repeated today against Latin Americans, Koreans, Vietnamese and others.

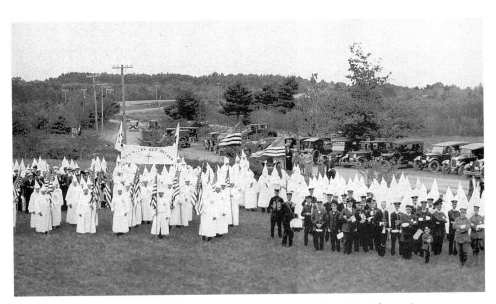

31. Ku Klux Klan meeting in North Hampton, September 1925. The anti-Catholic organization was active in New Hampshire during the 1920s. (Collection of Peter E. Randall)

32. The Most Rev. John B. Peterson was the fourth bishop of Manchester from 1932-1944. His episcopacy spanned most of the Great Depression and the greater part of World War II.

33. (right) Irene Farley of Manchester founded the Missionary Rosebushes of Ste. Therese in 1922 to raise funds for the education of a native clergy in mission lands. By 1997, over 2,100 had been ordained to the priesthood with financial assistance from her organization.

34. (below) Bishop Matthew F. Brady was installed as the fifth bishop of Manchester on January 17, 1945 during a snowstorm of 22 inches. Presiding at the throne in the background is the archbishop of Boston, Richard J. Cushing (later cardinal); behind Bishop Brady is a page dressed in white satin.

35. Bishop Brady, shown here in a relaxed moment, was the last bishop of Manchester to serve entirely before the Second Vatican Council which opened in Saint Peter's Basilica in Rome on October 11, 1962.

36. The first five bishops of the Diocese of Manchester are buried in this crypt beneath the main altar of Saint Joseph Cathedral. Top row: Bradley (+1903), Delany (+1906), and Guertin (+1931); bottom row, Peterson (+1944). Bishop Brady's vault is shown open just prior to burial. One space remains open. Bishops Primeau (+1989) and O'Neil (+1997) are buried in Saint Joseph Cemetery, Bedford.

37. The officers and members of the League of the Sacred Heart of Saint Francis Xavier Parish, Nashua, were photographed in 1945. Their dress and insignia are typical of the parish organizations of the time.

38. *Bishop Ernest J. Primeau is shown standing before St. Peter's Basilica in Rome during the Second Vatican Council. He served as the sixth bishop of Manchester from 1960 to 1974.*

39. *Before a session of the Second Vatican Council, Bishop Primeau discusses the day's agenda with his secretary and 'peritus' to the Council, Monsignor Wilfrid H. Paradis.*

40. Mrs. Margaret Loughlin Splaine after spending some four years in missionary work in Chile and Colombia passed an additional 29 years directing diocesan missionary activity from New Hampshire.

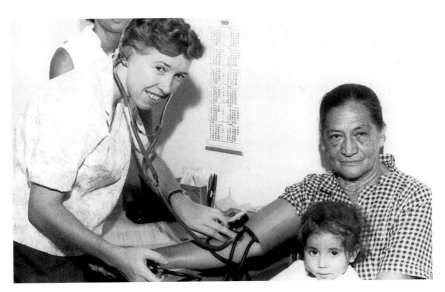

41. Miss Claire Aucoin, R.N., has been at the Manchester Mission in Cartago, Colombia, ministering to the poor, the sick, the orphan and the aged since 1966.

42. *Saint Casimir school, the parochial school of Saint Hedwig Parish, is located on the northwest corner of Union and Merrimack streets in Manchester. Constructed in 1906, it is most likely the only elementary school in New Hampshire where Polish was taught to the students. Since 1908, it has been conducted by the Felician Sisters of the Order of Saint Francis. (Note the silo shaped structure on the south wall of the school. It was an enclosed spiral-type slide to be used by the students and the faculty in case of fire. It has since been replaced by a conventional fire escape.)*

43. *Saint Mary Ukrainian Catholic Church (Protection of the Blessed Virgin Mary) on Lowell Street in Manchester, founded in 1906, is the oldest of three Oriental Catholic churches in New Hampshire. The other two are: Our Lady of the Cedars, a Melkite-Greek Catholic church in Manchester, and Saint George, a Maronite church in Dover. (Photo by the Rev. Albert G. Baillargeon.)*

44. *A new Diocesan Administration Building at 153 Ash Street in Manchester was dedicated on August 9, 1964. It brought together virtually all of the offices previously scattered all over the state. Since its dedication it has been enlarged twice. Catholic Charities occupies the left wing. (Photo by the Rev. Albert G. Baillargeon.)*

45. *Bishop Odore J. Gendron was bishop of the Diocese of Manchester from February 3, 1975 to June 12, 1990. He was the seventh to serve in this capacity. The photo above was taken early in 1997 on the occasion of his fiftieth anniversary of ordination to the priesthood. (Photo by Matthew J. McSorley.)*

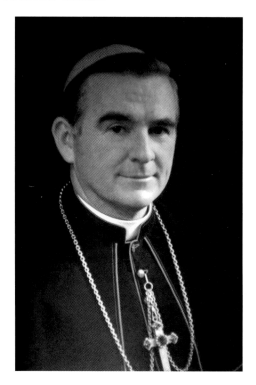

46. Bishop Robert E. Mulvee served as the first auxiliary bishop of Manchester between 1977 and 1985. Since then he has been successively Bishop of Wilmington (Delaware), Coadjutor of Providence, and Bishop of Providence.

47. Bishop Joseph J. Gerry, o.s.b., was auxiliary bishop of Manchester between 1986 and 1988. Since February 21, 1989, he has been Bishop of Portland (Maine).

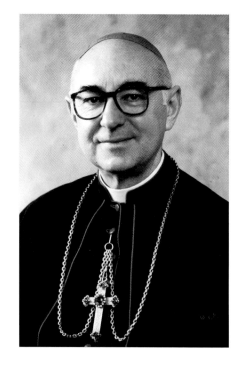

48. In full episcopal dress, Bishop Leo E. O'Neil gives an enthusiastic boy one of his typical greetings, a high-five! (Photo by Louis Dubois)

49. This Vietnamese family of Mr. Dau Hoang, shown arriving at Logan Airport, Boston, Massachusetts in March 1992, settled in Manchester. Contrast these immigrants with the French Canadians who arrived in the 1840s, shown earlier. (French Canadians emigrated mostly for economic reasons; the Vietnamese left their homes because of the brutish war in their country.) (Photograph from the Hoang family.)

50. At the conclusion of the Funeral Mass on December 5, 1997, Bishop Leo E. O'Neil was carried from the cathedral by six members of the Council of Priests. The bearers were on the left, from front to back, Fathers Agapit H. Jean, Jr., Leo A. Leblanc and Gerald R. Belanger, and on the right, A. Stephen Marcoux III, Joseph S. Klatka and W. Pierre Baker. (Photo by Tony Haley.)

240

51. *The Chapel of the Annunciation in Manchester, dedicated on March 25, 1896, served as the chapel of the motherhouse of the Sisters of Mercy until the community relocated in Windham, New Hampshire. On October 16, 1994, the chapel was dedicated as the new Diocesan Museum. (Photo by Gerald Durette.)*

52. *Mrs. Judith Hall Fosher, the founder and first director of the Diocesan Museum, is pictured near an old holy water container while unpacking a chalice that belonged to Bishop Denis M. Bradley. (Photo by Tidings.)*

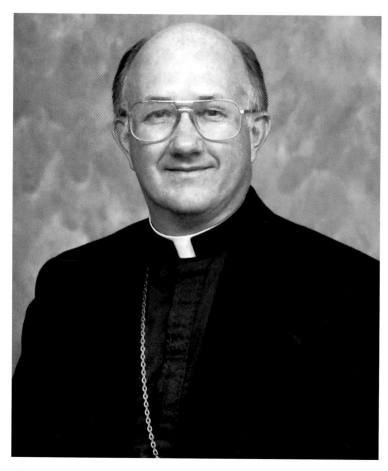

53. On May 14, 1996, Francis J. Christian became the third to be ordained an auxiliary bishop of the Diocese of Manchester, following Bishops Robert E. Mulvee and Joseph J. Gerry, o.s.b. Born in Jaffrey, he is only the third native of New Hampshire to assume Catholic episcopal functions in the state of New Hampshire, after Bishops George A. Guertin and Odore J. Gendron. He was elected the administrator of the diocese at the death of Bishop O'Neil. (Photo by Cote Photography.)

tion of the Catholic Church from being introduced, at least in print, into the public forum on issues that are, first and foremost, predominantly moral problems. An exception to this has been on matters dealing with sexual ethics, such as abortion, premarital sex, AIDS, and divorce.

This reluctance to become involved in social problems with a moral dimension by Catholic newspapers does not extend to the Office of Social Concerns of the Secretariat for Community Services. Among the many useful services of this office is the publication of a newsletter entitled *Creating a Community of Conscience*. Begun in 1990, with the encouragement of Bishop O'Neil, this newsletter provides a legislative update on all the bills presented before the senate and house of representatives in the state legislature at Concord that have a moral dimension. It also gives information on the time and place of hearings on these bills, as well as their compatibility with the teachings of the Church. This Office and Secretariat have done highly commendable work in presenting the moral dimensions of social problems before the state legislature as well as to the public at large.

In addition to greatly improving *Tidings,* the Office of Communications has been providing, on a yearly basis since 1986, a much needed comprehensive directory called the *New Hampshire Catholic Directory.* This valuable resource, long in use in other dioceses, was proposed and initially initiated by the then functioning, but now eliminated, Office of the Laity. A committee, under the leadership of Ms. Michelle Jones, director of the Office of the Laity, spent eight months in its preparation.

'The Four Hampton Nuns'

During an interview with *Tidings* on the occasion of the celebration of his fiftieth anniversary in the priesthood in 1997, Bishop Gendron referred to the case of "the Four Hampton Nuns," as it came to be known in the secular press, as one that disturbed him greatly because the "public was exposed to anger and negativity." For their part, the nuns involved were convinced, as they later said publicly, that as a matter of "conscience" they had to proceed.

This was, one cannot doubt, one of the more painful episodes in the recent history of the Catholic Church in New Hampshire. Not only did it attract local attention, but it drew the national and, to a lesser degree, the international media as well.

For a number of reasons, including the anguish caused to many, the still confidential nature of several aspects of the story, and the complexity of the issues involved, this particular case cannot be discussed or analyzed with certainty in all its dimensions. Because of these factors, it can only be related in summary and incomplete fashion.

This incident, if it may be so called, began with the nonrenewal of the teaching contracts with the four Sisters of Mercy employed at Sacred Heart School, Hampton—this institution being the parochial school of Our Lady of the Miraculous Medal parish. The notice of nonrenewal was hand-delivered to the sisters by the then diocesan superintendent of Catholic schools, Brother Roger Lemoyne, s.c., on January 28, 1982. The nonrenewal notice had been prepared in the form of an unsigned memorandum that was to take effect at the end of the current school year.

According to the memorandum, the principal reasons for the nonrenewal of the contracts of these sisters, who had been teaching at Sacred Heart for at least ten years, were their alleged "cliquishness," and the accusation that they were inaccessible to the parish. These charges were elaborated upon later to include such things as the lack of communication with the rest of the parish staff, and the ongoing attitude of the principal to ignore the parish school board and to do as she pleased.

On their own behalf, the four sisters asserted that they had been improperly terminated and the unproven reasons for their dismissal were not sufficient for not renewing their contracts. In brief, they sought reinstatement. After several months of maneuvering and charges, the sisters appealed to the Superior Court of Rockingham County to adjudicate this matter, claiming that the bishop and the diocese had violated the terms of their civil contracts and that their grievances had nothing to do with religion. For its part, the diocese took the position that this case was strictly an internal one and should be settled by the proper agencies of the Catholic Church. There was, it appears, at least a tendency for the diocese to view the matter as touching upon doctrinal issues.

This dissension, as was inevitable, split the parish of Our Lady of the Miraculous Medal into two camps. A group, taking the name Save Our Sisters (SOS), was formed. Some seven hundred people signed a petition in favor of the sisters, Sunday Mass attendance decreased at Our Lady of the Miraculous Medal, and some one hundred students—42 percent of the entire enrollment—were withdrawn from Sacred Heart School. In addition, four lay teachers at the school resigned in sympathy with the cause of the nuns.

Once in the hands of the Superior Court, the first judge assigned, Joseph Nadeau, now the chief justice of the Superior Court in New Hampshire, ruled on April 13, 1982, that the case could not be heard in civil court because it would require "impermissible inquiry" into church affairs. Through their attorney, John McEachern, the four sisters appealed this ruling to the State Supreme Court. On December 23, 1982, the Supreme Court, consisting of five members, unanimously overturned Judge Nadeau's ruling and remanded the case to the same lower court for a hearing on the merits of the nuns' dismissal.

While recognizing the difficulties, the State Supreme Court decided that the task could be accomplished by keeping in mind the distinction between nondoctrinal (in this case, civil) matters and those involving doctrine, faith, or internal organization. In summary, in matters of civil law, in this case four contracts, the Church is responsible to civil law and jurisdiction.

When the suit was returned to Judge Nadeau, he scheduled a hearing for January 24, 1983, and, given his position on "impermissible inquiry," he withdrew from the case. Soon thereafter, Judge Arthur E. Bean was named to replace him.

While the diocese continued to justify its position, and even to claim an element of victory in the decision of the Supreme Court, both the legal department of the United States Catholic Conference, the legal arm of the bishops, and the Apostolic Delegate, Archbishop Pio Laghi (the personal representative of the pope in this country), became involved. This was to be expected, as any court decision in New Hampshire would set a legal precedent for the whole country, a serious and far-reaching matter. In fact, Archbishop Laghi paid a personal visit to Bishop Gendron on his way to a speaking engagement before the boosters of the Berlin Regional Catholic School.

After a delay in the court hearing requested by the Diocese of Manchester,—better to prepare its case it said—an agreement was reached between the diocese and the four sisters. This agreement was made public by the parties and their legal counsel on the front steps of the Rockingham Superior Court on May 20, 1983, before a large gathering of the media, after sixteen months of controversy and legal action. Both sides claimed to be pleased with the terms of the settlement and agreed that is was time to build up the Church together.

Included in the terms of the settlement were the following: The diocese would not have to explain why the contracts were not renewed; all allegations against the sisters were to be held without foundation and expressly repudiated; the sisters could apply for teaching positions in the Diocese of Manchester, with the exception of Sacred Heart School, Hampton, and were to be assisted in this task; no mention was to be made about how the controversy started; and the sisters could continue to live at Sacred Heart Convent, if they so wished, until July 1984, or until reassigned. In addition, Bishop Gendron sent each nun a personal letter in which he affirmed that each was in good standing in the diocese. Finally, the legal fees for both the sisters and the diocese were to be assumed by the latter, except for a small share paid for by the organization Save Our Sisters. By the end of March 1983, the legal fees for the nuns has already climbed to $80,000.

Fallout from this incident was severe for both the sisters and the priests of the parish who were assigned there during this crisis. Eventually, two of the sisters left the Sisters of Mercy, and all four found it virtually impossible to obtain teaching positions in a Catholic school in New Hampshire. As for the parish clergy, two were transferred during the controversy and two more, including the pastor, were given new assignments the very day after the agreement was reached on the steps of the Superior Court House of Rockingham County. It was stated, however, that the last two transfers had nothing to do with the just–ended controversy.

During and following the litigation, the four sisters were given several honors. First, the journal *Seacoast Women* named the four "Seacoast Women of the Year" in 1982. On June 24, 1984, a group of their partisans in the town of Hampton held a banquet to acclaim them for their activities.

In January 1983, the National Coalition of Catholic Nuns (NCAN), a progressive group, praised the Hampton sisters for their stand. In their statement they wrote: "Too long have the sisters [i.e., everywhere] been shunted mercilessly by priests and bishops." In April 1983, the same Chicago-based association named the four sisters "Nuns of the Decade." Later the same year, on August 11, the sisters addressed an audience of two thousand at the National Assembly of Religious Women on the subject "Have We Abandoned You? Due Process in Our Church. A Response and Dialogue." It was subsequently reported that many women religious at that meeting shared the same fears as "the Four Hampton Nuns."

Reflecting on this experience, Bishop Gendron, in the interview with

Tidings already mentioned, observed that while the incident had been "painful," "[he] didn't lose an hour of sleep because [he] was doing what [he] believed [he] had to do."

While there was no malice involved in this unfortunate contretemps—each side believing that it was right—there were scar-leaving wounds inflicted on several individuals and groups: the four nuns who could not find employment in the diocese and who had, in the minds of some, betrayed their religious vow of obedience; the parish clergy, as noted, who were virtually forced to seek transfers; Our Lady of the Miraculous Medal parishioners, who inherited a serious division; the school-children of Sacred Heart, who were, in the true sense, the pawns in this litigation; and the diocese, which was seen by some as the insensitive and unjust oppressors of these nuns.

New Hampshire Council of Churches

Even while the case of "the Four Hampton Nuns" was dividing many in the diocese, major steps were being taken to further ecumenical dialogue and cooperation in New Hampshire.

Involvement in the movement for Christian unity—an initiative mandated by the Second Vatican Council and successfully launched by Bishop Primeau in New Hampshire in January 1963—expanded and prospered during the episcopacy of Bishop Gendron. By 1974, the experience of sharing that had taken place between Catholics and members of the United Church of Christ, Methodists, Episcopalians, American Baptists, and Unitarian Universalists, under the auspices of the New Hampshire Council of Churches, prompted the next development.

A change in the structure of the New Hampshire Council of Churches allowed the Diocese of Manchester to enter into associate membership. This structure change also replaced the broadly representative but unwieldy council assembly by a small executive board of about twenty-five members with Catholic representation. By this arrangement, Catholics also continued to have representatives on the various committees of the Council of Churches.

During that phase of the development of the council, the bishops or executive ministers of the several denominations strengthened the level of trust among one another, while increasing their own participation in the affairs of the council, by meeting regularly as a committee. They also began to come together once a year for a two-day retreat.

In 1983, the member churches decided that the time had come to conduct an in-depth evaluation of the council's structure and functioning. This led to the council's restructuring and restatement of purpose, which included the Catholic Church as an equal partner. As reorganized by the constitution of January 17, 1984, the council is presided over by an executive board made up of the bishops or executive ministers representing the member communions.

This new highest-level staffing of the executive board indicates that the council was now a major priority of the member churches. Essential to the functioning of the executive board is the assistance it receives from the advisory committee, which consists of ordained and lay representatives from the participating churches. Also, very significantly, the first purpose of the New Hampshire Council of Churches was stated to be to further Christian unity, life, and action in the Granite State.

Bishop Gendron became an ardent supporter of the New Hampshire Council of Churches and a faithful participant in its activities and meetings with his ordination to the episcopacy on February 3, 1975. In June 1983, he was elected vice president of the council. When the new constitution went into effect on January 17, 1984, allowing the diocese full membership in the council, Bishop Gendron had the honor of being elected president of the executive board by his peers.

His commitment to the ecumenical movement and his effectiveness as a leader in that movement were fraternally acknowledged in a letter to Bishop Gendron from the Reverend Frank H. Gross, then the executive secretary of the New Hampshire Council of Churches, dated May 22, 1984. In his remarks to Bishop Gendron, the Reverend Gross wrote: "I want you to know how much a joy it is for me to have you as our President, and to sit so frequently under your leadership. I clearly benefit—as do we all—from your clear vision of a Kingdom that both is and is to come in which we all may be one in our common Lord . . . It's a wonderful privilege to have you share so meaningfully in our life and work, and I'm honored that I am here now so that I may be a participant in this process of our reconciliation."

One important piece of evidence of the integration of the diocese into the New Hampshire Council of Churches is the fact that a Catholic layman, David LaMarre Vincent, was selected as executive secretary of the council to succeed the Reverend Frank H. Gross, a member of the United Church of Christ, in September 1990. Prior to his appointment, Mr. LaMarre Vincent served as assistant director for parish ministry in the office of New Hampshire Catholic Charities.

In order to establish a better working relationship with the New Hampshire Council of Churches and the totality of the other Christian communities in the state, Bishop Gendron in 1987 reorganized the Office for Ecumenical Affairs. This office had been founded in 1965 as the Commission on Ecumenism. Members of this new office were originally the bishop, four priests, including a brother who was also an ordained priest, one woman religious, two laywomen, and one layman.

Despite these major improvements in the structures to advance the apostolate for Christian unity, a Christ-mandated ministry, this work has languished and come to a near standstill in recent years, at least at the local level. The enthusiasm and high hopes of the period immediately following the Second Vatican Council, marked by joint prayer, shared study, and common ministry, have, for the greater part, hibernated or withered. This is one of the major responsibilities of the local church that must be revitalized and given the priority assigned to it not only by Christ but also by Popes John XXIII, Paul VI, and John Paul II, as well as the New Hampshire Council of Churches and the recent bishops of Manchester.

Differences with a Newspaper

Bishop Gendron's association with the New Hampshire Council of Churches brought him in confrontation with the newspaper the *Manchester Union Leader* for one of the few times in his more than fifteen years as bishop of the Diocese of Manchester. The issue was the cutting back of spending by the state of New Hampshire on social services. In a statement issued on June 12, 1981, Bishop Gendron deplored the slash in programs by the legislative and administrative branches of the state government to provide for children, families, the elderly, the handicapped, the mentally ill, and all those who require special care. He pointed out that by its very function the state had an obligation and a duty to care for and assist those in unfortunate circumstances. A concomitant duty of the state, he added, is to provide the revenues that are necessary so that all its citizens "receive the basic necessities of life to which they are entitled, and which they deserve." Consequently, he continued, if the state did not have the revenues necessary to provide these needed services, it had the duty to raise the funds required to fulfill its obligations. Bishop Gendron then made it clear that he did not wish to enter the political arena but that he was addressing this issue because of its "far-reaching moral implications." In conclusion, he wrote that until acceptable alternatives were found to provide the citizens of the state with the rights to which they were entitled, he was obliged to "wholeheartedly support," along with other members of the New Hampshire Council of Churches, a taxation that was fair, equitable, and as broad based as possible, so that these services could be provided and the people served.

A negative response to this statement appeared in an editorial of the *Manchester Union Leader* on June 18. After calling Bishop Gendron a "'good and holy man"—a good man "misled"—the editorial admonished him for getting involved in the highly controversial issue of broad-based taxes. The editorial believed that the bishop had gone beyond the moral dimension of Christian concern for necessary social services for the needy and was advocating a political solution—the broad-based tax—over other solutions. If such a tax were considered, the newspaper warned, the Church would become "fair game" for those who wanted to abolish tax exemptions on church buildings and land; the Church itself could be taxed in the future. The clergy, the editorial added, could not have the best of all worlds—that is, "play politics from a privileged sanctuary." No broad-based state tax has ever been implemented.

A First Centennial

A crowning moment among all the programs and activities of the 1980s was the celebration of the one hundredth anniversary of the creation of the Diocese of Manchester.

Organization of the centennial was placed in the hands of a Diocesan Centennial Committee consisting of sixteen people—laity, religious, and priests—under the leadership of Monsignor Edwin A. Francoeur. This committee held its first meeting on December 3, 1981, and, after a number of additional meetings during the winter and spring, compiled a list of recommendations for the celebration that was presented to Bishop Gendron.

This report proposed that the diocesan centennial be celebrated in three phases: Phase I, a period of evangelization and education supported by prayer; Phase II, the Centennial Mass at the cathedral; and Phase III, a Family Day celebration at Saint Anselm College.

A new steering committee of ten members and two consultants, with Father Francis J. Christian (now Bishop) as general chairman, was appointed by Bishop Gendron to implement the plan proposed by the original Diocesan Centennial Committee. The steering committee was then logically divided into three subcommittees corresponding to the above-mentioned phases of the centennial celebration. In order to established the essential liaison needed with the parishes, each of the eleven deaneries in the diocese was invited to appoint deanery coordinators.

Although it was generally left unsaid, this centennial was also the commemoration of close to 340 years of Catholicism, as well as anti-Catholicism, in what is now the state of New Hampshire.

After much discussion, the steering committee chose as the motto of the centennial "Remember, Rejoice, Renew," which incorporated the past by remembering, the present by rejoicing, and the future by renewing.

Phase I extended from Ash Wednesday of 1984 to Easter of the same year. This was a program to welcome lapsed Catholics back to the active practice of the faith, and to invite people who were unchurched to investigate the Roman Catholic Church. Some of the recommended activities were home visitation programs, an Easter outreach, and a come-home-for-Christmas appeal. These programs were supplemented by television and radio spots, automobile bumper stickers, and in a variety of other ways.

Phase II, the Centennial Mass at the cathedral, was celebrated on Sunday afternoon, April 29, 1984. This solemn and grandiose celebration was attended by the clergy, men and women religious, and three representatives from each parish of the diocese. Principal celebrant was Archbishop Pio Laghi, apostolic Pro-Nuncio of the Holy See to the United States, with the participation of the attending archbishops and bishops.

This Mass was the first public function in New Hampshire attended by the new archbishop of Boston, Bernard Law. Bishop Gendron delivered the homily. Miss Mary E. Bagnell directed a specially assembled choir of sixty voices, made up of adults from the parishes and religious communities of the Diocese of Manchester. The entire ceremony was televised live by Channel 9 (WMUR) of Manchester and was preceded by a brief segment on the history of Catholicism in New Hampshire from the seventeenth century. The Mass was followed by a very well-attended open house reception at the nearby St. Joseph Junior High School.

Phase III was a highly successful Diocesan Family Day celebration at Saint Anselm College on Sunday, June 3, 1984. Family Day began at noon with the concelebration of an outdoor Mass. This was followed by a variety of activities, many taking place simultaneously on the campus. There were singers, dancers, and many other kinds of entertainment, in addition to illustrated lectures of some aspects of the history of the diocese.

Much appreciated were the various ethnic foods—French, Hispanic, Polish, Portuguese, Italian, Irish, and American—on sale throughout the day. Major performances were given in the afternoon by the Muchachos, a well-known Manchester Boys' Club Drum and Bugle Corps, and in the evening by the 39th Army Band.

This exciting day was capped by a fireworks display sponsored by the Coca-Cola Company. At least five thousand attended this celebration at some point during the day or evening, and thousands more enjoyed the fireworks from various vantage points in Manchester and Goffstown.

This family celebration was the first of its kind in the history of the Diocese of Manchester and clearly the most enjoyed and appreciated event of the centennial year. In rounded figures, the celebration of the centennial cost $91,700 and income was $22,900. Overall, the diocese invested some $68,800 for this unique religious and social experience. A special collection in all the parishes to subsidize the Diocesan Centennial raised more than $90,000, which easily erased the remaining deficit for this memorable event.

Bishop's Summer Reception Fund

Another successful enterprise undertaken during the administration of Bishop Gendron was the Bishop's Summer Reception. The primary purpose of this reception was to raise funds that would make it possible for the bishop to respond to at least some of the many requests that he receives annually for donations from worthy organizations, secular as well as religious, particularly those devoted to charity or education.

Begun in 1985 under the direction of Monsignor John E. Molan, a vicar general, the reception—which is held either at the bishop's own residence or at that of a lay benefactor,—grew from an attendance of about 250 people who raised roughly $80,000 in 1987, to 500, who contributed $150,000 in 1995; to well over that number who donated in excess of $300,000 in 1997. In summary, these receptions raised more than $1.6 million during their first twelve years of existence. Not only has the fund raised money for charity, education, and other worthwhile religious and civic purposes, but it has also given the bishop an opportunity to meet socially many of his supporters from many faiths as well as many walks of life.

A New Auxiliary Bishop

With the departure of Bishop Mulvee to his new assignment as bishop of Wilmington, Delaware in the spring of 1985, Bishop Gendron soon began to petition the Holy See for a replacement. In a relatively short period of time for a request of this importance, the Apostolic Pro-Nuncio for the United States, Archbishop Pio Laghi, publicly announced on February 11, 1986, that Abbot Joseph J. Gerry, head of the Benedictine monastery and chancellor of Saint Anselm College, had been selected for that office.

Bishop Gendron's major reasons for requesting another auxiliary, he would explain later, was to have that person meet with the clergy and laity and serve as liaison between the local parishes and his own office "to allow him to get a better understanding through his eyes and his views."

The choice of Abbot Joseph (the name by which he wished to be known) made by the Sacred Congregation for Bishops and approved by Pope John Paul II, was received with both joy and surprise in New Hampshire. While not rare, elsewhere, few priests from religious orders had been selected in recent years as bishop or auxiliary bishop of dioceses in the northeastern part of the United States. Obviously, it was a first in the history of the Diocese of Manchester.

A common assumption was that the leadership in a diocese, where the primary goal is ministry with the people, usually in a parish setting, would be confided to priests with that pastoral background. Such a background, however, was not a necessity as the past had definitely proved, and as it would be demonstrated here in the next few years.

Whatever degree of surprise was registered in the Diocese of Manchester was greatly exceeded by an appreciation for the qualities of Bishop-select Joseph. All who knew him recognized his simple monastic charm, his accomplishments as a priest and Benedictine, as well as his sensitivity, concern, commitment, and spiritual demeanor. Equally noteworthy were his high intelligence, his leadership abilities, and the depth and brilliance of his sermons and public addresses.

Bishop-select Joseph was born John Gerry on September 12, 1928, in Millinocket, Maine, the son of Bernard and Blanche Gerry, both deceased at the time of his episcopal appointment. (John was given the name Joseph upon entering religious life.) He was one of a family of nine children. His father, a self-described "Yankee" and a convert to Catholicism, was distantly related to the historically famous Goffe family of New Hampshire. The story of the conversion of Theodore and Anna Goffe in 1834 has been related earlier. The ancestry on his mother's side was Irish.

Upon graduating from Stearns High School in his hometown in 1945, John decided to attend Saint Anselm College with the intention of becoming a teacher or doctor, or, possibly, a priest. As it turned out, he became both a priest and a teacher, and, by extension, a doctor, albeit a doctor of philosophy and not of medicine. As a student at Saint Anselm he became attracted to the Benedictine monastic life. During his second year at the college he decided to enter the monastery, and professed his vows in July 1948, at which time, as it has been indicated, he was given the name Joseph.

After graduating from Saint Anselm in 1950, he spent several additional years preparing for ordination to the priesthood at both Saint Vincent Archabbey in Latrobe, Pennsylvania, and at Saint Anselm Abbey Seminary. He was ordained to the priesthood in St. Joseph Cathedral by Bishop Matthew F. Brady on June 12, 1954.

In 1955, he was granted an M.A. degree in philosophy from the University Toronto (Ontario), and four years later, in 1959, a Ph.D. in the same subject from Fordham University in New York City.

One year before receiving his doctoral degree, he became a member of the faculty at Saint Anselm, teaching in the areas of philosophy and the humanities. In addition, he was given successively important administrative responsibilities: acting academic dean (1958–1959); academic dean (1971–1972); and, after being elected abbot, chancellor of the college. Since 1961, he has been a member of the Governing Board of the college, and a member of the National Advisory Board on Equality of Educational Opportunity from 1973 to 1976.

Apace with his academic advancement, Father Joseph became successively subprior of the abbey (1959–1961), and, from 1961 to his election as abbot, the prior of the Benedictine community.

Elected abbot on January 2, 1972, he became the third to hold this office, replacing the Right Reverend Gerald McCarthy, who had resigned for reasons of health. During his fourteen years as abbot, in addition to his highly skillful leadership of both the abbey and the college (as chancellor), he was elected by members of the General Chapters of the American Cassinese Federation of Benedictine Monasteries to serve on the five-member Council of the Abbot President. Within and without the Benedictine monasteries and priories in the United States, he was appreciated for his incisive and profound conferences and retreats.

Abbot Joseph, then fifty–seven years of age, was ordained the second auxiliary bishop of Manchester in St. Joseph Cathedral on the afternoon of Monday, April 27, 1986, by Bishop Gendron as principal consecrator and Bishops Ernest J. Primeau, retired bishop of the diocese, and Robert E. Mulvee, bishop of Wilmington, as co-consecrators. The ceremony was followed by a reception open to all at the nearby auditorium of St. Joseph Junior High School.

For his motto Bishop Joseph kept the very appropriate one that he had chosen when he was installed as abbot of Saint Anselm Abbey fourteen years previously: "To serve rather than to preside." Given his qualifications, it could not be expected that he would remain long as an auxiliary in Manchester.

Organizational Adjustments

While both the centennial preparations and its celebration were taking place and the search for an auxiliary bishop was in progress, plans continued to be made and implemented both to revise the organizational framework of the diocese and to create further new programs to meet the expanding needs of the faithful.

An area that appears to have caused some concern was that of some of the representative boards of the diocese. For example, Bishop Gendron found it necessary to issue, on March 28, 1985, a mandate to the 130 parishes in the state to develop a parish pastoral council, a directive originally given by Bishop Primeau in 1969, four years following the end of the Second Vatican Council.

A similar situation developed relative to the Diocesan Pastoral Council. This council, originally established in 1965, was allowed to lapse and was re-created between 1986 and 1989. Following the positive recommendation of an ad hoc committee, the first meeting of the new Diocesan Pastoral Council was held on June 24, 1989. Its original membership was composed of the following: a lay representative from each of the eleven deaneries; three additional appointed laypeople; seven religious (women and men); three diocesan priests; one permanent deacon and three ex-officio, that is, appointed by the bishop personally.

A Diocesan Pastoral Council has a role similar to that of the Parish Pastoral Council: It has the responsibility "to investigate under the authority of the bishop all those things which pertain to pastoral works, to ponder them and to propose practical conclusions about them" (Code of Canon Law, c. 511). While this council "enjoys only a consultative vote" (c. 514§1) and is not mandatory, it is considered "highly desirable" by the Church.

Another organization, founded by Bishop Primeau and approved by the then Senate of Priests, was the Board of Conciliation and Arbitration. Conciliation was designed to held find solutions in claims of alleged infringements of human and ecclesial rights, and its recommendations were not binding. On the other hand, the decisions achieved by Arbitration, by prior agreement of the contending parties, were binding. This board was also permitted to expire and was not active at the time of the case of "the Four Hampton Nuns." In the 1980s, this board was revived but in two parts: a separate Board of Conciliation and another as the Board of Arbitration; both are part of the Secretariat for Pastoral Services.

Another change brought about by the provisions of the new Code of Canon Law, which went into effect on Sunday, November 27, 1983, was in the name and composition of the Senate of Priests. The senate was renamed the Council of Priests (officially Presbyteral Council) and its membership was changed from an entirely elected body to one made up of both elected and appointed members (c. 497). The presiding officer is now the ordinary of the diocese himself rather than an elected member, as it was previously. A Presbyteral Council is mandatory and not optional in a diocese (c. 495).

Also made mandatory by the same Code of Canon Law were two

additional councils dealing with finances, one for the parishes and the other for the diocese. In accordance with the code, Bishop Gendron made parish finance councils obligatory (c. 537) shortly after the new law went into effect. While the conclusions reached by the parish finance council members are consultative only, this assembly of laity has already proved itself of invaluable assistance to the parishes in the state.

A corresponding finance council was established for the diocese (c. 492). It currently consists of, in addition to the ordinary, three laypeople and two priests supported by a staff of three.

In this consideration of diocesan structures, it is appropriate to observe that only four new parishes were established between February 1975 and June 1990, a period of slightly more than fifteen years. These were founded in Hampstead, Rye Beach, Londonderry, and Merrimack, in that order. For Hampstead and Rye Beach, this was the first Catholic parish in the town; for Londonderry and Merrimack, it was the second. Rye Beach, which is on the eastern seaboard, was the only new parish not in the southern sector of the state.

With the experience of the past and the changing needs of the present, it was to be expected that some modifications would be required in the organizational structure of the diocese that went into effect on January 12, 1969.

Following his visitation of all the parishes, the promulgation of the new Code of Canon Law (1983), and a broad consultation with the appropriate boards, Bishop Gendron instituted a number of changes in the diocesan structure to, as he stated, "better serve the personal and institutional needs of the People of God." The key provision of this change, which went into effect on January 1, 1986, was to allow for the first time the hiring of qualified laity and religious, as well as priests, to the highest positions in diocesan administration.

Another major innovation was to replace the three existing vicariates (Christian formation, community affairs, and administration) with five secretariats, which broadened Bishop Gendron's sharing of episcopal authority and responsibility. The five secretariats were for: administrative and canonical affairs, temporalities, education and youth services, ministries, and community affairs. Only one laywoman, however, Sister Pauline Lebel, c.s.c., was appointed to one of the positions, that of Secretary of Education. It was also decreed that the reorganization would be reviewed and evaluated after one year.

Six years later, under Bishop Leo E. O'Neil, further changes were made in the diocesan organizational chart because, it was explained, times had changed and so had the needs of the people. Paramount among these changes were the reduction of the five secretariats to four and the consolidation of a number of offices and functions. Two changes in name were also made: the Secretariat for Administrative and Canonical Affairs became the Secretariat for Pastoral Services, and the Secretariat for Education was renamed the Secretariat for Christian Formation. These two secretariats absorbed most of the departments and offices of the abolished Secretariat for Ministries. Only minor changes were effected in the other two secretariats, those of temporalities and community affairs.

In addition to streamlining the organization, the changes just mentioned produced a considerable economy by eliminating three priests (much needed elsewhere) and three full-time laypeople from diocesan administration. Financial savings by the diocese from these eliminations were estimated at $45,000 for 1991–1992, and $204,000 for 1992–1993.

New Programs 1985–1990

During the last third of his fifteen years as ordinary, Bishop Gendron continued to establish new programs to meet the contemporary spiritual needs of the people.

A well-attended program has been the celebration of wedding anniversaries, beginning in 1985. All married couples from around the state are invited to an anniversary Mass and the renewal of vows before the bishop on the occasion of a milestone anniversary, such as the twenty-fifth, fortieth, fiftieth, or, in some cases, more years of matrimony. The first celebration was held in the Abbey Church of Saint Anselm College. This wedding anniversary celebration is paralleled by a similar observance for men and women with religious vows. That service is held annually as well.

Two undertakings related to abortion were inaugurated in 1987 and 1990. The first, managed by New Hampshire Catholic Charities, is called Project Rachel. The objective of this project is to provide post-abortion counseling to women who have undergone this heart-wrenching experience, and are in need of psychological, physical, and spiritual support. In addition, in order to keep the memory of the aborted children alive and to remind the public to pray for them, their mothers, and other relatives, and for all those involved in this anti-human procedure, an impressive memorial monument was erected at Mount Calvary Cemetery, Manchester, and dedicated on December 28, 1991.

A second attack on abortion was the publication of a pastoral letter on that subject by Bishop Gendron in early 1990. Entitled *A Life Begins*, it is subtitled "Pastoral Reflections on the Pre-Born." While a great deal has been written on this subject by Catholic sources, the precise merit of this pastoral is the appeal to the citizens of the state to oppose abortion and petition the legislature to provide programs that will give women alternatives to this procedure.

Another statement of Bishop Gendron, in large measure related to sexual ethics, was a comprehensive policy with regard to AIDS. Developed by a diocesan AIDS committee after months of study and consultation, it was officially published in 1988. Taking a highly sensitive and understanding view of the victims of AIDS, the policy statement directs Catholic Charities to provide education on the subject, access to the sacraments for those afflicted, and confidentiality in every respect. It pledges no discrimination in hiring, no requirement of disclosure by victims, no firing because of the illness, and the granting of the same benefits as for any other illness.

In the fall of 1987, the Department of Spiritual Renewal Services established another office for the spiritual welfare of the Catholic population of New Hampshire: a Center for Spiritual Direction. Anyone—lay, religious, or clergy—may apply to one of some dozen spiritual directors (who are also lay, religious, and clergy) for religious guidance on the journey through life.

A Diocesan Museum

A major undertaking of the late 1980s was the establishment of a Diocesan Museum. Initially, virtually the sole proposer and supporter of this project was Mrs. Judith Hall Fosher, a housewife, mother, and archivist, who had an intense interest in preserving all that pertains to the past of the Catholic Church in New Hampshire. An ad hoc committee of nine, established in 1988 to consider the proposal for such a museum, gave an affirmative verdict. With the approval of Bishop Gendron, the museum was founded with a triple purpose: to collect, preserve, and interpret—through exhibits, lectures, seminars, and the like—the Catholic history of the Diocese of Manchester from the period of the first arrival of Catholic people to the present day.

At the invitation of the pastor of St. Anne parish, Manchester, Monsignor Joseph E. Desmond, the newly created Diocesan Museum began modestly in 1990 with a small collection of memorabilia in one of the sacristies of the church. Within a short time, the museum expanded into both sacristies, leaving little space for the liturgical ministers of the parish. Most of these historical materials came from individuals from Manchester and around the state who had them at home, in many cases as family heirlooms, and donated them gratis to the museum. Additional archives, books, memorabilia, and the like came from the various diocesan departments and religious orders in New Hampshire.

Fortunately, the search for a new locale ended with the offer of the beautiful Chapel of the Annunciation by the Sisters of Mercy. This Gothic-like church, designed by the architect Patrick W. Ford, had been dedicated on March 25, 1896, by Bishop Denis M. Bradley as the chapel of the then motherhouse of the Sisters of Mercy at 435 Union Street, Manchester. Mr. Ford was also the architect of the chapel at St. Joseph Cathedral and later the chapel (now the chapel museum) at Saint Anselm College.

The Chapel of the Annunciation still contains the eighty original stalls for the nuns in four rising tiers, three marble and onyx altars, a domed ceiling, and depictions of a particular saint on each stained-glass window. After the motherhouse of the Sisters of Mercy was moved to Windham, New Hampshire, several years ago to the grounds of the Searles Castle, the Union Street property was remodeled and renovated into apartments, and the chapel was scheduled for demolition. Instead, it was generously given outright to the diocese for the museum.

Bishop O'Neil blessed and dedicated the new museum on October 16, 1994. Since then, its collection has grown rapidly and the archives, lectures, and exhibits attract larger and larger audiences. The management, under its director, Mrs. Fosher, consists of an entirely volunteer staff, and the museum is funded, in addition to a diocesan subsidy, by the generosity of friends and benefactors.

A Coadjutor Bishop

During the final third of Bishop Gendron's administration, another major change in leadership took place in the diocese. On December 21, 1988, after only one year and eight months as auxiliary bishop of Manchester, Bishop Joseph Gerry, o.s.b., was promoted to bishop of Portland, Maine. This announcement was officially made by the Apostolic Pro-Nuncio in Washington, Archbishop Pio Laghi. Bishop Joseph was officially installed as the head of all Catholics in Maine on February 21, 1989. The Diocese of Portland extends over some 33,040 square miles—that is, more than three times the size of the Diocese of Manchester—and includes roughly 245,000 Catholics, some 77,000 fewer than in New Hampshire. Bishop Joseph's departure created a void not only in administration but also in the hearts of those who admired his gentleness, consideration, and superior intellectual and spiritual qualities.

A request to the Holy See for a replacement for Bishop Joseph began shortly after his departure for Maine, which was also the state of his birth. Again, with commendable rapidity, it was announced by the Apostolic Pro-Nuncio on October 17, 1989 that the Most Reverend Leo Edward O'Neil had been appointed coadjutor bishop of Manchester with the right of succession. He was welcomed to Manchester in that capacity at a ceremony held in St. Joseph Cathedral on November 30, 1989. Episcopal responsibility was not new to Bishop Leo (as he preferred to be called); he had been auxiliary bishop of Springfield, Massachusetts, since his episcopal ordination on August 22, 1980, a period of more than nine years. As Bishop O'Neil succeeded Bishop Gendron as ordinary of the Diocese of Manchester on June 12, 1990, his biography and accomplishments will be given in chapter 15.

One should note here, however, the major distinction between an auxiliary bishop and a coadjutor bishop. The Code of Canon Law specifies that an auxiliary bishop does not possess the right to succession (c. 403, § 1), while a coadjutor does have that right (c. 403, § 2). Consequently, as it shall be seen, Bishop O'Neil became ordinary at the very moment of his predecessor's retirement.

Bishop Leo E. O'Neil's arrival in Manchester was, in a sense, an exchange. On September 8, 1921, a priest of the Diocese of Manchester, Thomas M. O'Leary, had been ordained the third bishop of Springfield. In

New Hampshire, Father O'Leary had been chancellor (1904–1914), vicar general (1914–1921), and pastor of St. John the Evangelist Parish in Concord (1915–1921), then an elite parish of the diocese. Unfortunately, Bishop O'Leary was not a generally well-liked person in his new diocese; he was considered rigid, distant, and nearly unapproachable during his twenty-eight years of episcopacy. (He died on October 10, 1949.) Consequently, when the reverse occurred in 1989, with a Springfield priest-bishop being sent to Manchester, several clergy with a sense of humor whispered to Bishop O'Neil before his departure, "get even." His "getting even" was a delight to New Hampshire.

Retirement of the Seventh Bishop of Manchester

With the assurance of a coadjutor with the right of succession in place, Bishop Gendron petitioned the Holy See in the month of April 1990 for retirement, and in early June received word that his request had been approved effective June 12, 1990. On that day a public announcement was made and, as provided by canon law, he was immediately succeeded by Bishop O'Neil without additional ceremony.

In his retirement statement, Bishop Gendron explained that he was not, at the age of close to sixty-nine, retiring for reasons of health, as Bishop Primeau had before him. His principal reason was the length of his service as bishop, more than fifteen years. In addition to shedding the burden, he undoubtedly believed that a change in leadership would be an advantage for the more than 300,000 individuals under his spiritual care.

Bishop Gendron's retirement proved to be, in fact, simply a change in priestly employment. He continued to live in Manchester, first in his own home and then in the cathedral rectory, and busied himself with confirmations, replacing priests in parishes, visiting the sick, ministering to the handicapped, helping the poor, and, as in previous years, counseling women religious.

One month after his retirement, on July 12, Bishop Gendron was honored in a Vesper Service of Thanksgiving in the Abbey Chapel at Saint Anselm College, attended by Cardinal Law of Boston, sixteen New England bishops, numerous ecumenical leaders, a large number of clergy, and hundreds of appreciative well-wishers from around the state. This public display of appreciation was repeated even more expansively on the celebration of his fiftieth anniversary of ordination to the priesthood in 1997.

While it is obviously too soon to make a definitive evaluation of Bishop Gendron's episcopacy, one can be assured that he will be remembered for the following: his two-and-a-half-year visitation of all the parishes; his notable contributions to ecumenism, principally through the New Hampshire Council of Churches; his establishment of more diocesan programs and projects than any bishop before him; and his abilities as a coordinator, as he put it, of the "gifts" of others.

On a lighter note, Bishop Gendron was the first bishop of Manchester ever—ordinary, auxiliary, or coadjutor—to grow a beard. Over the years it progressed from long sideburns, to a narrow ribbon beard, to the full beard that he is shown wearing in his picture in the Photographs section of this history. Perhaps he is also the sole bishop of New England to have practiced the martial arts before replacing this activity with bicycling.

FIFTEEN

Preparing for the Third Millenium 1990–1997

A Millenium

Bishop Leo E. O'Neil's transfer to Manchester from Springfield coincided roughly with the remote preparation for the end of the second and the beginning of the third Christian millennium. Virtually all civilizations and many religions established their own calendars, usually based on their knowledge of astronomy and some significant date in their history or mythology. For example, at some time in our year 2000, the Jewish people, with whom we share so much, including the Old Testament, will celebrate the beginning of their year 5760; the Islamic world will commemorate the year 1420; and the Hindus will honor the beginning of their year 1921.

Even our own year 2000 is subject to criticism, as it appears to a majority of scholars to be based on an erroneous calculation of the year of the birth of Jesus. Many would compute that His birth occurred perhaps as many as four years before the year 1 A.D. Moreover, the date of His birth, given as December 25, is not mentioned anywhere in the New Testament. December 25 is most likely to have been chosen to coincide with the winter solstice (December 21) in order to compete with the celebrations that took place in the pagan Roman world at that time. Whatever variations are found in calendars and dates across historical time do not diminish the importance of a millennium for Christians.

The Eighth Bishop of Manchester: Leo. E. O'Neil

Leo Edward O'Neil was born in Holyoke, Massachusetts, on January 31, 1928, the son of Edward F. O'Neil and Bertha Doling. He was one of three children. Neither parent survived to the time of his ordination to the priesthood.

After twelve years of Catholic schooling, first at Blessed Sacrament Elementary School and then at Sacred Heart High School, both in Holyoke, he entered Maryknoll Junior Seminary in 1945, an institution at Clarks Summit in Pennsylvania dedicated primarily to the preparation of priests for the missions of the Maryknoll Order. Four years later, he spent one year (1949–1950) as a student at Saint Anselm College, Manchester. The next five years, 1950–1955, he prepared for the diocesan priesthood at the Seminary of Philosophy and the Grand Seminary in Montreal, Quebec, Canada.

Leo E. O'Neil was ordained to the priesthood on June 4, 1955, by the Most Reverend Christopher J. Weldon, bishop of Springfield, for ministry in that diocese. The newly ordained Father O'Neil's first assignment was to St. Mary parish, Westfield, Massachusetts, where he also served as director of both the parish elementary and high schools, chaplain at Westfield State College, and chaplain to the Hispanic community in that city.

One June 29, 1968, after thirteen years of priesthood, he became associate pastor at St. Catherine of Siena parish in the see city of Springfield. As at Westfield, he was given additional responsibilities: He taught religion at Ursuline Academy and served as chaplain to both the Sisters of the Good Shepherd and the Sisters of Holy Cross.

Nearly twenty years after his ordination to the priesthood, in May 1976, Bishop Weldon assigned him to what was to be his only pastorate, St. Mary of the Assumption in Haydenville, Massachusetts.

In 1975, Father O'Neil was named diocesan director of both Family Life and Parish Councils. Shortly thereafter, these positions were combined into the Office of Pastoral Ministry. Over the years, under his guidance, the Office of Pastoral Ministry expanded to include the following: victims of AIDS; the bereaved; black Catholics; the Blue Army; Camp Holy Cross; campus ministry; the Center for Spiritual Direction; charismatic prayer renewal; the Cursillo Movement; Hispanics; people in prison; liturgy and parish worship; pastoral planning; retreat houses; and ministries to the separated and divorced, the sick and elderly, and to youth.

Given this array of responsibilities, it was not surprising that his selection as the first ever auxiliary bishop of Springfield was announced on

June 3, 1980, by the Pro-Nuncio in Washington. On August 22, he was ordained to the episcopacy in St. Michael Cathedral in Springfield.

In 1989, the ordinary of Springfield, the Most Reverend Joseph F. Maguire, appointed him Moderator with the crucial task of forming a diocesan cabinet. During that same summer, Bishop O'Neil designed a program of spiritual, cultural, and linguistic study for seminarians of the Diocese of Springfield to prepare them for ministry with the rapidly growing Hispanic community in western Massachusetts. A phase of the program was spending six weeks in Puerto Rico both studying the language and culture and working in a summer school for disadvantaged local students. Bishop O'Neil shared these six weeks with the Springfield seminarians.

As related, Pope John Paul II appointed Bishop O'Neil as coadjutor of the Diocese of Manchester on October 17, 1989, and was welcomed in Manchester at a ceremony in St. Joseph Cathedral on November 30. Eight months later, on June 12, 1990, he succeeded Bishop Gendron automatically on the latter's retirement.

From his very first days in Manchester, Bishop Leo began to display his own personality and his own approach to episcopal ministry. Soon apparent were his sense of humor, his exceptional rapport with the young, and—another first for the diocese,—a flair for poetry.

Not long after the official Liturgy of Welcome for Bishop Leo on November 30, 1989, he visited St. Anthony School in Manchester, where he blessed the students (grades K–6) and, in characteristic fashion, exchanged "high fives" with many of them. This visit was followed by one to St. Teresa Manor, also in Manchester, a nursing home provided by New Hampshire Catholic Charities, where the exact form of the greeting between the bishop and elderly residents was not recorded.

On at least two occasions Bishop Leo surprised the people of the diocese by addressing them in poetic form. The first was his Advent Reflections, prepared for his welcoming liturgy on November 30, 1989. A second, longer message was his Epiphany Proclamation (January 6) for 1996. His poetry, by any objective standard, is graceful, clearly understandable, and spiritually compelling.

Of even greater importance was the agenda that he would initiate and pursue from June 12, 1990, onward. The plans and programs for the next seven years—1990–1997—proved to be well conceived, in logical sequence, and potentially salutary for all: laity, clergy, and men and women religious.

Renewing the Covenant

In the progression of major projects beginning in 1990, "Renewing the Covenant" was the first. It followed in the tradition of "Operation FIRE" in the late 1960s (cf. chapter 13) and "Renew" in the early 1980s (cf. chapter 14).

"Renewing the Covenant: New Hampshire Catholics in the 1990s," its full title, was the result of Bishop Gendron's visitation of all the parishes in the diocese in the early to mid-1980s; its purpose was to establish a common vision among all Catholics in the state. Primary responsibility for preparing this pastoral plan of action was given to then Monsignor Francis J. Christian, the chancellor of the diocese and secretary for Pastoral Services. After two years of extensive consultation with the parishes, diocesan personnel, clergy, lay representative bodies, school principals, and many others, a diocesan mission statement was prepared, describing in print for the first time the purpose of the Catholic Church in New Hampshire, and the pastoral plan "Renewing the Covenant" was completed. This extensive plan was presented to the Catholics of the diocese at a Eucharist celebration at 4 P.M. in St. Joseph Cathedral on September 23, 1990. About seven hundred people were present at this ceremony.

This plan, as its title implies, was to establish a vision that would guide the Diocese of Manchester into the next millennium by renewing itself in every possible manner. In the extensive materials published and distributed to explain, direct, and support the plan, the following key areas were identified for review and renewal: evangelization, education (in all its forms), service, ministries, worship, communications, stewardship, growth, and planning. Fundamental to this important enterprise was the renewal of each individual by calling upon the Holy Spirit for wisdom, vigor, insight, and especially divine grace.

Two other basic components of "Renewing the Covenant" were: (1) its duration—it was structured for five full years (1990–1995); and (2) the plan provided for both updating and evaluation. Unfortunately, as with a great many of the programs and projects of the Catholic Church in New Hampshire in the past, no provisions were made to implement either the proposed update or evaluation, two frequently fatal flaws. It seemed that in these many cases the producing of the plan, program, or project itself was the objective, and not the outcome that was desired. This same weakness has been frequently noted in all human enterprises, not only those of the Church.

As "Renewing the Covenant" was designed to encompass virtually every aspect of Catholic Church life, only a few subjects of particular relevance will be mentioned here. A great deal of emphasis was placed on the establishment of a new diocesan Office of Evangelization and the Catechumenate as well as the responsibility of each parish to develop a process and plan for the same purpose by June 1993. This injunction was given, without a doubt, not only because of the insistence of the Universal Church but also because of the obvious lack of priority given to this fundamental mission of the church, not only in New Hampshire but across the United States as well throughout much of its history.

Another unequivocal but not always recognized tool for ministry is a knowledge of the number of people in the territory of a parish and their religious affiliation and status. Primary in this information is their active or inactive status. Consequently, "Renewing the Covenant" mandated a parish census to be completed by July 1992 and then kept up-to-date thereafter. In 1994, eighty parishes reported that they had accomplished this task; at least fifty more (38 percent) submitted no report on this topic at that time.

A number of directives, as it could have been expected, concerned religious education. Catholic schools were requested to evaluate the effectiveness of their religious education offerings, and all other parish entities involved in this ministry, such as teaching children and youths not in Catholic schools, were required to do the same. In addition, deaneries were directed to expand their adult religious education programs either in Christian Life Centers or in individual parishes.

Great emphasis was placed on the centrality of the celebration of the Lord's Day Liturgy (as it was called in the document) and the need to develop full and active participation of priest-presiders, liturgical ministers, and the entire faith community. The plan goes on to give instructions on the proper preparation of the clergy and the laymen and laywomen who are to be involved in this ministry.

Recognizing the centrality and singular importance of the parish in the lives of a great majority of the faithful, "Renewing the Covenant" required that each parish had a pastoral council composed of a "majority" of lay members elected or selected through a process of discernment. It also mandated, as does canon law (c. 537), that a parish finance committee of at least, but not limited to, three members be created. While not obligatory, the plan recommends that a standing committee of the parish pastoral council on property and finance be founded, as it is "of great help." On the subject of church real estate and property, Bishop Leo observed in another pastoral letter, "A Splendid Opportunity," that "spending money to maintain buildings while religious instruction crumbles is not wise stewardship." The message is clearly that if something is to crumble, it should not be the teaching of the faith. On the Subject of stewardship, "Renewing the Covenant" advocated the development of such a process in each parish by September 1993. In the following year—1994—eighty parishes reported that they had implemented some form of stewardship, which had resulted in an increase of about 30 percent in parish revenues and, equally significant, a corresponding increase of involvement of parishioners in church activities. As with the mandate for a parish census, roughly fifty parishes, or about 38 percent, either chose not to or were not ready to take a report to the diocese on stewardship at that time. That more than one-third of the parishes in New Hampshire did not respond to this query, or to the one on a parish census, could not but be a cause of real concern for diocesan authorities.

Emphasis was also placed on multicultural ministries, especially the pastoral care of the newer immigrants such as Koreans, Vietnamese, and Latin Americans from Mexico, the Caribbean, and virtually all of the countries in Central and South America. A diocesan office for Multicultural Ministries was established in 1992 as part of the Secretariat for Community Affairs, and major efforts have since been made to care for the spiritual and other needs of these people, who are enriching the American church as well as our society as a whole. All Americans, save Native Americans who arrived from Asia some 12,000 or more years ago, need to recall their immigrant roots, many not older than three, four, or five generations ago.

In order to further clarify some issues dealing with the broad responsibilities of the Church in education, Bishop Leo elaborated on "Renewing the Covenant" with a nineteen-page pastoral entitled "To Whom Shall We Go?" in the fall of 1992. This document covers the teaching message of the

Church, the role of parents in the Catholic education of their children, the mission of the Catholic school, the duties of the parish, and youth ministry, the latter an area of concern for the young in which the Diocese of Manchester continues to exercise a "pioneer" role in the United States.

"To Whom Shall We Go?" also announced the following: a new program for youth ministry in the diocese; the formation of a board to study the organization and financing of Catholic schools; and the need for updating all religious education programs in the diocese, the latter a message much repeated in the implementation of "Renewing the Covenant."

In a novel ending for an episcopal pastoral letter, Bishop Leo addressed congenial and appropriate messages to elementary, junior high, and high school students, and to those who are on the state's college and university campuses. This most elaborate and encompassing program ever undertaken in the diocese, "Renewing the Covenant: New Hampshire Catholics in the 1990s," was officially concluded by a period of review and evaluation between 1993 and 1995, and the beginning of a new process of planning for the future was initiated by the diocesan secretaries and their staffs. Overall the review, evaluation, and the new process of planning have not had much effect on the diocese. However, the Church recognizes its continual need for renewal and reform as mandated in the "Decree on Ecumenism" of the Second Vatican Council (article 6). This mandate and resolve apply equally to every level of the local and diocesan church.

The Emmaus Journey

While "Renewing the Covenant" was taking its course, a special program was designed and implemented for the spiritual renewal of the clergy. This initiative was in response to a 1973 document of the National Conference of Catholic Bishops entitled "The Spiritual Renewal of the American Priesthood." In New Hampshire this was called the Emmaus Spiritual Program and was designed and supervised by the sixteen-member Emmaus Core Planning Committee under the direction of Monsignor Norman P. Bolduc and the Office of Priestly Life and Ministry.

As with "Renewing the Covenant," the Emmaus program was meticulously prepared, with ample printed materials available during each of the four phases of the plan. One of the initial documents elaborated on the purpose of the program: the personal spiritual renewal of all the priests and deacons of the diocese; the development of a deeper sense of community in the presbyteral body; and assistance for the clergy in union with their bishop to renew their corporate spirituality and their sense of mission. Basic to the endeavor was to involve the entire Catholic Church of New Hampshire through publicity and public relations, and particularly through the prayer-support of all—parishes, institutions, and religious and lay organizations—in the interior enrichment of their spiritual brothers and leaders.

The Emmaus Spiritual Program, scheduled to last for approximately one year, was launched at a meeting of the entire presbyterate—diocesan priests, priests of religious communities, transitional deacons, and permanent deacons—at the Red Jacket Inn in North Conway, New Hampshire, from June 17 through 20, 1991. The first two days were devoted entirely to the Emmaus program and the remainder to conferences on priestly spirituality, an open discussion on the subject, and the annual jubilarian celebration which honors those clergy who are celebrating significant anniversaries, such as twenty-five, forty, or fifty years of ordination. Two hundred and two people attended this opening convocation: 162 active diocesan priests (83% of the total), 16 retired diocesan priests, and 24 priests from religious orders and deacons.

This first phase was followed by Phase II, which consisted of seven separate retreat opportunities to give the participants the means and the time to reflect profoundly on life and ministry. As they are much involved in the ministries of their husbands, the wives of the permanent deacons participated in these retreats as well. More than 190 people, including the wives, attended one of these seven retreats.

Phase III, which extended between December 1991 and May 1992, consisted of eighteen freely constituted groups of between six and twelve individuals who pledged to meet six times for an overnight during that period to pray together and to discuss and reflect on assigned topics. These topics, one for each overnight, were prayer, study, personal growth, spiritual direction, growth with the people of God, and growth with brother priests and deacons. One hundred and eighty-four took part in these six overnight sessions. At the end of these meetings—108 in all, counting all eighteen groups assembled six times—the conveyer sent the recommendations of his group to the Emmaus office. These recommendations were published in booklet form and used as the basis for the concluding convocation, held again at the Red Jacket Inn in North Conway, June 8–11, 1992.

This meeting, Phase IV, had a four fold purpose: to renew and evaluate the Emmaus Journey of the past year; to identify the future priorities of the New Hampshire Catholic presbyterate; to reflect on priestly life and spirituality; and to celebrate God's goodness in their lives. Three of the conferences were led by Bishop Robert F. Morneau, auxiliary bishop of Green Bay, Wisconsin, a nationally known writer and lecturer on the subjects of the life and spirituality of priests. This final convocation was the best attended of any of the phases of the Emmaus Journey: 93 percent of all the active priests, 181 in all, were present, as were twenty-nine retired diocesan clergy, deacons (transitional and permanent), and religious priests.

After a lengthy but very systematic process of sifting through all the materials, including the recommendations accumulated between June 1991 and June 1992, notably those made by the eighteen discussion groups, fifty-four priorities were identified and then reduced to eight. Subsequently, by the vote of all those present at the convocation, these eight priorities were further reduced to a final three. Selected as the top three by the body of the clergy were: (1) that the diocese promote the spiritual, emotional, physical and health and growth of priests (five recommendations were appended on how to do this); (2) that the diocese promote the sharing of leadership and ministry in New Hampshire by enabling and utilizing the gifts of all the baptized so that they can better bring Christ's life to the world; and (3) that the diocese update and implement policies of financial accountability and adjustments on both the diocesan and parish levels.

A thorough final report on the entire process was submitted to Bishop O'Neil and the presbyterate on August 15, 1992, by the Priests' Continuing Formation Committee of the Office of Priestly Life and Ministry.

One of the major indications of the success of any program is the lasting effect that it has on those for whom it is intended. For the Emmaus Spiritual Program, the measurement of its effectiveness on the life and ministry of the clergy is quasi-impossible. While the four phases enjoyed outstanding participation by the clergy, the eighteen reflection groups formed during Phase III gradually deteriorated in membership from an original 157 to a relatively small, even minuscule, number by 1997. Most of the real benefits, as could be expected, remain intangible. It is also of some interest to note that the final report of August 15, 1992, to Bishop Leo and the clergy indicated that the total expenses for this project were $162,878.51.

New Programs 1990–1994

Concurrent with the major undertakings described above, Bishop Leo presided, as it has been mentioned, at the dedication of a monument commemorating all babies who were aborted while awaiting birth. This monument erected at Mount Calvary Cemetery in Manchester was the first of its kind in New Hampshire, remembering the many thousands who perished in this way. By design, it was blessed on the Feast of the Holy Innocents, December 28, 1991 (cf. chapter 14). Since then, similar memorial monuments have been erected in other Catholic cemeteries in New Hampshire.

Earlier in 1991, on Sunday, February 10, Bishop Leo inaugurated an annual blessing of engaged couples at the cathedral to correspond to the blessing of married couples celebrating anniversaries and another for men and women religious commemorating the anniversaries of their religious vows (cf. chapter 14).

In 1994, given the independent importance of each, the offices of evangelization and the catechumenate were separated and given autonomous existence under different leadership.

A Serious Illness

A major setback to the diocese occurred in the fall of 1993 with the serious illness of Bishop O'Neil. On November 30, he underwent surgery at the Catholic Medical Center in Manchester for the removal of a growth and part of his sternum because of a malignancy. Later, the diagnosis of multiple myeloma, a sometimes painful form of blood cancer that causes tumors to grow in the bones, was made public. According to newspaper accounts, this condition was not curable but could be held under control with chemotherapy. This condition occasionally flared up and temporarily afflicted and incapacitated Bishop Leo. Characteristically, at the time of his surgery in 1993, he asked that instead of get-well cards, messages, or gifts, donations be sent to the Santa Fund of the Salvation Army, a seasonal charity based in Manchester and well publicized by the *Manchester Union Leader* and the *New Hampshire Sunday News.*

A Splendid Opportunity

Bishop O'Neil published his next pastoral letter during the late summer of 1994; this one was given the title of "A Splendid Opportunity." It appeared as a four-page insert in the September 15 issue of the diocesan newspaper *Tidings.* Its purpose was to discuss how the vast talents and energies of all the baptized could and should be used to prepare the Diocese of Manchester for the next millennium and to do the work of the Church. While using all resources, human and physical, the bishop stressed that the plan that he was presenting had to be rooted deeply in faith. His plan outlined four elements: All the baptized are to assume the responsibilities of that sacrament (1) by professing the faith, (2) by sharing, (3) by celebrating the faith in the liturgy, and (4) by prayer. All, he emphasized, are to work together in shaping our parishes and diocese for the next century, which is also the next millennium. This general appeal to all, especially to the laity, to prepare for the future would be made more precise in subsequent letters to all the faithful.

Catholic Charities Celebrates Fifty Years

New Hampshire's largest nonprofit social service agency, New Hampshire Catholic Charities, celebrated its fiftieth anniversary in 1995. In addition to being the largest, it also has an excellent record with regard to the percentage of its gross income that is used for services and programs: In 1995 only 7 percent was expended on management and the remaining 93 percent on the purposes of the charity. In addition to what has been said about the organization in chapter 12, it should be noted that this charity addresses itself to a wide range of human problems in three basic categories: family services, parish social ministry, and institutional services. This assistance is provided to people of all ages, of all races, and of all religions, regardless of ability to pay. In addition to its headquarters at 215 Myrtle Street in Manchester, the services of Catholic Charities are available at a number of district offices around the state: in Berlin, Keene, Laconia, Lebanon, Littleton, Nashua, Rochester, and Salem.

One among the many enterprises of Catholic Charities that are of great service to the state is the New Hampshire Food Bank. This program, inaugurated in October 1984, solicits food in large quantities from producers, wholesalers, retailers, and private individuals. In most cases these are items, mostly food, that are deemed unsalable by the owners but still edible and usable. Most of it would probably end up as landfill.

During its very first year of operation, under the direction of Mr. Albert J. Tremblay, the Food Bank distributed some 250,000 pounds of goods statewide. Ten years later, in 1994, more than 2 million pounds were dispensed to more than four hundred soup kitchens, food pantries, shelters, day-care centers, elderly meal sites, substance-abuse programs, and group homes. This translates into more than 100,000 meals a month for the needy of New Hampshire.

In this latter year, 1994, the New Hampshire Food Bank was able to resolve a major distribution problem with the purchase of a refrigerated truck from Mack Sales, Inc. This essential purchase was made possible by financial support from a number of foundations, trusts, and companies. A refrigerated truck now allowed the delivery of perishable foods to northern and western areas of New Hampshire.

Catholic Charities' subsidy to the Food Bank has been consistently under $95,000 a year, with the remainder of the support coming from shared maintenance contributions from the nonprofit agencies that use this service. They contribute pennies per pound of food they receive to help offset the costs of transportation, administration, and warehousing. Some financial support also comes from other sources, such as Second Harvest, which is a national food solicitor that coordinates the work of some 185 food banks across the country. Despite the extensive reach of the New Hampshire Food Bank, in 1996 it employed only five paid staff, including an office manager. Most of the work is done by volunteers.

Catholic Hospitals in New Hampshire

One of the most visible, community-appreciated, and effective examples of charity by the Catholic Church in New Hampshire has been its services by its hospitals. Over time, beginning around 1886, there have been five established in the state; by 1997 only two remained.

The first of the five hospitals was what came to be known as Sacred

Heart Hospital in Manchester. In 1886, the national *Catholic Directory* listed St. Patrick Hospital as being directed by the Sisters of Mercy with Sister Mary Ligouri as superior. At that time the hospital cared for twenty patients. In 1893, the same directory noted the change in name from St. Patrick to Sacred Heart Hospital. The institution retained this name and continued to be managed by the Sisters of Mercy until it became the Catholic Medical Center, East Building, in 1974 as the result of a merger with Notre Dame Hospital on the west side of Manchester. The 1979 national *Catholic Directory* no longer listed the East Building, as all of the hospital services had been moved to the Catholic Medical Center west side building.

Notre Dame Hospital, the Manchester West facility, was blessed on October 18, 1894, under the title Hospital of Our Lady of Lourdes. In time it became known to the general public as Notre Dame Hospital. Under the ownership and care of the Sisters of Charity of Ste.-Hyacinthe (Gray Nuns), it grew from twelve patients in 1895 into a flourishing institution, as had Sacred Heart Hospital on the east side of the Merrimack River. By 1979, with all patients and services moved to its quarters, and with the discontinuation of the Manchester East facility, it became the Catholic Medical Center, the only Catholic hospital in Manchester.

In the expectation of further improving hospital care and lowering medical costs in Manchester and the surrounding communities, the Catholic Medical Center joined the Elliot Hospital in 1994, the latter a private and highly respected facility in East Manchester, under common ownership and management. Unfortunately, this merger has not been either entirely peaceful or acceptable by a significant part of the population. Serious disagreements have been strongly voiced on mainly two subjects. One was the plan to consolidate all services into one general-care hospital in Manchester at the Elliot site, with, basically, only emergency services and rehabilitation programs at the Catholic Medical Center building. The second and certainly the more serious dissension is in the area of medical ethics. While a few issues of this nature are involved, the most fundamental and controversial is that of abortion, which, it is said, has been allowed in rare, deemed medically necessary cases, at the Elliot Hospital. Both of these issues, the need, or desire, for one or two acute-care hospitals for Manchester, and the basic moral principal of the sanctity of life—abortion—have divided the community and remain unresolved at the publication of this history.

A third Catholic hospital was listed in the national *Catholic Directory* of 1894: This was St. Mary's Home for Aged and Hospital in Dover. Apparently begun by the "Gray Nuns," it had ten patients (most likely all elderly) in 1894. Two years later, twenty-nine orphans were being cared for by four Sisters of Mercy in a facility connected to the asylum of St. Mary's Home for Aged and Hospital, which at that time housed ten residents. By 1911, this institution was no longer listed in the national directory.

A fourth Catholic hospital was founded in Berlin on June 21, 1905, again by the Sisters of Charity of Ste.-Hyacinthe. From the beginning, this facility was known as St. Louis Hospital. It rendered praiseworthy service to the people of Berlin and its environs until it was ceded to secular management. It was no longer listed among the Catholic hospitals of the Diocese of Manchester in the national directory of 1971.

A fifth and still existing hospital was founded in Nashua by the Sisters of Charity of Montreal. This hospital was first listed in the national *Catholic Directory* of 1909 with nine "Gray Nuns" and nineteen patients. It had been dedicated the previous May 1908. After roughly one hundred years of existence, it still serves the medical, emotional, and spiritual needs of all in the southern part of the state. In recent years it joined in alliance with Optima Health, which controls both the Elliot Hospital and the Catholic Medical Center.

Saint Vincent de Paul Societies

Pre–dating New Hampshire Catholic Charities in some instances in the diocese is the ministry of the Societies of Saint Vincent de Paul. This movement was founded in Paris by Frederic Ozanam and his associates in 1833. Frederic Ozanam was beatified in the Cathedral of Notre Dame in Paris by Pope John Paul II during the 12th World Youth Day on August 22, 1997. This Catholic association of laymen and laywomen (since 1968) is devoted, usually on a parish basis, to the service of the poor through the practice of the spiritual and corporal works of mercy. Among its services in New Hampshire have been emergency donations of food, the founding of food pantries, the distribution of clothing, the providing of shelter and furniture, counseling, vouchers for stores, food baskets, and brown-bag lunches.

By 1996, there were seventeen individual Saint Vincent de Paul Conferences in the state involving more than 320 active men and women members. Ten of these conferences are in the city of Manchester. In addition to the services mentioned above, the conferences operate four thrift stores in Laconia, Berlin, Hampton, and Manchester, and fifteen food pantries. The Laconia conference, the largest in New Hampshire, is managed by some ninety volunteers. This conference provides nearly 55,000 free meals a year through its food pantry, more than $65,000 in financial assistance, and distributes the equivalent of $25,000 in clothing, furniture, and household items from its thrift store.

One of the great values of these societies is the practice of the spiritual and corporal works of mercy on a person-to-person basis, face to face, neighbor to neighbor.

The Care of Aged Priests and Sisters

With a rapidly aging clergy and even older women religious (this crisis is discussed below), it was inevitable that some provisions would have to be made for the care of both.

One of the pressing problems in the diocese was the nursing-home care needed by a good number of the sick diocesan clergy, most of them past retirement age. To remedy this urgent situation, New Hampshire Catholic Charities purchased and renovated the former Maple Leaf Residential Care facility directly across the street from the Mount Carmel Nursing Home in Manchester. Opened in late September 1995, this twenty-four-room home offers twenty-four-hour nursing care and medical supervision. Other in-house services are physical therapy, audiology, ophthalmology, podiatry, and dentistry. Mass, as could be expected, is offered daily in the chapel. Within a few months of its opening, this facility, named the Bishop Peterson Residence after the fourth bishop of Manchester, had fourteen patients and, given the average age of diocesan priests, could, unfortunately, expect many more in a relatively brief period of time.

Provisions were also made for the better administration of the nursing facilities of the religious communities in the diocese that requested it. This service, offered by New Hampshire Catholic Charities, was accepted quickly by two congregations of women religious, first by the Sisters of Mercy of the Americas (Regional Community of New Hampshire) and shortly thereafter by the Sisters of Presentation of Mary. According to the terms of the agreement, Catholic Charities assumed management in 1995 of the Warde Health Center, a nursing home, and the Frances Warde Center, a twenty-unit residential care/assisted living facility, both on the grounds of the motherhouse of the Sisters of Mercy at Searles Castle, Windham. On that occasion, the Sisters of Mercy announced that they would accept laywomen as residents should there be room either in their nursing home or in the residential care/assisted living facility. Should this occur, it would be the first time ever in New Hampshire that women religious and laywomen would be housed together in these circumstances.

Later in 1995, the Sisters of Presentation became the second congregation to accept the invitation of Catholic Charities. This organization assumed management of both St. Joseph infirmary, a nursing home caring for twenty-two sisters, and St. Joseph Residence, and assisted residence facility then housing twenty-two additional nuns. These facilities are on Mammoth Road in Manchester.

The Future of Our Faith

Capping such initiatives of the 1990s as "Renewing the Covenant," the Emmaus Spiritual Program, and "A Splendid Opportunity" was another project entitled The Future of Our Faith. The goal of this primarily fund-raising campaign, the first ever in the 110-year history of the Diocese of Manchester, was to generate between $15 million and $20 million of capital for the Catholic Church in New Hampshire. In his letter to the faithful announcing his decision, Bishop Leo explained that the current resources of the diocese and parishes were stretched to the limit and that "unless new funding is forthcoming, it will be impossible for us to undertake new and needed programs that are essential to the future." In brief, the insufficiency of funds would hamper the mission of the Church.

Planning for this unique and major campaign began with Bishop Leo consulting with the Council of Priests and the Diocesan Pastoral Council, the latter consisting mainly of laity. On December 6, 1994, he was able to announce that the Martin J. Moran Company, a nationally known fundraising consulting firm, had been employed to conduct a strategic planning study to determine the scope and dimensions of a major capital campaign to address a variety of diocesan needs.

During these early stages, two basic decisions were made. The first was that the fiftieth-anniversary appeal on behalf of Catholic Charities was to be "enfolded" by "The Future of Our Faith," and that $3 million from the campaign would be earmarked for that charity. A second and equally important determination was that after the Catholic Charities commitment had been met, 50 percent of all the funds raised in a parish during the campaign would belong to that parish exclusively, to be used according to its own discretion. This last provision was undoubtedly included to give an added incentive to generous contributions from those whose vision of Church, at least from the point of view of financial support, frequently ends at the parish boundary.

Having established these two conditions, the funds that were expected to be raised were designated for five separate purposes. The first was parish development with a goal of $7.5 million. In parish development were included debt reduction, plant restoration, church restorations, repairs, liturgical upgrading, building new facilities, and raising endowment funds.

Second was the retired clergy endowment fund, with an objective of $2 million. This endowment was to assist in housing retired diocesan clergy, providing for their personal needs, and—should they require it—to finance assisted living or skilled nursing-home care. The Bishop Peterson Residence mentioned above was one of the facilities the planners had in mind.

Next was a parish staffing endowment with a target of $2.5 million. This endowment had multiple goals: Assisting seminarians in paying their student loans and sponsoring programs to encourage additional vocations; structuring and conducting permanent deaconate programs; and sponsoring pastoral associate training programs to prepare lay and religious to work with the clergy in parishes.

A fourth endowment, with a goal of $2 million, was to be established for Catholic education. The proceeds were to be used for religious education assistance programs, to help support the continued growth and development of youth and adult religious education in the parishes, and a tuition-assistance program to provide annual grants to support financially the needy students in parish schools.

Finally, with a goal of $1 million, was a parish assistance fund. The objective of this fund was to assist the parishes in the diocese that were in need of special financial support for some specific purpose, or, as in the case of a few of them, to help meet their basic expenses if they were running into debt. Except for this fund for indigent parishes, all others were to be established as endowments.

Some may be surprised to note that "The Future of Our Faith" concerns only the needs of the Diocese of Manchester and does not extend to the entire Catholic Church, which is universal.

In summary, the financial goals of "The Future of Our Faith," including the $3 million for New Hampshire Catholic Charities, was set at $18 million. This figure was based on the total annual income of the diocese's parishes and agencies, which was about $19.2 million

Martin J. Moran Company also projected that based on the approximately 25,000 households that make an annual gift to the Catholic Charities appeal, "The Future of Our Faith" campaign would generate roughly an equal number of contributors. Pledges to the campaign were expected to be honored over a period of three years. Twenty parishes, for a variety of reasons, were given permission to delay the launching of the campaign until the fall of 1995, usually because some previous fund-raising activity was already in progress.

By the end of September 1997, 17,778 participants in this campaign had contributed a total of $11,042,758; and there remained another $2,898,259 still to be paid in pledges. In all, the total potential of "The Future of Our Faith" was $13,941,017 and not the $18 million established as the goal by Martin J. Moran Company; this was $4,058,983 short of the objective. It is also to be noted that the 17,778 contributors was 29 percent less than the 25,000 foreseen by the same company. On a more positive note, by August 1997, an additional $4,030,114.77 had been returned to the parishes based on the formula agreed upon for the financial drive.

In all, by September 1997, twelve parishes had met their goal, one hundred and one had not, and sixteen had not run the appeal. Of these sixteen, four have opted to make payments assessed by the diocese, and twelve have yet to participate at all. The five most successful parishes in exceeding their goals were: St. Patrick, Newport (190%); St. Paul, Franklin (185%); St. Rose of Lima, Littleton (177%); St. Joseph Cathedral, Manchester (155%); and St. Theresa, Rye Beach (153%). Once all unpaid pledges are honored, other parishes may exceed their goal as well.

Pastoring God's People

Another key factor in planning for the future of the Catholic Church in New Hampshire was the shortage of clergy, growing more acute with each passing year. This urgent problem was addressed in the diocesan plan entitled "Pastoring God's People Today and Tomorrow." The final plan was the result of a year and a half of work by eleven deanery groups and a diocesan planning committee. Their purpose was to build a comprehensive plan to meet the anticipated needs of the diocese for priests over the next five years. Once completed, the proposals were studied by both the Council of Priests and the Diocesan Pastoral Council. Each council recommended that the plan be accepted and implemented.

In summary, the plan proposes that permanent deacons and pastoral associates (lay or religious) be employed as fully as possible in the ministries that they are qualified to exercise. In order to protect priests from burnout or otherwise abusing their health, the plan proposed that they be limited to four or five weekend Masses (Saturday evening and Sunday), and a combined total of seventy-five weddings and funerals each year. Weddings, in particular, require several lengthy sessions of instructions with the parties to be married.

Several plans are advanced in the plan for the pastoral care of the parishes. These options include: the sharing of one pastor by two or more parishes, as already done by fifteen parishes by the fall of 1997; appointing a part-time pastor, already done in a few instances; and withdrawing a parochial vicar from parishes that could get by with one fewer priest. This last expedient has been in effect since shortly after the Second Vatican Council, which ended in 1965.

Of great usefulness in the plan is the identification of the parishes that need two priests, usually a pastor and an associate, and those that need weekend and/or summer help from retired priests or those who work in diocesan administration. Wisely, "Pastoring God's People," which went into effect in late 1995, was presented on an experimental basis and with the proviso that it be updated every five years. Given the role of the bishop in the Church, the entire matter of personnel assignment is ultimately left to his sole and final decision.

A New Auxiliary Bishop

Since 1977, during the administration of Bishop Gendron, the Diocese of Manchester has had two auxiliary bishops, Robert E. Mulvee and Joseph J. Gerry, o.s.b., and one coadjutor with right to succession, Leo E. O'Neil. It was not unexpected that these three would have a successor. On April 2, 1996, the Apostolic Pro-Nuncio in Washington announced that Monsignor Francis J. Christian, who had been chancellor of the diocese since June 1977 and secretary for administrative/canonical affairs since January 1986, had been selected for that office by the Holy See. Given the educational attainments of Monsignor Christian and his broad experience in ecclesiastical administration in the Diocese of Manchester, his appointment came as no surprise to the clergy of New Hampshire.

Francis J. Christian was born on October 8, 1942, in Peterborough, the only child of Joseph L. Christian and Dorothy Mary Parent. He attended the public schools of Jaffrey and graduated from Conant High School in 1960. During his high school years he was an athlete who lettered in three sports: baseball, basketball, and soccer. To this day he has retained his interest in sports, and is an avid and talented golfer.

After graduating from Conant High, Francis attended Saint Anselm College for two years. Having decided on his vocation to the priesthood, the Diocese of Manchester sent him to St. Paul Seminary in Ottawa, Ontario, where he spent an additional two years (1962–1964). During these same two years, he completed his undergraduate studies at the University of Ottawa, where he was granted two degrees, a bachelor of arts and a bachelor of philosophy. The next four years, for his theological studies, he was sent to the American College at the University of Louvain in Belgium, from which he earned a master's degree in theology in 1968.

On June 29, 1968, the feast of SS. Peter and Paul, Francis J. Christian had the privilege of being ordained to the priesthood in his home parish, that of St. Patrick in Jaffrey; the ordaining prelate was Bishop Ernest J. Primeau. Father Christian was to serve a relatively short period of time as an associate pastor. After being assigned for some three years at Our Lady of Mercy parish in Merrimack, he spent one year performing the same function at the Cathedral parish of St. Joseph in Manchester.

Obviously impressed by his intelligence and his other human and ecclesiastical qualities, he was assigned again to the University of Louvain for doctoral studies. After two years (1973–1975), he obtained a Ph.D., summa cum laude, in religious studies with a specialization in moral theology. With this degree, he joined a small number of priests in the diocese with doctorates, and became the first to do advanced studies in the important area of moral theology.

In March 1975, one month after his return from the University of Louvain, he was appointed assistant chancellor of the diocese, and was advanced to the head position of chancellor in June 1977. In January 1986, he was given the added responsibility of secretary for administrative/ canonical affairs. In that latter post he was responsible for the chancery, the office of communications, the office of planning, and the diocesan marriage tribunal. This title was changed to secretary for pastoral services in 1992, at which time his authority was broadened to further include the offices of pastoral ministry, the permanent deaconate, priestly life and ministry, worship, and vocations. Also in 1986, he was honored by Pope John Paul II by being named a prelate of honor, which included the title "Monsignor."

In addition to the above, Monsignor Christian was given other duties over the years. Among these were: defender of the bond in the diocesan marriage tribunal, executive secretary of the diocesan liturgical commission, member of the diocesan commission on Christian unity, judge on the matrimonial court, chairman of the diocesan centennial committee (mentioned earlier), diocesan consultor, member of the council of priests, and representative to the diocesan pastoral council.

From 1986 to 1996, he was involved in weekend parish ministry at St. Anne parish in Hampstead and its mission station, St. Michael in Sandown. During these years, he was much appreciated by the parishioners not only for celebrating the liturgy and his preaching but also for his ministry with youth in the confirmation program and for his involvement with adults in the Rite of Christian Initiation, the latter a detailed program for preparing converts for formal admission to the Catholic Church.

After twenty-one years in chancery and close involvement in the vast majority of the important events of the Diocese of Manchester during that period, Francis J. Christian was ordained to the episcopacy in St. Joseph Cathedral on May 14, 1996, by Bishop Leo. E. O'Neil. Speaking of his new auxiliary shortly after the latter's selection by the Holy See, Bishop Leo stated that he was an excellent choice for three reasons: "his personality, his experience, and his life of prayer and faith."

A 'Twinning' of Parishes Challenged

Toward the end of the parameters of this history (1647—1997), a division occurred concerning two matters of considerable importance to the Diocese of Manchester: The supposedly settled issue of ethnic strife and the necessity of "twinning" of parishes—that is, the sharing of a pastor by two or more parishes.

According to the diocesan plan "Pastoring God's People" (cf. above), one of the methods to be used to wisely and equitably share the rapidly dwindling number of priests, both diocesan and religious, was the assignment of a pastor to two or more parishes. After considerable discussion at several levels, including a special committee composed of Manchester's inner-city parishes, it was decided that St. Anne, the oldest parish in the city of Manchester founded, in 1848, and St. Augustine, the oldest French Canadian national parish in the entire state, founded in 1871, should share one pastor. In every other respect, it was emphasized, each parish was to remain separate, in finances, for example. All duplicating and unneeded parish buildings and real estate, such as parish halls, would be sold. Each parish church, as well as the parish name and identity, would be retained.

The basic criteria used in arriving at this decision for St. Anne and St. Augustine were: (1) both parishes would need to be independently solvent following the move, and (2) the workload of the pastor after the twinning could not be excessive. According to the financial calculation, $75,000 would be saved annually by this merger.

This merger plan, by all indications, was accepted with little or no dissension by the parishioners of St. Anne, many of whom could trace their ancestry to the founders of the parish some 150 years previously. For a few decades this parish had been slowly losing its membership to downtown erosion and had become the spiritual center for new immigrants, such as Hispanics and Vietnamese. For several years, the parish and its multicultural ministry had been confided to the Order of Friars Minor Capuchin, with an occasional interim diocesan priest administrator.

Announcement of the "twinning" under the conditions enumerated above was not well received by a significant segment of the parishioners of St. Augustine parish. From the heated comments made at a parish meeting convened by Bishop Christian in the early fall of 1997, it was made clear by those present that they wanted Mass celebrated in French, and preferably, it can be assumed, by a priest of French Canadian ancestry. Among the remarks made by a number of those present at the meeting was to the effect that St. Augustine was "a French parish and there should be a French priest there." Other comments were directed to the new immigrants under the care of St. Anne's. Some present said that they could not understand why the diocese should "cater to the Hispanic people and the Vietnamese people when the people over here [that is, St. Augustine] have spent all their lives living here." One participant even asserted that these immigrants could solve the problem by learning to speak the English language. Anyone one with a knowledge of history would recognize that this was the same complaint made about the French Canadians themselves when they arrived in Manchester three or four generations previously.

In summary, for many of the 140 who were said to be present at the meeting with Bishop Christian, it was difficult or impossible to accept (1) the priority needs of the new immigrants; (2) the demands placed on the diocese by the rapidly expanding Catholic population of the southern sector of the state of New Hampshire; and (3) the shortage of clergy, particularly those who are reasonably fluent in the French language.

This meeting ended with the assurance that efforts would be made to provide either a French–speaking Capuchin or a retired French-speaking diocesan priest to celebrate Mass in that language. The "twinning" itself was scheduled to take place when an appropriate assignment could be found for the current pastor of St. Augustine.

Preparations for the Jubilee 2000

Overarching the life of the Christian churches and communities in the 1990s is the coming of the third millennium and, consequently, their preparation for it. Despite inaccuracies in establishing both the year and the date of the birth of Jesus (cf. above), the year 2000, as observed in the Gregorian calendar established and followed by the Roman Catholic Church since 1582, gives all Christians a significant moment to remember its history, celebrate its good and expiate its sinfulness, and, above all, to prepare for a renewed future.

Pope John Paul II issued his apostolic letter on the subject on November 10, 1994, in what, he added, was the seventeenth year of his pontificate. This letter, entitled *Tertio Millennio Adveniente* ("On the Threshold of the Third Millenium"), was addressed to all the bishops, priests, and deacons, men and women religious, and "all the lay faithful."

In it he outlines the preparations that he expects to be made in the entire Catholic Church for the jubilee of the year 2000.

After explaining the importance of jubilees, particularly those in the Old Testament, and the steps already taken by the Church in the twentieth century to prepare for the third millennium (such as the Second Vatican Council, the series of Synods of Bishops since the council, his own ministry as bishop of Rome, his numerous pontifical documents, his frequent papal journeys, and several other initiatives), Pope John Paul II outlined three years of preparation for the year 2000. Year one, that is 1997, was to be devoted to reflection on Christ, the Word of God, made man by the power of the Holy Spirit. Year two, 1998, is to be dedicated in a particular way to the Holy Spirit and to His sanctifying presence within the community of Christ's disciples. The year 1999, he wrote, was to be aimed at broadening the horizons of believers, so that they will see things in the perspective of Christ: in the perspective of the Father who is in heaven (cf. Mt 5:45), from whom the Lord was sent and to whom he has returned (cf. Jn 16:28). These preparatory years, in summary, would highlight and focus on, in successive years, God the Son, God the Holy Spirit, and God the Father.

Pope John Paul II officially inaugurated the Year of Jesus Christ 1997 with vespers on the first Sunday of Advent, November 30, 1996. The actual Jubilee Year itself, after the three years of preparation, was designated as from Christmas 1999 through Easter 2001.

In order to provide leadership and to coordinate the implementation of the jubilee in this country, the Catholic bishops of the United States voted to establish and fund an office for the millennium beginning on June 21, 1996. Mr. Paul K. Henderson, a staff member of the Secretariat for Family, Laity, Women, and Youth of the National Conference of Catholic Bishops, was selected to be director of the new office effective August 5, 1996. Since then, the Secretariat for the Third Millenium and the Jubilee Year 2000, as this office is now called, has been very active in producing and supplying a variety of services and materials to the dioceses to assist them in their task.

On December 31, 1996, Bishop Leo E. O'Neil, in a letter to the clergy, announced the first steps to be taken for the millennium in the Diocese of Manchester. The Year of Jesus Christ, the first preparatory year, was to be inaugurated at the 10:30 A.M. Eucharistic Liturgy in the Cathedral Church of St. Joseph on the Feast of the Epiphany, January 5, 1997. All priests in New Hampshire who were able to attend were invited to concelebrate this Mass with the bishop.

In the same letter, he asked each of the eleven deaneries to prepare an annual community celebration appropriate to its circumstances throughout the three-year preparatory period and during the Jubilee Year (Christmas 1999–Easter 2001). All the eleven deaneries and 131 parishes were advised to use the "excellent materials" prepared by the diocesan Office of Worship. Most of these materials were prepared under the direction of the Reverend John M. Grace, director of the office. These materials, written and visual, were produced and made available throughout the early stages covered by this history.

Bishop Leo also announced in his letter of December 31 the formation of a Jubilee Year 2000 Steering Committee to plan diocesan pilgrimages of faith to sites within the United States and North America, as well as to Jerusalem, Rome, and the Marian shrines of Lourdes and Fatima. In addition, he commissioned this steering committee, under the chairmanship of Monsignor Charles E. Crosby, to plan and organize the Jubilee Year 2000 within the diocese.

This committee held its first meeting on May 19, 1996. In addition to the chairman, it consisted of twenty other people: lay, religious, and clerical, representing many of the departments in the administration of the diocese as well as representatives of the Catholic colleges, the major superiors of women religious, the deans, the council of priests, the diocesan pastoral council, Hispanic ministry, the Franco-American Center, campus ministry, and the diocesan historian.

This committee has met on an almost monthly basis since its foundation and has discussed and elaborated a large number of programs to carry out its mandate. Much of its time and energy have concentrated on a mega-celebration to be held at Saint Anselm College for all the people of the state of New Hampshire. This celebration, which is proposed to extend over three days, June 9, 10, 11, 2000, includes a marketplace for the exposition and sale of a variety of items, various ethnic foods representative of the Catholic population of the diocese, music areas for concerts, cultural displays, and specific events, such as lectures, plays, and sports. At the present stage of planning (late 1997), June 9 will be reserved for youth; Saturday, June 10, for family and interfaith interaction, including an ecumenical service; and June 11, Sunday, once again for the family, with a Jubilee Pentecost Mass, perhaps the administration of the sacrament of confirmation, and other spiritual, cultural, and social activities. An elaborate fireworks display is being planned for the climax of the activities on Saturday. The remainder of the plans and activities for the jubilee lie outside the chronological scope of this historical study.

Outside Activities of Bishop O'Neil

Since taking office as coadjutor bishop of Manchester with the right of succession on October 17, 1989, Bishop Leo had been frequently active beyond the range of his diocesan episcopal responsibilities. For example, he received numerous honors, including the John F. Kennedy Award in 1990 for his distinguished service in his chosen profession from the St. Patrick's Day Parade Committee of Holyoke, Massachusetts. In 1996, he was the first grand marshal ever of the newly reestablished St. Patrick's Day Parade in Manchester. He had the distinction of walking down Elm Street (the main thoroughfare of the city) with shillelagh in hand and a smile on his face. One of the reassuring aspects of this walk down the center of the main street of the largest city in New Hampshire was that a bishop could display legitimate pride in his ethnic and cultural heritage without causing a backlash of complaints or resentment among Catholics of other ethnic and cultural backgrounds.

Four Catholic educational institutions awarded him honorary doctorates: Saint Anselm, a doctor of law, and the College of Our Lady of the Elms, Chicopee, Massachusetts, also a doctor of law, both in 1990; in 1991 he was granted a doctor of divinity degree by Rivier College, Nashua; and in September 1992, Notre Dame College in Manchester gave him a third doctor of law diploma, honoris causa.

Bishop Leo, in the footsteps of several of his predecessors, was given several responsibilities on the regional and national levels. On the regional level, he was selected to represent Region I on the Administrative Committee Board of the National Conference of Catholic Bishops. This board is the most powerful structure of the bishops in this country. On the national plane, he was a member of the following: The priestly life and ministry committee; the communications committee; the campaign for human development; and the advisory committee of the tri-conference retirement project. This latter committee consists of representatives of both the conferences of women and men religious in addition to that of the American bishops.

Also of note is the fact that Bishop O'Neil was for many years a director of retreats for priests throughout the United States, an honor and a responsibility given to few.

Having essentially examined the major programs of the diocese from 1990 to 1997, this chapter will now consider some aspects of the status of the Catholic Church in New Hampshire in the last decade of the twentieth century, which is the end of the second millennium as well.

Signs of the Times

In order to carry out its mandate from Christ, the Catholic Church has the duty of scrutinizing "the signs of the times" and interpreting them in light of the gospel ("Pastoral Constitution on the Church in the Modern World," article 4). This apt expression, "signs of the times," a phrase frequently used by Pope John XXIII, particularly in his encyclical *Pacem in Terris* ("Peace on Earth"), and repeated in the previously quoted document of the Second Vatican Council, the "Constitution on the Church in the Modern World," requires that one must "recognize and understand the world in which we live, its expectations, its longings and its often dramatic characteristics." Recognizing and understanding the signs of the times does not apply solely to what is outside the Catholic Church in our modern world. It applies with equal strength to the very life of the Church at the local, diocesan, national, and international levels.

Some Positive Aspects

Even a confirmed pessimist regarding the present status and future direction of American society with respect to religion would be forced to accept some of the results of professional surveys on the subject. These polls indicate that 90 percent of Americans say that they believe in God, and more than 50 percent report that they pray at least once a day. More than 40 percent claim to have gone to church in any given week, although there has been no systematic attempt to verify this assertion. Some of these declarations of religiousness are diminished by the fact that surveys also show that one out of three does not belong to a religious organization, and that about the same percentage, another third, never attends religious services or does so only rarely.

Moreover, a great majority of Catholics in this country maintain that they will never leave the Church and an equally great majority state that they expect to bring up their children in their own faith. Those who expressed some disappointment with the Catholic Church explained that they would try to change it from within rather than criticize it in estrangement. Many other positive aspects uncovered in recent surveys could be mentioned as well.

Some Negative Aspects

However, much of the evidence available points unambiguously to a difficult future for religion in general in the United States. This ominous trend began to reveal itself more clearly during the decade of the 1960s: that is, the marginalization of virtually all Christian churches—in fact, of all religions. Religion, using a figure of speech currently common among some observers, has been eased out of "the public square." Religion is no longer considered by many to be a necessary and vital component of American society and its culture. From official religions in many of the English colonies and later in some of the original thirteen states, religion has evolved or, in a sense degraded, to a strictly private matter between the individual and God.

It would be nearly impossible to contest that one of the more visible substitutes for religion and its teachings and values is the media: television, movies, the Internet, and print in all of its forms. More than a little of what is seen, heard, or read is an assault on moral values and, frequently, a burlesque of religious teachings and practices.

One is even reluctant and embarrassed to mention that the churches themselves have contributed to the marginalization of religion in American society. Too often churches have failed to identify forcefully what is wrong or immoral around them, even in their own communities. Moreover, they can rightfully be accused of being too pusillanimous to speak about it from the pulpit or in the press, much less to propose remedies. Catholics may well ask themselves how often in recent years they have heard from the pulpit the "hard sayings" of the Scriptures and those of the teachings of the Catholic Church.

Another failing, certainly obvious in the Catholic Church, is the mediocrity, with obvious exceptions, of the religious education programs in Catholic schools and those designed for children and youth attending public grammar and high schools.

Levels of Belief among Catholics

Of major concern in the Catholic Church is the level of acceptance of its teachings among its members. There is, according to professional surveys, a rather solid consensus on matters that are essentially doctrinal in nature, such as credence in the Trinity, Incarnation, Virgin birth, Resurrection, Transubstantiation, and the like.

On subjects of morality, those requiring a specific conduct conditional upon a belief, many Catholics have a very different reaction. Some of the subjects that cause dissent or are ignored are: abortion, divorce and remarriage, premarital sex, birth control, a married clergy, and women priests. All of these topics involve sexual morality to some degree. Birth control has been the subject that has caused the greatest negative reaction for at least the past thirty years, and the opposition to it has grown stronger with the passing of time. For example, in 1967, some 41 percent of Catholics stated that they favored the use of birth-control devices, and 27 percent admitted that they used them. By 1993, only 13 percent said that they believed that birth control was morally wrong. In the age group eighteen to thirty-four, a diminutive 9 percent supported the magisterium on this point. In 1993, in fact, 73 percent said that one could be a good Catholic without obeying Catholic teaching on this subject; even the most loyal Catholics overall held the same view. This near consensus was formed, evidence indicates, in the late 1970s and still remains today.

Compounding the difficulties of the teaching authority of the Catholic Church is the statistic that only 12 percent of adult members say that they agree with all Church teachings on faith and morality. For those over the age of fifty, the level of agreement with the Church an all subjects reaches 28 percent, still not an encouraging figure. As all areas of disagreement have not been identified, nor the level of dissent on each topic measured, one cannot automatically attach an absolute level of importance to this statistic. Nevertheless, from this information one is not surprised to learn that the laity believes that it has the right to participate in decision making within the Church. This ranges from a high of 83 percent on the spending of parish money, to 74 percent on the selection of parish priests including the pastor, to 62 percent on the issue of birth control, and so on.

In the minds of many, however, the most reliable gauge of Catholic identity is attendance at Sunday Mass, or, since the late 1960s, at the weekend Eucharistic Liturgy. By this standard religious practice in the United States is also in a worrisome negative trend. Surveys at the time estimated that Sunday attendance at Mass in the later years of the 1950s was 71 percent; by the early 1970s, the first decade after the Second Vatican Council, weekend attendance had slipped to roughly 50 percent, or even slightly below; by 1997, some surveys indicated that in some areas of the United States the decline had dipped to as low as 28 percent of the church members. While no extensive survey has taken place in New Hampshire on this point, one can reasonably assume that regular weekend attendance at Mass is about equal to the current average across the nation.

Anyone involved in parish ministry, or who is an objective observer, has noted the precipitous plunge in the reception of the sacrament of penance, down to 17 percent by some estimates; the growing number of Catholics who do not choose to have a funeral Mass; and the disturbing number of couples who cohabit before receiving the sacrament of marriage.

Catholic Population

For the Christian churches that heed the mandate of Christ to "'Go therefore, and make disciples of all nations" (Mt 28:19), the number of its members becomes an important statistic, as it is one indication of its performance in carrying out this scriptural commission. From this point of view alone, which does not take into account the intensity of the knowledge, belief, or practice of its members, the Catholic Church has been successful. It counts nearly 2 billion adherents worldwide, over 60 million in this country, and 321,194 in the state of New Hampshire in 1997.

According to the calculations of the Diocese of Manchester, these 321,194 Catholics comprise roughly 28 percent of a total population of 1,148,000. These "registered" Catholics live in more than 111,000 households and are spread among 131 parishes. The highest percentage of Catholics in the population of New Hampshire appears to have been reached around 1970 when 36 percent—that is 268,685 out of a total of 737,575—professed membership in the Catholic Church.

An intriguing problem was revealed in 1990 during a survey conducted by the University of New Hampshire under the sponsorship of the New Hampshire Council of Churches. This professional survey concluded that an astonishing 42.5 percent of the state population claimed to be Catholic as opposed to 41.1 percent who professed to be Protestant. In terms of numbers, the survey further determined that 10 percent were members of the United Church of Christ, 7.1 percent were Baptists, and 5.2 percent were Episcopalians. No further action has been undertaken to verify the accuracy of the University of New Hampshire survey; nor of the statistics of the Diocese of Manchester, for that matter. The discrepancy of 14.5 percent between the two methods of counting remains unresolved.

Whatever the figure—28 or 42.5 percent—Catholic Church statistics also show that the number of marriages in its churches in New Hampshire has been declining in recent years, despite an increase in its total population. As a consequence, so have the number of infant Catholic baptisms. This points to the fact that the future growth of the Catholic Church in New Hampshire, as well as in the United States as a whole, will come mainly from new immigrants, very likely from Hispanic America.

Within the Catholic Church, its members can be divided into three basic groups: laity, religious, and clergy (the last group include bishops, priests, and deacons). A brief review of each group and its changing status and role in the Diocese of Manchester will give a clearer understanding of the evolution of the Catholic Church since the end of the Second Vatican Council (1962–1965).

Laywomen and Laymen in the Church

Among the major accomplishments of the Second Vatican Council was the clarification of the status and function of the laity in the Catholic Church. The intent of the council was summarized without ambiguity in the new Code of Canon Law promulgated in 1983. Canon 208 declares, "In virtue of their rebirth in Christ there exists among all the Christian faithful a true equality with regard to dignity and the activity whereby all cooperate in the building up of the Body of Christ in accord with each one's own condition and function." What differs in the Catholic Church is not dignity or equality but one's condition, one's abilities, and one's function—that is, the role that each has been called by God or the Church to fulfill.

The perception and understanding of this role has changed immensely and irreversibly in the Catholic Church since the end of that council in 1965. Formerly, the laity had been invited to perform roles such as groundskeepers, secretaries, housekeepers, organizers of parish fairs, and sellers or buyers of raffle tickets, and the like, with some being accepted as teachers of religion, but not in their own right as Christians but as helpers of the clergy. Since roughly the late 1960s, with this new understanding of the dignity and equality of all in the Church, the role of laywomen and laymen has expanded to virtually all the offices and functions not requiring ordination. Laypeople are now found as pastoral associates; religious educators; youth ministers; music ministers; in most aspects of preparing and performing the liturgy; ministries to the sick, including administering the Eucharist; in programs and activities related to spirituality; evangelization; care of the elderly and all other sectors of social ministry and works of charity; and so on. In fact, since 1985 a layman, Mr. Russell Sweeney, the father of four and the grandfather of six, has been involved in ministry at the New Hampshire State Prison in Concord; for approximately the past seven years he has been the full-time official chaplain to the prisoners and the staff.

In 1996, there were more than six thousand lay students in the United States studying to become full-time ministers in church–related organizations, or on college and university campuses. These academic entities provided 265 programs in 214 institutions in 135 dioceses around the United States. Lay students who are currently pursuing degrees in American graduate ministry programs now outnumber the seminarians enrolled in the nation's Catholic schools of theology. Nearly two-thirds of these students working for degrees in ministry hope to obtain salaried positions in ministry or religious education in the Church. It is significant to note that 70 percent of these ministry students are women.

A special effort in the professionalization of lay ministry in New Hampshire must be noted. This was the founding in 1988 of a Ministry Institute at Notre Dame College in Manchester. Its defined purpose was to "provide a solid theological and skills foundation for persons who are active or who are prospective ministers in parish and school contexts." Notre Dame College enhanced its ministry program in 1992 by offering as part of its Ministry Institute an accredited master of arts degree in theology, the first ever in New Hampshire. It is under the direction of Drs. Philip A. Cunningham and Barbara Radtke.

Another indication of the maturity of lay ministry in the Diocese of Manchester was the formal establishment on October 27, 1997, by Bishop Leo E. O'Neil of the New Hampshire Conference of Pastoral Associates.

This organization had its origin in a meeting called by the Reverend Robert E. Gorski in January 1988 of all the pastoral ministers in the diocese in order for them to get to know each other, to make plans for the future, and to form an advisory committee. From this initial meeting there gradually developed a professional organization of pastoral ministers well prepared to join the parish priests in service to the people of the diocese.

In order to ensure professionalization, a certification policy was completed in the summer of 1994, accepted by the membership that September, and approved by Bishop O'Neil on January 1, 1995. Certification requires formation and background in worship, spirituality, parish outreach, evangelization, adult enrichment, family life, peace and justice, organization and administration, youth ministry, religious education, and whatever else may be required by parish life.

In July 1995, Dr. Elise Tougas was appointed director of Pastoral Ministry, the first layperson to occupy that position, succeeding Fathers Gorski and Gerald R. Belanger. On October 5, 1997, Bishop O'Neil formally certified and commissioned thirty-seven people as pastoral associates in a ceremony at St. Joseph Cathedral. It is interesting to note that thirty-four of the thirty-seven associates are women, another forceful indication of the growing ministerial role being assumed by them in the Catholic Church in the United States.

Lay involvement in the ministry of the Catholic Church in the United States has been quite successful. In addition to what has been discussed, in 1996 there were at least 20,000 nonordained women and men already employed as ministers in some 19,000 parishes.

Diocesan Catholic Priests

While the number of laypeople involved in or training for the ministry continues to increase, the number of Catholic priests and those preparing for the priesthood in seminaries are in alarming decline in New Hampshire and across the United States, with few exceptions. This decline, for frequently different historical and sociological reasons, follows a pattern already evident in many countries of Western Europe for the past fifty years or so.

The number of diocesan priests in this country reached its peak between 1965 and 1975 at about 36,000. By 1995, the total number had slumped to roughly 27,000 on its way further down. By the year 2005 it has been projected that the figure will have dropped to 21,000 or so, a decline of 40 percent since 1966, the year following the end of the Second Vatican Council. During that same period, 1966–2005, it is predicted that there will be a 65 percent increase in demand for parish priests because of the growth in Catholic population. Some believe that by 2005, there may be as many as 74 million in the United States who will label themselves as belonging to this religious denomination. These calculations do not take into account the already noted decline in religious practice among American Catholics, and the equally described increase in the number of lay ministers who will be involved in all ministerial functions other than those requiring ordination.

New Hampshire has by no means escaped the decline in the number of Catholic diocesan priests, particularly those who are still active on a full-time basis in ministry. For example, in 1970 there were 260 diocesan priests and only 23 of these were retired. Twenty-six years later (1997), the overall number had declined to 247, with 80 of these either retired, sick, or on personal leave. Adding those who are on other assignments, in 1997 there were only 154 active diocesan priests in the diocese. Among these 106 were pastors, 6 were administrators, 12 were parochial vicars (curates), 5 were military chaplains, and the remainder were on other assignments.

As disturbing as the decrease in the number of priests, particularly those active in ministry, is the mounting average age of the diocesan clergy. In 1996, the average age of pastors was 56.6; that for administrators, 51.3; and for associates, 40.9. For the entire body of the diocesan clergy, including the retired and those who have resigned, the average age was, in 1996, fifty-nine years and five months.

A further worrisome fact needs to be mentioned. By the end of 1997, there will be an additional twenty-four pastors who will be eligible for retirement or for some nonadministrative position, and ten more who are already in some service to the diocese who will have the seniority to request retirement.

An almost taboo subject has been the number of diocesan priests who have completely left the ministry, thus contributing significantly to the decrease in clergy available for the religious service of the people. Between 1941 and 1996, the Catholic Church in New Hampshire has lost forty-five priests by way of resignation. The vast majority of these have occurred since 1965; only two, for example, left the ministry during the 1940s. Among the forty-five, at least twenty received a papal dispensation and entered a valid marriage. One of the forty-five is known to have become an Episcopalian priest and another a priest of the Polish National Catholic Church. (Whatever the circumstances of resignation, one can be grateful for their years of ministry in the Catholic Church and pray for them and their future.)

This diocese lost two very effective and admired priests by way of suicide, one in 1969 and the other in 1973. Another loss, by drowning in the Merrimack River in August 1929, was either an accident or a suicide; a final verdict has never been made. Another priest, a former Trappist, the Reverend Joseph J. Sands, was shot to death on May 11, 1979, in the rectory of St. Rose of Lima parish, Littleton, by a deranged man and his wife who had come for counseling. Father Sands had been called to the rectory in Littleton from his own assignment in Whitefield to substitute for the pastor, who was on vacation in Ireland. All of these priests merit our gratitude and prayers as well.

An unblinking look at the diocesan Catholic clergy of New Hampshire requires a mention of two priests who were arrested, tried by jury, and convicted on charges of sexually molesting young men, both in the 1990s. One is serving a sentence with a maximum of sixty-seven years in the state prison. At the writing of this history, a third has been arrested on similar charges and is now free on bail awaiting judiciary action. Previous incidents of sexual misconduct by priests had been dealt with internally by the diocese.

Along with these many changes in the priesthood, both diocesan and religious, some professional observers have perceived that the concept of ministry and service has been slipping from that of a vocation to that of a profession or a form of white-collar employment.

On a more positive note is the acknowledgment of the number of priests from New Hampshire who have been selected to serve the Church on the national level. The first was the Reverend Philip J. Kenney (now Monsignor), who worked for the American bishops in Washington for several years in the late 1940s and early 1950s, as assistant to the general secretary and then in the lay apostolate. Father Thomas S. Hansberry (later Monsignor), served as field representative for the Confraternity of Christian Doctrine from 1949 to 1953, and the Reverend Russell J. Neighbor acted in a similar capacity in religious education for several years beginning in 1962.

Serving longest in Washington was Monsignor Colin A. MacDonald, who became in 1971 director of the committee to implement the studies of the National Conference of Catholic Bishops on the American priesthood. Two years later he was appointed the first executive director of the newly founded committee on Priestly Life and Ministry. In that capacity he directed the preparation and publication of a number of the most important and influential studies ever made on the American Catholic priesthood between 1973 and 1988. In that latter year, he returned to the Diocese of Manchester.

Monsignor Wilfrid H. Paradis was assigned to several tasks in Washington between 1973 and 1980. In succession, he was project director for the preparation of a *National Catechetical Directory* (to guide the teaching of religion at all levels in the United States), associate secretary of the Office of Research, Planning, and Program Development of the Department of Education of the United States Catholic Conference, and, finally, secretary of the Department of Education. On the international level, Monsignor Paradis was a "peritus" (expert) at the Second Vatican Council, senior adviser at the World Synod of Bishops on catechesis in 1977, and a member of the Vatican Commission on Catechesis for five years (cf. "The Author.")

Another diocesan priest, Monsignor James J. Markham, served on the staff of the Military Ordinariate from 1965 to 1985. This organization administers the Church-related aspects of the Catholic chaplains of the Army, Navy, Air Force, and hospitals for veterans. From January 1986 to December 1990, he was chief chaplain at the veterans hospital in Newington, Connecticut, and then at that of the veterans hospital in Northport, New York.

Finally, between 1884, the year of the founding of the Diocese of Manchester, and 1996, 665 priests have been incardinated as members of its clergy. Of these, 373 are deceased and 292 are still living, including the 45 previously mentioned who have resigned from ministry. This does not include the scores of priests from outside the diocese who have served in the state, or the priests from religious orders who have, in addition to their other duties, staffed and now staff a number of parishes.

Treatment of the permanent deaconate from its inception in the Diocese of Manchester in 1980 to the present is included in chapter 14.

Diocesan Seminarians

Keeping pace with the decline in the number of diocesan priests has been the dramatic decrease in the number of seminarians studying for the diocesan priesthood. A look at a statistics illustrating the rise and fall of these vocations between 1955 and 1995 shows this very clearly. In rough figures, there were 33,000 seminarians nationwide in 1955, close to 50,000 in 1965, then a fall to about 18,000 in 1975, and to barely 11,000 in 1995.

This fluctuation in numbers of seminarians studying for the diocesan priesthood was clearly reflected in the Diocese of Manchester. In 1959, the year of the death of Bishop Brady, there were 77 diocesan seminarians; the number then rose to a peak of 108 by 1965, the year of the closing of the Second Vatican Council. This peak number included a few high school students, several in the first two years of college, and the majority in schools of theology, the latter usually a four-year program. From 108 students in 1965, there was a decline to 59 in 1969, to 38 in 1965 to 14 in 1997, just prior to the ordination of 4 at about midyear. In addition, two of the fourteen were listed as being in pre–theology and five as college affiliates. Obviously, this number of seminarians can replace only a small fraction of the diocesan priests lost by death, sick leave, retirement, resignation, or other causes.

A few other factors about seminarians should be mentioned. About 80 percent of the total for the United States are of European background, mostly Irish and German. Only 6 percent have Latin American roots, which does not bode well for an American Catholic Church that will have a notably Latin American future. On the local level, the Diocese of Manchester has never had a seminarian with Latin American antecedents.

In addition to ethnic background, the age of seminarians must be considered. In 1996–1997, the median age was thirty-two across the country, with almost as many in theology who were over forty as there were under the age of twenty-five. This far smaller number of seminarians and their clearly older age are not in themselves a firm guarantee of a better quality of priests in the future. A smaller pool of candidates would seem to generally militate against such a conclusion. Older seminarians, on the other hand, may project more maturity and experience in life, both basic qualities to sound ministry. However, being older in itself does not automatically confer on the candidate all the other qualities that are required for effective service to the Catholic Church and its members.

Those not familiar with the training of priests may be surprised to learn that by 1988, some 25 percent of all students in Catholic theological schools were women, and that by 1993 they made up one-third of that student population. From repeated recent assertions of the Holy See, including the Sovereign Pontiff and the Prefect of the Congregation for the Doctrine of the Faith, these women theology students have been made aware that they cannot be candidates for the priesthood. From this trend, however, a good number of laywomen will have not only an education equal to the diocesan priests but also the exact same training, and, consequently, essentially the same qualifications, except ordination.

Religious Orders of Priests and Brothers

Religious orders of priests and brothers have also decreased significantly in number, as have diocesan priests and seminarians. Religious orders of priests experienced an increase until 1965, when they reached a peak of about 23,000 in the United States. The decline in numbers was somewhat gentle until 1985 and then dropped rapidly to the vicinity of 17,000 around 1995. Overall, the number of religious priests has decreased by some 27 percent from its highest membership.

Brothers in religious life were never as numerous as priests, either diocesan or religious. Their total number in the United States over the past five years or so has fallen by an astonishing 45 percent from a high of 12,539 in 1965. Adding to the uncertainly of their future is the fact that in some orders the average age of the brothers has mounted to sixty-seven years.

According to the *New Hampshire Catholic Directory* for 1996–1997, there were 84 religious priests residing in the diocese compared to 127 in 1959, a loss of 43. These eighty-four priests belong to fifteen different religious orders, the most numerous being the Benedictines (o.s.b.) with twenty-nine, the Missionary Oblates of Mary Immaculate (o.m.i.) with fifteen, and the Missionaries of La Salette (m.s.) with eight. Of the fifteen orders, only the Benedictines are headquartered in New Hampshire.

With the exception of St. Raphael parish in Manchester, which has been staffed with Benedictines since its foundation in 1888, the confiding of parishes to religious orders in the Diocese of Manchester is a relatively new precedent. The major reason for this trend has been that on the one side there is the number of diminishing diocesan priests, and on the other the eroding of ministries for which the religious orders were founded, such as Catholic school education, the preaching of retreats, and so on.

By 1997, 10 of the 131 parishes in the diocese were staffed by the Order of Friars Minor Capuchin, the La Salettes, and the Vincentians (Congregation of the Mission), in addition to the Benedictines.

Religious brothers, never numerous in New Hampshire, fell from sixty-four in 1959, to fifty-four in 1983, to forty-one in 1996. These forty-one represent at least five communities, none native to the diocese, with fifteen Brothers of the Sacred Heart in Nashua centered on Bishop Guertin High School and six at Saint Anselm Abbey.

Women Religious

Women religious—sisters or nuns, as they are commonly called—have been the backbone of a great number of the apostolic endeavors of the Catholic Church in New Hampshire, as they have been all around the world. Their capable and generous hands have been obvious in virtually all the ministries of the diocese since the arrival of the first nuns, the Sisters of Mercy, in 1858, almost twenty-six years before the founding of the Diocese of Manchester (cf. chapter 7). A cursory examination of the history of Catholicism in New Hampshire will amply illustrate the extent and depth of their influence all over the state. An impressive portion of their numbers have also served in the missions of the Church all over the world.

At their peak in the American Catholic Church, their population exceeded by far the total combined number of diocesan priests, religious priests, and brothers. That was also true in New Hampshire.

Nationwide, the number of religious women reached nearly 140,000 in 1945, climbed to a peak of about 180,000 in 1965, fell to approximately

118,000 in 1985, and dropped to about 90,000 in 1995. This fall of approximately 40 percent in thirty years—barely more than a generation—is an unquestionable indication that the role of women religious in the Catholic Church and their training and styles of life should be most carefully examined. On a broad and intensive scale, this is being done in this country and all over the world where similar situations exist.

Equally dramatic is the aging of the population of nuns who have remained in community. With some exceptions, the average age in religious orders has reached from the mid-sixties to the late sixties.

Again, the Catholic sisters in New Hampshire have mirrored the national trend in every way: lower numbers, changed lifestyles, different dress, new areas of ministry, and a retreat from many of their traditional apostolates, such as teaching in Catholic schools, nursing, and the care of orphanages.

One further example of the change in religious lifestyle is the number of residences currently occupied by the sisters in the most numerous religious communities of women in the diocese. While they formerly lived in a relatively small number of large convents, by 1996 the Sisters of Mercy listed sixty-two separate addresses for their 154 members, with 34 of the sisters living alone, and the Sisters of Holy Cross occupied forty-seven different residences. The Sisters of Presentation, overall a more traditional order, had only five convents with fewer than three occupants.

The exact number of women religious in the state presents a somewhat erratic and perplexing pattern, although the trend has been clearly on the downside. The fluctuation of apparent growth and decline up to 1965 was due largely to the fact that only a small number of the thirty-nine religious orders (including three Pious Associations of the Faithful) of women serving in the diocese have their motherhouse in New Hampshire. For the most part, the orders are headquartered elsewhere and assign their subjects over several states and dioceses. Consequently, it is very difficult to determine the growth or decline of those specific orders solely from their number serving in this one state.

With this caution in mind, it is interesting to note the fluctuating trend in the population of Catholic nuns in New Hampshire over the years. For example, the total number of sisters listed in 1955 was 1,388; for 1958 it went up to 1,679; in 1960 it went down to 1,355; and for 1962 it went up again to 1,734, the highest number ever recorded. The following year (1963), it went down again to 1,538, and it went upward again to 1,609 in 1965. From that year onward, the number of women religious has declined steadily (except for minor rises in 1967 and 1972), to 1,324 in 1973 and to 1,110 in 1983. By 1996, their number was given as 823 in the *New Hampshire Catholic Directory*. Since their peak of 1,734 in 1962 to their present total of 823, the Diocese of Manchester has lost the services of 911 sisters. All of this has occurred in just thirty-four years, a relatively short period of time in the history of the Catholic Church in New Hampshire. As we shall see, the Catholic elementary and high schools of the diocese have been among the major casualties in this decrease in the number of women religious.

Among the thirty-nine religious orders of women exercising ministry in New Hampshire in 1996–1997, the three most numerous were the Sisters of Holy Cross, with 202 members; the Sisters of Presentation, with one less at 201; and the Sisters of Mercy, with 154. For more than one century prior to the Second Vatican Council the Sisters of Mercy had been the largest congregation of religious in the diocese. Following these three in order of members were the Daughters of Charity of the Sacred Heart of Jesus with forty-three, thirty-nine of these living in the provincial house in Colebrook; the Sister Adorers of the Precious Blood, a cloistered community, with thirty-one; and the Religious of Jesus and Mary with twenty-four, with only two of the latter not residing at Villa Augustina in Goffstown.

Of these thirty-nine communities of women religious in the diocese, two are considered cloistered orders. The one already mentioned, the Sister Adorers of the Precious Blood, is the older. They were introduced to the diocese by Bishop Bradley in 1898 and their history has been mentioned in chapter 8. A second, the Discalced Carmelites (o.c.d.), were introduced into New Hampshire during the episcopacy of Bishop Brady on June 19, 1946. The original group of five professed nuns, one novice, and one postulant who came from a monastery in Roxbury, Massachusetts, were first situated in a small farmhouse on Bridge Street in Concord. This monastery prospered, as did virtually all religious institutions in the United States in the period immediately following the Second World War (cf. chapter 12). These nuns enjoyed the added advantage of a superior, Mother Aloysius, who had a reputation for holiness and whose spiritual writings are still being distributed and read today. Mother Aloysius died in April 1961. Having outgrown their farmhouse-monastery, the

Carmelites purchased a piece of land on Pleasant Street, also in Concord, and despite some financial difficulties were able to move into their newly constructed quarters on the feast of St. Joseph, March 19, 1952. However, it was not until more than eleven years later, in September 1963, that the monastery and chapel were completed.

During this period of prosperity—1946–1965—these Carmelites of Concord, in addition to enriching the prayer life of the area, contributed in 1964 four nuns to strengthen a Carmelite monastery in Vermont, and in 1965, they allowed three others to form an experimental community in Maine with a more hermetic, or austere, spirit.

Like all religious communities, with few exceptions, the Carmelite monastery went into decline in the years following 1965, and by 1997 had been reduced to eleven nuns, virtually all of an older age. Even less encouraging for the future is that the monastery has not had one new solemn profession for the past twenty-five years.

Another branch of the Carmelite Order in New Hampshire, the Carmelite Sisters for the Aged and Infirm, was obliged to leave its remaining two facilities in the diocese, Mount Carmel Nursing Home in Manchester and St. Ann Home in Dover. After nearly fifty years of caring devotion to the aged and infirm, the last Carmelites turned their responsibilities over to qualified lay personnel in 1997. Like all the religious communities of women in New Hampshire, the number of Carmelite Sisters for the Aged and Infirm, headquartered in Germantown, New York, fell from about six hundred in the 1970s to fewer than three hundred in the mid-1990s.

In order to deal effectively with the more than one thousand women and men religious living in New Hampshire at the time, Bishop Gendron in October 1986 appointed nine religious as members of the newly formed Advisory Board for the diocesan Office for Religious. This initial board consisted of five women religious, two religious priests, and two brothers, one brother a La Salette and the other a Vincentian (Congregation of the Mission).

In addition, there is also a New Hampshire Leadership Conference composed of the major superiors of women religious serving in the diocese, whose purpose is to foster unity and collaboration among religious congregations and with the bishop and clergy. In 1996, this Leadership Conference consisted of eight superiors of religious congregations of women.

One element had not been factored in with regard to the future of the women and men religious in the Catholic Church in the United States in addition to their decrease in numbers, their aging, and the lack of replacements—that is, the drying up of vocations. Added to this, one is obliged to consider the extremely low stipends or salaries paid in the past to religious personnel, particularly to the nuns. A major consequence of these factors has been the inability of large numbers of religious congregations financially to support themselves, particularly the sick and aged members unable to work.

Faced with this unexpected situation, verging on disaster for many religious orders, the bishops of the United States mandated a special yearly collection to come to their assistance. The extent of the financial help to the religious can be judged by the fact that the total grants to them nationally in 1995 amounted to $25,750,000. The amount raised that year in New Hampshire by that collection was $164,749.66.

In return, the National Religious Retirement Office in Washington, created by the bishops, made the following grants: to the Sisters of Holy Cross, $169,006.53, primarily to care for more than one hundred religious in healthcare facilities in Manchester and Franklin; to the Sisters of Presentation, $144,792.26; to the Sisters of Mercy $87,434.59; and $3,622.55 to the eleven Discalced Carmelite nuns in Concord. In all, in 1996, religious congregations in New Hampshire received $468,705.51 in grants from this nationwide collection.

In conclusion, it may be said that the mental image of the Catholic sister of the past is very clear but that of the woman religious of the future has yet to be designed and, in turn, printed on the fabric of the Church. Judging from recent developments, many different images will emerge.

Elementary and Secondary Catholic Schools

Ever since the arrival of the Sisters of Mercy at St. Anne parish in Manchester in 1858, the elementary and secondary Catholic school systems in New Hampshire have been closely linked to the presence and expansion of the religious orders of women and to a lesser extent, to those of men. Because of this link between religious orders and Catholic schools, the decline of the first resulted in part in the decline of the latter. While other causes contributed to the shrinking in the number of Catholic schools, such as inflation, the need for more expensive educational materials and equipment, the requirement of new school buildings in the suburbs, a loss of interest in the Catholic school system by the parents in favor of public schools, the major cause was the diminishing number of sisters, brother's, and priests who provided an inexpensive labor force for the task.

As it has been related (cf. chapter 12), the Catholic grammar school population in the diocese in 1959 reached 23,651 students, who were enrolled in sixty-two schools—fifty-six parochial and six private. By 1973, thirty-nine elementary schools remained: thirty-three of these were parochial, and six private, with an enrollment of 11,636. On the eve of the diocesan centennial in 1983, there was a further dip to twenty-nine schools, twenty-six parochial, and three private, with 7,751 boys and girls. Between 1959 and 1983, thirty-three Catholic elementary schools in New Hampshire had closed and the student body had fallen by an astonishing 15,900. Fortunately, a slight rally from its lowest point began in the 1990s and by the school year 1996–1997 the diocese could count twenty-six elementary schools, twenty-three parochial and three private, with an enrollment of 7,487. Over 90 percent of the teachers in these schools are now laywomen and laymen.

On the high school level, there were twenty-one such schools—sixteen either diocesan or parochial and five private—with 4,297 students in 1959. These schools hit their high point in 1965–1966 with a student body of 5,797. Just eight years later, in 1973–1974, only three diocesan and three private high schools remained, with 2,954 students. These parochial high schools had been forced to close essentially for economic reasons. Ten years later, in 1983–1984, there were still three diocesan and three private high schools, but the number of students had fallen again, to 2,492. By 1996–1997, two private high schools had closed, leaving three diocesan and one private in the diocese. The student population, however, dropped just slightly during the previous ten years to 2,280.

In summary, there were 27,948 students receiving Catholic elementary and secondary school education in 1959. Their combined enrollment peaked at 30,230 in 1964–1965. From then on, it went down by steps to 16,100 in 1973–1974, to 10,644 in 1983–1984, to the current 9,767 in 1996–1997.

The combined Catholic elementary and secondary school population decreased by 20,463 between 1964–1965 and 1996–1997, in thirty years.

Catholic Elementary and Junior High Schools

A major and highly controversial issue for at least the past three decades in the Diocese of Manchester has been the financing of Catholic elementary, junior high, and senior high schools. Financing the six Catholic colleges in the state has always been the responsibility of the institution itself.

After years of debate, a decision was reached concerning elementary and junior high schools that is to go into effect on July 1, 1998. A financial formula is still under consideration for Catholic senior high schools. The new regulations relative to elementary and junior high schools will pertain to only those educational institutions that are directly under the jurisdiction of the Diocese of Manchester—that is, those owned and operated by it through agents or agencies designated by the bishop, such as parish schools and regional schools.

This new plan recognizes that the parents or guardians of Catholic school students are primarily responsible for the cost of educational services. It addition, it also acknowledges that the Church and community are also the present and future beneficiaries of Catholic schools and consequently should share to a proportionate extent in the cost of Catholic school education.

An additional premise of the developers of this plan was that all Catholic parents who wish to do so will be able to send their children to Catholic schools and that sufficient financial assistance will be provided to enable them to exercise "this right."

Using these principles as a foundation, it was decided that 75 percent of the cost of elementary and junior high school Catholic education would belong to the parent or guardian, that 20 percent would be the responsibility of the collaborative financial resources of all the parishes, and that 5 percent would be the share of the local communities served directly or indirectly by the school.

To assist the parishes in raising their share of the funds, it was enacted that beginning in January 1999 an annual Catholic school collection would be taken that would remain in the parish to offset the Catholic school assessment. It was also determined that 5 percent of the cost of operating the schools would be budgeted for financial aid, ideally given to those in economic hardship.

A complete evaluation of this plan to finance Catholic elementary and junior high schools has been scheduled for the school year 2000–2001.

Colleges and Universities

It is interesting to note that the Catholic college population in New Hampshire did not follow the downward trend of the Catholic elementary and secondary schools. In the school year 1996–1997, there were 6,690 students in the six Catholic colleges in the state up from 2,728 in 1965–1966.

On the campuses of both state and private colleges and universities in New Hampshire, the Diocese of Manchester maintains a Catholic presence through the assignment of priests, women religious, and laypersons as campus ministers. Campus ministry began in the state in 1922 with the appointment of the Reverend J. Desmond O'Connor to that office at the University of New Hampshire in Durham. There are now commodious and well-equipped Catholic student centers at both the University of New Hampshire and Dartmouth College in Hanover. Chaplains have also been assigned to the following state and private institutions of higher learning: New England College in Henniker; Keene State College in Keene; New Hampshire College in Manchester; Colby-Sawyer College in New London; and Plymouth State College in Plymouth. Each of the six Catholic colleges provides for its own chaplain services. Magdalen College, founded in 1973, and The Thomas More College of Liberal Arts, founded in 1978, are the two most recent Catholic colleges and each was established by laymen. Both are based on the classics and the traditional teachings of the Church.

Religious Education

As the vast majority of Catholic children and youth in the United States and in the Diocese of Manchester do not attend Catholic schools, most obtain their religious education from out-of-school programs generally offered by the local parish. Concerned and well-informed observers of these programs have concluded that in too many instances they are seriously lacking in the elements needed to accurately transmit the faith. It must be taken into account that these programs are of critical importance, as they will be the basic and almost sole instrument of religious instruction and Christian formation for most children and young people in the

Church for the foreseeable future.

Many would begin the criticism by lamenting the lack of substance in the most widely used textbooks from the end of the Second Vatican Council in 1965 to the publication of the *Catechism of the Catholic Church* by Pope John Paul II in October 1992. These critics expect an improvement in future religious education textbooks and other materials because of the detailed explanation of the Christian message, both doctrine and morality, in this universal catechism.

Numerous complaints have also been made about religious education at the local level. Foremost among these has been the lack of preparation of the teachers. In many cases, appeals for teachers are made from the pulpit or in the parish bulletin and little or no training is provided in the teachings of the Church (doctrine, morality, liturgy, social justice, and so on.), in the psychology of children and youth, and in methodology. Being an adult, or even a parent, does not, it is obvious, automatically confer all of these skills onto the teacher.

Other often-heard charges are the restricted number of classes presented each year, the short amount of time allotted for each class, and the lack of, or the poor quality of, the visual aids and other ancillary materials. In several instances, disappointment has been expressed concerning the lack of participation by the parish priest or priests in the process, and the absence of an invitation to the parents to become regularly involved, as they are the primary educators of their children. All of these combine, many are convinced, to form a young person who does not know in any detail what his or her Church teaches and, in many cases, will not care about or participate in its life.

Participation by children and youth in out-of-school religious education programs has not increased at the same rate as the loss of students in Catholic elementary and secondary schools.

Attendance at out-of-school elementary programs increased in this way: 1959—14,021 students; 1973—31,148; 1983—27,724; and 1996—28,242. Between 1959 and 1996 (thirty-seven years), therefore, the elementary out-of-school programs in the diocese gained 14,221 students while during the same period the elementary Catholic schools lost 16,164. In addition to what appears to be a relatively small loss of 2,000 in some form of religious education, one must take into consideration the leap in the total Catholic population in New Hampshire, from 220,000 in 1959 to

321,914 in 1996, a growth of 101,914 individuals, according to the statistics kept by the Church itself. This impressive growth in total Catholic population in New Hampshire was not reflected by a corresponding increase in elementary school age children attending either Catholic school or out-of-school religion classes, even taking into account any possible decline in the birth rate.

Given the situation just described, a good number of parents (their exact total is not known) have opted to provide the religious instruction of their children themselves at home. In some parishes, they are being encouraged to do this, and receive assistance and educational materials to help them in this important task.

High school out-of-school religious education, in many respects, fared even worse. Religious instruction for high school students in this out-of-school setting, to begin with, is almost always completed with confirmation, which is usually administered before the end of the tenth grade, the sophomore year. This means that the formal instruction of youth is terminated by the age of fifteen or sixteen, even before the young person can have an adult presentation and understanding of his or her faith to live in an adult world.

With this background information, it is not surprising to observe that attendance of high school age students at these programs has varied only slightly over the past thirty-six years, that is between 1959 and 1996. These figures are: for 1959—5,960 students; for 1973—5,863; for 1983—5,961; and for 1996—5,346. During the same period, Catholic high school enrollment fell by 2,017, and the total Catholic population of the state rose by over 100,000.

During this crisis in the religious instruction of Catholic children and youth, for it can be called no less than that, serious efforts have been made to understand and to rectify the situation. A good number of Roman documents and publications and of the American bishops have addressed this problem, such as the *General Catechetical Directory* (1971), the *National Catechetical Directory* (*Sharing the Light of Faith*) (1978), the already mentioned *Catechism of the Catholic Church* (1992), among many more.

With this guidance, the Diocese of Manchester has established structures and developed many strategies and programs to face this already critical, situation. Among these structures of the diocese are the Office of Adult Education and the Christian Life Centers, both designed to help prepare parents and the whole adult community not only in their own growth in faith but to assist the children and youth in theirs. Others are: (1) an Office for the Catechumenate, (2) Re-Membering Church, and, (3) a Small Church Communities Steering Committee, all established to assist in various circumstances to develop spiritually the Christian assembly.

To encourage and improve the teaching of religion in the Diocese of Manchester, a New Hampshire Conference of Religious Educators was organized a few years ago. This conference of professional religious educators "provides a forum for the exchange of information, programs, resources, and helps to surface goals and priorities for the renewal of the religious educator through ongoing dialogue."

At best, one can say that the future knowledge, belief, and practice of the faith by the American Catholic children and youth of today is still in the process of being resolved. A crucial factor in the resolution to this major problem in the Catholic Church in the United States will surely be the religious formation of the adult community, particularly the parents.

New Catholic Immigrants

While New Hampshire is far from having as varied a population as New York, California, or Illinois, for example, it has attracted quite a large number of racial and ethnic groups to settle within its borders. Some scholars have estimated that about eighty languages are still spoken, 7,000 Asians call the state home, and that roughly 9,000 African Americans and at least 15,000 Hispanics are domiciled there. In Manchester alone, according to a university professor of sociology, some forty ethnic groups reside within its boundaries; Portsmouth, a port city, very likely has even more.

Immigration into the United States reached its lowest point between 1924 and 1965 with the passage by Congress of several laws limiting the number of immigrants and the nations they came from. Since 1965, however, immigration to this country has resumed from nearly every part of the world at a pace, some believe, that rivals the great immigrations from Europe in the nineteenth century and the first twenty years or so of this one.

In a statement entitled "Cultural Pluralism in the United States," issued by the Committee on Social Development and World Peace of the United States Conference of Catholic Bishops in 1980, the American hierarchy welcomed ethnic and cultural diversity in this country and in the

Catholic Church. Fundamentally, it called for the "integration" rather than the "assimilation" of the multiple ethnic and cultural groups arriving and settling in America. This was a vastly different reaction and response from that given to the earlier immigrants, who were expected, by what appears to have been a majority of the bishops of the time, to integrate quickly into American society, and for Catholics to assimilate completely into the territorial parishes (predominantly Irish) as rapidly as possible. The 1980 document reminds the nation at large to understand and accept cultural differences and proposes a range of programs to ensure this diversity in the American Catholic Church. It further states that homogenization would be disastrous for the country, that the "melting pot" goal of the past was to be rejected, and confesses that ethnic and cultural discrimination can and had taken place within the Roman Catholic Church in the United States.

It was in this relatively new atmosphere of understanding and welcome that the new Catholic immigrants were received into New Hampshire and the Diocese of Manchester. The only new immigrants who were numerous enough to require special attention and organized ministry by the local Church were Hispanics, Vietnamese, Koreans, and Portuguese. As the Hispanics are by far the most numerous and varied among them, they will be discussed last.

Two of the groups mentioned are Asian and were for the most part displaced from their countries by the brutality and atrocities of wars in which the United States was deeply involved: These are the Koreans and the Vietnamese.

America's involvement in the Korean War lasted from 1950 to 1953. The war was fought against North Korea and subsequently China as well; after the war American troops remained to guard against another invasion from the north. The Korean War devastated most of that nation and created large numbers of refugees; many of them came to this country. In addition, since the end of the conflict, many of the American soldiers stationed there have married Korean women and returned to the United States with their brides.

A Korean Catholic community was not established in the Diocese of Manchester, however, until some forty-four years after the end of the conflict. After worshiping in Lexington, Massachusetts, for about ten years and in Newton, in the same state, for roughly a year and a half, a group of

Koreans, headed by Mr. Danny Chang, asked the pastor of St. Joseph parish in Salem, the Very Reverend Richard W. Connors, V.F., to use the parish church for worship. Salem was chosen because of its central location to the residences of many Koreans. Their request was granted, it is said, with pleasure by the pastor and the members of the parish. More than 150 Koreans from the area attended the first Mass in their language on Sunday, April 27, 1997. The Divine Liturgy was offered by Father Joseph Ryu, a Jesuit and a Korean, who was at that time a student in Cambridge, Massachusetts. Mass in Korean continues to be celebrated in Salem in what is named the St. Francis Xavier of New Hampshire Korean Community. Other Koreans around the state are served by the local parish or travel to Salem.

A second war that involved the United States, from roughly 1961 to 1973, that in Vietnam, brought another group of refugees and war brides to this country and to New Hampshire. Many of the Vietnamese Catholics who settled in this state are being ministered to in organized communities at St. Aloysius of Gonzaga parish in Nashua and St. Anne's in Manchester. The Nashua community has at least 130 members and that of Manchester more than 60. They too have a priest to serve them in their own language, Father John V. Tiep, a Vietnamese refugee like most of his communities in Nashua and Manchester. Vietnamese settled elsewhere in New Hampshire; a particularly significant number live on or near the seacoast and are served by the local priests and parishes. For the Vietnamese elderly, in particular, as it is for the Koreans, both the native language and their culture are critical to their worship and Catholic identity.

Since October 1994, a number of Portuguese, either natives or descendants of natives from Portugal and Brazil, have been worshiping at St. Aloysius of Gonzaga in Nashua, a parish founded by French Canadians who are particularly open and receptive to other ethnic communities. A year later, in October 1995, the diocese was able to obtain the services of Father Eusebio Silva, a diocesan priest from Portugal with twenty-three years of experience with both Portuguese and Brazilians in Lowell and Cambridge, both in Massachusetts. Unique in the Diocese of Manchester, St. Aloysius of Gonzaga parish harmoniously serves four linguistic communities: French, English, Vietnamese, and Portuguese.

While immigration from Korea and Vietnam has virtually ceased and that from Portugal and Brazil is at rather modest levels, that from Hispanic America—Mexico, Central and South America, and the Caribbean—is growing at a rapid rate and gives every indication of being the predominant immigration wave of the future.

Ministering to the Hispanic community in the United States presents some special challenges to the Catholic Church. One must consider first that these Spanish-speaking people come from scores of nations in Central and South America, the Caribbean, as well as Mexico, and have different cultures, customs, and traditions. There are considerable differences among them that must be recognized if one is to successfully minister to them in an American setting.

Another problem related to the first is the lack of vocations to the priesthood and to the religious life. It has been estimated that only 4 percent of the total number of Catholic priests in the United States have a Latino background, while it has been calculated that Hispanic Catholics constitute as much as 14 percent of the total Catholic population in the nation. Statistics also reveal that there are about three times as many Latinos enrolled in Protestant seminaries and schools of theology as there are in similar Catholic institutions. Among the reasons for this seems to be the great attachment and devotion of Hispanics to family and children and away from the celibate life, and the wide appeal of evangelical and charismatic Protestants to the Latin mind and spirit. In some Hispanic countries, Evangelicals already make up from 7 to 35 percent of the population. The American Catholic Church, therefore, cannot assume that all immigrants from Hispanic America are Catholics or that they will automatically remain so once they settle here. Many millions of Latin Americans have been joining evangelical Protestant churches and sects not only in their own country, but also later when they arrive in the United States. Moreover, as with many American youths, many Latin Americans of the same age do not identify themselves as Catholics, or at best as practicing ones, after they leave high school.

Three other factors need to be mentioned concerning Hispanic Catholics: (1) on average they are much younger than the general population of this country; (2) they are made up of larger families than those of Americans, with perhaps more children and with grandparents and other relatives living with them; and (3) unfortunately, one in four is living below the poverty level. While not all of the above considerations apply exactly to the Hispanics in New Hampshire, these considerations nonetheless must to be kept in mind as they are welcomed by the local

Catholic community.

A "Spanish Apostolate in New Hampshire" was formally established by Father Manuel Padilla, a priest refugee from Algeria, at a Spanish language Mass at St. Joseph Cathedral on Easter Sunday in 1969. Since then, consistent efforts have been made to meet the needs of the growing Hispanic population in New Hampshire, in addition to supplying personnel and financial assistance to the Manchester Mission in Cartago, Colombia, in South America (cf. chapter 13 and below). Over the years, a good number of New Hampshire priests, women religious, and laypeople studied Spanish and have learned about Hispanic culture in centers in Mexico, Santo Domingo, or here in the United States.

Among the structures established to guide this ministry has been the appointment in 1990 of Miss Shirley Brien, a former missionary to Cartago, Colombia, as stateside Hispanic outreach coordinator, a subsidiary of New Hampshire Catholic Charities. More recently, in early 1996, Project HOPE (Hispanics Organized for Personal Empowerment) was created by Catholic Charities and others to bring Hispanic women together to make a variety of marketable products for sale. Some of Project HOPE's goals are to minimize isolation among Hispanic women, to expose them to the American market system, and to help them become familiar with the English language.

Hispanics are also assisted by the Immigration and Refugee Services of the diocese, which offer's a variety of aids to all immigrants, including refugee sponsorship, family reunification, and orientation to the United States. Once the immigrant is in this country, this office provides counseling on a wide variety of subjects of vital importance to the recently arrived from all nations. In addition, the Multicultural Ministries Office oversees the actual pastoral care of the Hispanics, Vietnamese, and Portuguese through the parishes of the diocese. This office is currently directed by Sister Margaret Crosby, SNDdeN, who is also the very capable director of the Office of Social Concerns under New Hampshire Catholic Charities.

From the first Mass in Spanish in the cathedral on Easter 1969, ministry to the Hispanics has spread to a number of parishes around the state. Among those involved are: St. Francis Xavier parish, Nashua, where Father Daniel A. St. Laurent, Hispanic Ministry Coordinator for the diocese, inaugurated this ministry and has been assisted by a number of people, notably Sister Nancy Braceland, c.s.j.; St. Anne, Manchester, where in addition to Mass in Spanish, there is an office to coordinate this ministry directed by Sister Maria Luz Cervantes, m.s.c., and special feast days are celebrated according to Spanish custom; and St. Joseph, Dover, where the pastor, the Reverend Daniel O. Lamothe, extends his care to the entire seacoast area, to the far north of the state, and during the horse-racing season to the Hispanics, mostly grooms and stable hands, at Rockingham Racetrack in Salem. In the north country, Father Lamothe has been assisted since 1994 by some local personnel and by the North Country Hispanic Outreach of Catholic Charities.

Moreover, the entire Hispanic population of the Diocese of Manchester is invited to share a weekend at Camp Fatima at Gilmanton Iron Works on the Upper Suncook Lake, where the Liturgy is celebrated and the participants enjoy a fiesta with native food, music, and dancing. In Dover the Hispanic community publishes a monthly newsletter called *Periodico San Jose.*

Our Lady of Perpetual Help, Cartago, Colombia

While the Hispanic ministry within the diocese progressed, so did that of Our Lady of Perpetual Help Parish in Cartago, Colombia, South America, an enterprise originally staffed and financed by the Catholics of New Hampshire since October 1963.

Besides what has been written about the early years of that parish to approximately 1985 in chapter 13 under "Multicultural Ministries," the following needs to be added. Two missionaries, both laywomen, have been central to the success of that mission-parish: They are Mrs. Margaret Loughlin Splaine and Miss Claire Aucoin, R.N. While many other people have been important to that effort on the part of the diocese, these women have been the twin pillars of this missionary undertaking. (Some of these other selfless individuals are mentioned in chapter 13.) Key to the enterprise was Monsignor Thomas F. Duffy, who, as a volunteer, served twice as pastor of Our Lady of Perpetual Help, first as the founder from 1963 to 1968, and then from 1972 to 1978. This priest, it was clear, felt equally at home in the United States and in Colombia. He died in New Hampshire on February 16, 1994.

Margaret Loughlin, then unmarried, decided to volunteer while serving as an instructor in chemistry at the University of New Hampshire at Durham. In 1962 she became a papal volunteer for Latin America (PAVLA), and after four months of learning Spanish and instruction in Hispanic culture she was assigned to the Catholic University of Valparaiso in Chile, where she did research on the nutritional value of fish.

From there, she volunteered to work at the diocesan mission in Cartago, where she arrived in October 1965. At the mission, Miss Lough-lin concentrated on catechetical programs and on general education by radio to reach outlying areas of Colombia. In 1966, she returned to New Hampshire, where she began her most important ministry by becoming diocesan liaison for the missions in addition to working locally with groups of Hispanics. Now married, she persevered in these ministries from 1966 to her retirement in 1995. Mrs. Splaine spent some thirty-three years working in or for the missions.

Miss Claire Aucoin, a similarly motivated person and a registered nurse, who volunteered for three years, arrived at Our Lady of Perpetual Help in Cartago in 1966 and has been ministering there ever since, for thirty-one years.

As director of the Manchester Mission, Miss Aucoin manages a staff of thirteen paid workers who care habitually for at least three hundred peo-ple. These residents are housed in eleven separate buildings, each with a specific purpose: elderly men, elderly women, the sick, individuals with mental and emotional problems, children, and so forth. In addition, Man-chester Mission provides community healthcare services and developmen-tal and educational opportunities for the area. These ministries have been subsidized by the people of the Diocese of Manchester for the past thirty-four years. Priests from New Hampshire no longer provide the pastoral care of the parish; that duty is now in the hand's of the Colombian clergy.

Finances: the Parishes and the Diocese

Financing the Cartago mission is, obviously, only a small fraction of what the members of the Catholic Church in New Hampshire are expected to and actually do, support. These obligations all stem from the love of God and the love of neighbor—the two great commandments (Lv 19:18; Dt 6:5; Mt 22:37–40)—and extend outward from the individual to embrace the entire world. These duties are both of justice and of charity.

Money, for most clergy, is a distasteful subject to preach or write about and certainly the most unpleasant for the faithful to hear from the pulpit or read about in the parish bulletin. Yet, to fulfill the demands of the two great commandments, it is not only a valid but also a necessary theme. Money, in this context, is a basic component in carrying out the mission of the Church.

A few observations with regard to the Catholic Church and finances in the United States will help to keep the subject in perspective. It is with justifiable satisfaction that the Catholics of this country can view all that they have achieved, not only for the Church but also for society at large. For example, it has been noted that New Hampshire Catholic Charities is the largest nongovernmental provider of social services in the state. That is also true for similar Catholic organizations throughout the nation. If one includes the churches of all denominations, they still collectively receive about 51 percent of all the charitable giving in the United States.

Catholic parishes and other organizations must be aware, however, that religious giving as a percentage of family income has been on a downward course for at least the past two decades. Giving to churches nationally has fallen from an average of 3.1 percent in the late 1950s to 2.5 percent in the early 1990s. While this appears to be a small loss percentagewise (only 0.6 percent), it is a substantial drop in the amount of money involved.

One should also take into account that the upward trend in family income has, in great measure, been gained as a result of women either remaining employed after marriage or entering the labor force at or after that time. Two incomes per household has become the rule rather than the exception. Another nemesis to the family for many of the past years has been inflation, which played a role in decreasing purchasing power and lowering the standard of living. As the churches depend on the generosity of their members to survive and to carry out their mission, their good or bad fortune depends on the economic health of their contributors.

It is not pleasant to relate that on the national level, Catholics', contributions to their Church are the lowest of any major faith in the country; it has been calculated by sociologists of religion to be at about 1 percent of family income. Taking into account what appears to be a reluctance, or even an unwillingness, of the younger and future generations to support their churches, one can legitimately be concerned about the times to come. Studies, for example, have shown that shopping is now the number one pastime of teenagers. That is not surprising, as they and the rest of society are constantly "carpet-bombed" day by day, hour after hour, by all the media to buy while the Church is basically limited to about one hour each week to "sell" its message in the name of God.

Another basic failing of the churches is the fact that less than 5 percent of their budget nationwide goes to help the needy. An obvious interpretation is that the churches have not been sensitized to the common bond among human beings and their responsibility for each other. The old, famous, and disturbing question arises again: "Am I my brother's keeper?" (Gn 4:9). Church budgets, if they are to be meaningful and attractive, must reflect the responsibilities of the community of believers; the Church budget is one barometer of the spiritual values and health of the congregation.

Among the almost countless other issues involved in Church finances, one more will be briefly considered—parish buildings. This most frequently mentioned financial burden includes problems associated with overbuilding, the paying of interest, repayment of debt, mortgages, continued necessary repairs, and maintenance. In many cases, as a well-informed observer said, "word and sacrament," the core of the Church, gives way to "brick and mortar." A trap fallen into by many is to be able to find the finances to meet the needs of buildings but not those of human beings.

Another of the important factors to be considered is that, in times past, the churches could count on considerable volunteer help to save on paying parish employees. In examining the present and planning for the future, this option is fading away. Not only are husband and wife fully employed but also they now have so many personal commitments to children and their schools, their homes, relatives, friends, and, in a growing number of cases, to a second job that 70 percent in a recent poll stated that they have little or no energy for anything else.

By any standard, and despite the negative factors mentioned in this study, the Diocese of Manchester has been historically financially sound, except from roughly 1930 to around 1940, the period of the Great Depression. Even during that time, the financial measures taken mostly by Bishop Peterson, the ordinary from 1932 to 1944, were to lower the debt and were not brought about by panic or fear of the future.

A close examination of the archives of the diocese reveals that generally poor financial records were kept until roughly the end of the 1950s. An exception was the financial reports that were required from each parish every year. These were for the most part accurately kept and provided the bishop and his staff with considerable important information on the financial vitality of each parish, or lack thereof. Bishop Peterson was known to castigate soundly any pastor who did not comply fully with his expectations in this regard. Spiritual reports required by each parish at the same time as the financial were also of prime importance to the bishop and diocesan officers.

Enormous improvements in the recordkeeping and financial health of the diocese were the result of serendipity; that is, they were extremely fortunate but not directly intended. In 1956, the Reverend Albert W. Olkovikas (now Monsignor) returned to Manchester from his studies at the Catholic University of America in Washington with a doctorate in canon law, earned summa cum laude, and in October of that year was appointed an assistant vice chancellor by Bishop Matthew F. Brady. Working in that capacity, he took special interest in the finances and financial records of the diocese. Over the years, he became so knowledgeable and competent in those areas of expertise that he has been recognized by bankers and other professional financial managers as a natural "genius" for that work. Consequently, for roughly the past forty years, first unofficially and then officially, he has been directing the financial affairs of the Diocese of Manchester.

A second major step in firming up the financial administration of the diocese was the employment of Mr. Dana Hirst, a banker, as controller on January 1, 1984. Under his direction, the diocese began its transition to the use of computers for finances beginning in July 1984. Since then, even more extensive and sophisticated procedures have been introduced in the financial management of the entire diocese. (New Hampshire Catholic Charities, which is administered separately, had computerized its finances several years previously.)

For the sake of clarity, the finances of the diocesan offices and those of the parishes will be discussed separately.

As it has been noted, since 1983, with the promulgation of the Code of Canon Law (cc. 492–493), a diocesan finance council is mandatory in each diocese (cf. chapter 14, "Organizational Adjustments"). The functions of this five-person council are to establish a yearly diocesan budget and a financial report at the end of that year, and to "advise" the bishop in all areas of income and expenditures. It is interesting to note the proviso of canon 492 § 3, which states that no relative of the bishop "up to the fourth degree of consanguinity or affinity" may serve on this council. Memories of nepotism in times past were apparently still strong among the framers of the code.

At least since the appointment of Monsignor Olkovikas as a diocesan administrator in the late 1950s, its financial position has strengthened steadily. For example, as of June 30, 1996, the total assets of the Central Administration Funds and Diocesan Departments were $52,119,334.23 and their liabilities amounted to $43,009,846.88. In summary, the total assets over liabilities of those funds on June 30, 1996 was $9,109,487.35. The total revenues for these above-mentioned funds for the period July 1, 1995, to June 30, 1996, were $13,460,509.22 with only $2,954,401.32 derived from assessments on the parishes. A major outlay from these funds was to pay the salaries of lay personnel, clergy, and religious and the benefits of those who work for the diocese. This alone amounted to nearly $3 million, or, precisely, $2,777,972.72.

All of the other of the many financial accounts of the diocese, several designated by trust for specific purposes, are in similarly sound condition. In addition, for the fiscal year that ended on June 30, 1997, $1,001,175 was received by the diocese from the parishes from special mandated collections. Four of these collections were for use exclusively by the diocese: the diocesan missions (the poor parishes of New Hampshire); the Manchester Mission (Cartago, Colombia, and the apostolate to new immigrants in the diocese); the seminarians preparing for the priesthood for the diocese; and the Catholic school education fund, which is self-explanatory. Five of the collections go entirely to a national or international office: that for the bishops' national offices in Washington (NCCB/USCC) and The Catholic University of America, also in the nation's capital; aid for the Church in Eastern Europe; the propagation of the faith; the bishops' overseas relief fund; and for the Holy Father. The remaining three, while national in scope, allow the diocese to retain a specified share for local use. These are: the campaign for human development; the national drive for support of religious; and communications.

Of these twelve special collections, in the fiscal year 1996–1997, those with the most appeal were the national drive for the support of religious

($149,043), for diocesan seminarians ($109,720), and for the Holy Father ($91,138). Those with the least attraction were, aid for the Church in Eastern Europe ($45,723), communications ($55,563), and for the combined assistance of the national conferences of Catholic bishops (NCCB/USCC) and The Catholic University of America ($62,045).

A special collection is also taken up on Good Friday, not a holy day of obligation, for the Holy Places in the Holy Land. In 1997, it raised $50,789 for this purpose.

In all, one can count that thirteen mandated special collections are taken up each year in all the parishes, missions, and stations in the diocese.

When other charitable donations from the parishes are added, such as the relief of flood victims in Alton, New Hampshire ($20,824), and those along the Red River (North Dakota, Minnesota, and Manitoba in Canada), Rice Bowl, and collections for specific foreign missions, a total of $1,367,995 was raised by the parishes, missions, and stations for essentially outside purposes. Also used for many non-diocesan purposes is the bishop's summer reception fund (cf. chapter 14) which in 1997 brought in $299,265.

While the Diocese of Manchester has been and is currently in good financial condition, there is considerable concern for the future, particularly on the part of the bishop, the diocesan finance council, and the diocesan staff. After considering many of the recent developments related in this history, one can understand the reasons for their concern.

That is why Bishop O'Neil decided, after a broad consultation, to launch the project "The Future of Our Faith" in early 1995 with a goal of $18 million (cf. chapter 15, "The Future of Our Faith"). While this objective was not reached, the total potential of that drive has been established as $13,941,017 for the diocese, and an additional $4,030,114.77 for the use of the parishes.

Most of the parishes of the diocese have fared as well as the diocese in the matter of finances; there were some exceptions, as will be seen. Also, like the diocese, the parishes are obligated by canon law (c. 537) to have a parish finance committee to "advise" the pastor (cf. chapter 14, "Organizational Adjustments").

Taken collectively, the 131 parishes with their missions and stations during the fiscal year July 1, 1995, to June 30, 1996, had a total operating income of $27,189,181, with a full $24,870,839 derived from offertory and seat money. As expenses for the same period amounted to $25,739,300, there was a net operating income of $1,449,881. In addition to the total operating income mentioned above, another $1,320,109 was raised from capital fund drives, bequests, and so on. Thus, the total income from all sources of all the parishes for that fiscal period was $28,509,290.

Based on the information supplied by the parishes, it has been calculated that for the fiscal year ending June 30, 1996, the average donation per person per week was $1.62, and $4.99 per family.

As of June 30, 1996, the total debt of all the parishes was $9,431,640. Of this amount a full $9,095,701 was owed to the Central Fund of the diocese. This means that a fraction over 96 percent of the debts of the parishes is owed to the diocese and not to outside financial institutions. Among the parishes that are in debt, twenty-one owed more than $120,300; the greatest debt was $1,152,534 owed by a parish where a new church was built not many years ago.

On the same date, June 30, 1996, twenty-three parishes, a little more than 17.5 percent of the total number, received assistance from the Diocean Fund, a reserve of money raised principally, but not exclusively, from the collection taken annually in the parishes, usually in July (cf. above). In the year under consideration, income from all sources into that account was $125,532.58; total disbursements, however, amounted to $186,330.48. This created a deficit of $60,797.90 for that year.

The gifts from the fund ranged from $24,000 to two parishes, St. Mary, Claremont, and St. Patrick, Pelham, to a low of $575 given to St. Mark, Londonderry. Most of the subsidies to these parishes were for debt service; that is, they could not meet their expenses. Among these parishes one can very likely identify some that would be candidates for twinning or some other remedial action in the future. Other parishes, because of their relatively isolated location or some other factor, will undoubtedly continue to receive financial assistance and keep their independent parish status.

At the Portal of the Third Millenium

Over the past 350 years, Catholicism in New Hampshire has undergone numerous—almost unimaginable—transitions, many described in this history. While one can in large measure trace this past, the future lies greatly in the shadows, unclear and unseen. Present in the equation will certainly be a number of unexpected factors—both human and divine—that can alter, immensely or minutely, the trends of the past centuries or decades.

In preparing to cross into the next millennium, however, one must pay particular attention to the major transformations that have taken place in American society and the Catholic Church in the United States since the 1960s. Many of these changes, for better or for worse, have been described in chapters 13, 14, and 15. They will, with little doubt, be the base for the history of Catholicism in New Hampshire in the future.

As these last thirty-five to forty years are examined, however, they must be taken in context: The Catholic Church celebrates nearly 2,000 years of existence, and Catholicism in New Hampshire remembers, in some fashion, the last 350 years of the previous two millennia.

On this Thanksgiving Day, as these words are being written, approximately three hundred bishops representing all of the Americas (North, Central, South, and the Caribbean) are gathered in Vatican City with Pope John Paul II in a synod, the first ever of its kind, to discuss, pray over, and outline a course of apostolic action for the future of the faith in this part of the world.

Their objective, including that of the Catholics of New Hampshire to whom they are joined in faith, is to spread the evangelical message ever more widely and forcefully with renewed missionary zeal, whatever the prevailing circumstances.

Thanksgiving morning
November 27, 1997

Epilogue

Death of 'The People's Bishop'

On November 30, 1997, three days after Thanksgiving, eight years to the day after his installation as the first coadjutor of the Diocese of Manchester (November 30, 1989), and exactly the fourth year after the removal of a malignant tumor on his sternum, Bishop Leo Edward E. O'Neil, the eighth bishop of Manchester, died at his residence on River Road in the Queen City. At his bedside were his sister; a niece; a nephew and his wife; Sister Pauline Lebel, c.s.c.; his close friend Father John Burke of Worcester, Massachusetts; and Bishop Francis J. Christian. November 30 was also the First Sunday of Advent, which marked the beginning of a new liturgical year in the Roman Catholic Church.

One of the first major signs of the deterioration of the health of Bishop O'Neil occurred on November 30, 1993, when doctors at the Catholic Medical Center in Manchester removed a malignant tumor from his sternum. This surgery was followed by radiation and chemotherapy (cf. chapter 15, "A Serious Illness"). In April 1995, Bishop O'Neil fractured a bone in his leg while stepping awkwardly to avoid pain from another bone tumor. Approximately three months later, in July 1995, the diocese publicly announced that the diagnosis was multiple myeloma, a sometimes painful form of bone marrow cancer that causes tumors to grow. It is not curable, but is considered treatable with chemotherapy. Despite this somber diagnosis, the surgery in 1993, and the fractured leg in 1995, Bishop O'Neil continued his ministry nearly without interruption.

In September 1997 he was hospitalized again for several days with pneumonia, and again in November for the same reason. (Pneumonia is frequently a by-product of radiation and chemotherapy.) It was while being treated for pneumonia that it was discovered that Bishop O'Neil had a second form of blood cancer, acute leukemia. The specialists also informed the bishop that treatment for this condition would accelerate the development of the multiple myeloma. On learning this, Bishop O'Neil decided to discontinue treatment and returned to his residence on November 17 to wait, as he said, to die at home. To properly take care of him in these circumstances, his home was equipped with the necessary hospital furnishings, and around-the-clock nursing services were provided.

On November 18, the day after his return to his residence, Bishop O'Neil gave a press conference in his home. Wearing a nasal oxygen tube, he informed the members of the press of his condition, in his own whimsical and humorous fashion, in order to put rumors at rest. In his general statement and in his answers to questions, he explained the nature of his two forms of cancer, the lack of effective therapies, and that the physicians had placed "no time" on what remained of his life

After his emotional press conference—emotional for the bishop and for many of those present—his physical condition deteriorated rapidly. He was, however, able to do two things that were dear to his heart. The first was to hold a prayer service at St. Joseph Cathedral on Tuesday, November 25, at 11:30 A.M. with some two hundred priests from New Hampshire and other parts of New England. Still wearing a nasal oxygen mask and clearly weakened by his illness, he gave a personal and powerful message to those present.

Two days later, on Thanksgiving, November 27, 1997, he concelebrated Mass in a temporary chapel set up in a room next to his, and gave his eight-year-old grandniece, Hannah Moriarty, her first communion. Prior to the Mass, he had heard Hannah's first confession with, as someone who saw him at that time said, "tears coming down his face." His second wish, to spend Thanksgiving with his family, was thus realized in this very touching way.

Late on Saturday night, November 29, the eighth bishop of Manchester slipped into a coma. At about 3 A.M. on the first Sunday of the new liturgical year, he died to the accompaniment of the prayers of Bishop Christian, his family, and friends.

Bishop O'Neil was the first member of the Catholic episcopacy in New Hampshire to die, one could say, in a public way. From November 30, 1993, after the removal of the tumor on his sternum, he spoke freely of his cancer, particularly in his addresses on the value of human life and the assaults being made on it by abortion, euthanasia, assisted suicide, and the like. His press conference on November 18, twelve days before his death, was given wide coverage in all the media and clearly demonstrated his intention to teach about dying and death not only by his words but by his example as well. Those familiar with recent American Catholic Church history will recall the edifying "public" death of Joseph Cardinal Bernardin, the Archbishop of Chicago, who also died of cancer, on November 14, 1996.

Throughout his final illness, lasting some nineteen days, prayers were offered for him in many of the other Christian churches in the state and in the two Jewish synagogues in Manchester. At Temple Israel, the congregation was asked to pray for Bishop O'Neil every morning at the 7 o'clock service, and at Temple Adath Yeshurun he was included in a special prayer of healing during the Friday-night services. Bishop O'Neil's affinity and respect for the Jewish people had previously been demonstrated by his accepting an invitation from Rabbi Arthur Starr to speak at Temple Adath Yeshurun, the first Catholic bishop to do so, and by visiting Temple Israel in September 1997. Special prayers were also said for him at St. George Orthodox Cathedral at one of its feast day celebrations.

Even before his death, particularly during the final phase of his life, the community at large, through the media, began to express its respect, affection, and admiration for Bishop O'Neil. Much of the praise centered on two points: the Christian dignity with which he was preparing for death, and his spontaneously warm relationship with children and youth. Commenting on this latter quality, Sister Pauline Lebel, c.s.c., diocesan secretary for Christian Formation, said, "He was their [the children's] leader, but he was their friend at the same time." Tributes, in many instances, were also paid to his spiritual leadership and strong pastoral presence for everyone. One of the most fitting comments was that he was "The People's Bishop."

Also before his death, two major facilities in Manchester were named in his honor. The first was the recently established orthopedic clinic at Notre Dame College (Bishop Leo O'Neil Orthopedic Clinic), and the second was a youth center owned by the city of Manchester, a facility purchased from Blessed Sacrament parish at the south end of Elm Street in Manchester.

Funeral and Burial of Bishop O'Neil

As with all his deceased predecessors—bishops Bradley, Delany, Guertin, Peterson, Brady, and Primeau—Bishop O'Neil received the highest religious and civic tributes at the time of death and his funeral observances. One must recall that on the day of Bishop Bradley's funeral in December 1903, public schools in Manchester were closed and electric trolley cars came to a stop in place for two minutes at precisely noon out of respect for the bishop.

Bishop O'Neil's wake began with the rite of reception at St. Joseph Cathedral at 7 P.M. on Wednesday, December 3. This ceremony, which lasted about an hour, was presided over by the auxiliary, Bishop Francis J. Christian, and was attended by some four hundred people, including members of Bishop O'Neil's family, clergy, and mourners. The deceased, exposed in a casket opened full length, was vested in white garments worn to celebrate Mass and included his episcopal ring and miter. His rosary beads were intertwined in his fingers and under his hands was his liturgy of the hours (breviary), which he had prayed all his priestly life. To the side of the casket was displayed his shepherd's staff (crozier), the symbol of his episcopal leadership.

From approximately 8 to 9 P.M. that evening and from 9 A.M. to 9 P.M. on Thursday, December 4, the cathedral church was open for the viewing of his body. Hundreds of people from all over New Hampshire and other parts of the Northeast came to pay their respects and to pray for the former spiritual leader of the Catholics of New Hampshire. Prominent among the visitors were schoolchildren from various parts of the state, many of them arriving by bus.

On the same day, December 4, there were also two religious services to pray for Bishop O'Neil and for all those who shared in the sorrow of his death. At 12:15 P.M., a midday service was held, and at 7 P.M. solemn vespers were celebrated in his memory. Both were very well attended by hundreds of mourners.

The Mass of Christian burial for the bishop was held on Friday, December 5, beginning at approximately 11 A.M. The entire service, lasting slightly over two hours, was carried live by television station WMUR-TV as a public service, particularly to the more than 320,000 Catholics in the state. The print media, particularly the *Manchester Union Leader*, gave extensive coverage to the Mass, as it had to Bishop O'Neil's illness, death, and wake.

Particularly visible and welcomed were representatives from most of the Christian churches in New Hampshire and the Jewish community. Among these were the president of Temple Adath Yeshurun; the Episcopal bishop of New Hampshire, Douglas Theuner; leaders of the state Council of Churches; the United Church of Christ; Methodists; Lutherans; Baptists; and many others.

All of the major political officeholders in New Hampshire were also in attendance: The governor, the two U.S. senators, the two members of the U.S. House of Representatives, the mayor and the chief of police of Manchester, and numerous others. A surprise presence was that of the former ambassador to the Holy See and former mayor of Boston, Raymond Flynn.

In addition to about one hundred relatives and close friends of Bishop O'Neil, also in attendance were some three hundred priests, two abbots, thirty archbishops and bishops, and Bernard Cardinal Law. The latter was the main celebrant at the concelebrated Mass at which Bishop Joseph Maguire, the retired bishop of Springfield, Massachusetts, gave a highly personal and much appreciated twenty-three-minute homily. In addition to the solemnity of the service, the *Manchester Union Leader* commented on the "laughter, tears and the common touch" that accompanied it. Adding greatly to the beauty and dignity of the occasion was the music and singing of the seventy-member diocesan choir under the direction of Mary Bagnell. One of the renditions of the choir had been requested by Bishop O'Neil. This was the hymn "To Love and Serve," which had been composed by Ms. Bagnell on the theme of the motto on the coat of arms of Bishop O'Neil.

Also at the request of the bishop before his death, he was carried out of the cathedral at the end of the ceremony on the shoulders of six of the younger members of the council of priests, who represented the entire body of the Catholic clergy of the Diocese of Manchester. With this gesture, Bishop O'Neil wished to symbolize that as he had been carried symbolically on the shoulders of the priests in life, he was now being carried physically in death. This, his final exit from the cathedral church, was accompanied by sustained applause from a deeply moved and standing congregation.

Following the precedent of Bishop Primeau, who died on June 6, 1989, Bishop O'Neil chose to be buried in St. Joseph Cemetery in Bedford, rather than in the crypt reserved for bishops under the altar of the cathedral. Two reasons appear to have motivated this decision: the first was to indicate that as spiritual leader he believed that he should be buried among his people rather than apart, and second, that visitors to the cemetery would see his burial place and, it is hoped, remember him in their prayers.

At the gravesite, alongside that of Bishop Primeau, Bishop O'Neil's home diocese of Springfield as well as his hometown and the street on which he was raised in Holyoke—Davis Street—were not forgotten. Using soil dug from the yard of his boyhood home on Davis Street by his little grandnephew Joseph Moriarty, each of the members of Bishop O'Neil's family, including his grandnieces and grandnephews, threw this soil atop his casket, mingling it with that of New Hampshire, his final home.

Adding to the solemnity of the interment was the presence of the New Hampshire Police Pipe and Drum group, a volunteer organization of police from around the state, who touchingly played "Amazing Grace."

A Prayerful Tribute from Jerusalem

One of the most moving tributes to Bishop O'Neil came from Rabbi Arthur Starr of Temple Adath Yeshurun in Manchester. Rabbi Starr, who had left Manchester after the death but before the funeral and burial of Bishop O'Neil, to spend a three-month sabbatical as well as to attend a rabbinical meeting in Jerusalem, wrote to the *Manchester Union Leader* concerning the deceased bishop of Manchester. He related that he had gone to the Western Wall—the retaining wall of the great temple of the Jewish people destroyed by the Roman legions in 70 A.D.—a venerated structure that has received the silent, vocal, and written prayers of Jews for nearly two thousand years. At the Wailing Wall, with a prayer on his lips and, as he wrote, "in my hand," and with a "heart filled with thoughts and prayers," Rabbi Starr remembered "a friend, colleague, study partner and wonderful human being." This gracious memorial was augmented by the promise to plant a tree in Bishop Leo's honor in the Jerusalem forest. These fraternal remembrances at the Wailing Wall and in the planting of a tree in a land sacred to both Jews and Christians were received with emotion and gratitude by Bishop O'Neil's families, by both the bonds of blood and the ties of faith.

An Administrator for the Diocese

On Saturday, December 6, 1997, the day following the funeral and burial of Bishop O'Neil, the College of Consultors, composed of ten members selected by the bishop from the Council of Priests, met at 10 A.M. in the diocesan administration building at 153 Ash Street in Manchester to elect an administrator. In conformity with the requirements of the Code of Canon Law (cc. 416–430), the College of Consultors elected, as it had been unanimously expected, Bishop Francis J. Christian, the auxiliary bishop of the diocese since May 14, 1996 (cf. chapter 15, "A New Auxiliary Bishop").

It is the hands of this priest and bishop, whom Bishop O'Neil commended for "[h]is personality, his experience and his life of prayer and faith," that the College of Consultors, with the required notification to the Holy See (c. 422), has placed the administration (c. 427) of the Diocese of Manchester until a new bishop takes possession of the diocese (c. 430 §1).

This next bishop will be the ninth of the Diocese of Manchester and, going back through the prior jurisdictions of Portland, Boston, and Baltimore, the fifteenth Catholic bishop of New Hampshire.

A Bishop for the Third Millennium

Seven months and twenty-one days after the death of Bishop Leo Edward O'Neil, on the morning of July 21, 1998, Pope John Paul II, through the apostolic Pro-Nuncio to the United States Archbishop Agostino Cacciavillan, announced the appointment of the Most Reverend John Brennan McCormack as the ninth Bishop of the Diocese of Manchester. Bishop McCormack will be installed in that office on September 22, 1998 in the Cathedral Church of St. Joseph in Manchester.

John B. McCormack was born August 12, 1935 in Winthrop, Massachusetts, son of the late Cornelius McCormack and Eleanor Noonan McCormack. John was the youngest of three children. Maurice, the eldest, is the father of four and has a growing number of grandchildren. His sister Barbara was a Sister of Notre Dame until her death from cancer at the age of sixty-two.

All of John's education was received in the Boston area under Catholic auspices Successively he attended St. Mary Grammar School in Cambridge, Boston College High School, Cardinal O'Connell Seminary College, and St. John Seminary. He was ordained to the priesthood in Boston on February 2, 1960.

Since his ordination, Father McCormack has been involved in a variety of ministries. He has been an associate pastor; executive director of the North Shore Catholic Center (1967–1981); pastor of two large parishes; and vicar for ministerial personnel of the archdiocese with responsibilities for both priests and the women and men religious (1984–1994). In 1969, he earned a graduate degree from Boston College in social work.

After his ordination to the episcopacy as an auxiliary of the Archdiocese of Boston on December 27, 1995, he was assigned the pastoral responsibilities for the South region of the archdiocese which consists of eighty-two parishes and is served by two hundred and thirty priests, three hundred women and men religious and is populated by more than one half million Catholics.

In introducing him to the Catholics of New Hampshire, Bishop Francis J. Christian, who most ably served as administrator since the death of Bishop O'Neil, underlined the fact that Bishop McCormack values collaborative and cooperative ministry in which he includes not only the Catholic community but all Christians, those of the Jewish faith, members of other religions, and the civic community at every level. (Bishop Christian did not fail to mention that his episcopal colleague is also a skier and not unfamiliar with the slopes of Sunapee, Cannon, Waterville, and other Mountains in New Hampshire.)

As Bishop McCormack will serve only one year and one hundred and one days as Bishop of Manchester in the twentieth century and the second millennium (September 22, 1998 to December 31, 1999), he will essentially be a bishop of the twenty-first century and the third millennium— a bishop of the future history of Catholicism in New Hampshire.

Appendices

APPENDIX A

Catholic Population of New Hampshire 1785–1997

Year	Population
1785	*
1835	387
1884	45,000
1903	100,000
1959	220,000
1984	295,303
1997	321,914

* None listed in the report to the Holy See from the Reverend John Carroll, Superior of the American Missions.

APPENDIX B

Catholic Dioceses and Bishops with Jurisdiction Over New Hampshire*

Dioceses	Name of Bishop	Years
Baltimore	John Carroll	1790-1810 Diocese established November 6, 1789. Bishop consecrated in England August 5, 1790.
Boston	Jean Lefebvre de Cheverus	1810-1823 Diocese established April 8, 1808. Bishop consecrated November 1, 1810. Transferred to France in 1823.
	Benedict J. Fenwick S.J.	1825-1846
	John B. Fitzpatrick	1846-1855
Portland	David W. Bacon	1855-1874 Diocese established July 29, 1853. First candidate declined appointment. Bishop Bacon consecrated April 22, 1858.
	James Augustine Healy	1875-1884
Manchester	Denis M. Bradley	1884-1903 Diocese established April 15, 1884. Bishop consecrated June 11, 1884.
	John B. Delany	1904-1906

338

George A. Guertin   1907-1931

John B. Peterson   1932-1944

Matthew F. Brady   1945-1959

Ernest J. Primeau   1960-1974

Odore J. Gendron   1975-1990

Leo E. O'Neil   1990-1997

* In all, the Catholics of the State of New Hampshire have been under the jurisdiction of four dioceses and fourteen bishops.

APPENDIX C

Parishes of the Diocese of Manchester

In Chronological Order of Establishment

Order	Date	Location	
		Diocese of Boston	

Bishop Benedict J. Fenwick, S.J.

Order	Date	Location	
1.	December, 1822	Claremont	St. Mary. Closed 1827-1833; reopened 1833-1835; mission 1835-1856; parish 1856-1862; mission 1862–70; parish 1870
2.	November, 1830	Dover	St. Aloysius until 1872; since St. Mary

Bishop John Bernard Fitzpatrick

3.	1848	Manchester	St. Anne
4.	November 21, 1851	Portsmouth	St. Mary until 1874; since Immaculate Conception

Diocese of Portland

Bishop David W. Bacon

5.	Summer, 1855	Concord	St. John the Evangelist. Closed 1856–1865; parish again 1865.
6.	November 7, 1855	Nashua	Immaculate Conception to 1909; since St. Patrick
7.	August 24, 1856	Somersworth (formerly Great Falls)	Holy Trinity
8.	October 23, 1857	Lancaster	All Saints
9.	1859	Exeter	St. Bernard until 1879; since St. Michael
10.	1862	Keene	St. Bernard
11.	May, 1868	Milford	St. Patrick; mission 1874-1895; parish August 1895.
12.	April 19, 1869	Manchester	St. Joseph
13.	1870	Rollinsford (formerly Salmon Falls)	St. Mary
14.	May 11, 1871	Manchester	St. Augustine
15.	June 11, 1871	Nashua	St. Aloysius of Gonzaga (St. Louis de Gonzague)
16.	August 16, 1871	Laconia	St. Joseph
17.	February, 1872	Rochester	St. Mary
18.	1873	Suncook	St. John the Baptist
19.	1874	Wilton	Sacred Heart; mission 1874-1882; parish 1882
20.	1874	Peterborough	St. Peter; mission 1882-1885; parish 1885–1887; mission 1887–1900; parish 1900

Order	Date	Location	

Bishop James Augustine Healy

21.	1875	Lebanon	Scared Heart
22.	1875	Ashuelot (parish title moved to Winchester in 1962)	St. Michael; mission 1878-1902; parish 1901 (Winchester parish, St. Stanislaus)
23.	1876	Gorham	Holy Family
24.	1878	Newmarket	St. Mary
25.	November, 1878	North Walpole	St. Peter
26.	July, 1880	Penacook (formerly Fisherville)	St. John the Baptist to 1879; since Immaculate Conception
27.	September 13, 1880	Manchester	St. Mary (Ste. Marie)
28.	January, 1882	Littleton	St. Rose of Lima
29.	October 6, 1882	Somersworth (formerly Great Falls)	St. Martin
30.	March, 1883	Rochester	Holy Rosary
31.	February 2, 1884	Hinsdale	St. Joseph

Diocese of Manchester

Bishop Denis Mary Bradley

32.	July 21, 1884	Franklin	St. Paul
33.	June 17, 1885	Nashua	St. Francis Xavier
34.	August, 1885	Berlin	St. Anne
35.	May, 1886	Marlborough	Sacred Heart
36.	July, 1886	Whitefield	St. Matthew
37.	October, 1886	Hooksett	Holy Rosary
38.	1887	Jaffrey	St. Patrick
39.	February, 1888	Manchester	St. Raphael
40.	July, 1888	Greenville	Sacred Heart
41.	August, 1888	North Stratford	Sacred Heart
42.	September, 1888	Derry	St. Thomas Aquinas
43.	April 1, 1890	Manchester	St. George
44.	May, 1890	Ashland	St. Agnes; mission 1890-1904; parish September 30, 1904
45.	July ,1891	Laconia	Sacred Heart
46.	July, 1891	Tilton	Assumption
47.	1891	Canaan (parish title moved to Enfield, May 1901)	St. Mary; mission status from 1892; Enfield parish, St. Helena
48.	February, 1892	Concord	Sacred Heart
49.	1892	Plaistow (known as Westville)	Holy Angels
50.	October 19, 1892	Gonic	St. Leo
51.	1892	Hillsborough	St. Mary
52.	November 5, 1893	Dover	St. Charles Borromeo
53.	January, 1894	Berlin	St. Kieran
54.	January, 1896	Woodsville	St. Joseph
55.	December, 1897	Epping	St. Joseph
56.	January, 1898	Groveton	St. Francis Xavier
57.	February, 1898	Manchester	St. Patrick

Order	Date		Location
58.	1899	Manchester	St. Anthony
59.	January, 1900	Bristol	St. Timothy: mission 1901-1953; parish June 9, 1953
60.	1902	Manchester	St. Hedwig
61.	1902	Newport	St. Patrick
62.	1902	Bartlett (parish title moved to North Conway in 1903)	Sacred Heart; mission since 1903; titled St. Joseph since 1937; North Conway title Our Lady of the Mountains
63.	1902	Harrisville	St. Denis
64.	December, 1902	West Stewartstown	Our Lady of the Valley; Mission 1904-1926; titled St. Albert in 1911; parish February 27, 1926
65.	December 27, 1902	Lincoln	St. Joseph
66.	December 29, 1902	Troy	Immaculate Conception
67.	January 2, 1903	Manchester	St. Francis of Assisi; mission 1915–1953; parish again October 2, 1953; known as Goffs Falls

Bishop John B. Delany

68.	1904	Charlestown	St. Catherine of Siena
69.	1905	Lakeport	Our Lady of the Lakes

Bishop George Albert Guertin

70.	May 8, 1907	Hanover	St. Denis
71.	April 19, 1908	Nashua	St. Stanislaus
72.	September 6, 1908	Sanbornville	St. Anthony
73.	October 1, 1909	Nashua	St. Casimir
74.	October, 1909	Nashua	Infant Jesus
75.	May 29, 1910	Salem	St. Joseph
76.	April 23, 1911	Manchester	Sacred Heart
77.	September 15, 1911	Manchester	Our Lady of Perpetual Help
78.	July 19, 1914	Manchester	St. John the Baptist
79.	January 8, 1915	Manchester	St. Edmund
80.	1915	Manchester	Blessed Sacrament
81.	1916	Plymouth	St. Matthew
82.	August 12, 1917	Berlin	Guardian Angel
83.	February, 1920	Farmington	St. Peter
84.	June 30, 1921	Claremont	St. Joseph
85.	February 28, 1926	Pittsfield	Our Lady of Lourdes

Bishop John Bertram Peterson

86.	October 3, 1934	Manchester	St. Theresa
87.	June 24, 1936	Bennington	St. Patrick
88.	October 28, 1941	Berlin	St. Joseph

Bishop Matthew Francis Brady

89.	May 28, 1945	Wolfeboro	St. Cecilia
90.	October 14, 1945	Dover	St. Joseph
91.	October 14, 1945	Henniker	St. Theresa
92.	May 28, 1946	Meredith	St. Charles
93.	June 5, 1946	Concord	St. Peter

Order		Date	Location
94.	June 18,1946	Cascade	St. Benedict; last administrator in 1976; last building sold November 9, 1987; suppressed
95.	September 4, 1946	Pelham	St. Patrick
96.	July 19, 1947	Durham	St. Thomas More
97.	July 14, 1948	Auburn	St. Peter
98.	January 22, 1949	Hampton	Our Lady of the Miraculous Medal
99.	February 19, 1949	Belmont	St. Joseph
100.	March 30, 1949	Hudson	St. John the Evangelist
101.	July 21, 1950	Nashua	St. Christopher
102.	August 14, 1951	Portsmouth	St. Catherine of Siena
103.	October 31, 1952	New London	Our Lady of Fatima
104.	June 9, 1953	Colebrook	St. Brendan
105.	June 9, 1953	West Lebanon	Holy Redeemer
106.	June 25, 1954	Merrimack	Our Lady of Mercy
107.	September 24, 1954	Manchester	St. Catherine
108.	April 15, 1955	Goffstown	St. Lawrence
109.	November 8, 1955	Manchester	St. Pius X
110.	November 9, 1955	Keene	St. Margaret Mary
111.	November 9, 1955	Nashua	St. Joseph
112.	July 27, 1956	Concord	Immaculate Heart of Mary
113.	May 18, 1958	Portsmouth	St. James
114.	June 20, 1958	West Swansey	St. Anthony
115.	September 10, 1958	Lisbon	St. Catherine of Siena

Bishop Ernest J. Primeau

116.	June 14, 1961	Alton	St. Joan of Arc
117.	June 22, 1962	Londonderry	St. Jude
118.	June 22, 1962	Windham	St. Matthew
119.	April 8, 1965	Center Ossipee	St. Joseph
120.	January, 19, 1966	Bedford	St. Elizabeth Seton
121.	September 6, 1966	Salem	Mary, Queen if Peace
122.	January 4, 1967	Newton	Mary, Mother of the Church
123.	October 4, 1968	Hudson	St. Kathryn
124.	October 4, 1968	Nashua	Immaculate Conception
125.	June 3, 1970	Nashua	Parish of the Resurrection
126.	December 15, 1971	Candia	St. Paul

Bishop Odore J. Gendron

127.	June 18, 1979	Hampstead	St. Anne
128.	September 4, 1979	Rye Beach	St. Theresa
129.	November 1, 1981	Londonderry	St. Mark
130.	February 2. 1982	Merrimack	St. John Neumann

Bishop Leo E. O'Neil

131.	September 11, 1990	Derry	Holy Cross

Oldest National Parish for Each Ethnic Group

Year Established	Ethnic Group	Name	Location
1871	French Canadian	St. Augustine	Manchester
1888	German*	St. Raphael	Manchester
1902	Polish	St. Hedwig	Manchester
1906	Lithuanian	St. Casmir	Nashua

* Although Saint Raphael was established to minister to the German community, it was never canonically a National Parish. Catholic worship in New Hampshire is also celebrated regularly in Spanish, Korean, Vietnamese, and Portuguese.

Parishes Sharing a Pastor Since 1976

Since	Parish of the Residence of the Pastor	Other Parish
March 3, 1976	Sacred Heart* Marlborough	St. Denis Harrisville
May 9, 1980	St. Francis Xavier Groveton	Sacred Heart North Stratford
May 16, 1990	Holy Rosary Rochester	St. Leo Gonic
June 25, 1990	Sacred Heart* Marlborough	Immaculate Conception Troy
September 1, 1993	Holy Trinity Somersworth	St. Mary Rollinsford
August 1, 1995	St. Mary Manchester	Sacred Heart Manchester
June 17, 1996	St. Joseph Woodsville	St. Catherine of Siena Lisbon
June 17, 1996	Sacred Heart Greenville	Sacred Heart Wilton

* The pastor of Sacred Heart, Marlborough, is the pastor of two parishes: St. Denis, Harrisville, and Immaculate Conception, Troy. In summary, seven pastors are responsible for fifteen parishes. Plans are currently being drawn for numerous other parishes to share the same pastor because of the growing shortage of priests.

Enrollment of Catholic Schools in New Hampshire (Primary and Secondary) 1884-1997

Year	Enrollment
1884	3,000
1903	12,000
1931	23,800
1959	27,400
1964	30,230 (peak)
1973	16,100
1984	10,644
1997	9,767

APPENDIX G

Geographic Location
New Hampshire Catholic Schools
1997-1998

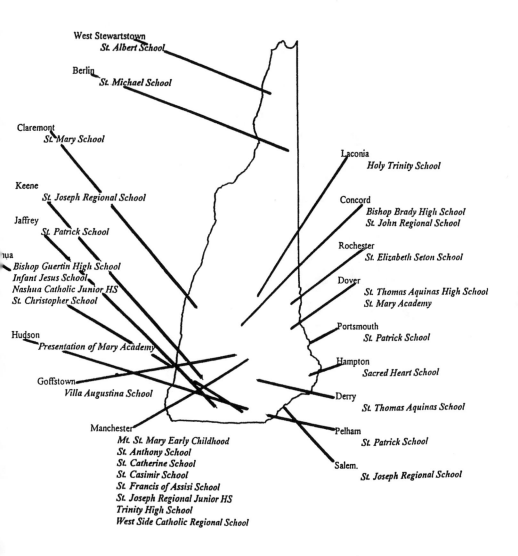

West Stewartstown
St. Albert School

Berlin
St. Michael School

Claremont
St. Mary School

Laconia
Holy Trinity School

Keene
St. Joseph Regional School

Concord
Bishop Brady High School
St. John Regional School

Jaffrey
St. Patrick School

Rochester
St. Elizabeth Seton School

ıua
Bishop Guertin High School
Infant Jesus School
Nashua Catholic Junior HS
St. Christopher School

Dover
St. Thomas Aquinas High School
St. Mary Academy

Hudson
Presentation of Mary Academy

Portsmouth
St. Patrick School

Hampton
Sacred Heart School

Goffstown
Villa Augustina School

Derry
St. Thomas Aquinas School

Manchester
Mt. St. Mary Early Childhood
St. Anthony School
St. Catherine School
St. Casimir School
St. Francis of Assisi School
St. Joseph Regional Junior HS
Trinity High School
West Side Catholic Regional School

Pelham
St. Patrick School

Salem.
St. Joseph Regional School

APPENDIX H

Catholic Colleges in New Hampshire

Year of Opening	Name of College	Present Location
1889	Saint Anselm	Goffstown
1933	Rivier	Nashua (since 1941)
1934	Mount Saint Mary	Hooksett (closed in 1978)
1950	Notre Dame	Manchester
1963*	Castle Junior College	Windham
1973	Magdalen	Warner (since 1991)
1978	The Thomas More College of Liberal Arts	Merrimack

*Opened as a secretarial school in 1963 and became a degree granting institution in 1973.

Oral Intervention of Bishop Ernest J. Primeau at the Second Vatican Council on the Relationship of the Hierarchy to the Laity, October 23, 1963

After situating his presentation in the proper document of the council and praising Pope John XXIII's remarks on the relationship between the hierarchy and the laity in his opening address to the Council on October 11, 1962, Bishop Primeau continued:

> To reach this goal, in dealing with the laity we have to keep before our eyes the growing concern which the laity has about its proper status in the apostolate of the Church. If this were not done, everything the Council has proposed or established would be spoken to deaf ears. Certainly we must avoid the danger of generalization; nonetheless we can affirm that lay people today, conscious of their capabilities, will not allow themselves to be treated as in past times as merely passive members of the Church, blindly bowing to authority, or as mute sheep.
>
> On the contrary, there are many well-educated faithful who ask to be heard on questions of undertakings in which they have a competence that clerics more often than not lack.
>
> They want to share in the apostolic work of the Church and they certainly intend to do this under the direction of the hierarchy, but not without previously being heard by the hierarchy concerning matters within their competence. They expect the confidence of the hierarchy.
>
> They have a great love for Holy Mother Church and manifest great reverence and confidence towards legitimate authority. They are also aware of their own dignity and competence, however, not only in temporal affairs, but also in the internal life of the Church. Above all, they consider dialogue between themselves and the hierarchy as absolutely necessary for promoting the common good of the Church and for defining the special role of the laity in the apostolate. By divine providence this Ecumenical Council has done a lot to make this dialogue possible. It has given the laity great hope and the opportunity for raising many questions. One important question concerns

the definition of the roles of freedom and authority. If the Council does not give an answer to this question, we can doubtless expect 1) a growing bitterness among the laity towards the Church's authority; 2) a growing indifference of laymen who passively keep the laws, but never share in the life and mission of the Church; 3) finally, sad to say, defections from the faith and the Church. The Church needs the help of the laity, especially those who are called "intellectuals," in order to grow. The Church can never use their help and advice unless it acknowledges their legitimate freedom of action, the meaning of "initiative" and is ready to consult them with due respect about matters within their competence.

If we keep all this in mind, it seems that some parts of chapter three hinder more than help the vital apostolate of the laity; for example, especially number 26, page 10. The text is too negative, perhaps too cautious, and too clerical.

The text insists too much on the need of obedience, reverence, and subjection and does not sufficiently emphasize proper responsibility and freedom of action, as the proper possession of laity who are true members of the Mystical Body of Christ. Let this constant talk of their duty of subjection and reverence cease-as if their only duty be stated in these terms: believe, pray, pay and obey.

Let us not forget that the faithful laity honor and love the Church just as we do. However, they also yearn to share actively in the mission of the Church, to be known not as mere representatives of the clergy and hierarchy, but as having their own unique part in the mission of the Church as laity whose proper role is defined and approved by the Church.

All this would have little value unless in this fundamental schema we affirm our sincere acknowledgment of the competency of the laity, show our readiness to hear them, and, above all, acknowledge clearly their right to exercise their proper spiritual activity in freedom and mutual confidence with hierarchical authority. In this sense, we, the bishops, must further expand and evolve the directives mentioned in number 26, so that in each diocese there would be a structure by which the laity, especially the more educated laity, could communicate with the bishop and pastors. Today I speak for the laity, and in the same way some other bishops have spoken for them, presenting their desires to the Council. But I also ask the Fathers to hear the laity, namely, that the auditors here in the aula would speak in the name of all the laity.

APPENDIX J

Diocese of Manchester Organizational Chart (1997)

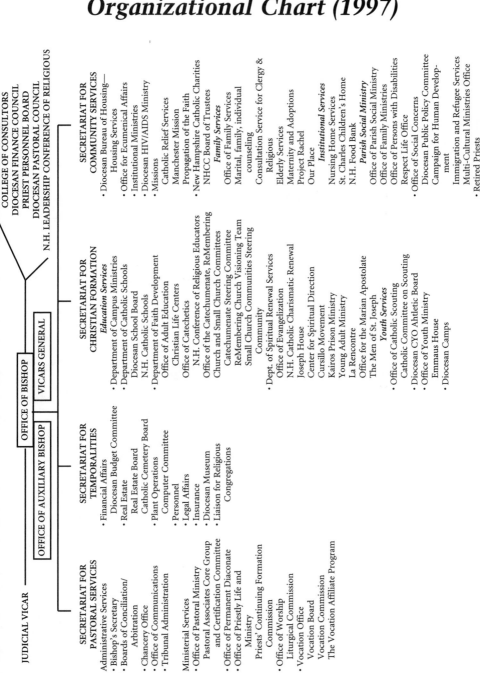

JUDICIAL VICAR

OFFICE OF AUXILIARY BISHOP

OFFICE OF BISHOP

VICARS GENERAL

COLLEGE OF CONSULTORS
DIOCESAN FINANCE COUNCIL
PRIEST PERSONNEL BOARD
DIOCESAN PASTORAL COUNCIL
N.H. LEADERSHIP CONFERENCE OF RELIGIOUS

SECRETARIAT FOR PASTORAL SERVICES

Administrative Services
· Bishop's Secretary
· Boards of Conciliation/Arbitration
· Chancery Office
· Office of Communications
· Tribunal Administration

Ministerial Services
· Office of Pastoral Ministry
  Pastoral Associates Core Group and Certification Committee
· Office of Permanent Diaconate
· Office of Priestly Life and Ministry
  Priests' Continuing Formation Commission
· Office of Worship
  Liturgical Commission
· Vocation Office
  Vocation Board
  Vocation Commission
  The Vocation Affiliate Program

SECRETARIAT FOR TEMPORALITIES

· Financial Affairs
  Diocesan Budget Committee
· Real Estate
  Real Estate Board
  Catholic Cemetery Board
· Plant Operations
  Computer Committee
· Personnel
· Legal Affairs
· Insurance
· Diocesan Museum
· Liaison for Religious Congregations

SECRETARIAT FOR CHRISTIAN FORMATION

Education Services
· Department of Campus Ministries
· Department of Catholic Schools
  Diocesan School Board
  N.H. Catholic Schools
· Department of Faith Development
  Office of Adult Education
  Christian Life Centers
  Office of Catechetics
  N.H. Conference of Religious Educators
  Office of the Catechumenate, ReMembering Church and Small Church Committees
  Catechumenate Steering Committee
  ReMembering Church Visioning Team
  Small Church Communities Steering Community
· Dept. of Spiritual Renewal Services
  Office of Evangelization
  N.H. Catholic Charismatic Renewal
  Joseph House
  Center for Spiritual Direction
  Cursillo Movement
  Kairos Prison Ministry
  Young Adult Ministry
  La Rencontre
  Office for the Marian Apostolate
  The Men of St. Joseph
Youth Services
· Office of Catholic Scouting
  Catholic Committee on Scouting
· Diocesan CYO Ahtletic Board
· Office of Youth Ministry
  Emmaus House
· Diocesan Camps

SECRETARIAT FOR COMMUNITY SERVICES

· Diocesan Bureau of Housing—
  Housing Services
· Office for Ecumenical Affairs
· Institutional Ministries
· Diocesan HIV/AIDS Ministry
· Missions
  Catholic Relief Services
  Manchester Mission
  Propagation of the Faith
· New Hampshire Catholic Charities
  NHCC Board of Trustees
Family Services
  Office of Family Services
  Marital, family, individual counseling
  Consultation Service for Clergy & Religious
  Elderly Services
  Maternity and Adoptions
  Project Rachel
  Our Place
Institutional Services
  Nursing Home Services
  St. Charles Children's Home
  N.H. Food Bank
Parish Social Ministry
  Office of Parish Social Ministry
  Office of Family Ministries
  Office of Persons with Disabilities
  Respect Life Office
· Office of Social Concerns
  Diocesan Public Policy Committee
  Campaign for Human Development
  Immigration and Refugee Services
  Multi-Cultural Ministries Office
· Retired Priests
  Retired Priests Committee

Bibliography

Lord, Robert H., Sexton, John E., and Harrington, Edward T. *History of the Archdiocese of Boston.* 3 vols. Boston; The Pilot Publishing Company, 1945

This remains one of the better diocesan histories in this country. Its shortcomings are that New Hampshire ceased to be a part of the Diocese of Boston in 1853 and that this history was published in 1945, that is some 52 years ago. A further deficiency is its more than occasional lack of objectivity with the episcopacy of William Cardinal O'Connell who financed the project.

Byrne, William et al. *The History of the Catholic Church in the New England States.* 2 vols. Boston: The Hurd & Everts Co, 1899. For the *Diocese of Manchester,* see Finen, John E. Vol I, pp. 562–679

This is frequently a self-serving and not always unprejudiced history of the Catholic Church in New England, including the section on the Diocese of Manchester by Father Finen. Its main value concerns the late nineteenth century, the period to which the author was an eyewitness and participant.

While there are other publications that cover some aspects of the subject, such as parish histories, there are no others that attempt to give an overall view of Catholicism in New Hampshire, save this history and its predecessor, the tabloid newspaper "Catholicism in New Hampshire: An Historical Summary," (28 pages), written by Wilfrid H. Paradis and published in 1985.

Index

About The Author

The Reverend Monsignor Wilfrid H. Paradis, a priest of the Diocese of Manchester, earned a doctorate in history from the University of Paris (Sorbonne) and one in canon law from the Catholic University of Paris (l'Institut Catholique). Both doctorates were awarded summa cum laude.

During his graduate studies, he was the recipient of seven scholarships including a Fulbright Grant and a Fulbright Prize Grant. In addition, he has received numerous citations and awards in both the fields of history and education. Monsignor Paradis has also published and lectured in France and Canada as well as the United states.

Among his several functions on the international level, he served as an official "peritus" (expert) at the Second Vatican Council (1962–1965), and as the senior advisor to the American bishops at the Vatican Synod of Bishops on catechesis in 1977. On the national plane, he was appointed Secretary of Education of the United States Catholic Conference, the highest administrative post in Catholic education in this country.

During World War II, he enlisted in the Army and served as a combat medic in France, Germany, and Austria. During these campaigns, he was awarded the Silver star, the Bronze star, the Combat Medical Badge, three Battle stars, and other citations for valor in action.